CLOSE ENCOUNTERS OF THE THIRD KIND

CLOSE ENCOUNTERS
OF THE THIRD KIND

The Making of
Steven Spielberg's
Classic Film

Ray Morton

APPLAUSE THEATRE & CINEMA BOOKS

AN IMPRINT OF HAL LEONARD CORPORATION

NEW YORK

Published in 2007 by Applause Theatre & Cinema Books
An Imprint of Hal Leonard Corporation
19 West 21st Street, New York, NY 10010

Printed in the United States of America

Book design by Mark Lerner

Library of Congress Cataloging-in-Publication Data
Morton, Ray, 1961-
  Close encounters of the third kind : the making of Steven Spielberg's classic film /
by Ray Morton.
      p. cm.
  Includes bibliographical references and index.
  ISBN 978-1-55783-710-3
  1. Close encounters of the third kind (Motion picture) I. Title.
PN1997.C6555M67 2007
791.43'72--dc22

                          2007036785

www.applausepub.com

This book is dedicated to M. F. Harmon—teacher, mentor, and friend.
"A piece of the glow belongs to you."

CONTENTS

Preface

SINCE THE BEGINNING OF TIME, mankind has looked to the heavens and dreamed of encountering life from beyond the stars. Depicted first in myth, then in literature, and finally on celluloid, many of these dreams were fearful ones in which the potential visitors were characterized as invading monsters intent on conquest and destruction. These frightening scenarios reached their apotheosis in the science fiction films of the 1950s and 1960s. Inspired by the rash of UFO sightings that began in the United States just after World War II, and further influenced by Cold War tensions and anxieties, these films portrayed the arrival of aliens on earth as doomsday events full of horror and catastrophe. These nightmarish notions were the standard until November 1977, when wunderkind filmmaker Steven Spielberg, fresh from the tremendous success of *Jaws*, gave us a startlingly new vision of extraterrestrial visitation.

Close Encounters of the Third Kind harnessed all of the power and the magic of cinema to tell a story of mankind's first meeting with beings from another world. Flying directly in the face of the fear and pessimism of the day, Spielberg boldly envisioned this event as peaceful, even spiritual, full of hope and wondrous possibility. This joyful, awe-inspiring message made a powerful impact on audiences of the time, weary from a decade of violence, scandal, and pervasive cynicism and desperate for something to believe in. The film was a big critical and commercial success and—along with *Star Wars* (which had opened six months earlier)—revolutionized the movie industry by helping to create the modern blockbuster; by initiating the late 1970s/early 1980s cycle of science fiction and fantasy movies that produced a number of classic works of imaginative cinema, including *Superman, Alien, The Empire Strikes Back, Raiders of the Lost Ark, Blade Runner,* and *ET: The Extra-Terrestrial*; and by ushering in a new era of high-tech visual and special effects.

Close Encounters is a landmark film for several other reasons as well. To begin with, it is the first true "Steven Spielberg movie," in which the preoccupations that would mark the director's later work—the awe of the cosmos, the magic and the terror inherent in everyday suburban life, families in crisis, children in peril, and the transcendent power of light, music, and sound—were front and center for the first time. It is a technically brilliant piece of filmmaking—one that made the most of the medium to tell its tale. When its maker decided to go back after the film was released and fix a few things that bothered him, it initiated the concept of the "director's cut" that is still with us today. It is also, and perhaps most importantly, enormously entertaining.

The story of how *Close Encounters* was made is almost as amazing as the movie itself. Filmed on a variety of far-flung locations, including Mobile, Alabama; Moorcroft, Wyoming; Hal, India; and Marina Del Rey, California, the production was extremely ambitious. With Spielberg attempting to create images that no one had ever seen before, the project was full of creative and logistical challenges that required a visionary application of technology to produce the desired celluloid magic. In addition, the production team had to overcome a tremendous series of obstacles, including heat, hurricanes, wave after wave of nonfunctioning aliens, and a budget that rapidly rose from $2.8 million to a then-astronomical $19 million, pushing Columbia Pictures, the financially strapped studio backing the film, to its fiscal edge. When the movie fell far behind its original production schedule and required a seemingly endless amount of additional shooting, doubts arose that the project could even be completed. Ultimately, however, Spielberg and his brilliant team pulled it off, delivering a film that was not only a critical and commercial smash but quickly came to be considered a true motion picture classic.

I first saw the film in December 1977 at the Ridgeway Theater in Stamford, Connecticut, and I was blown away. *Close Encounters* was simply unlike anything I had every seen before. The incredible combination of imagery and sound that makes up the last thirty or so minutes of the film, along with its incredible message of peace, goodwill, and dreams fulfilled, left me so mesmerized that my sisters Kathy and Nancy, who had accompanied me to the screening, literally had to nudge me to let me know that the movie was over. As we drove home (in a fog so thick that the headlights from our gray Grand Torino station wagon with the cracked front grille began replicating some of the visual effects from the film), I realized that my life had changed. For the first time I was truly aware of the power and potential of the cinema and the tremendous effect that it could have on an audience, and from that day on I was determined to make a life for myself—some way or another—in the movies. The result of that determination is another story, but when the opportunity arose to write this book, I was thrilled to have the chance to tell the story of the film that had made such an impact on me. In the course of my research, I had the honor of meeting many of the people who made *CE3K* (all of whom, as it turned out, were really terrific—generous, open, and incredibly supportive). As they shared their memories with me, I gained an even greater respect for the film and for the monumental effort it took to bring it to life. It became my goal to chronicle that effort as accurately and completely as I could. I hope they (and you) will feel that I succeeded.

Acknowledgments

I WANT TO THANK FOUR PEOPLE without whom this book would not have been possible:

The first is my editor, Michael Messina, who warmed to the initial idea and who has been extremely supportive of it every step of the way, even when I was driving him to distraction with a more delays than either of us probably wants to contemplate. The second is my agent, June Clark of the Peter Rubie Literary Agency, who set the book up and made it happen with her usual no-nonsense dispatch and sense of mission. Next, I want to thank Tim Partridge, who helped me make contact with many of the people interviewed in this book and who arranged and conducted the interviews with the U.K.-based subjects. In addition to his knowledge, wisdom, and just plain good sense about all matters cinematographic, Tim was—as he always is—incredibly supportive and encouraging to me throughout the sometimes arduous process of writing this book, even when he had things a lot more important to worry about than me and my tribulations. If you are lucky enough to have one friend in your life who is as true and steadfast as Tim, then you are a fortunate person indeed. Finally, I would like to thank Richard Yuricich, ASC. Richard was the director of photography for the photographic effects work on *Close Encounters*. He was kind enough to let me interview him about his work on the film and even kinder to allow me to continue to pepper him with what probably seemed like an unending series of questions about every aspect of the film and its making. Richard answered my every query with grace and good humor (as well as tremendous insight and knowledge) and gave me a tutorial in cinematography, visual effects, and the realities of movi-emaking that was better than ten years in any film school. His warmth, generosity, and support were boundless—and greatly appreciated.

I would also like to express my appreciation to six members of the *Close Encounters* production who not only allowed me to interview them but also made themselves available for ongoing consultation, fact-checking, and wise perspective: Robert Swarthe, Rocco Gioffre, Hal Barwood, Matthew Robbins, Jim Bloom, and Douglas Trumbull.

A heads-up and a high five is also due to the Brain Trust—those folks who provided me with excellent feedback on all matters editorial, technical, and grammatical: Andrew Morton, Raymond J. Morton Sr., and Rich Morton. For their technical facilitation, assistance, and support with various aspects of this book, I would like to thank Michael Apodaca, Carmen Apodaca, Denise Apodaca, Steve Bingen, Peter Buonadonna, Dharmesh Chauhan, Christine Czazasty at Devils Tower, Bob Coleman, Carol Ellis, Glenn Erickson, Gina Fénard, Hal Hickel, Will Huff, Jay Kanter, Richard H. Kline ASC, Glynis Lynn, Patsy Mack, Jeff Okun, Ilya Salkind, and John Scoleri. I would also like to acknowledge the following institutions and businesses for their help and assistance: The Margaret E. Herrick Library at the Academy of Motion Picture Arts and Sciences; The Louis B. Mayer Library at the American Film Institute, The Glendale (California) Public Library; The New Canaan (Connecticut) Public Library; The Hollywood Book and Poster Company; Jerry Ohlinger's Movie Material Store; and the Larry Edmunds Bookshop.

Tim Partridge would like to thank: Ignacio A. Aguilar; Manuel Alducin; the Cinema Audio Society; Harrison Ellenshaw; Kevin H. Martin; M. David Mullen, ASC; Jeffrey A. Okun; Frances Russell; and the BSC.

I would like to express my appreciation to Joe Alves, Hal Barwood, Jim Bloom, M. Kathryn Campbell, Glenn Erickson, Rocco Goiffre, John Hill, Nancy Hill, Andrew Morton, Michael Phillips, Matthew Robbins, Scott Squires, Robert Swarthe, Christine Van Bloem, and Paul Van Bloem for the use of photos from their private collections. Special thanks to Joe Alves and Glenn Erickson for the use of their personal behind-the-scenes snapshots of various aspects of the production of *CE3K* and to Gregory Jein and Robert Swarthe for the use of items from their memorabilia collections.

Finally, I would also like to thank all the people who worked on *Close*

Encounters and agreed to be interviewed for this book. They are (in alphabetical order) Joe Alves; Hal Barwood; Jerry Belson; Jim Bloom; Allen Daviau, ASC; Glenn Erickson; Richard Fields; William Fraker, ASC; Teri Garr; Rocco Gioffre; John Hill; Gregory Jein; Tom Koester; Alan Ladd Jr.; Al Miller; J. Patrick McNamara; Ralph McQuarrie; Dennis Muren; Michael Phillips; Steven Poster, ASC; Matthew Robbins; Douglas Slocombe, BSC; Scott Squires; Robert Swarthe; Douglas Trumbull; Pete Turner; Robin Vidgeon, BSC; Richard Yuricich, ASC; and Vilmos Zsigmond, ASC. My thanks as well to those who agreed to be interviewed off the record.

On a personal note, I would like to thank the members of my family for all their love and support: Raymond J. and Rita K. Morton; Kathy and Caitlin Bunting; Nancy, Kate, Maddie, and Carrie Lutian; Jim Lutian; Richard and Kendra Morton; William Morton; Ken Morton; Claire and Derek Masterbone; Andrew Morton; Tom, Lindsey, and Erin Moran Morton.

I would also like to thank the wonderful friends who supported me during the writing of this book: Maggie Morrisette; Tara, Kurt, Mia, and Mattius Johnson; Carmen and Dan Apodaca; Denise, Michael, Carina, Cecila, and Isabella Apodaca; Dharmesh Chauhan, Sara Chovan, Arslan Aziz, and Mabel Chovan-Aziz; Ron Barbagallo; Terri Barbagallo; Dana Bowden, Dave Cullen, and D.J. Cullen; Peter Buonadonna; Jim DeFelice and Linda Sanislo; Gina and David Fénard; the Fénard family; Brian Finn; Monsignor James Gehl; Faith Ginsberg; Steven Ginsberg and Steven Tropiano; M.F. and Linda Daudelin Harmon; Richard H. Kline; Michael Larobina; Janet McKenney and Holly Valero; John and Ali Nelson; Angel Orona; Joe and Donna Romeo; David Shaw; Paul Van Bloem; Erin, Andrew, and Malcolm Villaverde; and Brooklyn French Fry Apodaca (for biting me a lot when I was trying to write).

Finally, I would like to thank Ana Maria Apodaca—mi amiga, mi amor.

Synopsis

Sonora Desert, Mexico—Present Day. Led by French scientist Claude Lacombe, a team of investigators from the clandestine, U.N.-sponsored Mayflower Project arrives at this remote location in the middle of a raging sandstorm—and finds five World War II–era U.S. Navy Avenger Torpedo Bombers sitting in the middle of a junkyard. The ATBs were part of Flight 19, a Navy training mission that disappeared in the Bermuda Triangle in 1945. Although now over thirty years old, the ATBs look brand new. David Laughlin, a Mayflower Project cartographer who serves as Lacombe's unofficial translator, asks the obvious question—where did they come from? At the moment, the answer is unknown.

A few nights later, an air traffic controller in Indianapolis monitors an incident in which two passenger airliners encounter a strange set of brilliant lights while in flight. Moving non-ballistically, the lights buzz the planes and vanish into the sky. The air traffic controller asks the pilots if they want to report a UFO. They do not. Meanwhile, in Muncie, Indiana, four-year-old Barry Guiler is awakened when all of the battery-operated toys in his room come alive. Barry goes downstairs and discovers that something has ransacked the kitchen. Whatever it is appears to Barry off-screen, and a few minutes later his mother, Jillian, is awakened by the sound of her son's laughter as he gleefully follows whatever it is into the woods adjacent to the house.

A short time later, Muncie is hit by a major blackout. Department of Water & Power trouble foreman Roy Neary is sent out to supervise the replacement of the cut electrical lines that caused the failure. Traveling on unfamiliar country roads, Neary gets lost and ends up at an isolated rail-road crossing in the middle of nowhere. Suddenly, his truck loses power and then is hit by a beam of incredibly bright light coming from the sky above. As the gravity inside the truck cab diminishes, causing all of the items in the cab to fly up to the roof, Roy leans out the window in attempt to ascertain where the light is coming from, but the glow is too intense and burns his face. As Neary pulls back inside the truck, he goes into a brief trance. A few seconds later, the light beam switches off. Roy looks up and sees a mysterious craft floating in the sky above him. As it moves off down the road, the truck's power returns and Roy hears a report over his CB radio that the police are chasing a mysterious group of lights through a nearby area. Determined to find out what is going on, Roy speeds off to intercept them.

Meanwhile, runaway Barry Guiler makes his way to an isolated stretch of roadway on a hilltop called Crescendo Summit, where he meets an ec-centric farmer who sits by the side of the road with his family, seemingly waiting for something. Jillian finally catches up to her son just as Neary's truck comes speeding around the corner, heading straight for the boy. Roy swerves to avoid Barry, crashes his truck into a guardrail, and stops. As Neary rushes over to check on Barry, three large objects glowing with colorful light come flying around the bend just a few feet off the road and zoom past the startled onlookers. They are followed first by a smaller red object that struggles to keep up with its siblings and then by three police cruisers that come speeding around the bend in hot pursuit. Excited, Roy joins in the chase. After zipping through a toll plaza without paying the quarter, the UFOs leave the road and sail off into the sky. As they do, the lights start coming back on in the valley below.

The morning after his encounter, Neary finds that the shapes of cer-tain objects—a mound of shaving cream, a bunched-up pillow—strike him as being familiar, although he can't place what it is they remind him of. Roy's behavior alarms his wife, Ronnie, who is concerned about what their friends and neighbors will think if Roy tells them that he saw a fly-ing saucer. She becomes even more alarmed when the DWP fires Roy for abandoning his post the night before. That evening, Roy returns to Crescendo Summit armed with a camera, hoping the UFOs will return so he can get proof that he has not been imagining things. Upon arriving, he finds that a crowd of people has gathered, among them Jillian and Barry.

As Roy and Jillian get to know one another, lights are spotted approaching from a distance. As they come closer, the crowd's anticipation grows, but when the lights finally arrive overhead, it is immediately apparent that they are not from outer space after all but are instead just searchlights mounted to the front of two military helicopters that have come to shoo the people off the hillside.

Meanwhile, Lacombe and his team travel to a town in northern India where they find ten thousand villagers sitting on a hillside chanting the same five musical notes over and over again. As his team records the sounds, Lacombe asks a local official where they came from. When the official repeats Lacombe's question for the villagers, they respond by pointing their fingers at the sky. Back in the United States, Lacombe, convinced that the five tones are important, introduces them to the rest of the Mayflower Project using the hand signs normally utilized by the Kodály Method of music instruction. Lacombe then uses the Goldstone Radio Telescope to beam the tones out into space in the hope of getting a response. Unfortunately, the only reply is two sets of number patterns that no one can make any sense of—that is, until David Laughlin realizes they are map coordinates for a mountain in Wyoming called Devils Tower.

A few nights later, the three UFOs descend from a self-generated cloudbank and surround Jillian's house, causing all of the electrical appliances in the place to go haywire. As a terrified Jillian fights to keep the unseen occupants of the UFOs from gaining entry into the house, an excited Barry crawls through the doggie door to see his friends. Jillian tries to pull him back, but something on the other side of the door grabs him and yanks him through. Barry is gone. The next day, Roy goes to a nearby Air Force Base and along with a group of thirty other witnesses—many of them recognizable from Crescendo Summit—meets with one Major Benchley, who tries to persuade them that there are no such things as flying saucers. At that very moment, a van carrying a team of twelve Mayflower Project volunteers wearing red flight suits arrives at a secret warehouse located somewhere in the United States. The volunteers board a chartered bus headed for Wyoming as a Special Forces team led by Major Wild Bill Walsh loads crates full of top secret equipment into a convoy of tractor trailers disguised as delivery trucks from chain stores. Meanwhile, Walsh meets with a group of advisers and tries to come up with a scheme that will scare the residents out of the area around Devils Tower.

That night, Roy scares his family terribly when his obsession takes over and he begins sculpting the mashed potatoes on his dinner plate into the mysterious shape. He later tries to fashion the shape out of clay, but when he can't get it to come out right he runs outside and screams at the stars, demanding to know what the shape is supposed to be. Distraught and exhausted, Neary falls asleep in front of the model. When he wakes up the next morning, he finds his daughter watching a cartoon in which Daffy Duck squares off against Marvin Martian. The cartoon makes Roy laugh and realize how ridiculous his behavior has been. Starting to feel like his old self again, he begins pulling apart the clay model, but as he yanks at the upper portion of the model, it comes off in his hand, turning the formerly triangular sculpture into a rectangular shape with a flat top. Something about this new configuration strikes a chord with Neary. Inspired, he begins tearing up the backyard in order to gather material to build an even bigger model. Getting carried away, he begins tearing up the neighbors' yards as well. For Ronnie, this is the last straw. She loads the kids into the car and leaves Roy forever.

Consumed by his obsession, Neary locks himself in the house and constructs a giant, incredibly detailed model of a tall, square-topped mountain in the middle of the family room. When he finishes and beholds what he has done, he grows disgusted with himself and calls Ronnie to beg for a second chance. She refuses and they begin arguing. As they do, the evening news begins and the anchorman leads off with a story about the derailment of a train carrying a shipment of deadly nerve gas at Devils Tower, Wyoming. The gas has begun leaking, requiring that the whole area be evacuated. During the report, a shot of Devils Tower flashes on the screen. It looks exactly like the model Roy has built in his living room. It takes him a few minutes to see it, but when he finally does, Neary is transfixed.

Roy travels to Wyoming, rents a car, and heads for Devils Tower. He makes it as far as the small town of Reliance, which is being used as an evacuation center. An army roadblock prevents him from going any farther. As Roy tries to figure out a way around the roadblock, he hears someone calling his name. Following the voice to the railroad depot, he discovers Jillian, who saw the news report on television and has come to Wyoming in search of Barry, being loaded onto an evacuation train. Reunited, the two of them drive back down the highway, crash through a barbed wire fence and begin driving across the fields, determined to make it to the Tower. When they finally see the magnificent mountain looming on the horizon, they are both thrilled. Both express their conviction that the poison gas story is just a hoax, but when they see what appear to be several dead animals lying on the side of the road, they each don a gas mask just to be safe. They have almost reached their destination when they are arrested by sentries wearing hazmat suits and taken to a base camp that has been set up at the foot of Devils Tower. Roy is placed in an interrogation room, where he meets with Lacombe and Laughlin. As Lacombe interrogates Roy and tries to figure out why he has come to a place that he was told would endanger his life, Roy demands to be told what is going on. Instead, he is forced to don a gas mask and placed aboard an evacuation helicopter with a group of other "gatecrashers" that includes Jillian.

Lacombe tries to talk Wild Bill into letting the gatecrashers stay—he feels they have been invited to this spot by the same forces that have invited the Mayflower Project, a notion that Walsh dismisses as ridiculous. Meanwhile, Roy takes a leap of faith, removes his gas mask, and breathes deeply. The air is fine. Acting on Roy's suggestion that they make a break for it, he, Jillian, and another gatecrasher named Larry Butler jump out of the chopper and push past their guards. Pursued by Major Walsh's men, Roy, Jillian, and Larry climb Devils Tower, heading for a box canyon on the far side that Roy envisioned in his sculpture. They outdistance the soldiers, prompting Major Walsh to order a squad of helicopters to dust the mountain with a sleep aerosol. Jillian and Roy avoid the spray, but Larry is knocked out. Jillian and Roy make it over the mountain and find themselves on a ledge overlooking the box canyon, in which the Mayflower team has constructed an elaborate arena containing all manner of scientific equipment.

As night falls, Roy and Jillian join the Mayflower team as it turns its attention to the sky and watches as the stars forming the constellation of Orion suddenly rearrange themselves to form the Big Dipper. Following this, the three UFOs first seen at Crescendo Summit and their straggler buddy glide down from the sky and into the arena, where they hover above the runway. A keyboard artist plays the five tones on an ARP 2500 synthesizer that has been hooked up to a giant light board that lights up a different colored rectangular square each time a note is played. The UFOs respond by repeating the five tones and then begin flashing their lights in a signal pattern as a cloudbank forms in the sky over the Tower. Suddenly, dozens of UFOs explode from the clouds and zoom down, buzzing the arena and bathing the entire area in brilliant light. As the barnstorming continues, an excited Roy tells Jillian that he wants to go down into the arena. Jillian understands, but declines to go with him—Barry's not here and she needs to continue to search for her son. They kiss goodbye and Roy begins climbing down. As he does, the UFOs retreat and it appears that the event is over. But then something huge begins rising up from behind Devils Tower. It is a giant UFO—a brilliantly illuminated Mothership that moves into position over the canyon and then touches down in the arena. The keyboard artist tries to initiate contact by playing the five tones. After a few false starts, the Mothership responds by playing a note that is so loud it blows the glass out of one of the landing zone cubicles, thus beginning a joyful musical jam between synthesizer and spacecraft.

When the jam session ends, the Mothership's bottom hatch opens, emitting a blinding light. Several figures emerge from that light and Lacombe greets them. The figures turn out to be the pilots from Flight 19. They are followed by dozens of other humans who have been abducted over the years, Barry included. Jillian runs to her son and the two have a tearful, joyful reunion. When the last of the abductees have departed, the hatch closes. Lacombe finds Roy standing on the sidelines watching all of this and asks him what he wants. Roy says he just wants to know that this is all really happening. Lacombe smiles and nods—it is. The Mothership hatch opens again and an extremely tall, thin alien being emerges from the light and spreads its arms in greeting. A few minutes later, approximately one hundred small, humanoid extraterrestrials come walking down the ramp to greet the earthlings.

As Jillian uses her Instamatic camera to take pictures of this historic meeting between two worlds, Lacombe gathers the other Mayflower Project leaders to talk about Roy. A short time later, we see the group of twelve Mayflower Project volunteers, wearing their red flight suits and carrying travel packs, heading toward the Mothership to leave the planet with the aliens: pilgrims headed for a foreign land. As the line turns, it is revealed that Roy has joined them. As the pilgrims wait to go aboard the ship, a group of extraterrestrials surround Roy, pull him away from the other pilgrims, and lead him toward the hatch. It appears that the aliens have chosen Roy alone to go with them. Roy takes one last look around—at Lacombe, at Jillian, and Barry—and then enters the light.

The lead extraterrestrial comes forward and Lacombe uses the Kodály hand signs to greet it. The extraterrestrial responds using the same hand signals, then smiles. A few minutes later, the Mothership lifts off, flies up into the stars, and finally fades from view.

CHAPTER | **Invaders from Mars**

"I looked, and I saw a windstorm coming out of the north—an immense cloud with flashing lightning and surrounded by brilliant light. The center of the fire looked like glowing metal, and in the fire was what looked like four living creatures."

—Ezekiel 1:4–5

MANY PEOPLE BELIEVE that the mysterious flaming wheel the prophet Ezekiel encountered in this Old Testament passage was actually what today we would call a UFO. This is not an unreasonable assumption, given that Ezekiel's description of the wheel closely matches those given of the objects reported in many modern-day sightings: it emerged from behind a roiling cloud, was made of metal, emitted a blinding light, and appeared to be piloted by humanoid creatures that, later in the passage, are described as having extraordinary powers. While Ezekiel's account may have been one of the first UFO sightings in recorded history, it would not be the last. From the beginning of time until the present day, human beings have reported seeing strange objects in the sky:

- In the year 1450 B.C.E., "circles of fire" were seen flying over Egypt.

- In 1235 C.E., a Japanese army general and his troops watched for hours as "globes of light" zipped about in erratic patterns in the night sky above Kyoto.

- In 1561 C.E., dozens of large cylinders appeared over Nuremberg, Germany. Local residents watched as smaller, rounder objects emerged from the cylinders and appeared to engage one another in battle.

- In 1896 and 1897, "mystery airships" were spotted flying over twenty of the United States.

- During World War II, Allied and Axis airmen alike reported being followed by "foo fighters"—bright, round objects moving at incredible speeds—on dozens of occasions.

- In 1946, shortly after the end of the war, radar installations tracked several hundred cylindrical objects (nicknamed "ghost rockets") as they flew through the skies over Scandinavia and other parts of Europe.

So what were all these mysterious orbs and cylinders? Ancient observers assumed that they were supernatural manifestations: angry gods, mischievous spirits, or anthromorphized heavenly bodies. As mankind gained a greater understanding of science, many of these objects were identified as comets, meteors, or atmospheric phenomena, but just as many remained unexplained.

Curiosity about these aerial anomalies has always been strong, but our modern fascination with UFOs—a fascination that has led to the development of everything from serious scientific investigations to outrageous extraterrestrial-centered religions—did not begin until June 24, 1947. On that date, Kenneth Arnold, a thirty-two-year-old private pilot, was flying his CallAir A-2 near Mount Rainier in Washington State. A firefighting equipment engineer and salesman from Boise, Idaho, Arnold was also a volunteer search and rescue flyer. On June 24, he was looking for a downed Marine Corps transport plane when he spotted a bright blue flash in the sky in front of him. The flash came from a train of nine objects that were flying south toward nearby Mount Adams. Arnold described the objects as being crescent-shaped (concave in the front and convex in the rear) with shiny surfaces that reflected light in a brilliant (and sometimes blinding) fashion and that weaved back and forth "like the tail of a Chinese kite." Forty-five to fifty feet in length, with a wingspan of approximately one hundred feet, the objects moved at speeds Arnold estimated as being between 1,200 and 1,700 mph. He observed the train for approximately one minute and forty-two seconds as the objects swerved in and out between the mountaintops before they finally vanished into the distance.

After finishing his search, Arnold landed in Yakima, Washington, reported what he had seen to the Civil Aeronautics Administration, and then flew back home to Boise. During a refueling stop in Pendleton, Oregon, he told his story to several people, including a reporter who wrote about the incident for the *East Oregonian*, a local newspaper. The paper's editor submitted the story to the wire services, and it was quickly picked up by other newspapers and radio stations around the country and around the world. Arnold's tale was initially greeted with some degree of skepticism. When the pilot of a DC-4 that had been flying through the same airspace at the same time said he hadn't seen anything unusual, some accused Arnold of fabrication. Others were of the opinion that what he had seen was simply a mirage, but Arnold's account was corroborated when a prospector reported that he had been on Mount Adams and had seen six of the objects through a telescope at the same time Arnold had; when a Tacoma woman told a local newspaper that she had seen a chain of nine bright objects flying at high speed near Mount Rainier on the same day; and when many residents of nearby Bremerton, Washington reported seeing rapidly moving objects flash across the sky from early morning until late at night on June 24.

Arnold's encounter was the first ripple in what was soon to become a huge wave. In the days and weeks that followed, thousands of similar sightings were reported from all over the globe. Based upon several statements made by Arnold in which he described the objects as discs that moved in the same fashion that a saucer would if it were skipped across the water, these strange apparitions quickly became known as "flying discs" or, even more popularly, "flying saucers."

Efforts began immediately to determine just what these "saucers" actually were. Initially, many (including Kenneth Arnold himself) assumed they were some sort of top secret, experimental aircraft being test-piloted by the United States military, a notion both the armed forces and the government repeatedly and emphatically denied. In 1947, the U.S. Air Force—seemingly just as puzzled and as curious about the matter as the general public—gave weight to their denials by establishing a task force to investigate these mysterious craft. Begun as Project Sign, the unit was renamed Project Grudge a year later, and eventually became known as Project Blue Book. Feeling that the terms "flying discs" and "saucers" did not accurately characterize all of the items that were being sighted, Captain Edward J. Ruppelt, Project Blue Book's first director, suggested the use of the term "unidentified flying object"—abbreviated as UFO (and pronounced "you-foe")—instead. This term quickly became synonymous with and eventually supplanted the other two in the general vernacular.

Following the U.S. government's denials, fears arose in those early days of the Cold War that the UFOs were aircraft or weapons being deployed by hostile foreign governments. Before long, however, the great speed of the objects—which was well beyond any that was even conceivable at that time—as well as their bizarrely erratic movements—which seemed to defy many laws of aerodynamics and physics—caused some people to begin wondering if perhaps the objects were of otherworldly origin instead. Kenneth Arnold himself gave credence to this notion when he was quoted as saying that "being a natural-born American, if it's not made by our science or our Army Air Forces, I am inclined to believe it's... extra-terrestrial." Later reports of sightings of saucer occupants—usually described as four-foot-tall humanoids with blue/gray skin, short legs, long arms, and large, bulbous heads with big, dark eyes—reinforced this notion. Before long, the idea took root in the popular imagination, and it became commonly assumed that flying discs and flying saucers were indeed vehicles from outer space piloted by "little green men." It was also assumed—understandably given Cold War anxieties and tensions—that their motives must be sinister ones of invasion and conquest.

Sightings continued on a regular basis for most of the next decade, including the July 1947 sighting of five flying discs by the flight crew of a United Airlines DC-3; the appearance of "green fireballs" over a series of U.S. military bases in 1948; multiple sightings of a variety of objects over a period of several days over Washington, D.C., in 1952, which caused widespread alarm that reached the upper levels of the United States government and military; a similar incident in France in 1954; and the appearance of a glowing, egg-shaped object over Texas and New Mexico in 1957. During this time, UFOs and their occupants began infiltrating pop culture. The late 1940s and early 1950s saw the production of a steady stream of UFO and alien-related merchandise: toys, games, hats, candy, comic books and even ice cream (the Carvel ice cream chain introduced an ice cream sandwich made with round chocolate crackers called the "Flying Saucer"). Noted science fiction authors such as Arthur C. Clarke (*Childhood's End*) and Robert Heinlein (*The Puppet Masters*) wrote novels about UFOs and aliens, and pulp magazines such as *Amazing Stories*, *Astounding Science Fiction*, and *Galaxy* published hundreds of similarly themed stories. Newspapers ran UFO cartoons and carnivals, and amusement parks featured flying saucer rides and attractions. "Contactee cults," groups organized by people who claimed to be in communication with extraterrestrials, also began to pop up.

Given all of this popular interest in aliens, it wasn't long before Hollywood jumped on the UFO bandwagon. Encounters with creatures from outer space were not entirely new in the cinema. In 1901, French special effects pioneer Georges Méliès made *A Trip to the Moon*, a whimsical short film based on the Jules Verne novel *From the Earth to the Moon* about a group of earthlings who journey to the moon in a bullet-shaped spacecraft fired out of a miles-long cannon and then battle the satellite's monstrous native inhabitants. In 1913, the British-made comedy *A Message from Mars* told the story of an emissary from the Red Planet who pays a visit to a wealthy young man and uses his powers to persuade the young man to change his selfish ways. In the 1930s and 1940s, Flash Gordon and Buck Rogers (both played by Larry "Buster" Crabbe) encountered tiger-men, shark-men, Ming the Merciless, and a host of other alien beings in their famous movie serials, and in 1945 a Martian scout crash landed on Earth and tried to gain control of Earth's rocket technology in the serial *The Purple Monster Strikes*. However, it was only after Kenneth Arnold's sighting that the genre really took off.

Beginning in 1951 with the twelve-part serial *Flying Disc Man from Mars*, Hollywood began producing an entire series of UFO- and alien-themed feature films and chapter plays. Since science fiction was not considered a "serious" genre at the time, most of these were modestly budgeted "B" pictures. A few, such as *The Day the Earth Stood Still* (1951—about an alien named Klaatu who comes to Earth in order to warn the human race to curb its destructive ways), *The Thing from Another World* (1951—about the monstrous occupant of a crashed spacecraft that attacks the members of an Antarctic research expedition), and *Invasion of the Body Snatchers* (1956—about seed pods from outer space that attempt to take over the Earth by absorbing and replacing all of its inhabitants) were excellent films—well made, thought-provoking and extremely effective. Others, such as *War of the Worlds* (1953—based on H.G. Wells's 1898 novel about Martians that attempt to invade the Earth in cylinder-shaped spacecraft before being brought low by our indigenous microbes), *It Came from Outer Space* (1953—based on Ray Bradbury story about a small town's panicked reaction when a flying saucer lands in the nearby desert) and the Quartermass series (1955's *The Quartermass Experiment* and 1957's *Quartermass II*, both adapted from a British television series about an intrepid scientist who battles creatures from outer space) were solidly entertaining. Many, including *Invaders from Mars* (1953—in which a young boy dreams that aliens are taking over his family and his town), *Earth Versus the Flying Saucers* (1956—a film featuring stop-motion special effects by Ray Harryhausen about alien spaceships that attack Washington, D.C.), *Invasion of the Saucer Men* (1957—one of Hollywood's first depictions of little green men) and *I Married a Monster from Outer Space* (1958—about a young woman who discovers her fiancé has been "inhabited" by an alien), were a bit on the cheesy side. Others, including *Zombies of the Stratosphere* (a 1952 serial that featured a pre–Star Trek Leonard Nimoy as an extraterrestrial zombie), *Teenagers from Outer Space* (1959—about young aliens seeking to turn Earth into a farm for giant lobsters) and *Robot Monster* (1953—an alien invasion film whose less-than-terrifying titular villain was played by an actor wearing an antique diving helmet and a threadbare gorilla suit) were just plain bad. One—1959's *Plan 9 from Outer Space* (a grade-Z travesty about grave-robbing aliens who travel to Earth in flaming pie tins, directed by infamous bad movie auteur Ed Wood and featuring the final screen appearance of Bela Lugosi)—is considered by many to be the single worst motion picture ever made.

In keeping with the popular conception of the time, the portrayal of the extraterrestrials in most of these films was a negative one—most on-screen aliens were depicted as hostile monsters bent on conquering Earth and/or destroying humanity. While a few of these movies did show their otherworldly characters in a more sympathetic light (the ETs in *It Came from Outer Space* are peaceful beings who stop on Earth to repair their broken spacecraft, only to be persecuted by fearful humans, while *The Day the Earth Stood Still*'s Klaatu comes to Washington as a peaceful messenger), even they gave their visitors a threatening edge (the creatures in *It Came...* are hideous-looking, and Klaatu warns the Earthlings that if they don't shape up the citizens of outer space will destroy them). Whatever the approach, the message was clear—aliens were bad news.

Toward the end of the 1950s, the number of UFO sightings had begun to taper off. Compared to the previous decade, the early 1960s were a quiet time. There were relatively few sightings reported and the pop culture fascination with the subject cooled. Although there were a number of UFO-themed products produced during this period (including the Topps Company's notorious 1962 set of *Mars Attacks* trading cards, which told the graphically violent story of an invasion of the Earth by monstrous Martians and provoked considerable parental outrage), the level was nowhere near that of the 1950s. Only a few UFO-themed movies were produced in those years, and most that were, including 1960's *Visit to a Small Planet* (a Jerry Lewis vehicle based on a play by Gore Vidal about an alien who comes to Earth to study human emotions) and 1964's *Santa Claus Conquers the Martians* (in which Martians kidnap jolly old Saint Nick in order to bring Christmas to the children of the Red Planet), were played for laughs. The theme was more popular on television, but aside from a few excellent episodes of *The Twilight Zone* (including "To Serve Man," the notorious episode in which a group of aliens arrives on Earth posing as mankind's benefactors but are in fact looking to add humans to their grocery list), most of the shows were either aimed at children (such as the popular British series *Doctor Who*, whose main extraterrestrial villains, the Daleks, resembled giant salt and pepper shakers) or were comedic (1963's *My Favorite Martian*).

In the mid-1960s, the number of UFO sightings again began to increase. There were several significant incidents, including the so-called "Midwestern Flap"—a series of sightings by police and military officers of UFOs over several Midwestern states on August 1, 1965; the crash in October 1967 of an alleged UFO into Shag Harbor, Nova Scotia; and several reports by American astronauts while in space, including one from Neil Armstrong in which he claimed to have seen two unidentified flying objects while walking on the moon in 1969. Despite all of this activity, UFO and aliens were not popular subjects in the cinema of the 1960s. There were only a few such movies produced during the decade, although one of them—*2001: A Space Odyssey*, Stanley Kubrick's innovative 1968 masterpiece about mankind's first and ultimate encounters with an awesome extraterrestrial intelligence—is considered by many to be the best science fiction film ever made. Outer space–related topics were much more popular on 1960s television, where science fiction had become a very popular genre. On *Lost in Space* (1965–1968), the space family Robinson constantly encountered strange alien creatures and in one memorable episode time-traveled to 1960s Earth only to have the Jupiter 2 mistaken for a flying saucer. The crew of the *Star Trek*'s (1966–1969) starship Enterprise not only interacted with extraterrestrials on a regular basis, but also included one—the incredibly popular Mr. Spock—as a permanent member of the crew. In the pilot episode of *The Invaders* (1967–1968), star Roy Thinnes uncovered an alien plot to take over the world and spent the next forty-three episodes trying to expose and defeat it. With a few exceptions—most notably Mr. Spock—the portrayal of aliens in these films and television programs remained a negative, or at least intimidating one. (Even the unseen beings represented by the monolith in *2001*—whose actions transform humankind for the better on several significant occasions—**are** depicted as being chillingly remote and willing to manipulate entire races for their own mysterious purposes.)

The number of sightings continued to increase as the decade came to a close. Before long, the number of UFO- and alien-related incidents had reached levels comparable to those of the late 1940s and early 1950s (future president Jimmy Carter was one of thousands of people who reported seeing an unidentified flying object during this period). There was, however, an increasing variety in the types of those incidents. In the beginning of the UFO era, most reports were of simple sightings of spacecrafts and aliens. The 1960s, however, saw an increasing number of reports by people who claimed to have actually met and interacted with extraterrestrials, including many who said they had been abducted by aliens, taken aboard their vehicles, and subjected to examination and sometimes even torture. There were also many people who claimed to be receiving telepathic messages from ETs, either in person or from afar.

With all of this increased activity, UFOs and aliens once again began to take hold of the public's imagination. This time, however, they did so in a much more mystical manner than they had twenty years earlier. The publication of *Chariots of the Gods?: Unsolved Mysteries of the Past* by Erik von Däniken in 1968 popularized the idea that aliens had been visiting the Earth for millions of years and have been influencing human development and culture ever since. Based on this notion, many came to believe that aliens were behind many of the supernatural events depicted in the

Bible and other sacred and mythological lore and were perhaps even the gods worshipped by ancient man. Influenced by these theories, many believers, including some members of the developing New Age movement, came to regard aliens as spiritual beings with supernatural powers and started worshipping them as such. As a result, many of the "contactee cults" of the 1950s began transforming into actual UFO-based religions in the 1970s. In addition to these developments, the ongoing reports of alien abductions convinced people both in and out of the cults that extraterrestrials were behind many of the seemingly supernatural events that were occurring at the time—events such as the appearance of shapes and circles in fields all over the world; a wave of seemingly ritual slaying of cattle and livestock throughout the Midwest; and the disappearance of ships and planes in the Bermuda Triangle.

Another significant development in this era was the increasing belief in UFO conspiracy theories. In an era in which there was a great general suspicion and distrust of the United States government—fueled by its misleading handling of both the Kennedy assassination and the Vietnam War, and by the misconduct of the Nixon administration—it was easy for many people to become convinced that federal authorities knew the truth about the UFO phenomenon but were covering it up. This notion was reinforced in 1969 when the Air Force closed down Project Blue Book on the pretext that there was no evidence to support the belief that UFOs were real. In light of the ever-increasing number of reports of sightings, contact, and abductions, this decision aroused the suspicions of many.

By the dawn of the 1970s, UFOs had once again captured the public's imagination. Contemporary polls indicated that eleven million Americans claimed to have seen a UFO and more than fifty percent of the population believed them to be real. One place that no one was seeing UFOs, however, was on screen. Aside from *UFO* (a 1970 British series about an international team of agents that fights alien invaders), aliens were absent from television, and except for *Chariots of the Gods,* a 1970 documentary adaptation of von Däniken's book, they were pretty much absent from the big screen as well. Despite the resurgence in interest in the subject, it seemed that no one in Hollywood wanted to make a movie about UFOs.

Well, almost no one.

CHAPTER 2 | Steven Spielberg

STEVEN ALAN SPIELBERG was born on December 18, 1946 in Cincinnati, Ohio.

His father, Arnold, a former radio operator in the Army Air Corps who had been attached to a B-25 squadron stationed in Karachi and Calcutta during World War II, was studying electrical engineering at the University of Cincinnati. His mother, the former Leah Posner, had trained at the Cincinnati Conservatory of Music in preparation for a career as a concert pianist, a plan she put aside when she began having children. Arnold and Leah met in 1939 and were married on February 25, 1945. Steven was the Spielbergs' first child. He was followed by sisters Anne in 1949, Sue in 1953, and Nancy in 1956. After Arnold received his degree in 1949, he was hired by RCA and the Spielbergs moved to Camden, New Jersey. In 1952, the family moved to Haddon Township, New Jersey, and then again in 1957 to Phoenix, Arizona, where Arnold went to work for General Electric. Both Haddon and the Arcadia district of Phoenix, where the Spielbergs settled, were prime examples of postwar American middle-class suburbia, an environment that would have a profound impact on Steven's sensibilities and on his later work.

By all accounts, young Steven was a smart, energetic, and inquisitive child with an active imagination, a fast learner who lived to pull pranks and play practical jokes (mostly on his unsuspecting sisters), and could be insistent about getting his way. Extremely phobic, he was afraid of everything from his mother's piano (he would scream whenever she played it) to furniture with feet ("I wait for them to walk out of the room") to the tree outside his bedroom window (which he thought was a monster waiting to snatch him). Like many precocious children, Steven didn't do particularly well in school. An indifferent reader with a short attention span, he was a "C" student at best and aggravated many of his teachers by daydreaming and goofing off in class. Uninterested in sports, Spielberg remembers being considered something of a wimp by his classmates.

Young Steven loved music (he took up the clarinet in elementary school) and watching television. He enjoyed reading comic books, putting on puppet shows, building model railroads, and playing with the various electronic gadgets that his father brought home from work. He was interested in aviation, the history of World War II, and dinosaurs. He liked to write stories—clever, exciting tales, often with a macabre twist—and then read them aloud in class or tell them to his fellow Boy Scouts around the campfire. When he got older, he joined his high school drama club and the National Thespian Society, and occasionally acted in plays. As much as Steven enjoyed all of these activities and subjects (many of which he would reference in his future work), his enthusiasm for them paled in comparison to the passion he felt for his primary interest—an activity that began as a simple adolescent hobby and eventually developed into a life-changing vocation. That passion was filmmaking.

As all-encompassing as it would eventually become, Steven's interest in cinema took a while to develop. He remembers seeing his first movie in 1952, when his parents took him to a showing of Cecil B. DeMille's big-top extravaganza *The Greatest Show on Earth*. Under the impression that he was going to a real circus, the six-year-old was profoundly disappointed. For the rest of his childhood, Steven's movie diet consisted mostly of Disney films such as *Snow White* (1937), *Fantasia* (1940), and *Bambi* (1942), all of which scared him to death. When he got a little older, he began attending Saturday morning kiddie matinees, where he viewed a steady stream of cartoons, serials, B science fiction movies, and Westerns.

Soon after the Spielbergs moved to Phoenix, Leah gave Arnold a Brownie 8mm movie camera as a present. Arnold used the camera to film family outings, producing the shaky camera moves and bad exposures that have characterized home movies since private cinema began. When Arnold screened his travelogues for his wife and kids, Steven would mercilessly ridicule his father's amateurish technique. When he had finally had enough, Arnold turned the camera over to his prepubescent know-it-all and challenged him to do better. Steven took up that challenge, and before long a seemingly instinctive gift for cinematic storytelling began to emerge. Steven covered the events he filmed from different angles, cutting in the camera to create excitement and to give the scenes visual variety. He used creative framing to heighten the drama of the family's adventures and eventually even began to stage scenes in order to enhance their entertainment value.

As creative as Steven's endeavors were, filmmaking remained just an occasional pastime for him until the summer of 1958, when the eleven-year-old Boy Scout decided to earn a merit badge in photography by making a narrative film—a western called *The Last Gunfight*. Using his fellow scouts as actors, Steven shot the movie at a local steakhouse. The western-themed restaurant had a real stagecoach placed out in front and the management allowed Steven to use it as a set. When the movie was finished, Steven screened it for the other members of his troop, who responded with tremendous enthusiasm and, when the film was over, applauded the young auteur. The realization that he could create something that would move an audience and that he could be acclaimed for it was a powerful one for Steven, and from that moment on he was hooked on movies.

Steven's love of celluloid took several forms. He became an avid moviegoer, regularly checking out the latest Hollywood releases and carefully studying them for technical tips and creative inspiration. He liked all sorts of movies, but was especially fond of big films with epic stories and visuals such as *The Searchers* (1956), *The Bridge on the River Kwai* (1957), *Ben-Hur* (1959), *Psycho* (1960), *The Great Escape* (1963), and his favorite film of all—David Lean's *Lawrence of Arabia* (1962). He watched old movies on television, read books about film technique and history, and amassed a comprehensive collection of soundtrack albums. But mostly, Steven made movies—a dozen or more 8mm shorts that he used to develop his skills and experiment with technique.

When Steven was ready, he moved on to more ambitious fare. In 1959, Steven began making a fifteen-minute World War II action movie called *Fighter Squad* (1960), which he filmed aboard a vintage fighter and bomber that had been mothballed at a local airport. The centerpiece of the film was an aerial battle Steven created by employing a series of clever camera angles and then intercutting the results with documentary footage of real dogfights culled from a series of 8mm documentaries. Following *Fighter*

Squad, Steven began filming another WWII adventure. *Escape to Nowhere* (1962)—the story of a group of American soldiers battling the Germans in North Africa—contained a series of elaborate action sequences that required a generous number of stunts and special effects to realize. Shooting mostly on weekends, the forty-minute film took the young director three years to finish. Those who saw these films were struck by the sophistication of Steven's technique—the shots and the editing seemed to be the work of a mature veteran filmmaker rather than that of a high school amateur.

To finance his productions, Spielberg would screen 16mm prints of popular theatrical films in his living room and sell popcorn and candy on the side. He would donate the admission money to charity and use the snack money to buy film and supplies. He would also earn money by whitewashing his neighbors' fruit trees. When it came time to actually make the movies, Steven enlisted the help of everyone he knew. His father provided additional funding and helped Steven devise and execute the various physical and visual effects. His mother let him use the family home as a studio and helped him create sets and costumes. He tapped his sisters, friends, and classmates to crew the films and to act in them (one oft-repeated piece of Spielberg lore tells of how he got a notorious school bully off his back by casting him as the lead in *Escape to Nowhere*. Steven's classmates were amused indeed by the sight of the bruiser docilely taking orders from his former tormentee). Steven even involved the community at large—persuading local businesses and institutions to donate materials and allow him to use their premises for filming.

Spielberg was very serious about his filmmaking. The previously scattered adolescent brought a great sense of focus, determination, and maturity to his work. Once he embarked on a project, he would persevere, keeping at it until every detail of the production was exactly the way he wanted it to be. In the process he developed a great deal of confidence and self-assurance. Making movies paid off for Steven in other ways as well. To begin with, it helped him make friends—he became part of a group of young Phoenix filmmakers who helped each other out on their films. It also brought him respect—the same kids who had dismissed him as a wimp were impressed by seeing him confidently take command on his sets. Filmmaking also brought Steven acclaim (*Escape to Nowhere* won first prize at the 1962–1963 Canyon Films Junior Film Festival) and celebrity (he was interviewed several time by the area press, a local TV news crew did a story on the making of *Escape to Nowhere*, and he also appeared as a guest on "Home Movie Winners," a weekly segment of a popular Phoenix children's television show called *Wallace and Ladmo*). Unfortunately, it didn't help him much with school—Steven's obsession with film left him with less time and concentration for his studies than ever before. His teachers complained, his parents fretted, but Steven wasn't deterred.

Part of the prize Steven won for *Escape from Nowhere* was a 16mm movie camera. Unable to afford the cost of 16mm film, Steven traded it for a state-of-the-art 8mm camera. Arnold supplemented the camera with a Bolex Sonorizer—a device that enabled Steven to record sound on a magnetic strip that could be attached to the side of 8mm film and so add dialogue, music and sound effects to his movies. Arnold also bought a sound projector. With this equipment package in place, Steven decided to do something that few amateur filmmakers had ever attempted: make a feature-length film. It would be a science fiction epic about a subject that fascinated him—UFOs.

In many interviews Spielberg has given over the years, he has identified the start of his interest in unidentified flying objects as an incident that occurred in 1957, soon after his family moved to Phoenix. Late one evening, Arnold woke Steven up and bundled him into the car. Arnold had heard there was going to be a comet visible that night and wanted Steven to see it, so he drove them out into the desert, where the lights of the city would not obscure the sky. Finding an ideal spot, they lay down in the sand and gazed up at the heavens. Although they were unable to locate the comet, they were treated to a spectacular meteor shower. This was the first time Steven had seen such an amazing sight, and the brilliant display of falling stars absolutely enchanted him. This experience ("My first introduction to the world beyond the earth...") triggered a general interest in all things related to "out there." Steven got a telescope and began studying astronomy. He also began reading science fiction books and magazines (many borrowed from his father, who was also a fan) and watching a lot of science fiction movies and television shows (his favorites included *The Day the Earth Stood Still*, *Forbidden Planet*, and *The Twilight Zone*). He became fascinated by the idea that we might not be alone in the universe—that intelligent life might exist elsewhere in the cosmos and that we might someday have the chance to meet it.

Like all children of the 1950s, young Spielberg was captivated by the flying saucer craze and wished desperately to see one for himself. He didn't, but some of his friends did. While on a Boy Scout camping trip that Steven missed, his troopmates reported seeing a brilliant circle of red light rise up over the desert and fly off into the sky. When Steven learned that he had missed out on seeing a genuine UFO, he was devastated. He vented his frustration by writing a sixty-seven-page screenplay called *Firelight*—the story of three mysterious balls of light that descend on a small Arizona town and begin kidnapping the inhabitants. A team of scientists investigates the mystery and eventually discovers that the kidnappings are being perpetrated by members of an alien race called the Altarians, who transport the humans to their home planet and place them in a zoo. Typical for the era, the aliens are portrayed as menacing creatures who intend to have their way with the human race by brainwashing it into submission.

To produce *Firelight*, Arnold and Steven founded a partnership called American Artist Productions, with both chipping in to cover the $600 dollar cost of filming. Steven once again recruited family members, friends, and classmates to work on the movie and to perform in it. Beginning in June 1963, Steven shot scenes in his own home, in the homes of friends and neighbors, and in a variety of locations around Phoenix, including Camelback Mountain, Sky Harbor Airport (where Steven managed to persuade American Airlines to allow him to film on board one of its planes in between flights), and in the Baptist Hospital (where he was given the use of an empty room and an oxygen tank). The production attracted a great deal of attention, and the *Arizona Republic* published two articles and a photo spread about the movie. Steven used a wide range of effects, from miniatures to stop-motion animation to some simple but effective opticals (e.g., the firelights were created by putting gels over lights and then superimposing them on the live-action footage) to bring his story to life.

Filming wrapped in December 1963, after which Spielberg began four months of post-production. He edited all of his footage into a 135-minute final cut, often (with his mother's permission) faking sick and staying home from school to do so. He created a sound effects track and then recorded the actors' dialogue over it. Finally, he composed a score on his clarinet, which he then got his high school band to play while he taped it. By March 1964, the film was finished. Through a family friend, Steven arranged to premiere *Firelight* at the Phoenix Little Theatre. An extensive publicity campaign was mounted, programs were prepared, and a spotlight was borrowed from a local merchant. Steven and the cast arrived at the theater in a limo. The screening sold out (grossing an estimated $800 for a net profit of approximately $200—Steven Spielberg's first box office success). The film made a tremendous impact, earning cheers and applause from the enthusiastic audience.

By the time *Firelight* was finished, Steven knew that he had found his calling. He had become enthralled with the medium of film and the power it had to grab viewers and involve them in an immediate and visceral way. Moreover, he loved being the person who made that happen ("I love to grip an audience and watch them lean forward in their seats.... I like involving the audience on a level of total participation") and wanted to make doing so his life's work. "I knew after my third or fourth little 8mm epic that this was going to be a career, not just a hobby...."

The day after the *Firelight* premiere, the Spielbergs left Phoenix and moved to northern California—first to Los Gatos and then to Saratoga. Arnold had been hired by IBM to design computers. This was the beginning of an extremely unhappy period for Steven. He enrolled as a senior in Saratoga High, an upscale school with a lot of cliques. Although he joined the stage crew and the school newspaper, newcomer Steven felt ostracized. He also reported being the victim of a number of anti-Semitic taunts, which only made matters worse. To top it off, he continued to do poorly in his studies. Things weren't much better at home. Arnold and Leah's marriage was on the rocks. They were arguing a lot and talking about divorce. Arnold and Steven weren't getting along, either. Arnold's work had always taken a lot of his time and energy, causing Steven to feel neglected by his father. In turn, Arnold was frustrated by Steven's continually poor academic performance, as well as his plan to seek a career in show business. The senior Spielberg was happy enough to support his son's filmmaking as a hobby, but when it came to the future, Arnold wanted Steven to go to college and then do something practical with his life, such as become a doctor or an engineer. Steven's lack of interest in doing anything of the sort put the two at loggerheads. The young man's unhappiness was reflected in his creative output, which was minimal—he made only a few minor short films during this period and nothing on the scale of his previous endeavors.

In the spring of 1965, Arnold and Leah separated and began divorce proceedings, an event that devastated their children. Arnold took a new job and moved to Los Angeles. After graduating from high school, Steven joined him. Leah, Anne, Sue, and Nancy stayed in Saratoga for another year and then moved back to Arizona, where Leah would eventually marry Bernie Adler, a family friend who had been Arnold's assistant at General Electric.

As unhappy as Steven was over the breakup of his family, he was thrilled to be living in Southern California, the home of the movie business. Eager to study filmmaking, Steven applied to the legendary film programs at the University of Southern California and the University of California at Los Angeles, but his grades weren't good enough and he was refused admission. To please his father and to avoid the Viet Nam draft, he applied to the less demanding California State University at Long Beach and was accepted. He took classes in theater arts and creative writing (as well as a few basic film classes in the Department of Radio and Television that didn't do him much good, since he already knew more than most of his professors), but much to his parents' chagrin, he continued to be a lackluster student. Instead of studying, Steven spent a lot of time at the movies—frequenting the Los Angeles area's art and revival movie houses and catching up on the many classic and foreign films that never made it to suburban Arizona when he was growing up. He became a big fan of the work of John Ford, Alfred Hitchcock, Ingmar Bergman, Jacques Tati, and the director he has cited as being his all-time favorite, François Truffaut. He also began working toward his ultimate goal: to become a professional movie director.

CHAPTER 3 | From *Amblin'*
to *Sugarland*

WHEN STEVEN SPIELBERG first began his quest to enter the film industry, the odds were definitely against him. In the mid-1960s, Hollywood was pretty much a closed shop. The studios were fully staffed by mostly middle-aged people who had been in their positions for decades and were quite content to stay there. There were few, if any, job openings, and those positions that did become available were usually filled by the members of union-controlled apprentice programs, most of whom were relatives of those already working. Young people interested in film had almost no chance of finding significant work in the mainstream business and instead had to be content working on the fringes in non-union independent and exploitation features, educational and industrial films, commercials and documentaries.

By the late 1960s, however, things had begun to change. Hollywood was in serious trouble. The major studios had lost touch with an audience that, with the ascendancy of the Baby Boom generation, was growing increasingly younger. Production costs were rising, and more and more films—many of them overblown epics and stodgy musicals featuring fading stars from bygone eras—were failing at the box office. Having already been ravaged by the Supreme Court's 1948 anti-trust ruling that forced them to sell off their theater chains (thus robbing them of a guaranteed place to show their films and forcing them to split the box office take with the now-independent theater owners) and the arrival of television in the 1950s (which cut their weekly audience in half or more), the studios were on extremely shaky financial ground, with some teetering on the edge of bankruptcy. Help was desperately needed—and it came in the unlikely form of two motorcycle-riding drug dealers. The enormous and unexpected success of *Easy Rider* in 1969 caused the Hollywood powers-that-be to recognize the enormous potential of the heretofore-untapped youth market. Not having a clue themselves as to what would appeal to youthful moviegoers, studio executives began recruiting young talent they hoped would be able to connect to modern audiences.

This talent was recruited from a variety of areas, including television (William Friedkin, Bob Rafaelson, Robert Altman), acting (Dennis Hopper, Tony Bill, Peter Fonda), and journalism (Peter Bogdanovich). But most of the members of the so-called New Hollywood were recruited from the film departments of major universities such as USC, UCLA, New York University, and Columbia, as well as conservatories such as the American Film Institute. This group of young film school graduates was nicknamed the "Movie Brats" by authors Michael Pye and Linda Myles in their book of the same name. The Movie Brats were extremely close-knit. They worked on each other's scripts— contributing ideas and doing rewrites; they helped out on shoots—filming inserts and pickups and occasionally handling second-unit chores; they viewed one another's rough cuts and gave advice on editing, effects, and other post-production matters. All of this was done in the spirit of collaboration, without credit or compensation (although they would occasionally give one another "points"—profit percentages—in their films as thanks). Unlike the filmmakers of Hollywood's Golden Age, who drew their creative inspiration from the theater, classic literature, and journalism, the Movie Brats found their inspiration in the cinema itself. As a group, they were extremely interested in film technique and its role in on-screen storytelling. They were well versed in technology and eager to employ new processes and equipment in their work. They loved classic American films and enjoyed both celebrating and deconstructing traditional genres. They also loved foreign films, especially those by the directors of the French New Wave (Truffaut, Godard, Chabrol, Resnais, etc.), who rejected the formal traditions of conventional filmmaking in favor of a looser, more improvisational and experimental approach to making movies, one that addressed the social and political issues of the day in a frank and realistic manner. Like the great European directors, the Movie Brats saw filmmaking as a vehicle for personal expression, but they weren't interested in producing art house fare. Writer/

director/producer John Milius (*Apocalypse Now, The Wind and the Lion*), summed up their goals succinctly when he said: "We're not interested in making small, critical successes nobody goes to see. We're interested in well-crafted, intelligent movies that can appeal to millions of people."

Although Spielberg didn't go to film school, he is often identified as a Movie Brat because he was closely associated with many people who did. Sometime in 1967, Steven attended a student film festival and was impressed by a science fiction short called *THX: 4EB (Electronic Labyrinth)*. He sought out the film's director, a USC student named George Lucas, to congratulate him. The two became friends, and through Lucas Spielberg soon met an entire group of young filmmakers who were as passionate about movies as he was, including Milius, Francis Ford Coppola (*The Godfather, Apocalypse Now*), and the husband-and-wife screenwriting team of Gloria Katz and Willard Huyck (*American Graffiti*). Steven shared their passion for film history and film technique, and their interest in making popular, entertaining movies for the widest audience possible.

Unable to obtain entry into the same academic programs as his friends, Steven got his training in a very different and much more practical setting—on the backlot and soundstages of Universal Studios. For years the myth has circulated that Spielberg first gained access to Universal by jumping off the studio tour, setting himself up in an empty office, and then sneaking back onto the lot each day by dressing in a suit and tie and posing as a junior executive. As good a story as this is, the truth is a bit more protracted and a little less fanciful. When he was growing up, Steven used to spend part of his school vacations with relatives in the Los Angeles area. In the course of these trips, he visited several studios, including Warner Bros. (where he had the opportunity to observe the filming of a scene for the JFK biopic *PT 109*). Sometime in the spring of 1963, when Steven was sixteen years old, a friend of the Spielberg family with contacts at Universal's parent company, MCA, asked if Steven could be given a behind-the-scenes tour of the studio. Chuck Silvers, an assistant to the editorial supervisor for Universal Television, drew the assignment and showed Steven around the editorial department. Silvers was struck by the young man's passion for filmmaking and by his determination to become a professional director.

Steven stayed in touch with Silvers over the next year while he made *Firelight* and returned the following summer to show him the completed

film. Impressed by Steven's sci-fi epic, Silvers got him an unpaid intern-
ship as a clerical assistant in the editorial department. This position gave
Steven a chance to explore the lot, observe the workings of the various departments, and watch actual movies being made. After he and his father
moved to Los Angeles, Steven returned to Universal and resumed his in-
ternship. He would spend three days a week at the studio, often sleeping
overnight in Silvers' office. Taking advantage of his access, Steven would
introduce himself to major industry figures working on the lot, such as
Charlton Heston, Cary Grant, director William Wyler, and producer Sam
Spiegel, and invite them to lunch so that he could discuss the business
with them. He became friends with actor Tony Bill, with whom he took
acting classes, and actor/director John Cassavetes, who hired Spielberg
as a production assistant on his landmark independent film, *Faces*. As
invaluable as all of these experiences were, Steven knew that if he was
going to convince the industry to let him make movies, he was first going
to have to show it what he could do. Initially he tried to screen *Firelight* for
Universal executives and producers, but no one would look at an 8mm
film. Steven then made a series of 16mm shorts, including *Encounter*
(about a sailor on the run from someone who is trying to kill him) and
The Great Race (about a young man who chases his girlfriend around the
Cal State Long Beach campus). Although these projects were extremely
accomplished, Chuck Silvers told Steven that if he wanted the right people
to pay attention to him, he would need to make a film in the standard
industry format of 35mm.

Determined to create a professional audition piece, Steven first attempted to make a film about bicycle racing called *Slipstream*, which was
produced by his friend Ralph Burris, was financed by Burris's parents,
and starred Tony Bill. Unfortunately, although most of the shoot went
smoothly, the filming of the climactic race was rained out. Since there was
no money available for a reshoot, production was shut down and the film
was never finished. Soon after, Steven met Denis Hoffman, the thirty-
year-old owner of a Hollywood optical house and the manager of a rock
band called October Country. Learning that Hoffman was interested in
producing a film that could showcase the band's songs, Steven pitched
him an idea about a young man and woman who meet while hitchhiking
through the California desert. The story was designed to be told without
dialogue, leaving plenty of room for October Country's music. Hoffman

liked the idea and agreed to finance the film. *Amblin'* was filmed over eight straight days in July 1968 using a volunteer crew and novice actors. Steven edited the film at night at the Hal Mann Laboratories in Hollywood. The twenty-six-minute final cut (which was completed at a final cost of $20,000) had its world premiere on December 18, 1968 (Steven's twenty-second birthday) at the Loew's Crest Theater in Westwood Village, near the UCLA campus. The film brought Steven acclaim—it screened at the 1969 Venice Film Festival and won the award for Best Live Action Short at the 1969 Atlanta Film Festival—and got him an agent, Mike Medavoy (who also represented Tony Bill) at the General Artists Corporation. But, most importantly, it put him on the path to finally fulfilling his dream.

Shortly after *Amblin'* was finished, Steven showed it to Chuck Silvers, who loved it. Silvers screened the film for Sidney J. Sheinberg, the vice-president of production for Universal Television. Impressed by the enormous creative talent and technical prowess on display in the short, Sheinberg called Steven in for a meeting. "I think you should be a director," Sheinberg told young Spielberg. "I think so too," Steven replied. Sheinberg offered the twenty-one-year-old a seven-year contract to direct television with a starting salary of $275 per week, effective immediately. Taken by surprise (and not wanting to disappoint his father), Steven replied that he needed to finish college first. "Do you wanna graduate college or do you wanna be a film director?" Sheinberg shot back. Steven's answer was never in doubt. Although he was interested in directing movies, not television, Steven knew this was his big break and was determined to take advantage of it. Dropping out of college, Steven signed the contract in December 1968. Universal's hiring of Steven was big news, and the industry press ran many stories highlighting his extreme youth (he was the youngest person ever to join the Directors Guild of America) and his precocious talent.

His first assignment was to helm one segment of a multi-part television movie called *Night Gallery*. Written by *The Twilight Zone*'s Rod Serling, *Night Gallery* was an anthology of three supernatural tales that was designed to serve as a pilot for a possible series. The first two stories were going to be directed by Boris Sagal and Barry Shear. Steven's portion was called "Eyes"—the story of a wealthy blind woman (played by legendary Hollywood actress Joan Crawford) who pays a down-and-out man for his eyes so that she can have transplant surgery that will allow her to regain her sight for just twenty-four hours. In one of Serling's trademark ironic twists, a blackout strikes the city just as the woman's vision is restored. Flailing about in the dark, she ends up crashing through the window of her penthouse and falling to her death. Determined to make a good impression with his first professional assignment, Steven packed the episode with as many clever shots as he could, going a bit overboard in the process. When the final product aired on November 8, 1969, it received mixed reviews, but the ratings were good enough that the series was picked up by NBC. However, following *Night Gallery*, Steven couldn't get another assignment—none of the television producers on the Universal lot would hire him. There were reports that some of the more conservative producers were put off by his dynamic visual style (which proponents called "avant-garde" and detractors called "artsy fartsy"), others by his youth and presumed inexperience, and still others by the perception that he was being forced on them by Sid Sheinberg.

Although he was disappointed that he wasn't working, Steven didn't waste his downtime. Instead, with his eye on the big screen, he spent the next few months developing several feature film projects that he then pitched to Universal's movie division. One was *Snow White*, which was brought to him by producer Dick Berg. Adapted by screenwriter Larry Grusin from a novel by Donald Barthelme, this was a raunchy spoof about a young hippie girl who moves in with seven horny guys who run a Chinese food factory in San Francisco. The studio turned the project down because it was so bizarre and distasteful. Steven's other project was *Carte Blanche*, which was based on a story he had read in the *Hollywood Citizen-News* about a Texas ex-convict named Ila Fae Dent, who broke her husband Bobby out of a pre-release facility so that they could get their kids back from Ila Fae's parents, who had been awarded custody of the children. Along the way, they took a Texas state trooper named Kenneth Crone hostage and forced him to drive them to Wheelock, where Ila Fae's parents lived. Police officers and reporters from across the state began pursuing them, and the fugitives eventually found themselves being followed by a convoy of over one hundred vehicles. The incident ended seven hours later when Bobby entered his in-laws' house and was shot dead by an FBI agent and a county sheriff hiding inside. Steven thought of the story as a "tragic fairy tale," but the executives felt that it was too dark and depressing and turned it down. Frustrated by the rejection and the inactivity, Steven asked Sheinberg if he could take a leave of absence from Universal, and Sheinberg agreed.

Determined to get his feature career off the ground, Steven spent the second half of 1969 writing several story treatments (scene-by-scene outlines of a film's story) and developing a few full-length scripts. He worked with actor/screenwriter Carl Gottlieb on two concepts: a comedy about a Catskills resort and an action drama about World War II fighter pilots. He also worked with Claudia Salter on a screenplay about the relationship between a post–World War I barnstormer and his son, called *Ace Eli and Rodger of the Skies.* Spielberg's agent, Mike Medavoy (now working for the mammoth Creative Management Associates), tried to set these projects up at various studios with Steven as the director, but the studios' executives all felt that the twenty-three-year-old was too young and inexperienced to helm a feature film (Twentieth Century-Fox bought *Ace Eli,* but hired veteran John Erman to direct it. Steven disowned the final product, which was released in 1973). Frustrated, Steven then tried to raise the money to make an independent 16mm feature, but was unsuccessful. Discouraged and broke, he returned to Universal at the beginning of 1970.

With Sid Sheinberg's help, Spielberg began landing television assignments. Toning down his visual flamboyance, but never failing to find innovative and exciting ways to tell stories, he bounced back from his rocky start and soon became one of the busiest and best-regarded directors on the lot, helming episodes of *Night Gallery, Marcus Welby, M.D., The Psychiatrist, The Name of the Game, Owen Marshall: Counselor at Law,* and *Columbo.* Steven's work on these shows was very well received, and, in December 1970 Universal signed Spielberg to a new, six-year, non-exclusive television producing and directing deal that also gave him the option to make features, both for Universal and for other studios.

In the summer of 1971, Steven was offered the chance to direct his first full-length television movie. Based on a story by Richard Matheson, *Duel* was a suspense thriller about a mild-mannered businessman who is menaced by the unseen driver of a monstrous truck while driving through the desert. Excited by the cinematic possibilities of the script, which contained little dialogue and told the story primarily through action, Steven tried to convince Universal to allow him to make the film as a feature. The studio agreed if Steven could get Gregory Peck to star, but Peck turned him down and so the project returned to television with *McCloud* star Dennis Weaver in the lead. Steven did a masterful job on the film, generating intense visual excitement and Hitchcockian moments of thrills and suspense at every turn. When *Duel* was broadcast on ABC on November 13, 1971, to excellent reviews and respectable ratings, Steven's tour de force direction grabbed the attention of the industry. He considered several offers to direct feature films before selecting a Burt Reynolds action picture about moonshiners called *McKlusky*. After several months of pre-production, however, Spielberg decided that he wanted his feature film debut to be something of quality rather than just a run-of-the-mill action movie and bowed out. (He was replaced by Joseph Sargent, and the finished film— retitled *White Lightning*—was released in 1973.) Spielberg directed two additional television movies (1972's *Something Evil*—about a young boy possessed by a demon—and 1973's *Savage*—about a crusading reporter) and then decided to revive *Carte Blanche*. To help him, he recruited two young screenwriters named Hal Barwood and Matthew Robbins.

Hal Barwood was born and raised in Hanover, New Hampshire. His father was the booking manager of the local theater, so Hal became steeped in film at an early age. His first love was animation, and after completing an 8mm independent study project at Brown University he received a fellowship to the USC School of Cinema. There he met another young graduate student named Matthew Robbins. Born in New York City in 1945, Robbins had attended Johns Hopkins University, where he received his bachelor of arts degree in romance languages. After earning their master's degrees, both Barwood and Robbins found themselves working at a small commercial production company called Dove Films. Deciding that the best way to become filmmakers was to write scripts that people would let them make, Hal and Matthew started spending their lunch hours kicking around ideas for movies and eventually began writing together. Jeff Berg—now head of the powerhouse International Creative Management talent agency but then a junior agent at CMA charged with signing up young talent—took them on as clients, and they began setting up projects at various studios, selling six scripts in three years.

One of these was a science fiction thriller called *Home Free*. Written for producer Larry Tucker (*Bob & Carol & Ted & Alice* [1969]), *Home Free* was the story of a two-man expedition to a distant planet far outside our solar system. When the explorers detect signs of alien life on the planet, the senior member of the team is immediately whisked away to safety, while the junior officer is left behind as a decoy to face the aliens alone. Tucker set the project up at Universal and, following the success of *Duel*, invited Steven Spielberg to direct it. When Spielberg came in to discuss the script, he, Barwood, and Robbins hit it off immediately. The three became friends, and Hal and Matthew visited Steven on the set early in 1972 when he filmed additional sequences for *Duel*, which was being prepared for a theatrical release in Europe. Although Universal eventually decided not to go ahead with *Home Free*, the three men continued to develop projects together.

Spielberg, Barwood, and Robbins began work on *Carte Blanche* by writing a treatment that fictionalized the real-life events. Ila Fae and Bobby Dent became Lou Jean and Clovis Poplin, and Kenneth Crone became Officer Maxwell Slide. The Dents' two children became a single baby boy, the time of their odyssey was extended to several days, and their ultimate destination became a foster home in Sugarland. In the course of the story, Slide and the Poplins bond and become friends. The misguided couple's hapless antics create a media circus that turns them into unlikely folk heroes before the story comes to its tragic end.

The team submitted the treatment to United Artists, who initially agreed to develop the project, but then backed out. Following UA's rejection, Steven then pitched the idea to Universal's senior vice president in charge of production, Jennings Lang, who liked it and made a deal for Steven, Barwood, and Robbins to turn the treatment into a screenplay. After a quick research trip to Texas, Barwood and Robbins wrote a first draft in thirteen days. The studio promptly declined it, once again dismissing the project as depressing and downbeat. Spielberg's new agent, Guy McElwaine (Mike Medavoy wanted Steven to focus on features and dropped him when he returned to Universal Television), then submitted the script to several other studios and producers, including the team of Richard D. Zanuck and David Brown. Zanuck and Brown had met at Twentieth Century-Fox, when Zanuck, the son of legendary Fox chief Daryl F. Zanuck, was the head of production and Brown was a studio executive. Zanuck's father fired him in 1970, after which he moved over to Warner Bros. Brown went with him, and they spent eighteen months running the studio before leaving to establish their own independent production company. They were negotiating a financing and distribution deal with Universal when McElwaine gave them *Carte Blanche* in the spring of

1972. Zanuck and Brown liked the script, but when they informed Lew Wasserman, the head of Universal's parent company, MCA, that they wanted to make a project his studio had declined twice already, Wasserman wasn't excited. Although he had faith in Steven, he had none in the project. Still, wanting to maintain good relations with his new producers, Wasserman told Zanuck and Brown to go ahead, although he warned them that the finished film would probably play to empty theaters. With that, the deal was done and Steven Spielberg was signed to direct his first theatrical motion picture.

Carte Blanche, whose title was changed to Sugarland and then to The Sugarland Express, entered pre-production in October 1972. Pre-production is the period in which all of the necessary preparations—scheduling, casting, hiring a crew, designing and building sets and costumes, scouting and securing locations, and readying props, makeup, and special effects—are made to get a film reading for shooting. Academy Award–winning actress Goldie Hawn was signed to play Lou Jean Poplin. William Atherton was cast as Clovis, Michael Sacks as Slide, and veteran actor Ben Johnson as Captain Tanner, the officer in charge of the pursuit. Filming on the $2.5 million production began on January 15, 1973, on location in San Antonio. During production, Steven impressed everyone with his expert knowledge and command of the filmmaking process as well as what Richard Zanuck described as "an innate sense of the visual mechanics of how you put all [the] pieces together so that the result is very striking." Spielberg devised a series of wildly imaginative shots that required intricately choreographed movements of cameras, vehicles, and actors, impressing everyone with his ability to effortlessly stage massive action sequences and set pieces. As Vilmos Zsigmond, the film's director of photography, told American Cinematographer magazine, "The way he directs a film makes you think he must have...the experience of a man fifty years old...[with]...many features behind him." The sixty-day shoot wrapped at the end of March 1973 and the film entered post-production—the period in which the picture and sound effects are edited, optical effects are completed, and the musical score is composed and recorded. The plan was to work through the spring and summer in anticipation of fall previews and a Thanksgiving 1973 release.

As he began cutting Sugarland, Steven started thinking ahead to his next project. It is a common practice for directors to line up their next assignment before finishing a current one. Since no film is ever a sure thing until it actually begins shooting, most directors develop several projects at the same time, so that if one falls out, they'll have another ready to go. The project Steven was most interested in was a thriller based on a yet-to-be published novel by first-time author Peter Benchley about a giant great white shark that terrorizes a summer resort town on Long Island. The book was called *Jaws*, and Zanuck and Brown had just purchased the screen rights for $175,000. Steven became aware of the project when he spotted the manuscript on Richard Zanuck's desk and took it home to read. Struck by the story's similarity to *Duel* (both involved ferocious attacks on everyday people by seemingly unstoppable killing machines) and excited by its cinematic potential, Steven asked Zanuck and Brown if he could direct the film. When told him they had already hired a director, a disappointed Spielberg moved on. He considered a few other projects, including the New York subway hijack thriller *The Taking of Pelham One Two Three* and Zanuck/Brown's production of *MacArthur*, based on a script by Hal Barwood and Matthew Robbins (both films were eventually directed by Spielberg's *White Lightning* replacement, Joseph Sargent). Paul Newman asked him to direct *Lucky Lady* from a script by Spielberg's friends Willard Huyck and Gloria Katz, but he turned the project down because he didn't think Newman was right for the film. Steven, Katz and Huyck also worked on a treatment for a comedy about the man who invented the toilet, called *Flushed with Pride: The Story of Thomas Crapper*, but that project died when Guy McElwaine threatened to stop representing the trio if they went ahead with the bad-taste biopic.

Gradually, however, Spielberg's thoughts turned to another project, based on an idea he had been toying with for some time—a story that he described as being a thriller about "UFOs and Watergate."

CHAPTER 4 | *Watch the Skies*

STEVEN SPIELBERG'S INTEREST in making a feature film about UFOs dated back to the time of *Firelight*. In a newspaper interview he gave at the time of that film's Phoenix premiere, the seventeen-year-old director said that he hoped to interest Universal in producing a big-screen remake of his 8mm epic. That idea never came to fruition, of course, but Spielberg maintained his interest in the flying saucer phenomenon in the years that followed. He read books and articles on the subject, kept up with reports of the latest sightings, and talked to people he met about their own UFO-related experiences. In doing so, he was struck by how closely the descriptions of UFOs and sighting events from all over the world matched. He was also impressed by how widespread and strong the belief in UFOs and extraterrestrial life was. Spielberg found this belief intriguing: "I was just as interested in...why people looked to the skies, and want to believe, as I was in... [understanding what was] happening up there." In Spielberg's view, UFOs were as much a "cultural phenomenon" as they were a scientific one. "Whether they're real or not real, they have certainly affected everybody's life."

As for his own beliefs on the subject, Steven claimed to be an agnostic. "I'm convinced something's going on that's baffling people all over the world. Enough evidence has been collected for us to take UFOs seriously..." but, as for whether or not they were from outer space, Spielberg, never having seen a flying saucer for himself, declared that, for him, "the jury's still out." One thing he knew for sure, however, was that UFOs were a great subject for a movie, and at some point during the final stages of

Sugarland, his desire to do a feature film about them returned. Spielberg has never said what specifically prompted this renewed interest at that particular moment, but given the tenor of the time, it's not surprising that the topic was on his mind.

By the early 1970s, the intense interest in UFOs generated by the late 1960s spike in sightings inspired several young Movie Brats—members of the generation that had come of age during the first flying saucer craze—to begin thinking up ideas for UFO-themed movies. Riffing on a subplot from Ingmar Bergman's film *The Seventh Seal* about a man who sees visions but is not believed by the people around him, Hal Barwood and Matthew Robbins came up with a story about a police officer from a small town in the rural South who is sent out to investigate a disturbance at a remote farmhouse. Arriving on the scene, he sees a UFO, which quickly departs. The policeman reports the incident, but no one believes him and he becomes the object of ridicule. As he tries to persuade the world that what he saw was real, he grows increasingly estranged from his family and friends and eventually falls in with a group of UFO true believers. At the end of the story, the aliens return and the police officer—now feeling closer to the extraterrestrials than to the people in his own world—boards the spaceship and leaves the planet with his new friends.

Steven Spielberg had already come up with a few UFO-related ideas himself. In 1970, he wrote a short treatment called "Experiences." Reminiscent of his account of the evening that he and Arnold had spent watching the meteor shower many years before, the story was about a group of people parked in a lovers' lane who witness a display of UFOs in the night sky. On another occasion, he considered making a documentary about UFO witnesses. However, the catalyst for the project that ultimately became *Close Encounters of the Third Kind* appears to have been the 1972 publication of a book called *The UFO Experience: A Scientific Inquiry* by an astronomer from Northwestern University named Dr. J. Allen Hynek.

Josef Allen Hynek was born in Chicago on May 1, 1910. After graduating from the University of Chicago and completing his Ph.D. in astrophysics at the Yerkes Observatory, he began teaching at Ohio State University in 1936. During World War II, he joined the Applied Science Laboratory at Johns Hopkins and helped develop the U.S. Navy's radio proximity fuse. Following the war, he returned to Ohio State and became the director of the university's McMillan Observatory. In 1956, Hynek joined the Smithsonian Astrophysical Observatory to work on a satellite tracking program, and in 1960 he became the chairman of the astronomy department at Northwestern.

When the flying saucer craze first began in 1947, the United States military dismissed the initial reports as misinterpretations of natural atmospheric phenomena such as meteors, comets, St. Elmo's Fire, etc. When too many reports came in describing actual flying ships, the military officials changed their minds and decided that the UFOs had to be some sort of aircraft—probably foreign and possibly hostile. However, as more and more witnesses described the saucers' unconventional behaviors—their tremendous speeds, erratic non-ballistic movements, and silent, vaporless propulsion—it became apparent that there was something really unusual going on that needed to be investigated. So, in 1948, the Air Force started Project Sign.

Nicknamed Project Saucer, the unit was headquartered at Wright-Patterson Air Force Base in Dayton, Ohio (first as part of the Air Technical Intelligence Center and later as a division of the Foreign Technology Division). Its purpose was to investigate the various UFO sighting reports and to determine just what these flying saucers really were. In need of an astronomical expert who could identify and thus rule out those reported objects that were clearly natural atmospheric and celestial phenomena, the Air Force contacted Hynek, who agreed to become one of Project Sign's scientific consultants. As he began his duties, Hynek found that opinion about UFOs among project personnel was split. Some figured that the saucers were examples of foreign technology. A few believed they had to be extraterrestrial in origin. Most held that they were signs of some sort of mass public hysteria or psychosis. Hynek shared the latter view. As a serious scientist, he thought that the whole subject of UFOs was ridiculous, and that most reports were made by unstable or unreliable witnesses who mistook natural or man-made objects for flying saucers. This, he was sure, was a fad that would soon pass.

The longer that first wave of sightings went on, the more impatient some government officials became with it. They began to form the opinion that the focus on flying saucers was distracting people from real matters of national defense and security. The Air Force too became less inclined toward investigating the UFO phenomenon and more interested in ending it, and so, in 1949, Project Sign was reorganized as Project Grudge, and its mission became to debunk all of the reports that came in and to do whatever it took to disprove the existence of UFOs. In the summer of 1951, the unit was reorganized again. Project Grudge was now Project Blue Book and would remain so for the next eighteen years.

Project Blue Book was a curious mixture of Project Sign and Project Grudge. Like Project Sign, its stated purpose was to receive reports of UFO sightings from the public and to investigate the credible ones to determine just what it was that had been seen. In reality, however, Blue Book's purpose seemed to be to debunk all of the reports, no matter how credible. Although the Air Force liked to give the impression that Blue Book was a serious, full-scale operation, it was anything but. Headed by a series of low-ranking officers with little authority, the operation was actually quite small and understaffed. No report was ignored, but few were seriously investigated. It was automatically assumed that all of the UFO witnesses were either unstable or mistaken. The investigators would look for the simplest, most mundane and "normal" explanation for every sighting, even going to ludicrous lengths to do so (one Blue Book evaluation identified one particular UFO as being an airplane, a satellite, the planet Venus, and swamp gas all at the same time). Any facts that contradicted such explanations were ignored. Any case that really couldn't be explained would be labeled as "unidentified" and filed away, never to be looked at again. To aid its non-mission, Project Blue Book called frequently on Hynek, who was more than happy to oblige, although his willingness wouldn't last long.

In the course of his duties, Hynek reviewed every UFO report that came through Project Blue Book—a number that, as the wave of sightings continued, rose to over twelve thousand. While Hynek found that most of these sightings could be easily explained, he also found that a significant number couldn't be. Moreover, he found that a majority of these unexplainable reports were being made not by the confused and the crazy, but instead by witnesses that Hynek considered to be quite credible: scientists, pilots, police officers, and military personnel—people trained to be careful, astute observers and whose accounts needed to be taken seriously. All of this led Hynek to believe that there might actually be something to the UFO phenomenon. While he was not necessarily convinced that UFOs were, or even had to be, extraterrestrial in origin, he was starting to believe that they were indeed *something*—something that required thorough investigation.

Hynek began asking Project Blue Book investigators to take a closer look at the reports that he found credible, but his requests were continually rebuffed or ignored. When he pressed, he was asked not to pursue the matter further. Frustrated by this lack of action, Hynek was also troubled by the Air Force's seemingly contradictory public attitude toward the matter—promising to thoroughly investigate sightings, but then not doing so; claiming that UFOs didn't exist, but then classifying many of the official reports pertaining to them as "top secret"; housing unclassified UFO-related documents that were supposed to be open to the public in locations that required high-level security clearances. Although he attributed a lot of the confusion to simple bureaucratic incompetence, there was enough deliberateness in all of this that Hynek eventually became convinced that—as an increasing number of people were beginning to suggest—the Air Force knew that UFOs were real, but was covering up the truth about their existence.

As unhappy as he was, Hynek remained with Project Blue Book so that he could continue to have access to all of the reports. As the years went on, he became more and more vocal about his disagreements with the Air Force's tactics and conclusions. Hynek's complaints mostly fell on deaf ears until the mid-1960s, when Air Force officials finally asked for his ideas on how to improve the project. Hynek outlined an entire series of reforms aimed at making the program more serious, more thorough, and more scientific, but his recommendations came too late. In October 1966, the Air Force had established a committee headed by Edward U. Condon of the University of Colorado. The committee's mission was to review all of the information collected by Blue Book and come up with a valid explanation for the UFO phenomenon. In January 1969, the Condon Committee submitted its report, which dismissed the entire topic of UFOs by stating that: "No direct evidence whatever of a convincing nature now exists for the claim that any UFOs represent spacecraft visiting earth from another civilization... our general conclusion is that nothing has come from the study of UFOs in the last twenty-one years that has added to scientific knowledge..." and concluded that there was no good reason to continue investigating the phenomenon. Although Hynek felt that the report was poorly conceived, prejudiced (Condon made no secret of his anti-UFO bias before the committee had even begun its work), and sloppily executed, Robert C. Seamans, the Secretary of the Air Force, accepted Condon's recommendation and shut down Project Blue Book in December 1969.

Concerned that, without Project Blue Book to act as a central reporting station, a lot of valuable data was going to be lost, Hynek began collecting UFO reports himself, at first through his office at Northwestern and later through the Center for UFO Studies, which he founded in 1973. He developed strict criteria for evaluating reports, as well as a system for classifying the various types of sightings, which had six different categories: three for UFOs seen at a distance (Nocturnal Lights, Daytime Discs, and Radar/Visual) and three for closer sightings, which Hynek called "close encounters." According to Hynek:

- A Close Encounter of the First Kind is a UFO seen at close range but having no interaction with the surrounding environment.

- A Close Encounter of the Second Kind is similar to a Close Encounter of the First Kind, except that physical effects of the UFO—flattened, broken, or burned vegetation; frightened animals; power drains or interruptions that return to normal after the UFO passes by—are noted.

- A Close Encounter of the Third Kind is an encounter in which the presence of UFO occupants is reported.

Steven Spielberg has spoken on more than one occasion about the strong influence that Dr. Hynek had on his thinking about UFOs. Spielberg was particularly struck by Hynek's conviction that there was more than enough credible evidence to suggest that UFOs were real and by his conclusion that the U.S. government was hiding the true facts about them. As these ideas began percolating in Spielberg's imagination, he soon came up with the idea to do a thriller about a Project Blue Book official whose job, like Hynek's was, is to debunk eyewitness reports and disprove the existence of UFOs. As the plot developed, he would come to suspect that the Air Force has been covering up the truth about flying saucers. The official would investigate and make the awesome discovery that UFOs really *are* vehicles from outer space and that their alien occupants have been visiting our planet for some time. He would expose the conspiracy, and the film would end with the first meeting between human beings and extraterrestrials. Spielberg wrote a treatment outlining his idea. Borrowing the famous last line from 1951's *The Thing (From Another World)*, he titled it *Watch the Skies* and registered it with the Writers Guild of America, West. At this point, Steven's plan was to develop the treatment into a full-blown screenplay so that he could make *Watch the Skies* as his next picture. But before he could get started, *Jaws* came swimming back into his life.

After Spielberg had expressed his interest in directing the film, Zanuck and Brown had gone forward with Dick Richards (*The Culpepper Cattle Company*), the director they had originally attached to the project. Richards, however, lost the job when, during his initial meeting with author Peter Benchley and Zanuck and Brown to discuss the project, he repeatedly referred to the story's monstrous shark as a "whale." Realizing that Richards was the wrong man for the job, the producers started looking for another director. Knowing that the film would be technically challenging and complex, they thought at first to hire a veteran director with years of experience, but after considering several likely candidates they began to have second thoughts. Fearing that an old-timer would not be able to deliver the freshness of approach and visual excitement they were hoping for, they decided to hire someone who could, and in June 1973 they formally offered Steven Spielberg the opportunity to direct *Jaws*.

Despite his initial enthusiasm for the project, Steven had only a lukewarm response to Zanuck and Brown's offer. Having had some time to think about it, he realized that, as excited as he was by the last third of the book, which focused on the battle between man and shark, he wasn't all that thrilled with the rest of it, which in his opinion contained a lot of cardboard characters and a convoluted plot with too many soap opera elements. He was also concerned that the project was too blatantly commercial—Spielberg wanted to be known as a serious director of serious films, not as a technically adept director of monster movies, which is what he feared would happen if he directed *Jaws* so soon after *Duel* ("Who wants to be a shark and truck director?" was his famous quote). He was going to turn the project down, but Zanuck and Brown persuaded him that their intention was to produce a first-class motion picture, not a schlock horror film. They also reminded him that every director needed to make a few commercial hits to ensure funding for his more artistic endeavors.

Convinced, Spielberg signed on. The plan at that point was to have Peter Benchley spend the summer working on the screenplay under Steven's supervision while Spielberg continued to edit *Sugarland*, and then, in the fall of 1973, after *Sugarland* was finished, to begin pre-production on *Jaws*.

Spielberg and Benchley worked on three drafts of the *Jaws* script before Benchley completed his contractual obligation and moved on. Though they had addressed a number of Steven's concerns, the director still wasn't happy with the screenplay, which he felt had many of the same drawbacks as the novel. Concerned that the project didn't seem to be coming together despite its potential, Spielberg decided to quit. When he informed Zanuck and Brown of his decision, they asked him to give the script another shot. While in France for the European theatrical release of *Duel*, Spielberg met with the producers at Cannes, and together the three of them worked out a new, more cinematic treatment of the story that simplified Benchley's plot and reworked many of the characters. Steven wrote a quick draft outlining the new version, and then he, Zanuck and Brown went looking for new writers to carry on from there. They first approached Hal Barwood and Matthew Robbins, but the duo declined, claiming they couldn't figure out how to make a scary movie about a shark, since all one had to do to escape it was stay out of the water. Spielberg, Zanuck, and Brown then offered the job to Richard Levinson and William Link, the creators of *Columbo*, with whom Spielberg was friendly, but they turned it down because they didn't want to write what they saw as a schlocky "B" movie (both later regretted the decision tremendously). John Byrum (*Mahogany*) also declined the assignment. Finally, Zanuck and Brown brought in playwright Howard Sackler (*The Great White Hope*), who began what would turn out to be five weeks of work on the script. Although he had faith in Sackler, Spielberg still had serious doubts about the project. Thinking it would be a good idea to have something else in the works in case *Jaws* didn't pan out, Spielberg once again turned his attention to *Watch the Skies*.

It would not be an easy sell. In the early 1970s, science fiction was not particularly popular with most studio executives. It was considered a "B" genre consisting primarily of low-budget programmers generated by hack producers, writers, and directors; featuring wooden actors and cheesy special effects; and unworthy of serious attention by serious filmmakers. When A-level sci-fi pictures such as *The Day the Earth Stood Still*,

Forbidden Planet, Planet of the Apes, and *2001: A Space Odyssey* were made, the high cost of fantastic sets and costumes, exotic makeup, and elaborate optical and physical effects made them so expensive to produce that even when they were hits they never made much of a profit (it took *2001* five years to break even). To take the onus off the project, Steven began referring to *Watch the Skies* as "a political thriller."

He decided to pitch his story to Alan Ladd Jr. The son of the legendary actor and a former talent agent and producer, Ladd was currently a production executive in charge of developing feature film projects at Twentieth Century-Fox. He and Spielberg played poker together at a regular game hosted by Guy McElwaine. Ladd liked Steven, whom he felt was a major new talent, and wanted to be in business with him. Ladd was interested in *Watch the Skies,* but knew that before he could present it to Fox, the "package" was going to have to be made more attractive. At that point—with only one television movie and a modest, incomplete feature to his credit—Steven was not considered a "bankable" director, and it was highly unlikely that Fox (or any other studio) would allow him to make an ambitious film in a risky genre unless they were first able to attach a commercially proven "element"—a top star or a major producer—to the project. Luckily, Spielberg knew a producing team that fit the bill perfectly—a young husband and wife who were currently finishing work on their second major Hollywood production, a film about Depression-era con men starring Paul Newman and Robert Redford called *The Sting.*

CHAPTER 5 | **The Producers**

JULIA MILLER WAS BORN in New York City on April 7, 1944. Her mother, who had emigrated to the United States from Russia, was a housewife and occasional radio writer. Her father, who had graduated from Columbia University and had worked on the Manhattan Project during World War II, was a metallurgist. The family moved to Brooklyn in 1948 and then to the town of Great Neck on Long Island, where Julia was placed in an S.P. (Special Progress) track—an accelerated program for children with IQs over 135—in school. When Julia was in high school her family moved to Milwaukee, but after graduation she returned to the East Coast to attend Mount Holyoke College, where she majored in political science. During her junior year, the bold, brash Julia began dating a soft-spoken young student from Dartmouth College named Michael Phillips. Born in Brooklyn on June 29, 1943, as a boy Michael had often spent his Saturdays at the movies, where for a quarter he would watch two features and a string of cartoons. He became a big fan of science fiction films and has cited *The Day the Earth Stood Still* (1951) as having made a profound impression on him (greatly impressed by its message of universal peace and cooperation, he returned for a second and then a third viewing, all in one day). When Michael was in the fourth grade, his father, a successful clothing manufacturer, moved the family to Roslyn, an upscale town on Long Island. Although Michael dreamed of becoming a center fielder for the New York Yankees, after graduating from high school he headed for Dartmouth instead.

After dating for about a year, Michael and Julia broke up. Both graduated from their respective schools in June 1965 and returned separately to New York. Julia went to work as a production assistant at McCall's magazine,while Michael enrolled in the law school at New York University. They ran into each other a year or so later, got back together, and were married in 1966.

Following their marriage, Michael continued to attend law school, while Julia left McCall's to take a job first as an advertising copywriter for the college book division at Macmillan, Inc. and then as an editor at Ladies' Home Journal. After graduating from NYU, Michael was admitted to the New York State bar, but rather than practice law, he took a job as a financial analyst on Wall Street. Meanwhile, Julia got a job as a story editor working for a creative executive at Paramount Pictures named Marvin Birdt. Her job was to read and analyze the numerous scripts, books, magazine articles, and short stories that were submitted to the company to determine if any of them had the potential to make a good film. Birdt moved to the Mirisch Corporation (the production company behind films such as *The Magnificent Seven, The Great Escape,* and *In The Heat of the Night*) in 1968, and Julia went with him, but she lost her job a year later when Birdt was fired. She was unemployed for three months and then she met David Begelman, the New York head of Creative Management Associates, one of the industry's biggest talent agencies.

Begelman liked Julia's blunt, outspoken style and hired her as a creative executive at First Artists, an actor-driven production company that CMA had created for its clients Barbra Streisand, Paul Newman, and Sidney Poitier. Julia's job was to find and develop material for First Artists' principals to star in. She threw herself into the assignment and found several projects that she thought were promising, but she had a hard time getting any of the stars interested in them. After six months, Julia found herself becoming increasingly frustrated. Michael was unhappy with his job as well, and the two began talking about going into business for themselves. They were joined in these talks by actor Tony Bill, whom Julia had met in the CMA offices in 1970. The two of them hit it off, and Julia and Michael began socializing with Tony and his wife, Antoinette. Bill, born in 1940, graduated from the University of Notre Dame and made his professional acting debut alongside Frank Sinatra in the 1963 screen adaptation of Neil Simon's play *Come Blow Your Horn.* He followed this with roles on television and in other films, including Francis Ford Coppola's first major movie, *You're a Big Boy Now* (1966), and starred in his friend Steven Spielberg's aborted short *Slipstream*. Toward the end of the 1960s, Bill decided that he wanted to become a producer. Unable to afford to hire big-name talent or purchase high-profile material, he turned instead to the young artists coming out of the nation's film schools—filmmakers he figured would be willing to work cheaply in return for a chance to get their movies made. One of his first discoveries was AFI graduate Terence Malick, whom Bill hired to write the screenplay for his debut production—a comedy about an eccentric long-distance trucker, starring Alan Arkin, called *Deadhead Miles* (1972).

Tony, Michael, and Julia's initial idea was to create a venture capital firm that would provide seed money to filmmakers trying to get their movies off the ground in return for an equity position in the finished product. They began looking around for suitable projects, but their plans changed in January 1972, when Bill came across a script written by a young USC graduate named David S. Ward. *Steelyard Blues* was an anti-establishment comedy about a group of misfits who decide to repair a derelict Navy PBY flying boat and use it to fly off in search of paradise. Bill liked the script (which Ward had written as his USC thesis) and arranged to meet the author. During the meeting, Ward pitched Bill an idea he was working on about two con men in the 1930s who devise an elaborate ruse to bilk the notorious gangster who killed their friend. The fascinating tale built up to a surprise ending that Ward refused to reveal unless someone hired him to write the script. Intrigued, Bill recorded Ward's pitch and sent it to Julia and Michael. They loved it and decided to pay Ward to write the full screenplay, with the idea of producing it themselves if it turned out well. To this end, Bill put up $1,000 and the Phillipses put up $2,500 (their life savings), forming a company called Bill/Phillips Productions. They then gave Ward the money in exchange for an option on both *Steelyard Blues* and the con man story, which Ward called *The Sting* (after the grifter term for a con in which the mark never realizes he's been taken).

As Ward got to work on *The Sting*, Bill gave *Steelyard Blues* to Mike Medavoy, who passed the script along to another one of his clients—the actor Donald Sutherland. At the time, Sutherland was living with Jane Fonda and the two of them were looking for a project they could do together. *Steelyard*'s subversive humor appealed to Sutherland, who showed the script to Fonda, and the two agreed to star in the film. Having the two stars of the recent hit *Klute* made *Steelyard* a hot property, and in February

1972, just two weeks after acquiring the script, Bill/Phillips made a deal with Warner Bros. (then being run by Richard Zanuck and David Brown) to make it into a movie. As soon as the deal was finalized, Michael quit his Wall Street job. Since it was a conflict of interest for Julia to develop outside projects for herself when she was supposed to be developing films for First Artists, she initially kept her involvement in *Steelyard* a secret and let everyone think that Bill/Phillips was just a partnership between Tony and Michael, but when the Warner Bros. deal was announced, the truth came out and Julia was fired.

Steelyard Blues was rushed into production with very little preparation in order to accommodate Jane Fonda, who at the time had only a small window of availability. In addition, most of the key members of the crew—two of the producers, the writer, the director (Alan Myerson, a friend of Sutherland and Fonda who had been hired at their insistence), the cinematographer, and the art director—had never made a film before. The product of all of this hurrying and inexperience was, to be frank, a mess. At that point, Michael Phillips recalls, studio executives Richard Zanuck and David Brown "gave us [the three producers]—against editors guild rules—our own black-and-white print of the film and our own editing equipment and let us fiddle with the movie for a year. [We] didn't make [it] measurably better, but it really drove home why we had problems and what we would have needed to have done [during production] to make it work. I learned a lot from all of that recutting. To me, that was my [film school] education." When the film was finally released in January 1973, it bombed, but by then it didn't matter because production was about to begin on *The Sting*.

David Ward had finished the script for *The Sting* while *Steelyard* was being edited. As Bill and the Phillipses had hoped, it was wonderful, and the twist ending was a knockout. At that point, the plan was for Tony, Julia, and Michael to produce the film, with Ward directing and *Steelyard Blues* actor Peter Boyle costarring as washed-up con man Henry Gondorff. Mike Medavoy submitted the package to studios and producers all over town. Two of the recipients were Zanuck and Brown, who by then had left Warner Bros. and were looking for projects for their new Universal Studios-based production company. Zanuck and Brown loved *The Sting*, but were not interested in using either Ward or Boyle. Instead, they saw the project as an ideal vehicle to reunite the director and stars of *Butch Cassidy and the Sundance Kid* (a film that they had supervised while they were at Twentieth Century-Fox): George Roy Hill, Paul Newman, and Robert Redford. Zanuck made Bill/Phillips an offer, but the young producers were concerned that if they sold the project to veterans like Zanuck and Brown, they would be pushed aside. They briefly considered an offer from MGM, but after Zanuck agreed that he and Brown would executive produce and "present" the film and that Bill/Phillips could line produce it (do the day-to-day work on the set), they accepted his offer. The project was set up at Universal and, as Zanuck and Brown had hoped, Hill agreed to direct, and Redford and Newman agreed to star.

With filming set to start in early 1973, Julia and Michael decided to relocate permanently from New York to Los Angeles. They rented a beach house on Nicholas Beach Road in Trancas, just north of Malibu, and began hosting a series of regular weekend parties for the New Hollywood filmmakers. The get-togethers helped forge a sense of community among the up-and-comers and set the stage for numerous creatively fruitful and financially beneficial collaborations. Unfortunately, it was during this otherwise happy period that Julia began developing what would later become a serious addiction to cocaine.

The Sting began production on January 22, 1973. The shoot went smoothly. "Everything was carefully prepared, the antithesis of the *Steelyard Blues* experience," Michael Phillips reports. "You could see in the dailies that we were doing something wonderful." Unfortunately, things did not go as well for the Bill/Phillips team. As they originally feared, they were pushed aside during production, not by Zanuck and Brown but instead by George Roy Hill. A strong-willed director used to doing things his own way, Hill refused to let more than one of the team on the set at a time. His preferred choice was Michael, which created some tension between the partners. Personality conflicts and business disagreements added to the tension, and before shooting on *The Sting* wrapped in April 1973, Tony, Michael, and Julia had decided to end their partnership and the Phillipses began looking for projects that they could produce on their own.

During the summer of 1973, as *The Sting* was being edited, Michael and Julia saw some footage from *The Sugarland Express* that impressed them. A short time later, Michael met Steven Spielberg (it was almost inevitable that the two would meet, since they were both working with

Zanuck/Brown and both knew Tony Bill). Steven and Michael became friends and began having lunch together on a regular basis in the Universal commissary. In the course of these lunches, they discovered that they had a mutual interest in science fiction, especially the science fiction films of the 1950s. Steven began coming to the get-togethers at the Phillipses' beach house, where he met many other New Hollywood filmmakers, including Brian De Palma and Martin Scorsese, with whom he formed lasting friendships. When Steven found himself in need of a producer for *Watch the Skies*, it was logical for him to approach the Phillipses, not only because he knew that Michael would be interested in doing a science fiction film, but also because, thanks to the terrific buzz that *The Sting* was generating, the Phillipses were "hot" and so would be attractive to Twentieth Century-Fox (Michael says that Steven later told them that he'd wanted to "ride on our coattails"). During one of their lunches, Steven told Michael that he wanted to pitch him and Julia an idea. The Phillipses were eager to hear Spielberg's pitch because they "knew [he] was something special." They had both loved *Duel* and considered Steven to be by far the most talented of their contemporaries. Welcoming the opportunity to work with him, Julia and Michael invited Spielberg to dinner.

That night, Steven went out to Trancas and told Michael and Julia about his "UFOs and Watergate" idea. Although they were of different minds about UFOs (Michael believed in them, Julia didn't), they both loved Steven's concept and anticipated that —given all of the people out there who believed in UFOs and all of those who believed in conspiracies—it could attract a large audience. Excited, the three friends shook hands on a deal to make the film, agreeing to split all potential fees and profit shares, fifty-fifty. A short time later, they went to Twentieth Century-Fox and formally pitched the project to Alan Ladd Jr., who liked both the concept and the producer/director "package" and formally approved a deal for the trio to develop a screenplay.

Their next step was to hire a writer. As always, Spielberg thought first of Hal Barwood and Matthew Robbins. When the partners heard that Steven was doing a UFO movie, they were still planning to write their "small-town police officer sees a flying saucer" script, and didn't relish the idea of competing with Spielberg's film. They knew, given Spielberg's rising star status in the industry at the time, that his project stood a much better chance of being made than theirs did, so, hoping to ally rather than compete, they pitched him their story. He liked it, but preferred his own approach. Barwood and Robbins, in turn, thought *Watch the Skies* was a good idea, but they weren't available to write it. Shortly after *Sugarland* wrapped, they had made a deal with Universal for Matthew to direct and Hal to produce their first solo film, a science fiction adventure set in a post-apocalyptic Pacific Northwest, based on their own original screenplay called *Clearwater*—a story Barwood succinctly describes as "*The Road Warrior* with trains." In the midst of preparing the film for production, they could not take on *Watch the Skies*. (Although *Clearwater* got close enough to filming that Universal had actually prepared a teaser poster heralding its upcoming release, the studio ultimately canceled the project when the budget reached a then-untenable $7 million). Spielberg next approached Gloria Katz and Willard Huyck, but Katz thought the idea of doing a movie about UFOs was silly, so they turned the assignment down. Finally, Julia and Michael suggested that Steven consider a writer with whom they were currently working on a script about a deranged New York City taxi driver who plots to assassinate a presidential candidate.

Paul Schrader was born on July 22, 1946 in Grand Rapids, Michigan, and raised in the Christian Reformed Church, a strict Dutch Calvinist sect. As a child, young Paul was forbidden to watch movies, which, along with rock and roll music and television, his parents felt were the work of the devil. Paul did not see his first film until he was seventeen, but he soon became an avid moviegoer with an affinity for the work of intellectual filmmakers such as Ingmar Bergman, Robert Bresson, and Carl Theodor Dreyer. Planning to become a minister, Paul attended Calvin College, where he began writing movie reviews for the college newspaper and also started a campus film society. On the advice of legendary *New Yorker* film critic Pauline Kael, whom Schrader met while taking some summer classes at Columbia University, he decided to pursue a career as a film critic. Moving to Los Angeles, he earned a master's degree in film history from UCLA (eventually publishing his thesis as a book called *Transcendental Style in Film: Ozu, Bresson, Dreyer*) and then enrolled as a Critical Studies Fellow at the American Film Institute. He also became a movie reviewer for the *L.A. Free Press*—a job he lost when he panned *Easy Rider*—and then the editor of a small film magazine called *Cinema*.

Interested in becoming a screenwriter, Schrader took a job as a script analyst at Columbia Pictures so that he could learn what did and didn't work in a screenplay. After leaving the AFI, Schrader fell on hard times and became seriously depressed. To help purge his dark thoughts, he decided to pour them into a screenplay he was writing that had been inspired by the published diary of Arthur Bremer, a mentally ill man who stalked Richard Nixon with the intention of assassinating him, but who ended up shooting and permanently paralyzing Alabama governor George Wallace instead. The result was *Taxi Driver*. Schrader then collaborated with his older brother, Leonard, on a script about Japanese gangsters called *The Yakuza*, which Warner Bros. bought in February 1973 for the then-record sum of $325,000.

While he and Leonard were writing *The Yakuza*, Paul supported them by doing some freelance movie reviewing. In conjunction with a review of the suspense thriller *Sisters* (1973), Schrader interviewed the film's director, Brian De Palma, and the two became friends. Schrader showed De Palma *Taxi Driver*, which De Palma liked and passed along to Michael Phillips. Michael loved it—"It was an incredibly pure and true piece of work," he said later. Bill/Phillips optioned *Taxi Driver* from Paul for $1,000, and the partners set out to find a director and a star that would make the dark, disturbing project appealing to studio executives. The project stayed with Julia and Michael when Bill/Phillips split up (although the film is still credited as a Bill/Phillips production), and they were still trying to put together a suitable package when Steven approached them with *Watch the Skies*. According to Schrader, Julia and Michael recommended him to Spielberg because they thought he was a strong writer and because "they felt that my sensibility, being extremely Germanic and moralistic, was the proper counterpoint to Steve's [lighter] sensibility."

After reading *Taxi Driver*, Spielberg agreed to meet with Schrader to discuss *Watch the Skies*. The meeting took place at Paul and Leonard's house in Brentwood. Spielberg began by outlining his basic story, as well as some specific scenes and images that he wanted to include. He then described his ideas for the ending, which he wanted to take place on a mountain (a notion inspired by the "Night on Bald Mountain" segment of Walt Disney's *Fantasia*, which had terrified Steven when he saw it as a child). The sequence—reminiscent of the 1561 Nuremberg sighting and similar events in which groups of smaller objects were seen emerging from larger, cylindrical ones—would begin with the arrival of dozens of tiny UFOs and then climax with the touchdown of a giant alien Mothership over five miles wide. Paul and Leonard were excited by Steven's ideas. Paul also saw enormous philosophical implications in this story about mankind's first encounter with extraterrestrial life and suggested that, rather than focusing primarily on the thriller aspects of the story, they make it about a spiritual journey instead. Leonard suggested that they adapt the biblical tale of Saint Paul, who famously persecuted the early Christians as a Roman official named Saul until Jesus appeared to him in a blinding flash of light while he was traveling on the road to Damascus. Following this encounter, Saul changed his name, converted to Christianity, and spent the rest of his life as a missionary spreading the faith. Inspired by this idea, Paul suggested that they make the Project Blue Book official a skeptic who doesn't believe in UFOs until he encounters one himself. Following this experience, the officer would become a true believer and set out to make contact with the extraterrestrials. Spielberg's spectacular ending would be the fulfillment of that quest. Everyone thought that this was a terrific way to approach the story.

Steven, Michael, and Julia decided that they wanted Paul to create the script and informed Alan Ladd that they had found their writer. However, Ladd was not nearly as enthusiastic about their choice as they were. Although Ladd respected Schrader's talents, he thought that Paul was "too intense"—and, at $35,000, far too expensive—for this particular project. Ladd asked Steven, Michael, and Julia to find another writer, but they insisted on Schrader. Since neither side was willing to compromise, Ladd decided to put the project into turnaround (which meant that Spielberg and the Phillipses were free to take the project to another studio, as long as whoever picked it up reimbursed Fox for any money it had already invested). After a promising start, *Watch the Skies* was back to square one. At this point, Howard Sackler finished work on his draft of *Jaws*. Although Spielberg still had some serious reservations, he felt that the shark script was now good enough to proceed with. Needing to make some money, Spielberg asked Julia and Michael if they would mind if he did the film, estimating that it would take him about six months to complete the job. Knowing that it could take at least that long to get *Watch the Skies* set up at another studio, they told him to go ahead. With that, Steven Spielberg went to Universal and signed on to direct *Jaws*.

Meanwhile, Julia and Michael continued to look for a new home for *Watch the Skies*. Neither Spielberg nor the Phillipses wanted to offer the project to Universal (having been tied to MCA for his entire professional career, Steven wanted to make his next film at another studio. As for the Phillipses, they were reportedly unhappy with Universal for not doing more to support them during the making of *The Sting*), so they began to look elsewhere. After considering several possibilities, they decided to approach Julia's former boss David Begelman, who a few weeks earlier had become the new head of Columbia Pictures.

CHAPTER 6 | Columbia

In the fall of 1973, Columbia Pictures was in serious trouble. The once grand studio had been felled by serious financial problems and its very future was now much in doubt.

The company was founded in 1919 as the CBC Film Sales Corporation by brothers Harry and Jack Cohn and their associate Joe Brandt—three former employees of Carl Laemmle's Universal Pictures (the Cohns had produced short films for Universal, while Brandt was the head of its East Coast operations). CBC (for Cohn-Brandt-Cohn) began by making short films, but, starting with *More to Be Pitied Than Scorned* (1922), moved into features. Jack and Joe ran the sales, distribution, and marketing divisions of the company from Manhattan, while Harry supervised the production of CBC's films in a studio they rented (and eventually bought) from Laemmle on Gower Street in Hollywood. Gower Street was located along a stretch of Sunset Boulevard that was nicknamed "Poverty Row," as it was home to many companies that specialized in producing low-budget films. With its slate of cheapo westerns and quickie adventure movies, CBC fit right in with its illustrious neighbors. The quality of its product was so poor that many industry insiders joked that the company's initials stood for "Corned Beef and Cabbage." In an attempt to improve its image, CBC changed its name to the Columbia Pictures Corporation in 1924 (its reputation stayed the same, however—riffing on the title of the popular patriotic song "Columbia: Gem of the Ocean," naysayers now dubbed the studio "the Germ of the Ocean"). Harry and Jack Cohn fought constantly over control of the company, and in 1931 Harry (a crass bully of a man whose various nicknames included "King Cohn," "Harry The Horror," "White Fang," and "His Crudeness") finally won the battle by buying out Joe Brandt's shares and becoming Columbia's president as well as its head of production (making him the only studio chief to ever hold both positions at the same time).

Columbia's transformation from a Poverty Row quickie house into a major motion picture studio began in 1927, when Cohn hired an ambitious young director named Frank Capra. Although Capra began by directing typical Columbia fare such as *Submarine* (1928) and *Dirigible* (1931), he urged Cohn to let him direct higher-quality material. At first Cohn resisted, but when Capra-helmed pictures such as *Ladies of Leisure* (1930), *Platinum Blonde* (1931), and *Lady for a Day* (1933) started making money, Cohn relented and let the young director have his way. Throughout the 1930s, Capra turned out a string of artistic and commercial successes that included classics such as *Mr. Deeds Goes to Town* (1936), *Lost Horizon* (1937), *You Can't Take It With You* (1938), *Mr. Smith Goes to Washington* (1939), *Meet John Doe* (1941), and the film that won Columbia its first Academy Award for Best Picture—*It Happened One Night* (1936). The quality and success of Capra's pictures allowed Columbia to attract big-name stars (Clark Gable, Barbara Stanwyck, Gary Cooper, Cary Grant, Claudette Colbert, and James Stewart) and directors (Howard Hawks, Joseph Von Sternberg, and Leo McCarey), and the studio began turning out high-level pictures such as *Twentieth Century* (1934), *The Awful Truth* (1937), and *Only Angels Have Wings* (1939). By the end of the 1930s, the studio had lost its tawdry image and become known as one of Hollywood's top companies. Columbia's success continued throughout the 1940s and 1950s with a string of memorable films, including *His Girl Friday* (1940), *Gilda* (1946), *The Lady from Shanghai* (1948), *All The King's Men* (1949), *Born Yesterday* (1950), *The Caine Mutiny* (1954), *The Wild One* (1954), *Picnic* (1955), *Pal Joey* (1957), *The Last Hurrah* (1958), *Bell, Book, and Candle* (1958), and three more Academy Award winners for Best Picture: *From Here To Eternity* (1953), *On the Waterfront* (1954), and *The Bridge on the River Kwai* (1957).

Jack Cohn died in 1956 and Harry in 1958 (the large crowd at Harry's funeral allegedly prompted comedian Red Skelton to quip: "Give the people what they want and they'll turn out for it"). Following Harry's death, his vice-president, Abe Schneider, became Columbia's new president, and

Leo Jaffe, who had started with the company as an accountant in 1930, became head of production. Together, Schneider and Jaffe continued Columbia's winning streak with a string of popular and critical successes that included *The Guns of Navarone* (1961), *Lawrence of Arabia* (1962), *Bye Bye Birdie* (1963), *Dr. Strangelove or How I Learned to Stop Worrying and Love the Bomb* (1964), *Cat Ballou* (1965), *A Man for All Seasons* (1966), *Born Free* (1966), *Guess Who's Coming to Dinner* (1967), *In Cold Blood* (1967), *Funny Girl* (1968), and *Oliver!* (1968). Things were going so well that in 1968 Columbia posted a record profit of $21 million.

That same year, Matthew Rosenhaus, the former head of the J.B. Williams Pharmaceutical Company (the manufacturer of Geritol) bought a controlling share of stock in the company, which was reorganized and renamed Columbia Pictures Industries. Abe Schneider became the chairman of the board and CEO; Leo Jaffe became CPI's president, and Abe's son Stanley was put in charge of the motion picture division. In the three years that followed, the company produced more solidly successful films, including *Bob & Carol & Ted & Alice* (1969), *Cactus Flower* (1969), *I Never Sang for My Father* (1970), and *Nicholas and Alexandra* (1971). CPI also inaugurated Hollywood's youth craze when it released *Easy Rider* (1969). The film had been produced by Bert Schneider, another of Abe's sons, whose BBS Productions made some of the most important films of the New Hollywood era, including *Five Easy Pieces* (1970) and *The Last Picture Show* (1971), all of which were released by Columbia.

However, the good times were not to last. By the early 1970s, the same problems that were affecting the rest of the industry had begun to plague Columbia, and the company lost $40 million in fiscal 1971. To stem the flow of red ink, the company slashed overhead, reduced salaries, and fired three hundred employees. Columbia sold its Gower Street complex and moved to the Warner Bros. lot in Burbank. (CPI had bought a half-interest in the Warner studio, and the two companies jointly operated the facility, which was renamed The Burbank Studios.) These measures helped, but the company's fortunes took another hit in 1973 when three of its biggest and most expensive productions—the musicals *1776* and *Lost Horizon* and the Churchill biopic *Young Winston*—flopped at the box office. The studio lost $50 million, its stock dropped from $9.00 to $5.00 per share, and it was carrying an enormous debt of $220 million. Columbia's bankers were giving serious consideration to forcing the company into bankruptcy.

This dire state of affairs alarmed producer Ray Stark, whose Rastar company had made *Funny Girl*, one of company's biggest hits. Stark was concerned that if Columbia went bankrupt, he wouldn't be able to collect his profits from the picture. To help save the studio, Stark contacted his close friend Herbert Allen Jr., the thirty-three-year-old president of Allen & Company, a New York–based investment banking company that had been founded by Herbert's father, Herbert Sr., and his uncle, Charles, in 1922. Following a careful analysis of the situation, Herbert Jr. became convinced that he could save Columbia by bringing in a new management team. With the support of Columbia's bankers and of Matthew Rosenhaus, Herbert Jr. directed Allen & Co. to buy a large block of CPI stock (approximately seven hundred thousand shares at a cost of $2.5 million) and took control of the company in July 1973. Abe Schneider retired, Leo Jaffe became chairman of the board, and Herbert, Jr. hired his friend Alan J. Hirschfield—who had worked for Allen & Company as an investment banker since 1959 and was currently managing the Allen family's personal finances— to be CPI's new president and chief executive officer.

One of Hirschfield's first tasks was to find someone to run the company's motion picture division. Knowing that they needed a person with skill and experience in making deals and assembling successful movie packages, Ray Stark recommended his old friend David Begelman. A native of the Bronx, the fifty-two-year-old Begelman had served in the Army Air Corps during World War II. After the war, he attended NYU and then got a job in the insurance industry. Knowing that Begelman was unhappy working in insurance, his friend Freddie Fields, an agent at MCA (Music Corporation of America)—at that time the biggest talent agency in show business—persuaded him to change careers. Begelman joined MCA and quickly became one of its top agents, representing stars such as Milton Berle and Jack Paar. In 1961, Begelman and Fields left MCA and started Creative Management Associates. Their first major client was Judy Garland, but they quickly signed others, including Barbra Streisand, Steve McQueen, Robert Redford, and Cliff Robertson. Begelman and Fields were both extremely sharp and aggressive agents, and, with the departure of MCA from the field (the company stopped representing talent when it bought Universal Studios in 1962), CMA soon became one of the industry's dominant agencies. When Begelman accepted Columbia's offer, he became one of the first agents to take charge of a Hollywood studio, a practice that would soon become commonplace.

Working together, Hirschfield and Begelman devised a strategy that was designed to turn Columbia around. The company's bankers had imposed a strict budget limit of $3 million per picture—the average cost of an average film in 1973. Working within this restriction, Hirschfield and Begelman came up with a plan to forgo expensive blockbusters and to instead make a series of small and medium-sized movies on tightly controlled budgets, aiming for a consistent series of modest hits rather than risking everything on the occasional smash. With this plan in place, Begelman began looking for projects that they could use to save the floundering studio.

When Julia Phillips contacted Begelman and asked if she, Michael, and Steven could pitch him an idea, he immediately said yes. Apart from his good relationship with Julia and his desire to be in business with the producers of *The Sting*, Begelman had been very impressed with *Duel* and was eager to work with Steven. A meeting was arranged, and in the fall of 1973, Steven, Michael, and Julia, along with Guy McElwaine, met with Begelman and presented *Watch the Skies*. David liked Steven's idea and agreed with the choice of Schrader as the writer, but Columbia's shaky finances made cost a major concern, so Begelman asked the trio how much they thought the movie was going to cost. Since they hadn't discussed the film's budget even between themselves (in the absence of a script upon which to base an estimate), Michael and Julia felt they couldn't answer this question. Before they were able to say so, however, Steven surprised them both by telling Begelman that the film would cost $2.8 million. Julia and Michael, stunned, knew that $2.8 million was an incredibly low figure for such an ambitious movie. However, when they saw that Begelman was comfortable with Steven's response, they kept their astonishment to themselves. As the meeting came to an end, Begelman—in one of his first official acts as head of the studio—agreed to a deal: Columbia would finance the development of a script and, if it turned out well, make the movie. After they left Begelman's office, Julia and Michael asked Steven where he had come up with the $2.8 million figure. Steven replied that, considering Columbia's problems, he'd figured that it was the highest number that Begelman would listen to without objecting. Realizing that Steven was probably right, the Phillipses decided that they would concentrate on getting a great script and then cross the budget bridge when they came to it.

As fall 1973 turned to winter, things were looking good for everyone. For the Phillipses, advance word on *The Sting* had been excellent. When the film opened on Christmas Day, it became a smash hit that would eventually gross over $150 million and be nominated for ten Academy Awards. As for Steven, the buzz on *The Sugarland Express* was terrific, and word began to spread that a major new director was about to burst onto the Hollywood scene. And on December 12, 1973, Columbia Pictures signed Paul Schrader to write the script for *Watch the Skies* for a fee of $35,000. Steven Spielberg's dream to do a feature film about UFOs was becoming a reality. Or so it seemed.

| *Kingdom Come* and *Meeting of the Minds*

STEVEN, PAUL, JULIA, AND MICHAEL met several times in early 1974 to discuss *Watch the Skies*. In the course of these meetings, they worked out how best to blend Steven's "UFOs and Watergate" concept with Paul's "Road to Damascus" approach. As the story came together, they incorporated an idea contributed by Brian De Palma, who, to solve the problem of how the Project Blue Book officer would know where to meet the UFOs when they landed at the end of the story, suggested that the aliens should psychically implant the location of the encounter in the officer's mind. Apart from the contactee cults, psychic phenomena are not a significant part of UFO lore, but the team adopted De Palma's notion because, as Michael Phillips candidly admits, it "solved a big story issue." Once the basic concept had been laid out, Paul went off to write while Julia and Michael turned their attention to *Taxi Driver* and Steven began work on *Jaws*. Schrader was a fast writer, and it only took him a few weeks to finish his first draft, which he called *Kingdom Come*.

Schrader's script told the story of Major Paul Van Owen, a Project Blue Book officer whose job it is to travel around the country debunking UFO sightings. One night, while driving along a lonely country road, Van Owen encounters an actual UFO. Shocked to discover that these objects he has been paid for years to deny are in fact real, Van Owen reports the sighting, drawing ridicule from his friends and coworkers. Van Owen becomes depressed and isolated, and eventually his marriage breaks up. Realizing that the government has been using him to cover up the truth, Van Owen goes to the head of Project Blue Book and threatens to expose the entire conspiracy. Before he can act on that threat, however, he is offered a chance to join a secret organization called Project Grief. The members of Project Grief go to great lengths to keep the public from finding out the truth about UFOs while at the same time working to make contact with the extraterrestrials who pilot them. Van Owen joins the organization and spends the next fifteen years trying to connect with the aliens. His efforts are fruitless until he finally realizes that UFOs are not actually physical objects, but instead are mental projections of a memory that the aliens implanted into mankind's collective subconscious millions of years ago. Van Owen makes a spiritual journey into his own subconscious and connects with the alien memory, which directs him to a rendezvous point at Idaho's Black Mountain. There Van Owen—having been transformed from a doubter to a believer— greets the aliens when they arrive. In the end, he climbs aboard the Mothership and leaves the planet with the extraterrestrials.

Rather than the requested thriller, Schrader's script turned out to be a dark and, at times, grim supernatural drama with heavy religious overtones. Told in flashbacks (as Van Owen prepares for his rendezvous with the aliens), it was convoluted and hard to follow, and the special effects–filled journey into Van Owen's subconscious was bizarre and abstract. Steven hated it, saying later, "It was a bad script.... Paul went so far away on his own tangent, a terribly guilt-ridden story.... It had little to do with the UFO phenomenon and nothing to do with the movie I wanted to make. It was...horrendous. Absolutely horrendous." Michael and Julia didn't like it, either. Michael felt the script "...wasn't joyful... [and] we weren't getting the excitement." Julia thought that the screenplay was so far off the track that she refused to show it to David Begelman, worried that if he read it he wouldn't want to make the movie. Schrader left the project. Starting over, Spielberg and the Phillipses decided to return to Steven's original concept and do a straight thriller about Project Blue Book's UFO cover-up. They began looking for another writer, but the search went slowly because the spring of 1974 was a busy time for the trio:

- On March 31, 1974, *The Sugarland Express* opened in New York City, and on April 5, 1974, it opened around the country. The film received excellent notices, most of which focused on Spielberg himself. Paul D. Zimmerman of *Newsweek* called

Sugarland "the arrival of an extraordinary young filmmaker."
In *The New Yorker*, Pauline Kael said the film was "...one of
the most phenomenal debuts in the history of movies." As
good as the reviews were, however, the film was a financial
disappointment, earning only $7.5 million in the United States
and Canada and an additional $5.3 million overseas.

• On April 8, 1974, *The Sting* won seven Academy Awards,
including one for Best Picture. As the film's producers,
Michael, Julia, and Tony Bill accepted the award onstage
during the ceremonies at the Dorothy Chandler Pavilion in
Los Angeles. Julia was the first woman ever to win an Oscar
for Best Picture.

• On May 2 1974, Steven began shooting *Jaws*. The production
he had expected to be able to wrap up in six months turned
into a long, protracted nightmare. Still without a finished
script, Steven recruited his friend and onetime collaborator
Carl Gottlieb, whom he had cast in a small role in the picture,
to rewrite the script as the movie was being shot. He received
additional input from Hal Barwood and Matthew Robbins
(who worked on scenes back in Spielberg's office at Universal
while watching the Watergate hearings on television) and also
from John Milius. Due to the difficulties of working on the
ocean, and to problems with the weather and the mechanical
shark, the filming went way over schedule and way over
budget. Filming had been scheduled to wrap by the end of
July but continued through the summer. Things got so out of
hand that Universal considered pulling the plug on the whole
project, but Spielberg, Zanuck, and Brown convinced Sid
Sheinberg to let them keep going.

While *Jaws* was shooting, Michael and Julia continued searching for a
new writer for *Watch the Skies*, bringing the promising candidates to Martha's Vineyard to meet with Steven. Some of the people they considered
were Tracy Keenan Wynn (*The Longest Yard*), David Gerrold (*Star Trek,
Land of the Lost*), and John Landis (later the director of *Animal House* and
The Blues Brothers, but then the precocious twenty-five-year-old author of

an inventive horror/comedy screenplay for which he was trying to find backing, called *An American Werewolf in London*). None of these folks got the job, although Landis—after hanging around the Vineyard for several weeks waiting in vain to meet with the impossibly busy Spielberg—did land another gig when *Jaws* production manager James Fargo hired him to help build a breakaway dock for the famous scene in which the shark yanks the dock free from its pilings, causing two hapless fisherman to plunge into the deadly water.

Sometime in June, Julia and Michael read a script about an aging buffalo hunter called *Far as the Eye Can See*, by a twenty-seven-year-old writer from Kansas City named John Hill. Inspired to become a screenwriter after reading a paperback edition of William Goldman's screenplay for *Butch Cassidy and the Sundance Kid*, Hill moved to Los Angeles in 1971 (arriving on April Fools Day, which is, he says, "the correct day of the year to try to become a screenwriter") and spent three years working as an advertising copywriter and writing sample scripts. Impressed by Hill's work, Michael and Julia met with him, showed him *Kingdom Come*, and explained the changes they wanted to make to it. Hill, a science fiction fan and a believer in UFOs (he had already written a UFO-themed script called *Something Landed in the North Pasture*), was receptive and enthusiastic. Michael and Julia passed *Far as the Eye Can See* on to Spielberg, who also liked it, and they decided to offer Hill the assignment to rewrite *Watch the Skies*. By that time, Steven had come up with a new title: borrowing J. Allen Hynek's term for contact with alien life, he had changed the name of the project to *Close Encounters of the Third Kind*.

Hill describes what happened next in his unpublished article "My Close Encounters with *Close Encounters*":

> I was informed by my agent that I got the job to write CLOSE EN-
> COUNTERS for Columbia Studios at 3:00 P.M. July 19, 1974, while
> I was at work at an L.A. ad agency. As I hung up the phone, all in
> one smooth happy automatic motion, I remember, I was on my feet,
> walked in and quit my job, two minutes later.
>
> I kept expecting the two producers or the studio to have me get
> started writing right away, but they kept deferring to the fact that Ste-
> ven Spielberg had "the idea more in his head than anyone's, so let's
> wait and meet with him." They did, however, give me UFO data to

study from J. Allen Hynek and also some possibly semi-secret U.S. Air Force Project Blue Book information to study.

So I did my research homework. Weeks later, in August, 1974, Michael and Julia Phillips and I flew to Martha's Vineyard to stay at Spielberg's rented-for-the-duration-of-JAWS-filming house, for a long weekend's worth of meetings about CLOSE ENCOUNTERS.

We get to Spielberg's house on Martha's Vineyard, prior to our "work" weekend. It was a rustic, log cabin-esque, big six-bedroom home, up on a hill, overlooking the sea. He was busy, off somewhere, filming JAWS, and "trying to get the shark to work," a refrain one would hear a lot there.

He was drowning in JAWS problems: weather problems, the challenge of filming on the sea anytime (shots never match since waves, the sun, and clouds are always in motion), mechanical shark problems, deadline/budget problems, thus studio pressure. So it wasn't just that Spielberg was busy filming JAWS while we were there for a short three-day weekend for me to get debriefed—it was that he was OVERWHELMED and TOTALLY DISTRACTED by JAWS while I was there. Timing, sadly, in life, really is everything.

But I was extremely eager to work, roll up my screenwriting sleeves, learn all I can from them about what they wanted, then do my very best job possible. I was all business, eager for any opportunity for Steven, Michael, and Julia and I to meet. I wanted all possible input and guidance before I started writing.

But the seventy-two hours of our time there, however, passed quite differently.

Steven was gone, somewhere out to sea, trying, yes, to get his shark to work, during the days and some into the night. Then he'd have meetings with his staff in his living room that Saturday, going over the storyboards for JAWS, with the shark, orange barrels, etc., different angles, drawn in cartoon panels; the script to JAWS was never in sight, by the way. Steven had this big house, big open living room, great ocean views, so I just sort of hung out, and waited. And waited.

Richard Dreyfuss was around a lot. For the long summer of filming, Dreyfuss and Spielberg had purchased a big brand-new gadget they kept in Spielberg's living room. It was PONG, a simple electronic game of ping-pong, great-great-great-grandfather of today's video games. It was one of the first on the market; I had never seen one. But at the time, since I had to wait around, I learned to play. My middle class/Kansas work ethic was amused that Columbia Studios had flown me out here, first class, to spend hours playing Richard Dreyfuss in PONG. Since Dreyfuss won't remember or care, I'll now claim I beat him a lot.

As I kept being available, but forced to wait, the obvious finally sunk in: Spielberg's vision was the key for this UFO movie I was supposed to write, and he didn't have time to really think about it the weekend I was there.

But finally, we had a CLOSE ENCOUNTERS meeting. Michael, Julia, me and Spielberg, in his living room.

They told me the plot they wanted, basically similar to the story direction of the Paul Schrader first draft: an Air Force officer who is routinely sent out to "investigate" UFO sightings—but actually debunks each sighting. This was done in subtle ways with the nervous civilians who reported lights in the sky. ("Well, you're very brave to go on record with this." "Why?" the farmer would say. "Well, you've heard what happens to others who have gone on record as having seen a UFO, and I admire your courage." "What do you mean?" "Oh, you know, becoming the town nutcase, teased for years, ostracized. I've seen marriages end, businesses go under. People even crack up. So you're very brave. Now, what size light would you say it was?" "Well...I'm not that sure what I saw....") So this Air Force officer, the protagonist, did this routinely, without much thought either way to whether UFOs are real or not—until one night, HE has a UFO sighting/experience in his car on a lonely road. And he finds himself wanting to truthfully and officially go on record. But the Air Force now shuts him out. He suspects that the government has always known that UFOs exist—hiding it from the public! And he's been part of it!

Anyway, the Air Force officer who saw this then has nightmares, then maniacally creates the mountain image from his dreams with a sculptured pile of dirt in the living room, really scaring his family. Disheveled, on a forced leave of absence, he tries to get proof of what he saw, runs around, studies books on mountains, wife leaves him, etc., he then ironically gets "debunked/threatened" by Air Force, etc. He's having a breakdown—but then he sees on TV news of a train derailment out West with nerve gas, the Army securing the area. And he sees the familiar dream-image of the mountain—so he must go there, sneak in, to PROVE the Air Force is hiding a known connection with UFOs. He is after a personal redemption through discovering the truth to a cover-up. So the last part of the movie is him sneaking in, past all Army sentries, etc., climbing down into the edge of the canyon at the top of a mountain, where he sees more soldiers, then limos, and a red carpet rolled out to nothing. Then a giant UFO, the mothership, slowly, majestically, lands, and we see an alien come out, greeted by some official, and our hero, the Air Force colonel in hiding, smiles, vindicated. Steven also described some scenes, without linking them up within the story, and he said he wasn't sure how but he wanted the Air Force officer to go a little nuts and build a mountain of dirt in his living room, simulating the image of the mountain he'd later see, plus some other images. The meeting ended, and everyone scattered. I was left to piece it together. (It was presented to me more much confusingly than I've explained above, more in unconnected scenes and ideas.)

I was eager to talk more about it, with questions, but everyone had scattered that Saturday afternoon, Steven to JAWS, Michael joining him to watch filming, etc. I was frustrated, since the pieces of this story didn't really fit and I didn't yet have enough of a feel for it to write it. Certain scenes, like an airplane's encounter with a UFO, and the air traffic controller's confusion, etc., weren't clear to me where they went, etc.

One of the things I then did was try to talk Julia Phillips out of was the title/concept! I had been a science fiction fan all my life and I explained to Julia, probably patronizingly, how mixing ESP and UFO was not a good idea at all. I said the first rule of good science fiction is that you ask the reader or audience to accept ONE fantastical plot premise—but everything else, including human behavior, then has to feel real. I said you just can't mix witchcraft and Bigfoot, or the Loch Ness monster and time travel— or UFOs and ESP. Then (further digging myself into this hole I cringe at remembering) I said I had just spent almost five years in advertising, and you don't want to go out with a "blind title" (no one knows what it means until AFTER they buy the product) and a clumsy title like CLOSE ENCOUNTERS OF THE THIRD KIND. Quite obviously, I explained to Julia Phillips, who

humored me in a nice way, that title was not memorable, didn't communicate anything to the average moviegoer, etc. I said a better title/
concept would be A MEETING OF THE MINDS, which is the title of
the draft I put on the script I wrote months later.

But I wasn't able to fully engage any of the three of them again, let
alone together, about the script, so I probably beat Dreyfuss at PONG
again that evening. (Talk about winning a battle but losing the war....)

The next day, Sunday, I was really ready to work—it was our last
full day here, I was scheduled to fly back to L.A. on Monday. Sunday
was an official day off from filming JAWS, so finally, I assumed, we'd
all really get back into the story meetings for CLOSE ENCOUNTERS.
I had many questions and even Michael, Julia, and Steven knew many
aspects of the story were not at all settled or clear. So there I am, right
after breakfast, pen and pad and notes in hand, ready to go, assuming
Sunday would finally be a long, good, serious UFO work day.

Wrong.

On Sundays, Spielberg liked to relax (he was working intense four-
teen-hour days, six days a week) and the way he liked to do this was a
big traditional Sunday softball game, where the island-invading JAWS
crew played the local townies in a big softball game. Everyone was going and it would take all afternoon and into the evening, etc.

I couldn't believe it.

I was invited to play too, but I politely passed; I was eager to work
so, using a typewriter, I worked hard for hours and knocked out a fast,
rough story treatment of the random images and scenes I'd been debriefed on, plus my own ideas, giving it all a rough beginning, middle
and end. I added a sergeant buddy to the Air Force officer protagonist,
trying to steer it all into my comfort zone a little: Butch and Sundance
go after UFOs.

That evening, I showed the treatment to Michael, Julia and Steven. They said, fine, looks good, and we'd all talk some more. My deal
was for a first draft, a second draft and a polish probably, so this was
a process—I'd read enough about screenwriting to know the writer
writes a draft, gets notes (changes), does another draft, etc. and they
all go on to glory this way. On Monday, with Michael and Julia staying
behind, I said goodbye to the three of them and flew back to L.A. by
myself, eager to work.

In my eagerness, I had said to Michael, Julia and Steven that even though there were still many unanswered story questions, why don't I try to piece this all together by writing a first draft and get us going? It was premature, we all knew it, but who turns down progress? They said okay. So once I was back in L.A., I started writing the script.

While Hill worked on his draft, Julia and Michael were preoccupied with other matters. At the end of July, they had decided to get a divorce. Although they were ending their personal relationship, they intended to continue as business partners on the projects they currently had in the works, which by now included *Taxi Driver*. After considering several directors (including Brian De Palma, Lamont Johnson, and their former producing partner Tony Bill) and actors (including Jeff Bridges), they had finally chosen Martin Scorsese (who had made a big splash the year before with *Mean Streets*) to direct and Robert De Niro (who had delivered a startling performance in the same film) to star, and convinced David Begelman to back the production. Scorsese was currently directing *Alice Doesn't Live Here Any More* at Warner Bros., and De Niro was playing the young Vito Corleone in Francis Coppola's *The Godfather, Part II*, so the project was put on hold until they were both available. Meanwhile, *Jaws* finished shooting on September 15, 1974—an incredible one hundred days over schedule and one hundred percent over its original $4 million budget. Spielberg returned to Los Angeles and began cutting the movie together with editor Verna Fields.

In November 1974, John Hill finished his script, which he had indeed called *Meeting of the Minds*, and turned it in. Steven, Michael, and Julia read it, and although they thought that it was well done, they realized that they were no longer interested in "UFOs and Watergate." The concept had seemed quite vital early in 1973, but by this point in time—three months after Richard Nixon's resignation and a short time before the final collapse of the United States adventure in Viet Nam—they and most of the rest of the country were burned out on the whole sordid topic of government lies and cover-ups. In addition, one movie with an "uncovering a conspiracy" theme had already come out—*The Parallax View* (1974)—and there were two more (1975's *Three Days of the Condor* and 1976's *All The President's Men*) on the way. The idea had lost its freshness, so they decided to drop it. Michael, for one, was relieved. He had never really believed in the notion that the government was covering up the facts about UFOs. "I mean, why would they? It always struck me as ridiculous to theorize that the government was holding back the truth here." It was up to Michael to deliver the bad news to John Hill, who describes their conversation in his article:

> So I finished my first draft, which I called A MEETING OF THE MINDS, because, obviously, CLOSE ENCOUNTERS OF THE THIRD KIND could never catch on as a title or a catch phrase. And I was very aware I contractually had more drafts to go, so I could include their reactions to it in the next draft, per the system, and called Michael Phillips, turned it in to them, and waited.
>
> Michael Phillips phoned me sometime later and said that they had read it.
>
> "John, you did the assignment and took us down the road we said, but that has let us see clearly now, that is not the direction we want to go. So thank for you helping us in that way. You're a really good writer, you know I'm a fan, but we're taking you off the project now, so we can go in a new direction with a fresh new writer."
>
> And that was that. I got paid by the studio for later drafts no one ever wanted.
>
> And I was off the project.
>
> And life moved on and years later, when the beautiful mothership rose into the night sky and cinematic history, I was left behind, a footnote.

Steven, Michael, and Julia still wanted to make a movie about UFOs, but they realized that they were going to have to come up with an entirely new approach. At this point, however, they didn't have time to think about it—Steven was busy with post-production on *Jaws*, and Julia and Michael were occupied with their personal issues and professional obligations. None of them had time to think about *Watch the Skies/Kingdom Come/ Close Encounters of the Third Kind/Meeting of the Minds*, and the project was temporarily shelved.

EARLY IN 1975, as Spielberg continued to edit *Jaws*, he had more on his mind than just a shark. He had already begun to think about what he was going to do next. Ideally, of course, he wanted to make *Close Encounters*, but the difficulty he, Michael, and Julia were having in developing a workable script had cast serious doubt on the project's future. Even if they were able to come up with an acceptable screenplay, Spielberg wasn't sure that Columbia would let him direct it. In fact, he was worried that no studio would ever hire him to direct any film ever again. By now, everyone in Hollywood had heard about the horrendous problems that had plagued *Jaws*. Many people not in the know laid the blame for many of these problems on Steven—saying that he was too inexperienced to handle a production of that size and scope and had let things get out of control. This wasn't true, of course, but Spielberg knew that in Hollywood rumors were often taken as fact, and if enough producers and studios believed them, his career could be in trouble. His first film had failed at the box office. If *Jaws* failed too, then the problem would only intensify. For these reasons, Spielberg's main priority was to get another directing job lined up as soon as possible, preferably before *Jaws* came out. With *Close Encounters* stalled, he began looking around for another assignment.

Around this time, he received an offer to direct a film adaptation of one of his favorite comic books: *Superman*. In early 1975, that superhero epic was in its nascent stages. A screenplay had already been written by Mario Puzo, and the film's executive producer, Ilya Salkind, and its producer, Pierre Spengler (the makers of 1973's *The Three Musketeers* and 1974's

The Four Musketeers), were looking for a director. Salkind and Spengler had both seen *Duel* and had been impressed by it. After screening *Sugarland*, they were convinced they had found their man and contacted Guy McElwaine to see if Steven was interested. He was, so Ilya and Pierre then approached Ilya's Paris-based father, Alexander, the film's financier and "presenter." The elder Salkind hadn't heard of Steven or seen any of his films and wanted to know what he had done lately. Ilya told his father that Spielberg had just finished making a film about a shark. Alexander decided to wait and see how the "fish movie" did before making a decision. In the months that followed, Guy McElwaine continued to lobby the Salkinds on Steven's behalf, but was continually rebuffed by them.

The next project Steven considered was a Depression-era comedy/drama about a Negro League baseball team called *The Bingo Long Traveling All-Stars & Motor Kings*. Steven had heard about *Bingo Long* from Matthew Robbins and Hal Barwood, who had written the screenplay (based on a novel by William Brashler). It was being produced for Universal by another Movie Brat, twenty-five-year-old Rob Cohen (*Mahogany*), and was scheduled to start shooting in the summer of 1975. After reading the script (which he loved), Spielberg called Cohen and said he was interested in directing the film. Cohen immediately offered him the job and, although no contracts were signed, began meeting with Steven to plan the production.

To design *Bingo Long*, Steven hired Joe Alves. Joseph Alves Jr. was born in San Leandro, California, on May 21, 1936. A talented artist, Joe had moved to Los Angeles after high school to attend the Chouinard Art Institute. In need of a summer job, he applied to the Walt Disney Company and was hired to assist veteran special effects animator Joshua Meador. Meador had worked on many Disney classics (he had created the fire effects for *Bambi* and worked on the "Night on Bald Mountain" sequence of *Fantasia* that had so frightened young Steven Spielberg) and was currently animating the Monster from the Id for *Forbidden Planet* (1956). After *Planet*, Joe spent two years at Disney working on a number of animated films, including *Sleeping Beauty* (1959). Interested in moving into live-action filmmaking, Joe began designing sets for theatrical productions at the Hollywood Playhouse. His work got him noticed, and he soon began working as a junior set designer at several studios, including Warner Bros. and Twentieth Century-Fox, on films such as *My Fair Lady* (1964), *How* the West Was Won (1962), and *Mutiny on the Bounty* (1962). He became a regular at Universal as a senior set designer and eventually advanced to the position of assistant art director (a set designer works on individual sets; an art director is responsible for the look of the entire production) on television series such as *McHale's Navy* and *Dragnet* and features such as *Torn Curtain* (1966) and *Winning* (1969).

After several years Alves became a full art director and was given his own series, *Night Gallery*. It was while working on an episode called "Make Me Laugh" in 1971 that he first met Steven Spielberg, who had been hired to direct it. As the two worked together on several episodes of Alves's next series, *The Psychiatrist*, they became friends. When *The Sugarland Express* went into production, Spielberg asked Alves to be the film's art director, a role he repeated (with a change in title to Production Designer) on *Jaws*, where, in addition to supervising the creation of the film's sets, he was also responsible for designing the appearance of its star—the giant great white shark. When *Bingo Long* came along, Steven asked Joe if he wanted to work on it. Having enjoyed their previous collaborations, Alves immediately said yes.

To get the ball rolling, Spielberg requested that Alves assemble some preliminary research on the time period and subject matter. The two of them then went to comedian Tom Smothers' condo in the popular resort area of Mammoth, California (Alves was friends with Smothers, who owned a Formula 2 racecar that Alves, a sports car enthusiast who had become a professional racer in his spare time, had driven for him in several competitions). The plan was to spend a few days skiing and reviewing the *Bingo Long* research. Sometime during the course of the trip, Steven told Joe about *Close Encounters*, which he was once again calling *Watch the Skies*. Joe recalls, "I said 'Boy, that sounds a lot more interesting than this baseball thing. Maybe you should do that.'" As the two talked about the project's possibilities, Steven's enthusiasm for his UFO movie began to return.

Sometime later, Steven met with Michael and Julia, who by now were in pre-production on *Taxi Driver*, and tried to figure out how to proceed with *Watch the Skies*. Having found the previous drafts of the script to be cold and uninvolving, Steven knew he wanted to humanize the story, to make it warmer and more personal. He also wanted to capture the magic and wonder of UFOs and of outer space, elements he felt were missing in both *Kingdom Come* and *Meeting of the Minds*. With these points in mind, he began rethinking the piece:

- Since he had already dropped the "uncovering a conspiracy" premise, Steven also eliminated the Project Blue Book aspect of the story. He kept the concept of a secret unit that investigates UFO sightings and tries to make contact with extraterrestrials, but decided that it would no longer be an Air Force operation. Instead, it would now be an international team of scientists and UFO experts operating under UN auspices. This idea apparently sprang from a suggestion that J. Allen Hynek made in his book that the UN establish just such a group. The leader of the team would be an inquisitive, enthusiastic UFO expert based on Hynek, and the group's work would now be characterized as positive rather than sinister. The government element would remain only for one short sequence in which the protagonist visits an Air Force base to report his sighting, only to be debunked by a Project Blue Book representative (whom Spielberg named Major Benchley, apparently after *Jaws* author Peter Benchley).

- Steven retained the "Road to Damascus" concept of a man whose life is transformed by an encounter with a UFO, but decided that the main character would no longer be an Air Force officer. Spielberg found the military protagonist of the previous drafts off-putting—he had a hard time identifying with people in uniform and believed that audiences tended to see them as remote authority figures rather than equals. Because Steven wanted viewers to feel as if this story could happen to them, he decided to make his protagonist a very ordinary, forty-five-year-old suburban husband and father named Norman Greenhouse, whose wife, Ronnie, doesn't understand him and whose kids ignore him. Norman's increasing obsession with UFOs would widen the already-existing gap between him and his family.

- Based on many reports that described electrical power interruptions during UFO appearances, Steven decided to begin the story with a UFO-provoked blackout. To give Norman a reason to journey out into the disturbance so that he could have his first encounter, Spielberg gave him a job as a power company trouble foreman.

- To guide Norman to the site of the final encounter, Spielberg retained the notion of an alien-implanted vision and Norman's resulting obsession with a mountain that he's never seen before. Greenhouse's attempts to make sense of his obsession would be the focus of the second act. To visually express Norman's preoccupation, Spielberg also retained a sequence that had been featured in both *Kingdom Come* and *Meeting of the Minds* in which the protagonist creates a massive model of the mountain landing site in his living room (Paul Schrader has claimed that he originated this scene, although some have credited it to Spielberg and others to Brian De Palma). This seemingly crazy act would permanently drive Norman's increasingly estranged family away from him.

- Finally, Steven decided to retain the climactic sequence in which the giant Mothership arrives at the mountain.

The next step was to find a writer to properly realize all of this. The question was, who? Steven wanted someone who would understand his vision for the project and be able to capture all of the qualities he was looking for. After considering several possibilities, he realized that there was really only one logical candidate for the job. Michael Phillips recalls: "There was a moment when he [Steven] said, 'I have to write this. I think that's the only way I'll get the script I want.'" Julia and Michael concurred—so much of the concept was in Steven's head that it made sense for him to be the one to put it down on paper.

With the three of them in agreement, Spielberg and the Phillipses went back to David Begelman and told him what they wanted to do. Begelman approved the new approach and agreed to let Steven write the screenplay. His only stipulation was that Spielberg had to write a script that could be produced on a modest budget. Although by 1975 Columbia's fortunes had improved somewhat (thanks to the success of films such as 1973's *The Way We Were* and 1975's *Shampoo*), it was still in extremely poor financial health. The banks continued to restrict the company's production expenses, and Alan Hirschfield and Begelman were holding to their "no blockbuster" policy. Columbia couldn't and wouldn't take on an expensive project. Since the ending of the story required a mountain setting, one trip to an appropriate location would be permitted, but otherwise *Close Encounters* was going to have to be made in-house—on the soundstages and backlot of The Burbank Studios. Steven was amenable to Begelman's request—after the difficulties he had encountered making *Jaws*, he wasn't eager to do another location-based picture. Not that he had much choice—given his spotty box office record at that point, Spielberg wasn't in a position to make too many demands. If *Close Encounters* was going to be made, it was going to have to be in accordance with Columbia's strictures.

Guy McElwaine negotiated a script fee with Columbia for Steven, while Spielberg and the Phillipses agreed to amend their personal handshake deal. Since Steven was now taking on an additional role in the project, they agreed to change their fifty-fifty split of the fees and profits to a sixty-forty split in his favor. (Their deal with Columbia stipulated that Spielberg and the Phillipses were to receive approximately thirty percent of the film's net profits. With the sixty-forty split, Steven's share was approximately eighteen percent.)

Watch the Skies was off the shelf.

CHAPTER 9 | The Screenplay

AS POST-PRODUCTION on *Jaws* entered the final stretch, Steven began writing his screenplay. In an interview with writer Dick Tracy in the May 20, 1978 issue of *New Musical Express*, he described his method of attack: "The first step was writing a series of encounter sequences. I just sat behind the typewriter and wrote seven or eight scenes that never got into the movie, but it put fire under me. Then I sat and wrote the story—the structure, the idea, the plot points, the characters and, in parting, the final encounter."

The writing process proved to be very difficult for Spielberg. "I'm not a writer and I don't enjoy writing," Steven admitted to *Sight and Sound*. "I find it much more difficult than directing," he said in an *American Cinematographer* interview, "because it requires a lot of concentration and I'm not the most concentrated of people. It took me a long time to write the screenplay because I would rev up and for two or three days I would go great guns. Then suddenly I'd lie fallow for months—after which I'd come back at it again in a burst of inspiration and write for forty-eight hours. Then nothing for two weeks." It is possible that these struggles gave Steven second thoughts about the task he had undertaken—in *Easy Riders, Raging Bulls*, author Peter Biskind's 1998 book about Hollywood in the 1970s, Rob Cohen reported that at one point Steven asked him to get Universal to hold him to his contract (under which he owed the studio another picture) and force him to direct *Bingo Long* so that he wouldn't have to continue writing his UFO script. But whatever anxiety he may have had proved to be temporary, and Spielberg gradually began to make progress on his opus.

To enhance the script's verisimilitude, Spielberg incorporated a great many details that he had culled from eyewitness reports and other UFO-related data and research, including the notion that most UFO encounters take place in isolated settings such as fields, wooded areas, or on lonely stretches of highway; that all natural sounds stop just prior to an encounter and resume immediately afterward; that car engines stall out at the beginning of a UFO incident and then start up again as soon as it is over; and that UFOs frequently use clouds as cover. The depiction of UFOs as cone-, saucer-, vee-, and crescent-shaped objects that glow with a brilliant and often blinding light that often shifts from color to color; that generate magnetic fields intense enough to cause metallic objects such as mailboxes and railroad crossing signs to vibrate intensely; that produce reduced-gravity and weightless conditions in their immediate vicinity; and that project probing beams of light from their underbellies that generate enough heat to leave burn marks on the surrounding environment and on witnesses also comes from this research.

Steven also developed a few scenes and elements based on his own personal interests and experiences:

- Inspired by his one great passion apart from cinema,
  Spielberg decided that the extraterrestrials and the humans
  in *Close Encounters* would communicate with one another
  using music. When Steven first began thinking about the final
  encounter, he knew he didn't want his ETs to speak in stilted
  English the way the aliens did in so many bad science fiction
  films. He also didn't want them to use mental telepathy, which
  he felt was also a sci-fi cliché. Inspired by a conversation he
  had with John Williams about the solfège method of music
  instruction, in which tones are represented by syllables (Do,
  Re, Mi, etc.), Steven decided that it would be original, unique,
  and beautiful to have terrestrials and extraterrestrials talk to
  one another using music—specifically through four seemingly
  random notes that would acquire more and more meaning
  as the story went on. Spielberg's interest in gadgets led him
  to show the humans generating their part of the musical
  conversation with a Moog synthesizer—a new and cutting-
  edge piece of technology at the time.

- The feeling of awe that Spielberg has described experiencing when he watched the meteor shower in the skies over Phoenix when he was a boy was reflected in a scene in which Norman stares up at the sky with tears in his eyes as UFOs cavort in the clouds above him.

- Steven's interest in astronomy influenced the creation of a playful scene in which the UFOs, masquerading as stars, make it appear as if the constellations are rearranging themselves.

- It is likely that the scenes of the Greenhouse family's strife were influenced by Steven's memories of his own family's difficulties.

When it came time to write the final encounter, Spielberg experienced a small crisis of creative confidence. Based on data indicating that most reported human/alien encounters have been nonviolent and tranquil, as well as his own optimistic sense of wonder about the universe's infinite and awesome possibilities, Steven's plan was to characterize the extraterrestrials as gentle creatures and to depict their climactic meeting with the humans as a peaceful, friendly one—an idea that flew directly in the face of the traditional Hollywood depiction of aliens as violent, monstrous beings bent on invasion and destruction. Steven's decision to give his story a hopeful conclusion was a risky one—the prevailing aesthetics of the cinema of the early 1970s were a gritty and hopelessly pessimistic "realism," along with an overwhelming attitude of cynicism and despair. By making such an unabashedly positive and uplifting statement, Spielberg was setting himself up for possible ridicule and accusations of being corny, naïve, and out of touch. He knew this, but chose to proceed anyway. However, as Steven began to sketch out his revolutionary idea, he started to worry that it wouldn't be exciting enough—that audiences would expect a more traditional ending that featured a confrontation between good guys and bad guys. As Michael Phillips notes, "I think he was a little bit unsure because he didn't have the formal, classical dramatic resolution with the adversary being defeated...."

Steven began to wonder if perhaps he should recast the aliens as villains and create some sort of climactic struggle between them and the humans. In what he considers his most significant creative contribution to the project, Michael Phillips, a self-described "believer in benevolent aliens," encouraged Steven to stick with his original conception. "I was always a strong advocate of that if they [the aliens] are smart enough to get here...[then] they're advanced. They're not coming to conquer us." Convinced, Steven decided to go forward with his boldly benign vision for his ETs. Michael also urged Spielberg to forgo any sort of showdown between the two races. "Steven was always asking the question: 'Do you think it's enough for it to end with just the arrival? Y'know—the meeting?' And I said, 'Yes, I think it's great...it's the meeting of two species...it's fantastic.' But I think he never really trusted it, which is why I think he drove himself to give us like six different endings... He...[realized he]...was gonna have to give us something else and he did and it was great." Instead of an epic battle featuring death rays and laser guns, Steven turned the final meeting into a series of exciting, occasionally playful, and at times awe-inspiring vignettes that Michael describes as "...a cornucopia. It just kind of washes over you. There are many moments where it's kind of enough to wrap up the story, but surprise after surprise, he keeps it coming. He really outdid himself."

Steven also struggled to come up with a satisfactory resolution for Norman's personal story. His original intention was to use a variation of the ending he had pitched for *Meeting of the Minds*: Greenhouse would make his way to the mountain landing site and witness the arrival of the Mothership and the meeting between the members of the Mayflower Project and the extraterrestrials. Norman would photograph these events, which would give him the evidence he needed to prove to the world that UFOs were real and that he wasn't crazy after all. However, as Spielberg continued to develop the theme of his protagonist's estrangement from his family and from his everyday life, it began to seem more logical and dramatically satisfying to have Norman, with nothing left for him on Earth, accept an invitation to join the aliens and journey off with them into space. This seemed to be the conclusion of choice for UFO stories. Hal Barwood and Matthew Robbins had devised a similar climax for their "small-town policeman sees a flying saucer" tale, as had Schrader for *Kingdom Come* (although Schrader's finale had more of a missionary theme—when Paul Van Owen left the earth, it was to establish a human presence in the cosmos). For Hal Barwood, the logic and appeal of such an ending is obvious: "Being enthusiastic about flying saucers makes one separated from the rest of humanity. If you're rejected by people, then your only refuge is [with the extraterrestrials]." At one point, Barwood asked Spielberg to stick with his "Norman proves he's not crazy" ending so that he and Robbins could still use the "going aboard the UFO" ending for their project if they were ever able to get it going. Initially Steven agreed, but ultimately the notion of having Greenhouse fly off in the Mothership proved too perfect to not use. Although he was disappointed, Barwood understood. "It's...[the ideal ending]...and it's really hard to resist." Since, as things turned out, Barwood and Robbins never wrote their UFO script, Barwood says that he is "glad that [Steven's movie] got made and that these ideas got expressed as well as they did." (In recent years, Steven—who in the decades since *CE3K* has become a father many times over—has expressed misgivings about allowing his protagonist to leave his family behind at the end of the movie, feeling now that no loving, responsible father would do such a thing. He has said that if he had it to do all over again, he would not end the story in this way.) Since Norman was now going to depart with the aliens, the task of taking the photographs that would prove to the world that UFOs were real was assigned to another character—a young woman named Jillian Guiler. One of Norman's fellow believers, Jillian would accompany him on his climb up the mountain and witness the climactic events alongside him.

Although the content of the finale was now locked, Spielberg still needed a location to set it in. He knew he wanted the ending to occur at a mountain, but not just any mountain—he wanted a visually spectacular peak, someplace that was both unique and memorable. To find it, Spielberg persuaded Columbia to bring Joe Alves (who had just finished work on a horror film called *Embryo* [1976]) on board early. Alves and Spielberg spent a few days in Steven's office at Universal poring over numerous picture books and maps and compiling an extensive list of potential sites. When they were done, Joe set out on an extensive scouting trip, eventually traveling over 3,500 miles to check out and photograph each of the locations.

Alves left Los Angeles on June 20, 1975, which, quite coincidentally, was also the day *Jaws* opened in movie theaters around the country. Despite all the naysayers' dire predictions, the film was a sensation. Spielberg had triumphed over all of the production's monumental problems to create a wonderful motion picture. Brilliantly realized in every respect,

Jaws was a tremendously exciting film—alternately thrilling, frightening, and funny, and never anything less than supremely entertaining. The reviews were strong and audiences loved it—the film began breaking box office records from the minute it opened. *Jaws* also became a cultural phenomenon—it sold millions of dollars in shark-related merchandise, was referenced in everything from political cartoons to records to late night television comedy shows, and kept millions of people out of the water for several summers running.

Thanks to a virtuoso job of direction, Spielberg, who a few months earlier had been worried that his career might be over, vaulted to the top of Hollywood's A-list. Praised for his masterful command of the cinematic medium, his powerful ability to enthrall and entertain audiences, and his keen commercial instincts, he was inundated with offers, including one from Alexander Salkind to direct *Superman* (impressed by the incredible success of *Jaws*, Salkind finally gave his son the go-ahead to return Guy McElwaine's calls) and another from Universal to direct the inevitable *Jaws 2*. Now able to write his own ticket, Spielberg turned them all down, dropped out of *Bingo Long*, and focused all of his creative energies on *Watch the Skies*. (*Superman* would eventually be directed by Richard Donner, the *Jaws* sequel by Jeannot Szwarc, and *Bingo Long* by John Badham.)

At the end of June, Steven flew to New York to do some press for *Jaws* and to meet with Julia Phillips, Herbert Allen, and Alan Hirschfield to discuss *Watch the Skies*. In between appointments, Steven and Julia did some field research for the script, visiting a Con Ed station to learn how an electrical plant works and how a power outage is dealt with so that they could give the blackout sequence the proper authenticity. (They also took some time to check up on their other films—Steven and comedian Albert Brooks rode around Manhattan in a cab, taking 8mm movies of people waiting in line to see *Jaws*, while Julia touched base with the *Taxi Driver* crew, which was currently shooting in the city under Michael's supervision.) By the time they got back to Los Angeles, Joe Alves had returned from his mountain-hunting expedition. Steven and Joe got together and looked at all of the pictures Joe had taken of the locations he had visited, which included Arches National Park, Bryce Canyon, and Canyonlands (all in Utah), Badlands National Park (South Dakota), Chimney Rock (Nebraska), Monument Valley (Arizona/Utah), Ship Rock (New Mexico), and a 1,267-foot-tall monolith in the Black Hills of Wyoming called Devils Tower.

Located in eastern Wyoming above the Belle Fourche River, Devils Tower was formed millions of years ago when an extinct volcano eroded away, leaving a central core of hardened lava behind. Shaped like a giant tree stump, it is flat on the top and has a series of distinctive flutes running up and down its sides. At the base is a pile of rubble consisting of boulders, small rocks, and stones that have fallen from the peak. Surrounded by 1,347 acres of pine forests and prairies, Devils Tower is a sacred site for many Native American tribes, including the Sioux, Arapaho, Crow, Cheyenne, Kiowa, Lakota, and Shoshone. The folklore of these tribes contains many legends of how the Tower came into existence. The best known tells the tale of six Sioux girls who went out to pick flowers and were chased by bears. Frightened, the young women prayed to the Great Spirit to save them. The Great Spirit responded by raising the ground beneath them up into the sky. The bears tried to climb the rock, leaving scratch marks on the sides, but it had risen too high and the bears fell off.

On September 26, 1906, President Theodore Roosevelt designated Devils Tower as the United States' first national monument. Hal Barwood had visited the Tower on a family vacation in 1971 and, feeling that it had "an otherworldly, totemic feeling," recommended it to Steven and Joe when he heard that they were searching for a unique-looking mountain. Upon seeing the monument, Alves concurred: "It was a very strange... very impressive...piece of topography." When Spielberg saw the pictures, Alves reports that he "...immediately chose Devils Tower. [The decision] was pretty much hands down." Steven incorporated the massive igneous intrusion into the script, identifying it as Wamsutter Mountain (Wamsutter is a small town in Wyoming)—apparently to keep the identity of the location a secret in case the script somehow leaked out.

As the story came together, Steven looked for a theme—a thread that would connect all of the ideas and elements he had assembled and meld them into a unified whole. He found it in one of his favorite childhood songs: "When I heard...'When You Wish Upon a Star' from Walt Disney's *Pinocchio* (1940), sung by Cliff Edwards, everything kind of fell into place." The gentle, wistful tune gave Spielberg the hook he was looking for ("I pretty much hung my story on the mood that song created, the way it affected me emotionally") and he incorporated it into the script, laying the lyrics in over Norman's final ascent into the Mothership. As soon as he did this, the script found its soul. Steven had taken a story that had begun as cynical thriller about a sinister act and transformed it into a sweet-natured fable about the pursuit of a belief and the fulfillment of a dream. "It became," Michael Phillips says, "what we now recognize as a Steven Spielberg film—a joyous roller coaster." By August 1975, Spielberg had finished his first draft. Although it was still extremely rough, it laid out the story that he wanted to tell, which went as follows:

A massive blackout strikes suburban Indiana. Norman Greenhouse, a trouble foreman for the Tolano Department of Water and Power, is sent out to determine the cause of the outage. Arriving at the site where the failure occurred, Norman discovers that all of the electric lines have been stolen from the poles. As he prepares to replace the lines so that the system can be rebooted, Norman receives reports of lights appearing in a nearby area that the sensors at the DWP command center indicate is still without power. Worried that the sensors have somehow failed to detect that the lines have been reenergized, Norman heads out to warn the unsuspecting DWP crews working in the zone that they may be dealing with live wires. Driving through farm country on his way to the affected area, Norman gets lost and stops at a four-way intersection to get his bearings. As he does, the lights in his car suddenly fail and then the entire area for thirty yards around is suddenly bathed in a beam of extremely intense light coming from the sky above. Norman tries to look up to identify the source, but the light is too bright and he can't see a thing. A few seconds later, the beam switches off and Norman's car comes back to life.

As Norman recovers, he hears reports over his radio that the local police are chasing six orange flares traveling southwest in a wing-like formation down the highway. Suspecting that these flares may be connected to what has just happened to him, Norman sets out to find them. He drives to a hilltop area called Crescendo Summit, from which he can survey the countryside for miles around. As Norman searches the horizon looking for the flares, four of them suddenly come zooming up the road heading right toward him. Traveling a mere two feet above the asphalt, the flares zip around Norman and disappear into the distance. A few seconds later, three police cars come barreling along in hot pursuit. Excited, Norman follows the cops as they chase the UFOs through a tollbooth and on into Ohio. At a hairpin turn in the road, the UFOs keep going straight and sail off into the sky. The lead police car is so intent on the chase that it misses the turn, leaves the highway, and crashes into a gully below.

As the flares fly up into the clouds, a team of air traffic controllers at Ohio's Cox Municipal Airport deals with the sudden appearance of several unidentified objects on their radar. At the same time, two approaching airliners report seeing the group of mysterious flares fly past them in the sky. After the flares disappear into the distance, the air traffic controllers ask the pilots if they want to make a UFO report. Not wanting to deal with the paperwork headache, the pilots say no. When told that some of the passengers on one of the planes took pictures of the lights, Cox's Director of Ground Operations, acting on orders from nearby Wright-Patterson Air Force Base (home of Project Blue Book), orders the plane to land. A short time later, the airliner touches down and is met by a mysterious team of very official-looking people. As the team confiscates all cameras and tape recorders, a friendly public relations man informs the passengers that they have flown through restricted government airspace and inadvertently witnessed some classified government testing. The PR man assures the irate travelers that his team will develop their pictures and return them along with their cameras in a few weeks' time.

Dawn finds Norman sitting in a cornfield, looking up at the sky and crying as hundreds of puffy white clouds drift by overhead. The clouds are lit up from within by some mysterious lights. As several military jets approach, all of the lights turn off except for one. The jets chase the solo light, which performs some moves that violate the laws of physics before it finally zooms off toward the horizon, leaving the jets behind. Profoundly moved by his experience, Norman returns home and tries to tell his wife, Ronnie, about what has happened, but she is preoccupied with the concerns of her very average suburban existence and can't understand what he is trying to tell her. Norman goes to the Civilian Information Center at Pease Air Force Base to report his sighting. He is interviewed by an Air Force officer who insinuates that Norman was hallucinating when he saw the UFOs. Norman protests, but the officer tells him that there isn't enough evidence to warrant any sort of investigation and that the only way to get one would be to present some sort of proof of what he saw. Otherwise, nothing can be done. To get that proof, Norman returns to Crescendo Summit with a movie camera, hoping to capture a UFO on film. Seeing some lights rise above a dense thicket, Norman runs into the foliage, where he encounters several weird, spindly figures wearing metallic suits. He chases after them, but quickly realizes that they are just mischievous kids wearing costumes and that the lights are only small hot air balloons powered by flickering burners.

In the days that follow, Norman begins to crack up. Plagued by visions of a mountain that he can't identify, he builds a clay model of it atop a model railroad landscape in the Greenhouse family room. He hopes that doing this will help him identify what the mountain is, but it doesn't—there's something not quite right about the model. Disturbed by Norman's behavior, Ronnie insists that he go to see a psychiatrist. When he refuses, Ronnie tells Norman that she is going to take the children and move in with her parents until he does. After his family leaves, Norman stares morosely at his mountain. Suddenly, something clicks in his mind and he becomes inspired. When Ronnie returns a few days later to check on Norman, she finds that he has constructed a giant model of a uniquely shaped mountain, reaching to the ceiling of the family room, out of dirt, mud, and items collected from the yard. For Ronnie, this is the last straw and she leaves Norman for good. Following Ronnie's departure, a depressed Norman gets drunk and spends a long day in front of the TV, catatonically watching mindless television programming and trying to figure out what has happened to him. The evening news begins and Walter Cronkite leads off with a story about a nerve gas leak in the Wyoming wilderness area near Wamsutter Mountain. A picture of Wamsutter Mountain appears on the television screen. Much to Norman's surprise, it looks exactly like the model he has just built. The mystery has been solved.

Norman travels to Wyoming and makes his way past hordes of evacuees who are heading in the opposite direction. He slips into the restricted area and heads for Wamsutter Mountain, but is captured by a group of men wearing life support suits, who take him to a base camp at the foot of the distinctive-looking mountain. Norman is taken to an interrogation room where he is interviewed by the friendly PR man from the airplane scene, who we learn is actually Robert Lacombe, the leader of a secret team that has been investigating UFO sightings and attempting to make contact with the extraterrestrial race that is responsible for them. A rendezvous between humans and aliens has been arranged and is set to take place that evening in a canyon on the other side of Wamsutter Mountain. The nerve gas leak was faked in order to keep civilians away while the encounter takes place. The sincerely curious Lacombe asks Norman why he has come to an area where he was told his life would be in danger, but Norman can't explain it. Their interview is cut short when Wild Bill Walsh, the military leader of the project, orders that Norman be shipped out of the area. Norman is put into a helicopter along with the group of other "gatecrashers" who have also made their way to the area. One of the gatecrashers is a young woman named Jillian Guiler. Meanwhile, Lacombe tries to convince Wild Bill to let the gatecrashers stay because he feels that they have been invited, but Wild Bill thinks this is nonsense and orders the evacuation to proceed.

Back at the helicopter, Norman leads a mass escape. The gatecrashers force their way out of the chopper and head for Wamsutter Mountain. Most are recaptured, but Norman, Jillian, and an Irishman named Collin O'Connor get away. Their goal is to make it to the valley on the other side. To stop them, Wild Bill orders a team of helicopters to dust the mountain with a sleep aerosol that will render the gatecrashers unconscious. Collin is knocked out, but Norman and Jillian elude the spray, make it over the mountain, and scramble down to the canyon, where they discover that the UFO team has set up a makeshift landing zone.

By now, night has fallen. As Norman and Jillian watch, the members of the UFO team turn their attention to the sky, where the stars forming the constellation of Orion suddenly rearrange themselves to form the Big Dipper. The stars—which we now realize are the UFOs—then surround a lone cloud and begin spinning around it until the cloud swirls into the shape of Messier 51, the famous whirlpool galaxy of the Canes Venatici constellation. One of the UFOs takes up a position on the outer edge of the whirlpool, indicating the location of the alien home world. Three of the orange UFOs seen earlier drop down from the sky and hover over the landing zone. Lacombe directs a Moog synthesizer operator to begin playing a series of atonal notes. The UFOs respond to the notes by altering their color from orange to ultraviolet. Following this, three hundred ice cube–sized cuboids zoom down from the sky and put on a show for the UFO team by forming a series of three-dimensional shapes in the air above the landing zone. The cuboids then dispense a cloud of luminous dust—pinpoint-sized cubes that settle over the landing zone like a swarm of fireflies and then dissolve. One of the micro-cubes melts into Norman's hand and enters his bloodstream before it finally fades away. Suddenly, a series of delightful chimes is heard from the sky. The cuboids ring the valley and begin glowing brightly. We realize now that they are landing lights. A fire-orange object at least fifty yards long appears over the rim of the canyon. As it continues to move up over the rim, we realize that the object is just a protrusion on top of a superstructure that is over two hundred yards long. Before long, the entire craft comes into view and we see that the superstructure is set atop a giant, brilliantly illuminated UFO Mothership. The Mothership is eccentrically designed—like something out of a Dr. Seuss book—with light pouring from thousands of portholes.

As the Mothership lands, it blasts four musical tones at a deafening volume. The Moog synthesizer operator responds and so begins a joyful musical jam between the synthesizer operator and the Mothership. We realize that the notes are meant to be some sort of greeting. As this is happening, Norman leaves Jillian and makes his way down to the landing zone, where he sees a group of nine young men wearing hospital gowns being given the last rites by a Catholic priest. Norman realizes that they are preparing to go aboard the Mothership. Lacombe discovers Norman and asks him what he wants. Norman says that he just wants to know that this is all really happening. Lacombe smiles and nods. A hatch opens and one hundred humanoid aliens emerge from the Mothership. They fan out in all directions to investigate the landing area—excitedly interacting with humans, playing with equipment, and having a delightful time. The robed young men emerge from their tent and approach the Mothership. As they do, we see that Norman has joined them. Some of the aliens surround Norman and lead him to the Mothership so that he can be the first aboard. As the original recording of Jiminy Cricket singing "When You Wish Upon a

Star" plays on the soundtrack, Norman boards the Mothership as Jillian takes pictures of the monumental event.

Wary of announcing his authorship until he was sure the team was
actually going forward with his screenplay, Steven decided to use a pseud-
onym and humorously identified the author of the script—which he had
once again decided to call *Close Encounters of the Third Kind*—as Sam Irvin, the North Carolina senator who led the United States Senate investigation into the Watergate scandal and a folk hero to the exposers of cover-
ups everywhere (although Spielberg spelled the esteemed Senator's name
wrong—it's actually "Ervin").

Steven and the Phillipses submitted the script to Columbia, whose
budgeting department estimated that it would cost approximately $4.5
million to produce—considerably more than the $2.8 million that Steven
had proposed to Begelman back in 1973. (Michael Phillips reports that
Steven's hastily improvised figure haunted them throughout the life of
the project. Although the $2.8 million had been pulled out of thin air and
had never been attached to any version of the screenplay, many people
at Columbia and in the press continually cited it as the film's starting
budget, making it seem as if the film had been over budget from the very
beginning.). Although not an unreasonable amount for a large-scale film
at the time, $4.5 million was a hefty sum for the still-struggling Columbia.
Even so, Begelman wasn't dissuaded—he liked the script, and his faith in
Steven was strong and growing stronger as *Jaws* continued its incredible
run.

Since the budget exceeded the strict $3 million per picture limit
imposed by Columbia's bankers, the company was required to obtain
a waiver in order for the expenditure to be approved. Begelman and
Hirschfield made an appeal to the bankers, expressing their confidence
in Spielberg and his film, and the waiver was granted. With that hurdle
cleared, *Close Encounters of the Third Kind* was given a yellow light. In
Hollywood parlance, this meant that the project had been tentatively
approved and the film could now enter pre-production. Once all of the
necessary preparations had been made to get ready for shooting, a final
budget would be drawn up. If the budget met with the studio's approval,
then the project would be given a green light and enter production. If
it didn't, then it would be canceled. (In the event that the film was can-

celed, any money spent on the production up until that point would be written off. No matter how high the amount, it would be cheap compared to the cost of production, which could run into the tens of thousands of dollars per day.)

Close Encounters was assigned an official Columbia production number (#132215) and offices were opened in a series of trailers set up in a parking lot at The Burbank Studios. Steven imposed a strict secrecy policy regarding the project—he didn't want the plot or the concept ripped off for a quickie exploitation film or television movie. Everyone associated with the project was required to agree to a nondisclosure policy. They weren't allowed to talk about the movie, even to their friends and family.

Begelman assigned executives Peter Guber and John Veitch to supervise the making of the movie for Columbia. Born on March 1, 1942 in Boston, Guber graduated from New York University Law School and joined CPI as an assistant management trainee in 1968. In a few short years he became the vice president of business affairs and was then named the studio's head of production by Stanley Schneider. One of the few members of the former management team retained by Begelman when he took over, Guber was promoted to the position of executive vice president in charge of worldwide production in August 1973.

A former actor who played bit parts in *Stalag 17* (1953) and *From Here to Eternity* (1952), John Veitch, born in New York City on June 22, 1920, moved behind the camera in the late 1950s as an assistant director and production manager. He joined Columbia as an executive assistant production manager in 1961 and eventually worked his way up to the position of senior vice president and executive production manager. Veitch's job was to oversee the practical and logistical aspects of the studio's filmmaking. He and his staff budgeted each production, assigned the use of studio facilities and made sure that each unit had all of the technical equipment and support it needed to make its film.

On August 12, 1975, Guber announced to the press that pre-production on *Close Encounters of the Third Kind*—which he described as "a science fiction thriller based on an original story by Steven Spielberg"—would begin in the fall. Production was scheduled to start in November, and the finished film would be released at Easter 1977. Before pre-production could begin, Steven needed to rewrite his rough draft script. In the process, he made a number of significant changes and additions:

- Robert Lacombe—an American in the first draft—was transformed into a Frenchman. This change was made to better demonstrate the international makeup of the team and the international scope of the UFO phenomenon. It has been said that Steven based Lacombe on French UFO expert Jacques F. Vallée, an associate of Dr. J. Allen Hynek, although Spielberg himself has never confirmed this (he did not actually meet Vallée until the film was almost finished). It is possible that Spielberg meant Lacombe to be a tribute to the French in general, whose serious and scientific approach to the UFO phenomenon Hynek applauded in his book as a model of how such research should be conducted.

- To assist Lacombe in communicating with the other members of the team, Steven gave him an unnamed American translator with a heavy Brooklyn accent.

- To flesh out the UFO team's mission, Spielberg developed a subplot based on a theory that had captured the popular imagination in the mid-1970s—the notion that UFOs and aliens were behind the mysterious disappearances of boats and planes in the area of the Atlantic Ocean off of Florida known as the Bermuda Triangle. The subplot referenced two of the more famous Triangle disappearances by having the five Avenger Torpedo Bombers of Navy Flight 19 (which vanished off Fort Lauderdale on December 5, 1945) and the tanker ship M.S. Marine Sulphur Queen (which was reported missing on February 4, 1963) reappear in unusual settings around the world, returned by the extraterrestrials as a prelude to their arrival. Lacombe would find the ATBs sitting in some crop circles—another phenomenon allegedly caused by UFOs—in the middle of the dense Brazilian jungle and the Sulphur Queen leaning against a sand dune in the remote reaches of Mongolia's Gobi Desert. Flight 19's missing pilots, the Sulphur Queen's crew, and hundreds of other people abducted by the extraterrestrials over the years would also return, emerging from the Mothership at the end of the film.

- To further emphasize Norman's estrangement from his previous life in the aftermath of his encounter, Steven had the power company fire Norman for deserting his post on the night of the blackout. A sequence was also added in which Norman is interviewed by a television news crew about his encounter and made to look like a nut in the final on-air report.

- Several more scenes set at Crescendo Summit were added to the script. In one, Norman takes Ronnie out to the isolated spot to neck, but keeps his eyes on the sky the whole time. In the other, Norman joins a group of true believers who are waiting for UFOs to make an encore appearance, only to be shooed away by a pair of Air Force helicopters. Apparently, some elements of Steven's UFO story "Experiences" were incorporated into these scenes.

- The character of Jillian Guiler was significantly enhanced in the second draft. She was given an identity as an artist and single mother to a four-year-old son named Barry, and introduced early in the story, in a scene in which she chases after her son, who has run out of the house in the middle of the night in pursuit of some unseen alien intruders that have ransacked their kitchen. Jillian and Norman become acquainted in the Crescendo Summit scenes and then meet up again at the UFO team's base camp. They climb the mountain together and witness the arrival of the Mothership. Because of her obligations to her son (who is being looked after by Jillian's father), Jillian declines to go with Norman when he journeys down into the landing zone to get closer to the action, but she does bid him farewell as he boards the Mothership in the end.

- The four musical tones that the humans use to communicate with the aliens became five, and a scene was added in which the members of the UN team assemble in an auditorium and are introduced to the sounds by a French synthesizer player named Jean-Claude, who is described as looking like William Shakespeare. Wild Bill Walsh, the UFO project's military leader in the first draft (where he was also referred to on occasion as Wild Bill McLaughlin), was renamed Wild Bill Hickcock and introduced in this scene as the Lyndon Johnson–like leader of the entire UFO investigative team.

The second draft—again credited to Sam Irvin—was finished on September 2, 1975 and submitted to Columbia. The enhanced scope and additional sequences caused the budget to rise to $5.4 million. Begelman wasn't thrilled with this newer, higher number, but when *Jaws* supplanted *The Godfather* to become the highest-grossing film of all time (it would eventually gross almost half a billion dollars worldwide) after just seventy-eight days in release, he decided to stay the course.

| # Assembling the Team

Pre-production on *Close Encounters* formally got under way in the fall of 1975. When it did, one of the producers was noticeably absent. In the midst of their divorce proceedings, Michael and Julia found it increasingly difficult to work together on a daily basis, so they decided to split up their projects. They agreed that Michael would supervise the production of *Taxi Driver* and Julia would oversee the making of *Close Encounters*.

To assist her, she needed an experienced production manager. The PM is responsible for all of the nuts-and-bolts aspects of making a movie—he or she organizes the shooting schedule and makes sure that the company sticks to it; controls expenditures to keep the project on budget; hires the below-the-line crew; rents or purchases equipment; secures locations; negotiates contracts; and signs all of the checks. After interviewing several candidates, Julia hired Clark Paylow. Born on December 16, 1918, Paylow began his Hollywood career in the 1940s as an assistant director on a series of low-budget Westerns and adventure movies. As a production manager, he worked on the 1960s television series *I, Spy* and on numerous features, including *Cold Turkey* (1971), *The Organization* (1971), and Francis Ford Coppola's *The Conversation* (1974). He had just finished *Hearts of the West* (1975) for MGM when he signed on to *Close Encounters* as both production manager and associate producer.

As Phillips and Paylow began laying out the logistics of the production, Joe Alves began designing sets and scouting locations. Steven felt that if the audience accepted the world the story took place in as absolutely real, they would believe that the fantastic events that took place there were absolutely real as well. Therefore, he wanted the settings to look as normal and everyday as possible, and asked Joe not to design anything that looked futuristic. Instead, Spielberg instructed Alves to create a typical, suburban American environment full of brand names, plastic, and polyester.

Meanwhile, Steven began storyboarding the film's action and special effects scenes. A storyboard is a visual interpretation of a script—a series of drawings that depict each shot planned for a particular sequence. Storyboards (a.k.a. continuity sketches) are usually prepared for complex action and special effects scenes in order to give all members of the production team a clear idea of the images and illusions the director wants them to achieve. Spielberg had been a meticulous storyboarder since his amateur filmmaker days. For him, thorough preparation was the road to creative freedom: "I try to work from my imagination day-to-day...[but storyboarding] makes me feel secure in knowing that if I'm bone dry and nothing new hits me, I can fall back on a good idea that already works on paper."

Steven devised his shots in accordance with a self-imposed guideline: "When I was first planning the movie, I felt like I had to frame everything with more sky than ground....I felt the sky was as important to the surprise and mystery of *Close Encounters* as the water was to *Jaws*." To keep the film's fantastic elements rooted in the down-to-earth reality he was trying to so hard to create, Spielberg used another guideline—when creating shots that included the flying saucers, he never showed them alone against a star field, but instead made sure to always include them in the same frame with some sort of earthbound object such as a person, a roadway, a mountain, or a tree.

By his own admission, Spielberg wasn't much of an artist, so he relied on an accomplished production illustrator named George Jensen to do the actual drawing. To produce the storyboards, Jensen and Spielberg began by working their way through the script. Steven would describe the composition, action, and camera movement he envisioned for each shot and George would then translate these ideas into finished pieces of art. Continuity sketches are usually done in black and white, but because so many scenes in *Close Encounters* were going to employ multihued lighting effects, Jensen rendered his boards in color. When all of the sketches for each sequence were completed, they were placed in a three-ring binder and distributed to the key members of the production staff.

In between his sessions with George, Steven began to assemble the rest of his creative team. He recruited several of his key collaborators from *The Sugarland Express* and *Jaws*, including:

Vilmos Zsigmond (Director of Photography): Zsigmond was born in Szeged, Hungary on June 16, 1930. When he was seventeen, an uncle gave him a book about photography called *The Art of Light* by photographer Eugene Dulovits. Inspired by the book's beautiful black-and-white pictures, Vilmos began studying photography and became an accomplished amateur. He later studied cinematography at the State Academy of Theatre and Film Art in Budapest. Following his graduation in 1955, Zsigmond went to work as an assistant cameraman and camera operator at a Budapest film studio. After photographing the events of the Hungarian people's 1956 uprising against their Communist leaders and the subsequent invasion by the Soviet army to crush the revolt, Vilmos fled the country and came to the United States as a political refugee. He made his way to Hollywood, where he found work as a technician in a film lab and also as a home portrait photographer. After shooting a few student films, Vilmos began working on documentaries and commercials, then (using the name William Zsigmond) moved into features in the early 1960s as the director of photography on a series of low-budget horror and exploitation films, including *The Incredibly Strange Creatures Who Stopped Living and Became Mixed-Up Zombies* (1964), *The Nasty Rabbit* (1964), *Psycho a Go-Go* (1965), *The Name of the Game is Kill* (1968), and *Futz!* (1969).

Zsigmond's mainstream studio career was launched in 1971 when he shot *The Hired Hand* for Universal Pictures. Once again calling himself Vilmos, he went on to photograph *Red Sky at Morning* (1971), *McCabe & Mrs. Miller* (1971), *Deliverance* (1972), *Images* (1972), *Cinderella Liberty* (1973), and *The Long Goodbye* (1973)—quickly gaining a reputation for being an extremely creative and daring cinematographer who used a variety of innovative and sometimes risky techniques to create striking images on film. Zsigmond first met Steven Spielberg in 1972 when Spielberg, impressed with his work on *McCabe & Mrs. Miller*, asked him to be the director of photography on *The Sugarland Express*. The two men enjoyed a close creative relationship on *Sugarland* (Spielberg described them as "brothers"), the result of which was an extremely kinetic and visually stunning film. Busy on another project, Zsigmond did not work on *Jaws* (*Something Evil* DP Bill Butler—who also shot the second unit on *Deliverance*—was the cinematographer on that film), but he was eager to do *Close Encounters* because he loved the story and was excited by the photographic challenges the film presented.

Once Vilmos was on board, he and Steven discussed what they wanted the movie to look like. In his quest for realism, Spielberg thought at first to shoot *Close Encounters* like a documentary—using a handheld camera and available light to give the film a gritty, naturalistic look. This would be familiar territory for Zsigmond, who had made his reputation by eschewing artificial illumination and shooting with natural or available light whenever possible. In order to generate an acceptable image when light levels were low, Vilmos would often "flash" his film—pre-expose the negative, which reduced the contrast to the point where only minimal light was required to get a picture—or "push" it—underexpose the negative during shooting and then increase the development time during processing, which added an additional degree of exposure to the final image.

The drawbacks to these techniques were that flashing made it hard to generate solid blacks on the negative, and pushing usually resulted in a very grainy picture. Because *Close Encounters'* visual effects were going to require images that were as crisp and sharp as possible, with little to no diffusion, a full range of color, and a minimal amount of grain, Spielberg and Zsigmond eventually realized that they would have to forgo the documentary look and employ more traditional techniques—formal compositions and artificial lighting—instead, although their goal was still to keep the look of the film as realistic as possible. The film would be shot on 35mm film using the Panavision anamorphic process—a method that uses a special camera lens to squeeze a widescreen image onto regular 35mm film and a special projector lens to unsqueeze the image when it is shown on a wide theater screen.

Verna Fields (Editor/Associate Producer): The daughter of screenwriter Sam Hellman (*Little Miss Marker, My Darling Clementine*), Verna was born March 21, 1918. After earning a B.A. in journalism from USC, she entered the film industry as an apprentice sound editor and worked her way up to full sound editor. Verna retired to have children, but when her husband, film editor Sam Fields, died suddenly in 1954, she returned to work in order to support her two sons. After editing the sound for several television series and for features such as *While the City Sleeps* (1956), *How to Make a*

Monster (1958), and *El Cid* (1961), Fields earned her first credit as a picture editor on *Studs Lonigan* (1960) and continued in this capacity on *An Affair of the Skin* (1963), *Deathwatch* (1966), *Medium Cool* (1969), *What's Up, Doc* (1972), and *Paper Moon* (1973).

During the 1960s, she also produced and edited documentaries for the federal government and taught editing at USC. In 1973, Fields coedited (with Marcia Lucas) *American Graffiti* for her former student George Lucas, who recommended her to Steven for *Sugarland* (which she coedited with *Savage* editor Edward Abroms). After *Sugarland*, Verna joined Steven on *Jaws*. Her spectacular work on that film prompted Universal to hire her as a production executive. Fields worked on *Close Encounters* in an unofficial capacity during its formative stages when she, Steven, and Joe Alves had offices next to one another at Universal. When the production began to ramp up, Spielberg asked Universal if he could "borrow" Fields to act as editor and associate producer for his new film and Universal agreed. Verna's son Rick also joined the team as Steven's personal assistant, a position he had also held on *Jaws*.

John Williams (Composer): Williams was born on February 8, 1932, in Floral Park, New York. The son of jazz drummer Johnny Williams, John began playing the piano at an early age and dreamed of becoming a concert pianist. In 1948, the Williams family moved to Los Angeles, where John attended Los Angeles City College and UCLA. Following a two-year hitch in the Air Force, Williams became a student at the Juilliard School of Music, studying piano during the day and supporting himself by playing in a jazz band at night. After graduating from Juilliard, John returned to Los Angeles and became a staff arranger, first at Columbia Pictures and then at Twentieth Century-Fox. He also played piano on the soundtracks of *South Pacific* (1958), *Some Like It Hot* (1959), *The Apartment* (1960), and *To Kill a Mockingbird* (1962), and arranged songs for singers Vic Damone, Doris Day, Mahalia Jackson, and Frankie Laine. In the mid-1950s, John began writing music for television, composing themes and scores for shows such as *General Electric Theater*, *Playhouse 90*, *Gilligan's Island*, *Wagon Train*, *Lost in Space*, and *Land of the Giants*. He won two Emmy Awards for his work on the television movies *Heidi* (1968) and *Jane Eyre* (1970).

Williams composed his first motion picture score for 1958's *Daddy-O*. He followed this with music for many films, including *I Passed for*

White (1960), *Diamond Head* (1963), *The Killers* (1964), *How to Steal a Million* (1966), *Valley of the Dolls* (1967), *Goodbye, Mr. Chips* (1972), *The Cowboys* (1972), *The Poseidon Adventure* (1972), *Images* (1972), *The Long Goodbye* (1973), *The Paper Chase* (1973), *Cinderella Liberty* (1973), and *The Towering Inferno* (1974)—and won an Academy Award for his adaptation of the music for *Fiddler on the Roof* (1971).

John met Steven Spielberg in 1973. Spielberg admired the music Williams had written for *The Reivers* (1969)—"It was a fantastic score...a very American score...a cross between Aaron Copland and Debussy"—and asked him to write similarly sweeping music for *Sugarland*. Williams demurred—he felt that *Sugarland* was a simple film that required simple music, and so proceeded to compose a score based on a harmonica riff (performed by Toots Thielman)—a choice that proved tremendously effective. Spielberg and Williams, who had become good friends, worked together again on *Jaws*, and Spielberg attributed much of that film's success to William's now-classic two-note "shark" theme and to the sweeping "pirate movie" score that accompanied it.

Charlsie Bryant (Script Supervisor): The script supervisor's job is to keep track of each element of every shot taken during production. She or he records the scene and take number, the camera position, and the running time of each shot, as well as which portion of the scene's action and dialogue has been covered by the setup, and notes any changes made to these elements during filming. The script supervisor also makes sure that props, action, and costumes match from shot to shot within a scene and keeps a detailed record of every event that happens on and off camera during each day of production. Bryant, who earned her first script supervisor credit on Alfred Hitchcock's *Rope* (1948) and who also worked on *Portrait of Jennie* (1948), *In a Lonely Place* (1950), *Barefoot in the Park* (1967), *The Sting* (1973), and *The Great Waldo Pepper* (1975), had done a masterful job on *Jaws*, and Steven eagerly invited her back for *Close Encounters*.

There were some new faces as well:

Charles "Chuck" Meyers (First Assistant Director): The First AD runs the set for the director. He or she prepares each shot for filming by making sure that all personnel (including the actors) and equipment are in position and that all stunts and effects have been prepared and rehearsed, and are ready to go on schedule. The First AD calls for the camera and sound to begin rolling and on occasion will direct crowd scenes and extras. The son of production manager Frank E. Meyers, Charles was born on January 9, 1939. A former marine, he worked on films such as *American Graffiti* (1973), *The Conversation* (1974), and *The Godfather: Part II* (1974) and had just wrapped the Woody Guthrie biopic *Bound for Glory* (1976) when Steven asked him to work on *Close Encounters*.

Jim Bloom (Second Assistant Director): After attending the University of California at Berkeley, Bloom began his film career as a production assistant on *American Graffiti* and then joined the Directors Guild of America's trainee program. He served as an assistant director trainee under Chuck Meyers on *The Conversation* and then worked on Sam Peckinpah's *The Killer Elite* (1975) and on the television series *The Streets of San Francisco* before rejoining Meyers on *Bound for Glory*. Knowing he would need a reliable assistant, Meyers brought Bloom with him to *CE3K*.

Gene S. Cantamessa (Production Sound Mixer): A sound mixer's job is to record dialogue and other pertinent sound effects during production. Born in 1931, Cantamessa began his film industry career in the mid-1950s erasing old tapes at the Ryder Sound Company. After joining the union, he became a sound transfer technician at MGM and moved into production—first as a cable runner, then as a boom microphone operator, and finally as a mixer. He worked on a number of television series (*Peyton Place, Wanted: Dead or Alive, The Many Loves of Dobie Gillis*) and features (*Blazing Saddles* [1974], *Young Frankenstein* [1974], *Smile* [1975]), and received an Academy Award nomination for his work on *The Candidate* (1972). Prior to *Close Encounters*, Cantamessa recorded the sound on *Black Sunday* (1977) for director John Frankenheimer, who recommended him to Spielberg.

Buddy Joe Hooker (Stunt Coordinator): Veteran stunt man and second unit director Hooker (*The Omega Man* [1971], *Harold and Maude* [1971], *Bound for Glory*) was hired to supervise the film's stunt work. His job was to determine what techniques and equipment would be used to realize a particular bit, make all of the required preparations (including choosing and training the stunt men and women to perform the piece and ensuring that all safety precautions were attended to), and oversee its execution on the set. Hooker doubled for Richard Dreyfuss in a number of scenes and performed many of the stunts himself.

James Linn (Wardrobe Supervisor): Linn (*Marnie* [1964], *Bound for Glory*) assembled and maintained the show's costumes. Since *Close Encounters* was set in contemporary reality, most of the clothes the actors wore were bought off the rack rather than specially created. **Vicki Sanchez** joined him as the women's wardrober.

Bob Westmoreland (Makeup): An experienced makeup artist (*Alice Doesn't Live Here Anymore* [1974], *Stay Hungry* [1976], *Bound for Glory*), Westmoreland was also an actor who had bit parts in *Molly and Lawless John* (1972) and *Stay Hungry*. He would appear in *Close Encounters* both as a power company dispatcher and as one of the returnees (a British sea captain) at the end of the film.

Edie Panda: Panda (*All in the Family*) supervised and maintained the actors' hairstyles, a task that grew increasingly complicated when production stretched out for over a year.

As pre-production continued, more people joined the crew. To staff the art department, Joe Alves hired **Daniel A. Lomino** (*American Raspberry* [1977]) as his art director and **Phil Abramson** (*Finian's Rainbow* [1968], *Bullit* [1968], *The Other Side of the Mountain* [1975]) as his set decorator. **Sam Gordon** (*The Magnificent Seven* [1960], *West Side Story* [1961], *Blazing Saddles*) was put in charge of props.

To fill out the camera crew, Vilmos Zsigmond hired **Nick McLean**, who had been his assistant on *Cinderella Liberty* and *The Sugarland Express*, to be his camera operator (the CO physically maneuvers the camera and maintains the framing of a shot throughout filming) and **Mike Genne** and **Louis Noto** as his assistants (a first assistant maintains and mounts the camera and adjusts the lens during filming to make sure that a shot remains in focus. A second assistant loads and unloads the film and prepares the slate for each take). Industry veteran **Earl Gilbert** came aboard as the production's gaffer (the chief electrician who sets the lights for the director of photography). **Bob Moore** was hired as key grip (supervisor of the team that moves scenery and equipment, devises rigs for lights and cameras, and lays the dolly tracks), and **Tim Ryan** as dolly grip (who maintains and operates the various camera dollies and cranes).

Buddy Joe Hooker's stunt team included **Bobby Bass**, **Steven Burnett**, **Jeannie Epper**, **Monty Jordan**, and **Stephen Powers** (most of whom were members of Stunts Unlimited, a elite organization made up of Hollywood's top stunt performers and arrangers).

Steve Warner came aboard as the location auditor (in charge of managing day-to-day expenses) and **Joe O'Har** as the location manager. **Bill Bethea** coordinated all of the vehicles used to transport the production equipment and personnel. **Al Ebner** and **Murray Weissman** were the unit publicists, and **Peter Sorel** and **Jim Coe** were the on-set still photographers. **Kendall Cooper** and **Judy Bornstein** assisted Julia and Michael Phillips. **Janet Healy**, **Pat Burns**, and **Sally Dennison** were hired as production assistants, and American Film Institute Fellow **Seth Winston** joined the production as an intern.

Columbia assigned a new executive to oversee the project when Peter Guber left the company in the last quarter of 1975. His replacement was **Stanley R. Jaffe**, the son of Leo Jaffe. Born on July 31, 1940, Jaffe began his entertainment industry career as an executive assistant to the president of the Seven Arts Associates television production company and eventually became the head of East Coast programming. In 1967 he resigned to become an independent producer. His first feature was the British-made *I Start Counting* (1969), which he followed with *Goodbye, Columbus* (1969). In 1970 Jaffe became the executive vice president and chief corporate officer of Paramount Pictures, and it was on his watch that the studio made *The Godfather*. He returned to independent production in 1972 with the revisionist western *Bad Company* and the Little League comedy *The Bad News Bears* (1976), which was released several months after Begelman invited him to join Columbia.

| # The Box Canyon and Beyond

AS THE PREP PERIOD PROGRESSED, the plan was still to mount a relatively modest production. Aside from a quick trip to Devils Tower (planned for the end of the schedule, since it was too cold to film in Wyoming in the winter), the majority of the filming was going to be done at The Burbank Studios. The Mongolia and Brazilian sequences would be shot on locations in Southern California. Before long, however, the scope of the production began to expand.

This expansion started with the Box Canyon set—the landing zone at the foot of Devils Tower where the Mothership would touch down at the end of the film (also referred to as the Base of Operations and code-named "The Dark Side of the Moon" in the film). In the original drafts of the script, the landing zone was described as a temporary encampment consisting primarily of a bunch of hastily erected tents. As Spielberg and Alves began working on designs, however, they decided that the tent city idea wasn't very exciting and started playing around with other concepts. Interested in keeping the film as rooted in everyday reality as possible, Steven suggested that perhaps the Mothership should land in a parking lot in between a McDonald's and a Jack in the Box restaurant, but after Joe worked up a preliminary design, Steven decided that the idea was too silly. The drive-through runway hit the trash and the two men continued to brainstorm. Eventually they decided that the landing zone should resemble a sports arena.

With this in mind, Alves began building a model of the proposed set (Joe always made models of his designs rather than drawings because he felt that a three-dimensional representation was a much more effective way of selling a concept). The design included a large display board that was positioned at one end of the arena. This board was the result of discussions between the members of the creative team about how to best visualize the process of communication between the humans and the extraterrestrials. Inspired by Russian composer Alexander Nikolayevich Scriabin (1872–1915), who had theorized that specific musical notes prompted listeners to think of specific colors, Spielberg came up with the idea of connecting the Moog synthesizer to an array of colored lights so that each time a note was played on the Moog, a corresponding color would flash in the array. Alves suggested that the colors appear on a huge video screen, but Spielberg wanted something resembling an athletic field scoreboard. Developing this idea, Alves decided to segment the board into several rows of colored rectangular panels. He then needed to find a logical way to relate the colors on the lightboard with the musical notes being played on the synthesizer. He wasn't quite sure how to do this until he saw a television program that featured Leonard Bernstein talking about composer Arnold Schoenberg (1874–1951).

Schoenberg had devised a method of musical composition that utilized all twelve tones in the chromatic scale. Realizing that there were also twelve colors in a secondary progression on the color wheel, Alves decided to link the tones and the colors (beginning with middle C and yellow), which gave him a row of twelve rectangles running across the board. He then added three more rows on top, consisting of lighter tones and higher octaves, and two more rows on the bottom, consisting of darker tones and lower octaves, for a total of seventy-two rectangles. A full-scale version of this color board would be created when the actual set was built.

Although Box Canyon was supposed to be outdoors, Spielberg and Alves intended from the very beginning to build the set on an enclosed soundstage. They did not want to be at the mercy of the elements, as they had been on *Jaws*, and they wanted to be able to film the final sequence—which is set entirely at night—during the day (because extended night shooting can be very hard on a film crew). The set obviously needed to be big, which meant that a very large structure was going to be needed to house it. At the start of pre-production, John Veitch told Joe Alves that he could build Box Canyon on Soundstages 15 and 16 at The Burbank Studios. Two of the biggest stages in Hollywood, 15 and 16 are adjacent to one another and are connected by a gigantic door that can be opened to create a huge interior space. Initially this was deemed to be more than sufficient, but as the design developed, it became apparent that in order to really do the arena concept justice, the set would need to be about four times bigger than originally conceived. When Steven and Joe explained this to John Veitch, he laughed. Accusing them of letting the success of *Jaws* go to their heads and give them delusions of grandeur, Veitch told Spielberg and Alves that they would have to make do with the space they had been given. Joe complied and scaled down his design so that it would fit inside the tandem soundstages.

Joe started constructing a model of the scaled-down Box Canyon set. As he worked, he began receiving visits from David Begelman, Alan Hirschfield, Leo Jaffe, and other members of Columbia's top brass, often with bankers in tow. It is not regular practice for a studio's corporate officers and financiers to drop in on production designers while they are working, but it was quickly becoming apparent that *Close Encounters* was no longer a regular movie. With more and more of the company's limited resources being committed to the project, Columbia's management team became keenly interested in the film's progress. The executives were intrigued with Alves's design, but when they asked him how he felt about it, Joe was honest and said that he felt the set needed to be much bigger. Although increasing the size would also increase the film's budget, the executives, beginning to sense the film's potential, told Joe to go ahead and make the set as big as he thought it should be. He proceeded to construct a model that was so large that it took up almost half of the trailer he was working in.

Steven Spielberg was delighted with the finished product and used it to storyboard the final sequence, walking around the model with a tape recorder and describing the shots he wanted to see. His secretary then typed up a transcript of the tape, which Spielberg and George Jensen used to create the necessary sketches and diagrams. Jensen translated these diagrams into exquisitely beautiful drawings that emphasized the lush, backlit look that Steven wanted for the Mothership scenes, prompting Spielberg to rave to *American Cinematographer*: "The sheer luminescence of his [Jensen's] style was like seeing the entire movie for the first time."

With the design for this enormous set completed, they now had to find a place to build it. Joe Alves figured, "I needed [a space] 300 feet by 450 feet, something like that—a football field wide and a football field and a half long." No movie studio in the world had a soundstage that big, so Joe and Clark Paylow began looking around for an alternative facility. They traveled to several states (Ohio, Texas, and Connecticut) and looked at a number of warehouses, gymnasiums, aircraft hangars, and other buildings. They found an ideal structure in Tillamook, Oregon—a former U.S. Army zeppelin hangar. At 300 feet by 900 feet, the hangar was more than big enough. Unfortunately, half of the enormous shed was occupied by the Georgia Pacific lumber company. The set could have fit comfortably in the other half, but the noise from the sawmill would have made filming impossible.

Alves and Paylow continued their search and eventually came across an abandoned former Air Force base in the port city of Mobile, Alabama. During World War II, Brookley Army Air Field had served as a fighter plane overhaul and maintenance facility, as well as a supply depot. Renamed Brookley Air Force Base after the war, the facility remained active until the mid-1960s, when the government decommissioned it and turned the airfield over to the city of Mobile. Since the city had no use for it, the place had remained derelict ever since. Standing alongside the base's runway were two large hangars. At 300 by 300 feet, each of these hangars was certainly wide enough to house Box Canyon, but not long enough. However, seeing that the hangars' doors could be opened fully, Joe realized that he could add a tent onto the end of one of them that would extend it an additional 150 feet. Steven and Julia checked out the facility, and, although no one relished the thought of spending a hot summer in the south, they agreed that it would work for them. Julia presented the idea to Begelman. Although shooting in Mobile would push the film's budget to approximately $7 million, he approved the plan. Clark began negotiating with the city of Mobile and soon concluded a deal for the production to lease Brookley from January until September of 1976. The production plan was then revised—the company would begin shooting in Southern California, move to Alabama to film the final sequence, and then finish up in Wyoming. Before long, however, the plan was changed yet again.

Columbia had originally wanted the exteriors of the Greenhouse family's home to be shot on one of the suburban streets on The Burbank Studios' backlot. This idea was dismissed early on because the creative team thought the backlot didn't look realistic enough. Instead, they decided to film on location in a real suburban neighborhood somewhere in the Los Angeles area. Joe Alves began scouting for a suitable spot, but quickly realized that Southern California neighborhoods, with their Spanish-style houses and fenced-in yards, didn't look anything like Midwestern neighborhoods, which tended to have ranch or Colonial style homes and fenceless yards that flowed freely into one another. Alves suggested that they give some thought to filming on location in Indiana, but that idea was dismissed as being too expensive. Steven and Julia wanted to stick with Los Angeles, but Joe still thought they could do better. Figuring that he would have a better chance of finding a suitably Midwestern-looking neighborhood in the South than in the Southwest, Alves decided to see if he could find a viable location in Alabama near where they would be shooting. Without telling anyone, Alves and Clark Paylow flew to Indiana and took pictures of typical suburban tract homes in the Muncie area. They then flew to Mobile, drove around until they found a neighborhood that matched the ones they had seen in Indiana, and took some pictures of it. When Steven and Julia saw the pictures, they were convinced, and it was decided that the Greenhouse home would be filmed in Alabama.

Since so much of the movie was now going to be shot in the Yellow-hammer State, everyone agreed that it made sense to shift the entire production from Burbank to Mobile. Production offices would be opened in Brookley Field's vacant administration blocks. The sets that would have been constructed on The Burbank Studios' soundstages would now be built in the second hangar at the former military base. Scenes that would have been filmed in Southern California locations would now be filmed in and around the Mobile area. Some supporting roles and bit parts would be filled by actors cast locally—many from the New Orleans theatrical community. The expense of switching from a studio-based shoot to a location shoot caused the budget to rise again—this time to almost $9 million. It would rise further still.

When the film was first yellow-lit, Spielberg worked very hard to keep the budget as low as possible. Knowing that Columbia's management was extremely anxious about money, he did not want to do anything that would cause the executives to get cold feet and cancel the project. He limited the scope and scale of the film and pressed his collaborators to spend as little money as possible. As the pre-production process wore on, however, Steven's ambitions for the project grew.

First, he added the Flight 19 and MS Sulphur Queen scenes to the second draft, which gave the previously U.S.-bound story a broader, more international dimension. Next he decided that it would give those scenes (which he had originally planned to film in Southern California) greater authenticity if they were actually shot on location in Brazil and Mongolia. Then he added yet another scene to the script to explain that the five musical tones that the humans use to communicate with the extraterrestrials have actually been given to mankind by the aliens, using the same psychic implant process that they used to give Norman his mountainous visions. Spielberg planned to dramatize this idea by showing an entire crowd of people singing the five notes in unison. To continue to underscore the worldwide scope of the UFO phenomenon, Steven wanted to set this scene in yet another exotic foreign land. As exciting as all of these new scenes and locations were, they were also extremely expensive.

In adding these fresh set pieces to the film, Steven's goal was not to spend more money—he was motivated primarily by his enthusiasm for the project and his desire to develop it to its fullest potential—but he also knew that by now he was in a position to be able to do so without much opposition. In Hollywood, success brings a filmmaker a tremendous degree of leverage. Studios will often provide the director of a hit movie with enormous amounts of money, resources, and freedom to produce his or her next one in the hope that he or she will be able to make box office lighting strike twice. Interested in making the best films possible, most directors are more than happy to take advantage of this motivated generosity. Steven certainly was. He knew that the incredible success of *Jaws* gave him more sway than most, and he was determined to use it to make his dream project as grand and as perfect as he possibly could. He admitted as much in a 1978 interview in *Cinefantastique* magazine: "I figured... that I might as well take advantage of that success and get all the money I needed to make this picture right." Columbia was willing to give Steven the resources he needed, but it couldn't afford to give him a blank check. Discussions took place and concessions were made:

- Since the Brazil and Mongolian scenes contained similar content (the mysterious reappearance of large missing objects in incongruous locations), it was decided that one of them would be discarded. Since the Sulphur Queen scene was judged to be more spectacular, the return of Flight 19 was cut from the script.

- It was also agreed that the scene of the crowd singing the five tones would be shot in India. Despite the fact that the nation reports the least number of UFO sightings of any country the world, India was chosen because its government had frozen the nation's currency (the rupee) in 1969, which meant that foreign companies were not allowed to take any money they made out of the country. All profits had to remain in India and be spent there. Columbia had accrued a lot of funds from films it had released in India, and if Steven filmed his crowd scene there the company could finally get some use out of money that would otherwise be lost. It was decided that the scene would be shot in the fall of 1976, after the completion of principal photography.

By now, the film's budget had reached $10 million, and David Begelman had become extremely concerned. Julia was concerned by his concern and tried to assuage it by expressing her conviction that *Close Encounters* had the potential to make more money than any other movie in history (a declaration that—because of the tremendous pressure it put on him to deliver a blockbuster—unnerved Spielberg as much as his assertion that the film could be made for $2.8 million had unnerved the Phillipses). Begelman didn't require much arm-twisting—his love of the project and his faith in Steven convinced him to let them continue, but he made it clear to Julia that the budget couldn't go much higher or the film would never be greenlit.

Because it was going to take a lot of time to prepare for an extensive location shoot, the decision was made to push the start date of the picture back from November 1975 to April 1976 (meaning that the Wyoming sequences would now be shot at the beginning of the schedule rather than at the end). This gave the production team some necessary breathing room, but it produced yet another financial crisis. In the mid-1970s, many Hollywood studios raised a significant portion of the money they used to finance their movies from tax shelters—investment plans that allowed participants to write off money invested in film production. If Columbia decided to make *Close Encounters*, the ailing studio was going to need tax shelter money to cover a significant portion of the film's budget. However, the company would only have access to that money if the film started production before January 1, 1976 (thus allowing the tax shelter participants to write off their investments on their 1975 tax returns). If filming began any later than December 31, 1975, the funds would no longer be available. For this reason, the studio decreed that at least one scene from *Close Encounters* had to be shot before the end of 1975. This would qualify the film as being "in production," which would allow the tax shelter participants to write off their investments and preserve Columbia's access to their cash.

The question then became, what scene could they shoot? Since no principal actors had yet been cast (and wouldn't be unless the film was greenlit) and no sets constructed (ditto), the options were limited. After reviewing the script, Steven, Julia, and Clark realized that the only real candidate was the scene in which a group of air traffic controllers tracks two airliners as they encounter a UFO while in flight. Since the scene was going to be filmed in a real air traffic control facility—the Los Angeles Air Route Traffic Control Center in Palmdale, California—no sets needed to be built, and since the only characters in the scene were the air traffic controllers, none of the main stars would be required. Actors David Anderson, Richard L. Hawkins, Craig Shreeve, and Bill Thurman were cast to play the controllers, and after a few days of preparation, filming began on the evening of Monday, December 29. It wrapped the following evening, and by New Year's Eve 1975, the first scene of *Close Encounters of the Third Kind* was complete.

| **Black Backings and Green Lights**

As 1976 BEGAN, *Close Encounters* had still not been greenlit. One of the reasons for this was that the budget had not been finalized. It couldn't be, because no one yet knew how much the film's special photographic effects were going to cost. And that was because no one had been hired yet to produce them.

There is a vast difference between special effects and special photographic effects. Special effects (sometimes called physical effects) are those produced through mechanical or pyrotechnical means on the set during principal photography—wind, rain, explosions, etc. On *Close Encounters*, the special effects included helicopter downdrafts, UFO-generated static electrical charges and low-gravity zones, vibrating mailboxes and railroad crossing signs, exploding glass, and topsy-turvy truck cabs. The man charged with conjuring up all of these effects was Roy Arbogast. A former construction worker, Arbogast broke into Hollywood in the early 1960s as a set builder and prop maker. After working on movies such as *Fantastic Voyage* (1966), *Bonnie and Clyde* (1967), and *Finian's Rainbow* (1968), Roy was hired by Warner Bros. Television and eventually became involved in "rigging"—the process of setting up a mechanical effect (also called a "gag") in preparation for filming. He moved over to Universal Television in the early 1970s and met Joe Alves while working on an episode of *Night Gallery*. Arbogast had experience with plastics (having left the film business for a time in the mid-1960s to start a plastic paneling company), so when production began on *Jaws*, Joe brought Roy in to help develop a realistic skin for Bruce, the mechanical great white shark. Arbogast joined the film's special effects team as well and helped prepare gags such as the sinking of the Orca and the final exploding of the shark. His work impressed Steven Spielberg, and when it came time to assemble the crew for *Close Encounters*, Spielberg accepted Alves's recommendation that they make Arbogast the head of the film's physical effects team. Arbogast assembled a team that included John Belieu, Johnny Borgese, Ray Cline, Don Courtney, Curt Dickson, Kevin Grimsley, Russell Hessey, Kevin Pike, Tom Ryba, LeRoy Smith, Dave Wood, Max Wood, and Mike Wood.

Special photographic effects (also called optical effects, visual effects, and sometimes even "trick photography"), on the other hand, are those produced by manipulating various aspects of the photochemical process: photography, developing, and printing. Usually produced during post-production, photographic effects include shooting miniatures and models to make them look full- or giant-sized; using matte paintings to enhance sets or to place actors into inaccessible or nonexistent locations; utilizing optical printing techniques—split screens, traveling mattes, double exposures, and superimposition—to combine separately filmed images into a single new one; and employing animation and animation techniques to enhance live-action footage. With numerous scenes involving spaceships, spontaneously generating clouds, and hordes of alien beings, it was obvious that *Close Encounters* was going to require the use of most if not all of these techniques. Moreover, their quality needed to be excellent—if audiences weren't convinced that what they were seeing was absolutely real, then the film would fail miserably. Unfortunately, no one on the production team knew how to create these effects. Steven Spielberg certainly didn't: "I'm not a special effects person," he said at the time. "I could conceive of these things, but couldn't engineer them or even take them further." Joe Alves puts it more bluntly: "We didn't know what the hell we were doing."

They needed someone who did. A few years earlier, they could have turned to Columbia's in-house special effects department. During Hollywood's heyday, each studio maintained its own mechanical and optical effects divisions staffed by experts in each area. By the mid-1970s, however, most of those departments had been downsized or eliminated. Most of the specialists had either retired or gone freelance, so whenever a film project required effects, a team had to be assembled from scratch. When *Close*

Encounters got under way, John Veitch brought in Lawrence W. Butler as a consultant. The former head of Columbia's special effects department, Butler had created optical and physical effects for dozens of films in his long career, including *Hell's Angels* (1930), *Things to Come* (1936), *Destination Tokyo* (1943), *Casablanca* (1943), *The Lady from Shanghai* (1947), *Robinson Crusoe on Mars* (1964), and *Marooned* (1969). He received Academy Award nominations for his work on *That Hamilton Woman* (1941) and *Jungle Book* (1942) and won Oscars for *The Thief of Baghdad* (1940) and *A Thousand and One Nights* (1945). Butler had retired in the early 1970s, but when John Veitch called, the sixty-eight-year-old returned to Columbia one more time. Butler gave Steven and the rest of the *Close Encounters* team a crash course in special photographic effects. He explained all of the various techniques, screened old films to show how they had been used in the past, and helped Steven, Joe, and the others figure out how they could be applied to *Close Encounters*.

Steven appreciated Butler's tutorial but was dissatisfied with the degree of realism and believability that could be achieved using traditional effects methods and began looking around for an alternative. On the recommendation of George Lucas, animator Colin J. Cantwell was brought onto the project. A USC graduate, Cantwell had worked on *2001: A Space Odyssey* (1968) and had also done some of the preliminary spaceship designs for *Star Wars*. By the mid-1970s, Cantwell had become interested in computers and their ability to generate graphics and was exploring ways to utilize this ability to create animation and visual effects for the movies. Cantwell was confident that he could use computers to create *Close Encounters'* flying saucers and magical clouds digitally. (He was also confident that he could construct the Box Canyon landing zone in the computer, thus eliminating the need to actually build the set or maintain the art department—a proposal that did little to endear him to Joe Alves.) Intrigued, Steven and Julia hired Colin to do a test to see how feasible his ideas were. Cantwell set to work to create a shot of three UFOs flying over the stadium landing zone. The shot took weeks to complete, much longer than originally scheduled, and the results were disappointing. Although Colin's ideas concerning the use of computers to create cinematic visual effects turned out to be remarkably prescient, mid-1970s digital technology simply wasn't up to the task—it took too much time to generate a single shot, the resolution and clarity weren't sharp enough, and the whole process proved to be far too expensive. Cantwell departed (although he would later contribute some technical dialogue to the film's final sequence) and Steven turned his attention back to traditional visual effects techniques. Since Larry Butler was only a part-time adviser, they needed to find someone to supervise the opticals on a full-time basis. Steven knew exactly whom he wanted.

Like everyone else in the film industry, Spielberg had been terrifically impressed by the groundbreaking photographic effects in *2001: A Space Odyssey*. There were several effects supervisors on that film, including Wally Veevers, Con Pederson, and Tom Howard (with Stanley Kubrick himself receiving a credit for effects design), but the person who received the lion's share of the credit for the film's most innovative visuals was a young Californian named Douglas Trumbull. Born in Los Angeles on April 8, 1942, Doug was the son of Don Trumbull, a mechanical designer and engineer who had begun his career in the 1930s as a special effects rigger on *The Wizard of Oz* (1939) but had left Hollywood during World War II to join the aviation industry. Doug had originally wanted to become an architect, but switched to illustration while attending El Camino College. In need of money to continue his education, he took a job as a background artist at Graphic Films, a company that produced animated films for NASA and the U.S. Air Force. In 1963 Graphic was hired to produce a movie about space exploration, called *To the Moon and Beyond*, for the 1964 New York World's Fair. Kubrick saw the film and, impressed with Graphic's work, contracted the company to do concept art and preliminary design work for a project he was developing for Metro-Goldwyn-Mayer called *Journey Beyond the Stars*. Trumbull worked as an illustrator on the project until mid-1965, when Kubrick moved the production to the MGM British Studios in Borehamwood, England. The six-thousand-mile distance between the U.K. and L.A. made effective collaboration in those pre-fax, pre-email days impossible, so Kubrick established his own in-house design department and terminated the contract with Graphic. The loss of the contract prompted Graphic to lay off a number of workers, including Doug. In need of work and eager to continue with *Journey*, which he thought was a very intriguing project, Doug called Kubrick and asked him for a job. Kubrick was amenable, and before long Trumbull was on his way to England.

Doug was initially hired as an airbrush artist, part of a team responsible for creating a series of short films featuring animated graphics that would be used to simulate computer readouts on the many monitors featured in the film. This assignment required Trumbull, who had never worked in the production end of filmmaking before, to learn the basics of photography, cinematography, and animation. As the production went on, however, the filmmakers found themselves faced with a series of visual effects problems that required innovative combinations of art, photography, and technology to solve. Well versed in all three areas, Doug made a number of innovative contributions to the production: he detailed miniatures, painted star backgrounds, developed new animation techniques, and helped devise an automated system for photographing the spacecraft models. His most significant accomplishment was the development of the Slit-Scan process. Based on techniques devised by computer animation pioneer John Whitney, Slit-Scan was a method of photographing backlit pieces of artwork through a long, narrow opening in an otherwise blacked-out piece of glass, using a combination of lengthy exposures and moving cameras to create the dramatically abstract panels of lights featured in the film's "stargate" sequence. Trumbull's contributions to *2001* earned the twenty-six-year-old great acclaim and helped the film win an Academy Award for Best Special Visual Effects.

When *2001* was finished, Trumbull returned to Los Angeles and started a company called Trumbull Film Effects, where he used the techniques and the expertise he had honed on *2001* to produce visual effects for television commercials and to create distinctive identifications and program intros for the ABC television network. In 1971 he was hired (along with James Shourt) to create effects for Robert Wise's *The Andromeda Strain*. Following *Andromeda*, Doug made the leap to directing with an offbeat science fiction film called *Silent Running* (1971). Based on Trumbull's own original story, *Silent Running* was set in a future in which the Earth has become so polluted that its last remaining forests have been placed aboard space freighters and sent into orbit around Saturn for safekeeping. When the crew of one of the freighters is ordered to destroy the forests, the mission's botanist kills the other members of the team, hijacks the ship, and sails it into deep space in an attempt to preserve our planet's last remaining flora. With a minuscule $1.3 million budget, Trumbull and his crew (which included his father, Don, who had returned to the film business to work with his son) created an endearing film that featured some surprisingly elaborate mechanical and visual effects.

Following *Silent Running*, Trumbull, who had made deal with several studios to develop new film projects, appeared poised to begin a successful directing career. His first project was a science fiction film called *Pyramid* that he was going to make for Metro-Goldwyn-Mayer. The script—which told the story of how mankind survives when the sun enters its death throes sometime in the distant future—had been finished and work on the sets and special effects begun when the financially strapped MGM decided to drastically curtail its filmmaking operations and canceled the project. His next project—another science-fiction film called *The Ride*—was also canceled after a management change at Warner Bros., when the incoming regime dropped all of the movies that had been initiated by the outgoing one. More disappointments followed: when the producer of *Journey of the Oceanauts*, *Planet of the Apes* impresario Arthur P. Jacobs, died before filming could begin, the rights to the project became entangled in his estate. Two other movies—*Damnation Alley* and *Hiero's Journey*—also failed to get off the ground (*Alley*, based on Roger Zelazny's novel, was later made by director Jack Smight using a completely different script. *Journey* was developed for Columbia but the studio, unable to afford to produce two big-budget science fiction films at the same time, cancelled the project when it decided to proceed with *Close Encounters*). During this period, Doug had also signed on to be the executive producer of a Canadian-produced sci-fi television series called *The Starlost*, but departed from the poorly organized and under-funded production after just a few weeks.

By 1974, a frustrated and disappointed Trumbull was in desperate need of cash ("You can't live on development deals," he says. "You have to make the movies to get your fees.") and began looking for a way to earn a steady paycheck. Over the years, he had come up with a number of ideas for expanding the potential of the cinematic medium. Interested in developing these ideas and finding practical applications for them, he made a deal with Frank Yablans, the president of Paramount Pictures, to start a research and development company called the Future General Corporation. Located at 4241 Redwood Avenue in the Marina Del Rey section of Los Angeles, Future General's mission was to create new motion picture technologies, alternative film formats, and innovative entertainment concepts. Under the terms of the deal, Paramount would finance the company and Trumbull, signed to an exclusive employment contract, would run it.

Future General got off to a smashing start. During its first year, the company developed Magicam (a real-time video compositing system that allowed the image of a performer positioned in front of a blue screen to be filmed simultaneously with that of a miniature background set—thus inserting the actor believably into the set). It also developed the prototype for a simulator ride—a device that consisted of several rows of seats bolted to a stationary platform that could be made to pitch and yaw in synchronization with an image being projected on a large wraparound movie screen. The device gave viewers the impression that they were taking a roller coaster ride through a series of wild environments and adventures when in reality they hadn't moved an inch. Future General also developed an interactive 3D arcade game that utilized computer graphics and came complete with a story and characters. The company's primary focus, however, was a unique large-format film system called Showscan.

Trumbull was a huge fan of the various widescreen processes that Hollywood had introduced in the 1950s and 1960s as a way of enticing the large portion of its audience that had defected to the new medium of television back into theaters. Systems such as Cinerama, Todd-AO, and Ultra-Panavision 70 all utilized 65mm film (instead of the usual 35mm) to create a rectangular picture that was much bigger and more detailed than a traditional square movie image (an additional 2.5mm soundtrack was added to each side of the 65mm image to create a 70mm stereo release print). Many spectacular event films such as *Around the World in Eighty Days*, *How the West Was Won*, and *2001* had been produced using these formats, but by the mid-1970s, most of the major studios had stopped using 65mm, opting instead to use cheaper 35mm-based widescreen formats, such as Panavision and Super 35, that used special lenses to create their expanded images rather than oversized film. In spite of this, Doug maintained his interest in 65mm and wanted to take the concept to a new level.

While making some tests, Trumbull and his colleagues discovered that something unusual happens when 65mm film is shot and projected at sixty frames per second as opposed to the usual twenty-four. As Trumbull describes it, "The surface of the screen disappears. It becomes completely fluid; it's like a window on reality." Doug was extremely excited by the possibilities of Showscan and wanted to make a full-length feature utilizing the process. To do so, Future General needed to create a fully equipped large-format production studio, complete with 65mm cameras, projectors, editing machines, and printers. The cost of all this equipment was considerable, and Paramount was reluctant to provide the necessary funds. Since the founding of Future General, the studio had undergone a management change and the new executives weren't nearly as supportive of Trumbull's efforts as Yablans had been. They didn't really understand Future General's innovations, couldn't grasp their artistic or commercial potential, and made it clear that they didn't want to go forward with any of them. Disappointed, Doug asked to be let out of his contract, but Paramount, not wanting him to go off and develop his ideas for its competitors, refused and Trumbull found himself in limbo: "I was just sitting around, twiddling my thumbs and collecting a paycheck." It was at this point that Spielberg called and asked Doug if he would consider producing the special photographic effects for *Close Encounters*.

After *Silent Running*, Trumbull had decided that he was no longer interested in producing visual effects, except for his own projects. Since then he had received many offers from other directors to create effects for their movies (including one from George Lucas, who wanted him to work on *Star Wars*), but he turned them all down (Trumbull recommended that Lucas hire John Dykstra, one of his assistants on *Silent Running*, which Lucas did). However, Doug had been very impressed with *Jaws* and thought that Spielberg was an amazing filmmaker, so he agreed to meet with him. When he did, Doug found that he really liked Steven personally and thought that he was somebody that he would enjoy working with. He then read the script, which he thought was "terrific. I liked what the movie had to say and I thought it was worthwhile." Trumbull began to seriously consider Steven's offer.

Aside from the chance to work with Spielberg and the tremendous creative challenges the project offered, Trumbull realized that there was another good reason to take the *Close Encounters* job. A major part of optical effects work involves the combination of a number of previously photographed images into a single new picture by copying all or part of those images onto one fresh piece of film. Unfortunately, each time a photographic image is duped (duplicated), it degrades in quality, gaining more grain and contrast with each additional generation. Because of this, the image quality of visual effects shots has traditionally been much worse than that of non-effects shots. When the widescreen film formats were introduced, many effects supervisors began opting to use them to generate their visual effects because they generated a higher-quality picture that could be copied several times over and (when reduced and intercut with the production footage) still match the image quality of regular 35mm film.

For reasons of cost and efficiency, some supervisors used 35mm widescreen formats such as VistaVision, but for *Close Encounters* Trumbull wanted to use 65mm because its aspect ratio (the height: width ratio of the film frame) was compatible with that of the 35mm anamorphic format that was going to be used to shoot the film. Columbia agreed, and a portion of the effects budget was earmarked for the purchase of a full complement of 65mm equipment, equipment that Future General could keep and then later use to move forward with Showscan. Taking all of this into consideration, Trumbull decided to accept the assignment. With Paramount's permission, Future General made a deal with Columbia to produce the effects for *Close Encounters*. There were several reasons why Paramount was willing to let its exclusive research and development division do work for a rival studio. The first was that the job would allow Future General to generate income that it could use to fund its ongoing operations, money Paramount then wouldn't have to provide. The second was that Columbia agreed to pay Trumbull's salary for the duration of the project. The third was that Columbia agreed to give Paramount a percentage of *Close Encounters'* net profits.

The first order of business was to prepare a budget. To do so, Trumbull first reviewed the script and the storyboards with his partner, Richard Yuricich. Born in Lorain, Ohio, Yuricich began his career just out of high school as a part-time second assistant in the MGM matte department, working on *The Greatest Story Ever Told* (1965), a film that featured paintings created by his older brother, renowned matte artist Matthew Yuricich (*Ben Hur* [1959], *North by Northwest* [1959]). Richard then spent several years working in the aerospace industry before being hired as a rostrum (animation stand) cameraman by cinematographer Nick Vasu, whose eponymous company specialized in doing the photography for cartoons (the *Peanuts* television specials, Dr. Seuss's *How the Grinch Stole Christmas*) and animated commercials, as well as title and opticals for film and television shows. Yuricich remained with Vasu after the latter joined forces with cinematographer Jim Dickson (another alumnus of Graphic Films) to create the Dickson-Vasu Company. A short time later, Dickson, who had spent some time working on *2001: A Space Odyssey*, received a call from *2001* effects supervisor Con

Pederson asking if he could recommend a good rostrum cameraman. Yuricich put himself up for the position and spent the next year in England shooting star fields for Kubrick's epic.

During his time on *Space Odyssey*, Richard met and got to know Doug Trumbull. When *2001* finished production, Yuricich returned to Dickson-Vasu and then moved over to Trumbull Film Effects, where he worked on a number of commercials and opticals before becoming one of the special photographic effects supervisors on *Silent Running*. After that film was finished, Yuricich worked as an assistant cameraman on films such as *Idaho Transfer* (1973) and *The Drowning Pool* (1975) and also joined Future General, where he served as the cinematographer for Showscan and the company's other projects. Yuricich's title on *Close Encounters* was to be Director of Photography for Special Photographic Effects, but this was only one of his responsibilities. In actuality, he would function as Trumbull's coproducer and would help supervise every aspect of the visual effects work.

Together, Trumbull and Yuricich determined that it would cost approximately $3 million to produce the visual effects. This was a very large amount for the time, and when Julia Phillips heard it, she was shocked. Certain that if she presented that figure to Columbia it would immediately cancel the project, she made a rather daring strategic decision. In her bestselling 1991 autobiography, *You'll Never Eat Lunch in This Town Again*, Julia wrote that she asked Trumbull to name the smallest amount of money that he would need to start production on the photographic effects. Doug replied that he would need at least $1 million to get up and running. Knowing that it was easier to get a studio to put more money into a movie after it has started shooting (when it needs to protect its by-then considerable investment by making sure that the film gets finished) rather than before, Julia decided to tell Columbia that the effects were going to cost approximately $1 million and then ask them for the balance of the money after they were in production. In her book, Julia admits that she was deceptive, but made it clear that if she hadn't been, the movie never would have been made. Although she knew Columbia wouldn't be happy about having to pony up additional funds, she also figured that no one would care about the deception or the extra money if the movie turned out to be even half as successful as she was confident it would be.

Even with the fudged photographic effects number, the budget was now up to approximately $11 million—the cost of almost four "normal" movies at the time. Michael Phillips reports that when Columbia's top brass got wind of this "they freaked out." Some members of the board wanted to cancel *Close Encounters* right then and there. In 1976, an $11 million movie would have been a big risk even for a healthy studio. For a company that had come as close to bankruptcy as Columbia, it was a potentially disastrous one, because if the movie failed the company would go down with it. Begelman urged the board members not to cancel the project for one simple reason: Columbia needed a hit—a big one that could pull the studio back from the financial abyss and restore its lost luster by showing the industry and the world that it was still capable of producing a successful high-profile event picture by big-name talent. This would, in turn, attract even more big-name talent to the studio, talent that would (it was hoped) produce even more successful pictures. Begelman was confident that Spielberg could give them that hit. Some of the board members were persuaded by Begelman's argument, some were not, and some were still on the fence.

As the board continued to debate, preparatory work on *Close Encounters* continued, but slowly and under a cloud of increasing uncertainty, because no one was sure if they were really going to make the movie or not. The issue finally came to a head over a piece of cloth—a really big piece of cloth. Joe Alves's Box Canyon design called for the set to be surrounded by a pitch-black scenic backing to give the impression that it was always nighttime. There was nothing unusual about this—scenic backgrounds are a comment element in many movie sets. What was unusual was the amount of backing that was required. The Box Canyon set was so big that it required more than a mile of material to fully envelop it—much more than had ever been used on a single set. Alves could not simply go into a store and buy this much backing off the shelf; an order this size needed to be specially manufactured. Alves found a company in Texas that could handle the order, but was told that it would take at least four months to produce the required five thousand-plus feet of material. That meant that the order needed to be placed as soon as possible if it was going to be ready on time. An order that big was going to be expensive—so expensive that it only made sense to place it if they were actually going to make the movie. Upon hearing this, Julia went to Begelman and told him that Columbia had to stop dithering and decide right then if it was going to greenlight *Close Encounters* or not.

Begelman went to the Columbia board. To persuade the board members to approve the film, he expressed his belief that *Close Encounters* had the potential to make $80 million or more, a rather stunning claim in a time when only one film in history (*Jaws*) had ever made more than $100 million. In making this statement, Begelman, a gambler by nature, was putting his career on the line, because if the film failed, he would certainly lose his job. This was a risk he was willing to take because he truly believed in the film, in its makers, and in its box office potential. The Columbia board wasn't quite as daring as Begelman. A suggestion was made that the studio bring in a partner—another film company to cofinance the project and share the risk. Begelman was adamantly opposed to this idea—certain that *Close Encounters* was going to be huge, he didn't want to share the glory or the profits with anyone. The board dropped the partner idea, but some of members still wanted to bring in outside investors to help lighten the load. Begelman was willing to go along with this proposal. (Time, Inc. and EMI, Ltd.—the British entertainment conglomerate—would eventually invest a total of $7 million in the film. EMI invested the lion's share of this amount, earning itself a copresentation credit in the process.)

At the beginning of February 1976, the Columbia board told Begelman he could greenlight the film at an approved budget of $11.5 million—the highest budget Columbia Pictures had ever approved in its fifty-year history. The start of production was pushed back—this time to Monday, May 17, 1976. After three years of inspiration, struggle, creation, and frustration, *Close Encounters* was officially a "go."

ABOVE: Director Steven Spielberg, *center*, consults with special photographic effects supervisor Douglas Trumbull at the Future General workshop. Project manager Robert Shepherd is on the left. *Photograph by Glenn Erickson.*

BELOW: Producer Michael Phillips. *Photograph courtesy of Michael Phillips.*

ABOVE: A contemporary photograph of Warner Bros. Studios. In the 1970s this facility was known as The Burbank Studios and was home to both Warner Bros. Pictures and Columbia Pictures, the company that produced *Close Encounters of the Third Kind*.

BELOW: Sylvester Stallone presents *CE3K* star Richard Dreyfuss with his Academy Award as Best Actor for *The Goodbye Girl* on March 29, 1978, the same night *Close Encounters* received an Oscar for Best Cinematography and a Special Achievement Award for Sound Effects Editing. *Photofest.*

ABOVE: Associate producer/unit production manager Clark Paylow.

Photograph by Joe Alves.

LEFT: Yul Brynner presents François Truffaut with the Academy Award for Best Foreign Film for *La Nuit américaine* (*Day for Night*) on April 2, 1974. *Photofest.*

RIGHT: A contemporary photograph of project assistant Scott Squires, who helped develop the cloud tank and assisted Dennis Muren with the Mothership photography. *Photograph courtesy of Scott Squires.*

BELOW: Vilmos Zsigmond is embraced by Jon Voight and Goldie Hawn after winning the Academy Award for Best Cinematography for his work on *Close Encounters*. *Photofest.*

ABOVE: Music composer/conductor John Williams. *Photofest.*

LEFT: Screenwriter John Hill stands beside his life's work—a stack of all the scripts and novels he has written, topped by the Emmy he won for his work on *L.A. Law*—while holding

RIGHT: Screenwriter
Matthew Robbins in 1986.
Photograph courtesy of Matthew Robbins.

BELOW: Screenwriter Hal
Barwood today. *Photograph
courtesy of Hal Barwood.*

LEFT: Second assistant director Jim Bloom. *Photograph courtesy of Jim Bloom.*

BELOW: Devils Tower National Monument, Wyoming. *Photograph courtesy of the National Park Service.*

ABOVE: Vilmos Zsigmond, Steven Spielberg, Clark Paylow, and other crew members ponder their next move during a location scouting trip to Devils Tower. *Photograph by Joe Alves.*

BELOW: An exuberant Vilmos Zsigmond climbs the Tower. *Photograph by Joe Alves.*

ABOVE: A vintage photograph of two hangars on the former Brookley Air Force Base in Mobile, Alabama. The Box Canyon set was constructed in the hangar on the right. The hangar on the left housed the Crescendo Summit and Notch sets. *U.S. Air Force Photograph courtesy of the University of South Alabama Archives.*

BELOW: An aerial view of the hangars. *U.S. Air Force Photograph courtesy of the University of South Alabama Archives.*

ABOVE: Joe Alves's big model of the "Big Set." *Photograph by Joe Alves.*

BELOW: The Box Canyon set nears completion. *Photograph by Joe Alves.*

ABOVE: Model of the Crescendo Summit set. *Photograph by Joe Alves.*

BELOW: Production designer Joe Alves in the pre-renovated kitchen of the Guiler House. *Photograph*

LEFT: The flight suit worn by Richard Dreyfuss in the final sequence of the film.

BELOW: The Mayflower Project patch on the left arm of the flight suit.

ABOVE: A contemporary photograph of the Warner Bros. Studio Ranch. In the 1970s this facility—which was originally owned by Columbia Pictures—was named the Burbank Studios Ranch. Many of the additional scenes for *Close Encounters* were filmed there in May 1977.

BELOW: A contemporary photograph of 4094 Glencoe Avenue in Marina Del Rey, California. In 1976/1977 this was the Future General photographic effects workshop and housed the cloud tank, the smoke room, the matte and optical camera rooms, a miniature shop, and a machine shop.

ABOVE: The left side of this building housed the Future General "Annex" (the right side was home to Bose speakers). The Annex contained the animation department, the insert stage, a projection room, and the small smoke room where the Mothership was filmed.

BELOW: Animation supervisor Robert Swarthe in April 1977. *Photograph courtesy of Robert Swarthe.*

ABOVE: Matte artist Matthew Yuricich. *Photograph by Glenn Erickson.*

LEFT: Assistant matte artist Rocco Gioffre. *Photograph courtesy of Rocco Gioffre.*

CHAPTER 13

Casting

AS SOON AS THE FILM WAS GREENLIT, work on *Close Encounters* began to ramp up: Joe Alves placed the order for the black backing and began set construction and location scouting in Wyoming and Alabama; Vilmos Zsigmond began shooting a series of tests to determine how best to achieve the many lighting effects that he would be required to generate during shooting; Roy Arbogast began working out the mechanical effects. Meanwhile, casting got under way in Los Angeles, supervised by Shari Rhodes, who had done location casting (the auditioning and selection of actors outside of the Los Angeles and New York areas) for Spielberg on *Sugarland* and *Jaws*. The first item on their agenda was to find a star to play Norman Greenhouse.

Richard Dreyfuss wanted the part. Born in Brooklyn in 1947, Dreyfuss moved with his family to Los Angeles in 1956 and began acting in community theater. He made his professional debut in 1964—on stage in the play *In Mama's House* and on television in the situation comedy *Karen*. After appearing in a number of other television programs, including *Gidget*, *Bewitched*, and *That Girl*, Richard made his film debut in *Valley of the Dolls* (1967). Over the next seven years, Dreyfuss continued to act in the theater (on Broadway in Julius J. Epstein's *But Seriously...* and off-Broadway in Israel Horovitz's *Line*), on television (*Room 222*, *The Mod Squad*, and *Gunsmoke*), and in film (*The Graduate* [1967], *Dillinger* [1973], and *American Graffiti* [1973]). During this period Richard met Steven Spielberg for the first time when he auditioned for a role in *Savage*. In 1974, Richard landed his first starring role in a film adaptation of Mordecai Richler's novel *The

Apprenticeship of Duddy Kravitz. After *Kravitz*, Steven asked Richard to play ichthyologist Matt Hooper in *Jaws*. Dreyfuss didn't like the part (which he felt was nothing but a device for delivering shark exposition) and turned it down. A few weeks later, however, he attended an advance screening of *Kravitz* and was appalled by his performance in the film. Fearing that he would never get another acting job as long as he lived, Dreyfuss called Spielberg back and told him he would take the part of Hooper if it was still available. It was.

During the long and arduous *Jaws* shoot, Spielberg and Dreyfuss became friends, and Steven told Richard about *Watch the Skies*. Dreyfuss loved the concept and kicked in a few story ideas, but since the main character was a middle-aged Air Force officer, Richard never gave any thought to appearing in the film. However, when Steven changed the character into more of an everyman, Dreyfuss began to give a lot of thought to it. Aside from the chance to work with Steven again, Dreyfuss wanted to be part of the film because "I felt...that this particular project had a noble agenda. This was a big idea that Steven was talking about. It wasn't just a sci-fi movie, it wasn't just about monsters from the id. It was that we are not only not alone, but that we have relatively little to fear...That really was a huge statement and I...wanted to participate in that."

Dreyfuss told Steven that he wanted to play Norman, but Steven didn't think the twenty-eight-year-old was right for the part of the middle-aged Greenhouse and began looking for a more age-appropriate actor. Steven's first choice was forty-five-year-old Steve McQueen, whom Spielberg had admired ever since seeing him in *The Great Escape*. McQueen liked the script but didn't think he could play Norman, because the script called for the character to cry, and, as McQueen told Spielberg when they met at a rough-and-tumble roadhouse in Trancas, California, he had never been able to cry on film. Spielberg offered to eliminate the crying, but McQueen told him not to. He thought the crying scenes were extremely effective; he just wasn't the guy to do them. Disappointed, Spielberg approached a number of other actors, including James Caan, Jack Nicholson, Al Pacino, and Dustin Hoffman, all of whom turned him down. While Steven continued his search, Richard Dreyfuss campaigned tirelessly for the part (mostly by bad-mouthing Steven's other choices). Spielberg wasn't persuaded until Dreyfuss suggested that, in order to capture Norman's sense of wonder, Steven needed to cast "a child...a child and yet a man" for the part. Spielberg realized that his friend was right and, as this was a quality that Dreyfuss possessed in abundance, gave him the role.

The search for someone to play Ronnie Greenhouse was much less extensive. Steven gave the part to an actress he had seen in an MJB coffee commercial portraying a "typical American housewife." Terry Ann Garr was born to two show business parents: her father, Eddie, was an actor and comedian, and her mother, Phyllis, was a former Rockette who went to work as a seamstress in the costume department at NBC after Eddie died in 1955. Terry started taking dance lessons when she was a young girl and aimed to become a ballerina. In need of money, she got a job as a chorus girl in a production of *Finian's Rainbow* when she was sixteen, then—after performing in a production of *West Side Story* and in shows at Disneyland—began dancing in movies, including *A Swingin' Affair* (1963), *What a Way to Go!* (1964), *Red Line 7000* (1965), and a string of Elvis Presley films. Having developed an interest in acting, Terry started going out on auditions and soon landed small parts on television shows such as *Batman*, *That Girl*, *The Andy Griffith Show*, *Star Trek*, and *McCloud*, and in the movies *For Pete's Sake* (1968), *Head* (1968), and *The Moonshine War* (1970). After changing the spelling of her name to Teri (on the advice of a numerologist who told her she wouldn't have any success if she had double consonants in both her names), Garr was hired as a featured player on the *The Sonny and Cher Comedy Hour* and then appeared in her first major film role—as Gene Hackman's girlfriend in Francis Ford Coppola's *The Conversation* (1974). She followed *The Conversation* with roles in *Young Frankenstein* (1974), *Won Ton Ton: The Dog Who Saved Hollywood* (1976), and *Oh, God!* (1977). She also appeared in a long string of commercials, one of which was the MJB spot that got Spielberg's attention.

Impressed with Teri's quirky comedic timing and the fullness of the characterization that she was able to create in just thirty seconds, Steven asked her to come in and audition. Garr was excited by the chance to appear in a big movie directed by the man who had made *Jaws*, but she didn't want to play a housewife, a part very far from her own experience. She wanted to play Jillian instead. But Steven wanted her to stick with Ronnie, so Teri threw herself into the task of preparing for the part. In an interview with the author, Garr remembers: "I worked very hard in developing this character, with Steven's help. Steven said these were middle-class people and the wife was very worried about not being able to make payments on things, so to have my husband go crazy and lose his job would have been terrible. I went from there." Teri didn't want Ronnie to be a stereotype. Having no idea what it was like to be a real suburban housewife, Garr moved in with her brother's family and followed her sister-in-law around for a few weeks, observing her and her friends. She also went shopping at Sears for appliances, haggled with a salesman over the price of a bedroom set, and when it came time to select Ronnie's wardrobe, refused to buy any clothing that wasn't made out of polyester.

February 1976 was a busy month for the production. On February 5, Columbia announced to the press that the title of the film had been changed (once again) to *Watch the Skies*. This switch appears to have been prompted by a letter Columbia received from Dr. J. Allen Hynek's lawyer. When Hynek heard that the studio was making a movie named after one of his sighting classifications, he was upset and had his attorney contact the company and complain that it was using his material without permission (sources familiar with the situation have said that Steven and Columbia didn't realize the "close encounters" terms belonged to Hynek, but were under the impression that they were common usage phrases in the public domain). To avoid legal action, the studio decided to revert to Spielberg's original appellation. Steven responded to Hynek's letter by inviting him to join the project as a technical adviser and consultant. Feeling that the movie could be a great tool for promoting the cause of serious UFO study, Hynek accepted. Columbia then made a deal with the good doctor to acquire the rights to *The UFO Experience* for $10,000, and the title of the movie was switched back to *Close Encounters of the Third Kind*, this time for good.

Hynek reviewed the script and helped make the scenes involving the UFOs, and those featuring the Air Force and its debunking techniques, as accurate as possible. On February 8, *Taxi Driver* opened, and Steven and Richard Dreyfuss accompanied Julia Phillips to Manhattan for the premiere (the film went on to become both a critical and commercial smash, which was something of a surprise given its dark and violent nature). While there, Steven, Julia, and Richard met with New York casting director Juliette Taylor and began auditioning actresses for the part of Jillian. They met with Kathryn Walker, Mary Beth Hurt, and a twenty-six-year-old graduate of the Yale School of Drama named Meryl Streep. Steven didn't feel any of them were right, so the search continued.

During this Big Apple sojourn, Steven did another rewrite on the script. He had already made a few changes (some reportedly with the help of screenwriter David Giler [*The Parallax View*]), and, although he was happy with the basic story and structure, he wanted to improve the characterizations and dialogue and add more humor to the piece. With this last goal in mind, Julia suggested that they bring in her friend, the renowned television comedy writer Jerry Belson, to help with the rewrite. Born on July 8, 1938 in El Centro, California, Belson moved to Hollywood immediately after graduating from high school and worked as a magician, a drummer, and a comic book writer before selling his first television script to *The Danny Thomas Show*. In 1963, Belson teamed up with Garry Marshall and together the duo wrote dozens of scripts for situation comedies such as *The Dick Van Dyke Show*, *The Lucy Show*, *The Danny Thomas Show*, *Gomer Pyle, U.S.M.C.*, and *The Joey Bishop Show*, and for specials starring Bob Hope, Bing Crosby, Fred Astaire, and Danny Thomas. In 1966 they created their own sitcom called *Hey Landlord*, and then in 1970 adapted Neil Simon's play *The Odd Couple* for television. After Marshall and Belson ended their formal partnership in 1973, Jerry became interested in breaking into features. He took the *Close Encounters* gig in part so that he could "learn to write movies." Belson and Spielberg spent three weeks at the Sherry Netherland hotel (much of the time in Francis Ford Coppola's private apartment) working on the script. In the course of the rewrite, many changes were made to the characters:

- Norman Greenhouse was renamed Roy Neary.

- Robert Lacombe was renamed Claude Lacombe, after Claude Poher, the director of the Scientific Systems and Projects Division at the Centre National d'Etudes des Spatiales (CNES)—France's version of NASA. Introduced to the UFO phenomenon by J. Allen Hynek, Poher began pushing CNES president Hubert Curien to form an official UFO study group. Poher get his wish in 1977 when CNES established the Groupe d'Etude des Phénomènes Aerospatiaux Non-Identifies (GEPAN)—the Group for the Study of Unidentified Aerospace Phenomena, which Poher would head.

- Lacombe's Brooklyn-accented translator was given a name: David Laughlin. A comedic scene was added in which in an increasingly uncomfortable Laughlin auditions for Lacombe by translating a steamy passage from a racy paperback novel. Lacombe was also given a taciturn driver named Robert.

- Lacombe's UFO team was given a name: the Mayflower Project, an apt moniker for an organization whose ultimate goal is to send a group of pilgrims on a long journey to a new world.

- Wild Bill Hickcock was split into two characters: the Mayflower Project's leader—a man known only as "Texas"—and Major Wild Bill Walsh—the Project's military leader.

- Irishman Collin O'Connor was transformed into laid-back Larry Butler from Los Angeles. Apparently named for visual effects consultant Lawrence Butler, Larry accompanies Roy and Jillian in their escape from the Mayflower Project base camp and in the first part of their climb up the mountain.

- Wamsutter Mountain was properly identified as Devils Tower, and the description of the base of operations was revised to conform to the design of Joe Alves's set.

Spielberg and Belson put a lot of their energy into the family scenes, fleshing out the Neary kids' reactions to their father's strange behavior and adding depth and humor to the exchanges between Roy and Ronnie. As part of this process, Steven contributed a bit from his own childhood to a revision of the scene in which Roy takes Ronnie to Crescendo Summit and scans the heavens for UFOs while they make out. In the new version, Roy—as Arnold Spielberg had done with Steven years before—wakes his entire family up in the middle of the night and takes them all out to Crescendo Summit so they can see something amazing in the sky. Belson gave the ETs more to do. As a surprise for Steven, Jerry concocted a scene in which several UFOs descend on Jillian's home. The saucers' magnetic fields cause all of the appliances in the house to go haywire as some unseen aliens attempt to gain entry to the house, terrifying Jillian (but not Barry, who thinks that his friends have come to play with him). Unable to get in, the aliens ultimately depart. Steven loved the scene and inserted it in the script. In an interview with the author, Belson recalled the rewrite experience as being, "...a lot of fun. We'd get together in the morning and pitch. He [Steven] had lots to do, I had nothing to do. So, I'd say half the time I went off and wrote what we pitched and about half the time we'd write it together. I got $35,000 for a picture that made about $8 billion." Steven was happy with the revised script—so happy that he finally retired Sam Irvin. From then on, all of the drafts were identified as being written "by Steven Spielberg."

In early February, the Academy Award nominations for 1975 were an-nounced. *Jaws* was nominated for Best Picture, Best Original Score, Best Sound, and Best Film Editing. To everyone's surprise, Steven was not nominated as Best Director. By all reports, he was terribly disappointed, especially since the film was widely regarded as being a director's picture. Interpreting his omission as a backlash against his film's incredible finan-cial success, Steven tabled his disappointment and got on with his new movie.

As the casting process continued, Bob Balaban was selected to play David Laughlin. Balaban was born on August 16, 1945 in Chicago. His father, Elmer, owned and operated a chain of art theaters in the Chicago area (and would later buy a series of television and radio stations and become involved in the cable television industry), and his uncle Barney was the president of Paramount Pictures from 1936 until 1964. Bob was a theater and movie fan from a very young age. He first appeared onstage as a troll in a second-grade production of *The Three Billy Goats Gruff* and im-mediately fell in love with acting. He continued to perform in high school and college and then moved to New York to act professionally. He ap-peared in many plays on and off-Broadway, including *You're a Good Man, Charlie Brown, Plaza Suite,* and *The Basic Training of Pavlo Hummel,* and on television in shows such as *Room 222, Love, American Style, The Mod Squad,* and *Maude.* He made his big screen debut in *Midnight Cowboy* (1969) and then appeared in *Me, Natalie* (1969), *The Strawberry Statement* (1970), *Catch-22* (1970), *Making It* (1971), *Bank Shot* (1974), and *Report to the Commissioner* (1975).

Steven had enjoyed Balaban's performance in *Midnight Cowboy* and thought he would be a good choice to play Laughlin if he could speak French. Balaban went to Juliette Taylor's office on March 24, 1976, where he met with Steven, Juliette, Julia, and Richard Dreyfuss (Balaban and Drey-fuss were old friends, and both were friends with Teri Garr). Balaban had taken French in high school, but had forgotten most of it, so when Steven asked him to say a few words, he said, "Il y a avait longtemps depuis que j'aie parlé français, et si vous me donnez ce rôle, je devrais beaucoup étudier. En effet, je ne sais pas si je pourrais le faire," which means (approximately), "I haven't spoken French in years, and if you give me the job I don't know that I'll be able to do it." Not being able to speak French himself, Steven thought Bob sounded terrific and gave him the part. (Balaban immediately signed up for a refresher course at Berlitz.) Balaban and Dreyfuss were similar physical types, and since both also had beards and wore glasses, they looked a lot alike. Dreyfuss was going to shave his beard for the movie, so to differentiate the two, Steven told Bob that he had to keep his. This meant that Balaban now looked more like the Dreyfuss that the public knew from *Jaws* than Dreyfuss did himself. As a result, Bob was constantly being mistaken for Richard throughout the filming of *Close Encounters*.

Shari Rhodes spent several months traveling around the country looking for children to appear in the film. She videotaped dozens of auditions and screened them for Steven and Julia. Out of this process, twelve-year-old New Orleans actor Shawn Bishop was cast to play Roy and Ronnie's oldest son, Brad, and three-year-old Adrienne Campbell was hired to play their daughter, Sylvia. For the role of Toby, the Nearys' middle child, who allies himself with Roy when Ronnie and Brad turn against him, Richard Dreyfuss suggested his nephew Justin. When Steven saw how closely Justin resembled Richard, he agreed. At first, the eight-year-old wasn't interested—he wanted to spend his summer vacation playing baseball— but Steven managed to convince Justin he'd have a good time making a movie and he finally agreed to take the part. During her travels, Shari also came up with two candidates to play the role of Jillian's son, Barry—one young boy named Zachariah and another named Cary. Steven auditioned both but couldn't make up his mind, so he decided to have them both come to Mobile. He would direct each boy in Barry's first scene and then make his choice.

To play Major Wild Bill Walsh, Steven hired veteran character actor Warren J. Kemmerling. Born in St. Louis in 1924, Kemmerling had a long career on television (*The Twilight Zone, The Untouchables, I Dream of Jeannie, Mission: Impossible, Bonanza, Gunsmoke, The Six Million Dollar Man, The Waltons, The Rockford Files,* and *The Execution of Private Slovik*) and features (*Incident in an Alley* [1962], *The Loved One* [1965], *The Cheyenne Social Club* [1970], *92 in the Shade* [1975], *Family Plot* [1976], and *Eat My Dust* [1976]). He had played a police officer in *Savage*, so Spielberg knew he was well suited to play an authority figure like Wild Bill.

Lance Henriksen was cast as Lacombe's driver, Robert. After an itinerant childhood, Henriksen, who was born in Manhattan on May 5, 1940, spent a few years in the Navy and the Merchant Marine and then returned to New York to study at the Actors Studio. His first work in the theater was as a set builder and painter, but he eventually landed a leading role in an off-Broadway production of Eugene O'Neill's *Three Plays of the Sea*. He appeared in his first film (*It Ain't Easy*) in 1972 and went on to play parts in *Emperor of the North Pole* (1973), *Dog Day Afternoon* (1975), *The Next Man* (1976), and *Network* (1976).

New York–based actor Josef Sommer was engaged to play laid-back Larry from Los Angeles. Sommer was born in Germany in 1934 and soon after moved to the United States with his family, where his father became a history professor at the University of North Carolina. Josef first appeared on stage at the age of nine in the Carolina Playmakers production of *Watch on the Rhine*. After leaving the Army, Sommer trained as an actor at the American Shakespeare Festival in Stratford, Connecticut and performed with the Seattle Repertory Theatre before making his Broadway debut in 1970 in a production of *Othello*. He went on to appear in productions of *The Trial of the Catonsville Nine* (1971), *Children! Children!* (1972), *Enemies* (1972), *The Merchant of Venice* (1973), *Full Circle* (1973), and *Who's Who in Hell* (1974), and in the films *Dirty Harry* (1971), *The Stepford Wives* (1975), and *The Front* (1976).

A key role in the Crescendo Summit scene was that of an eccentric old farmer with a fervid belief in UFOs and other supernatural phenomena. Steven gave the part to a distinctive-looking character actor and poet with the equally distinctive name of Roberts Blossom. Born in 1924 in New Haven, Connecticut, Blossom was educated at Harvard and planned to become a therapist, but turned to acting in the 1950s and won Obie awards for his performances in *A Village Wooing* (1955), *Do Not Pass Go* (1964), and *Ice Age* (1975). He also appeared on television in episodes of *Naked City*, *The Defenders*, and *Beacon Hill*. He made his film debut in 1961's *The Sin of Jesus* and had roles in *The Hospital* (1971), *Slaughterhouse-Five* (1972), *Deranged* (1974), and *The Great Gatsby* (1974).

George DiCenzo (TV's *Dark Shadows, Across 110th Street* [1972], *Helter Skelter* [1976]) came aboard to play Major Benchley, an Air Force debunker, and Matt Emery (*Funny Lady* [1975]) joined the cast as a the Mayflower Project's Support Leader, a mysterious civilian who claims to have spent fifteen years searching for UFOs. Together, the two characters represent the last remaining vestiges of the Paul Van Owen character. *Duel* cast member Gene Dynarski (*Airport 1975* [1974], *Earthquake* [1974], *All the President's Men* [1976]) was hired to play Ike, the harried load dispatcher who sends Roy out to help restore power during the blackout; and New Orleans actress Mary Gafrey was selected to play Mrs. Harris, the Neary family's nosy next-door neighbor. Football player turned actor Carl Weathers was hired to play the part of a soldier who suspects Roy of being a looter during the evacuation scene. Born in 1948, Weathers played football in the United States and Canada for several years before turning to acting in 1975. He appeared in episodes of *Good Times, Kung Fu, S.W.A.T., The Six Million Dollar Man,* and the blaxploitation films *Bucktown* (1975) and *Friday Foster* (1975) before landing the role of Apollo Creed in *Rocky*. That film had just finished shooting (it would be released in November 1976) when Weathers was cast in *Close Encounters.*

For the cameo role of the network news anchorman whose report on a train derailment at Devils Tower finally identifies the object of Roy's obsession, Steven and Julia approached the era's preeminent television newsman, Walter Cronkite. There was some question as to whether a journalist of Cronkite's stature would be willing to appear in a movie, but, as it turned out, Cronkite was open to the idea. He and his wife owned a house on Martha's Vineyard and had spent a lot of time the previous year watching Spielberg shoot *Jaws* there. Cronkite loved the finished film and was interested in working with Steven; however, he was under contract with CBS News, which barred its reporters from acting in movies and television shows. There was one potential loophole—Cronkite's contract expired on June 30, 1976, which was the Wednesday before the long Bicentennial Fourth of July weekend. If Cronkite put off signing his new contract until after the holiday weekend, then he would technically be available to perform for those few days. After a period of deliberation, Cronkite ultimately decided not to do this, and ABC's news anchor Howard K. Smith took the part instead (ABC permitted its reporters to make outside appearances), but not before several scenes had already been shot in which Cronkite was referenced.

The film's biggest casting challenge was to find someone to play Claude Lacombe. Steven had considered most of the big-name French actors of the time: he initially offered the part to Lino Ventura, who turned it down, and then approached Yves Montand, Jean-Louis Trintignant, and Philippe Noiret, all of whom also declined. It was at this point that Spielberg began considering a rather unusual candidate: legendary French film director François Truffaut. Born in Paris on February 6, 1932 to Janine de Monferrand, an unwed mother, the infant François was immediately turned over to a wet nurse, in whose care he remained for several years, even after his mother married architect Roland Truffaut, who legitimized the boy by giving him his name. When François was three, his grandmother brought him to live with her, a happy arrangement that lasted until her death in 1942, at which point he was given over to his parents. Regarding the boy as a burden, Janine and Roland ignored him and frequently left him alone—often for days at a time—while they went off to pursue their own interests. Young François took refuge in the cinema. He began going to the movies an average of three times a week, but eventually reached the point where he was going three times a day, skipping school and sneaking into the theaters or, occasionally, pilfering money from his parents in order to buy tickets.

Cinema clubs—groups that would rent older and classic movies from distributors and private collections and screen them for their members—were very popular in post-war Paris, and as a teenager Truffaut started his own. When he found that his proceeds weren't covering the cost of theater and print rentals, Truffaut began borrowing money (which he neglected to pay back) and defaulting on bills. On one occasion he even stole a typewriter from his father's office and sold it to raise funds. Learning of his stepson's delinquent behavior, Roland had François arrested and sent to a facility for juvenile offenders. After he was released, Truffaut met acclaimed film critic André Bazin, founder of the prestigious film journal *Cahiers du Cinema*. Impressed by François's passion for film, Bazin hired Truffaut to write for his magazine and eventually made him the editor. Truffaut quickly earned a reputation as a harsh and outspoken critic. His primary target was mainstream French cinema, which he regarded as boringly conventional and hopelessly out of touch. Instead, Truffaut and his *Cahiers* compatriots Jean-Luc Godard and Eric Rohmer championed the work of American directors such as Howard Hawks, John Ford, and

Alfred Hitchcock—a revolutionary position at a time when these directors were considered nothing more than studio journeymen. The *Cahiers*
group also formulated the *politique des auteurs*, a theory that championed
the notion that the director is the author of a movie and that every director
has a personal signature that is visible from project to project.

Truffaut eventually became interested in making movies as well as
writing about them. After directing two short films (1955's *Une Visite* and
1958's *Les Mistons*), he began work on his first full-length feature, an auto-
biographical film about a young boy who is neglected by his parents, drifts
into delinquency, and ends up in an institution. *Les Quatre cents coups*
(*The Four Hundred Blows*, 1959) was a great critical and commercial success, won Truffaut a Best Director award at the Cannes Film Festival, and,
along with Godard's *A bout de souffle* (*Breathless*, 1960, which was based
on a story by Truffaut) and Claude Chabrol's *Le Beau Serge* (*Handsome
Serge*, 1958), kicked off the French *Nouvelle Vague* (New Wave) movement
of the early 1960s. Over the next seventeen years, Truffaut created a series
of extremely popular and influential films, including *Jules et Jim* (*Jules and
Jim*, 1962), *Fahrenheit 451* (1966), *La Mariée était en noir* (*The Bride Wore
Black*, 1968), *Les Deux anglaises et le continent* (*Two English Girls*, 1971),
L'Histoire d'Adele H. (*The Story of Adele H.*, 1975), and a trio of films that
continued the story of Antoine Doinel, the youthful protagonist of *Les
Quatre cents coups*: *Antoine et Colette* (*Antoine and Colette*, 1962), *Baisers
volés* (*Stolen Kisses*, 1968), and *Domicile conjugal* (*Bed and Board*, 1970).
In 1973, Truffaut's joyful film about filmmaking, *La Nuit americaine* (*Day
for Night*), earned Academy Award nominations for Best Director, Best
Screenplay, and Best Supporting Actress, and won an Oscar for Best
Foreign Language Film. On March 2, 1976, Truffaut was at his home in
Paris preparing for the March 17 release of his latest film, *L'argent de poche*
(*Small Change*), when he received a call from Steven Spielberg.

Although known primarily as a director, Truffaut had acted in a few
of his own films, including *La Nuit americaine* (in which he played, aptly
enough, a film director). Steven had seen and liked all of François's performances, but had been especially impressed by his work in 1970's *L' Enfant
sauvage* (*The Wild Child*), in which Truffaut played a doctor attempting to
humanize a feral boy found living in the wilds of eighteenth-century Avey-
ron: "I felt that he was a tremendous human presence in that film...he just
radiated so much compassion. And I felt that, rather than just putting the

face of government on this movie [*Close Encounters*]...I wanted the face that led the way to be extremely charitable and kind and optimistic." For Spielberg, Truffaut was the ideal Lacombe: "I needed a man who would have the soul of a child, someone kindly, warm, who completely accepts the extraordinary, the irrational."

Steven knew that the chances of landing Truffaut—who had never acted for another director and was constantly busy making his own films—were slim. That he would even consider taking time out to appear in an American science fiction movie about flying saucers seemed unlikely, but Spielberg wanted to at least make the attempt and so contacted Truffaut's agent. Having seen and greatly admired both *Duel* and *Jaws*, François agreed to take Steven's call. Speaking through Truffaut's assistant (who knew English), Steven asked François if he would read the script and, if he liked it, consider playing Lacombe. Flattered by Steven's interest in him, Truffaut agreed, so the next day Julia Phillips sent him the script, along with French translations for all of his scenes. On March 15, Truffaut responded to Steven via telegram: "I like the script and I like Lacombe," but he warned Spielberg that he didn't speak English and that he wasn't an actor—he could only play himself. Since Spielberg wanted Truffaut precisely because of his warm and appealing personality, this was fine with him. Although Truffaut had no interest in UFOs, he was intrigued by the idea of working with Spielberg and wanted to see how a massive Hollywood movie so unlike his own extremely modest productions was mounted and managed. François told Steven that he was interested in playing the part, but warned that he needed to be finished by the middle of August—he was shooting a new film (*L'Homme qui aimait les femmes/The Man Who Loved Women*) in the fall and was scheduled to work on the final shooting script with his collaborator Suzanne Schiffman at the end of the summer. Steven promised Truffaut that the *Close Encounters* shoot wouldn't exceed fourteen weeks and that he would be released on time. With this assurance, François accepted the role. (At the time, Truffaut claimed that the main reason he agreed to take the job was so that he could use the experience as research for a book he was writing about film acting. Since he never actually wrote such a book, there has been some speculation that François only said this so that he wouldn't be accused of "selling out" to the Americans by his fellow French filmmakers.) Truffaut's American lawyer, Louis Blau, and his agent, Rupert Allen, negotiated a salary of $75,000 for him and the deal was set.

François flew to California on May 5, 1976 and reported to The Burbank Studios for his costume fittings. It was at one of those fittings that he and Steven met for the first time. Since Spielberg didn't speak much French and Truffaut didn't speak much English, the encounter was an awkward one. As Spielberg told *Film Comment*, "Mostly, I stood around smiling stupidly; he returned the smile; we smiled at each other for about an hour."

Despite his anxiety, Steven was extremely pleased that Truffaut had joined the production. "I was absolutely certain that he was the Lacombe I had envisioned...and that the film was going to turn out really well because he was in it."

CHAPTER 14 | # Music, Aliens, and Melinda Dillon

WITH THE BULK OF HIS CAST ASSEMBLED, Steven turned his attention to the film's other stars: the extraterrestrials. Spielberg wanted the look of his ETs to match the description of alien beings given by the majority of people who claimed to have had close encounters of the third kind— he wanted them to be small, humanoid creatures with elongated limbs and digits, oversized heads, blue-gray bodies, and tiny facial features. If *Close Encounters* had been made in the twenty-first century, Steven would have been able to use a variety of sophisticated techniques to bring the aliens to life: animatronics, full-body-makeup appliances, or computer-generated imagery. Back in 1976, however, his choices were limited—his only real option was to use performers wearing costumes and masks.

Since most witnesses had estimated the ETs' height as being four feet or less, Spielberg knew he was going to have to use diminutive performers. After allegedly toying with and then dismissing the idea of using trained apes to play the aliens, Steven had some tests made with little people, but it quickly became apparent that they would not be able to provide the sleek, tapered look mentioned in the most encounter reports. His only other alternative was to use children. Wanting the aliens to look delicate and petite, Steven decided to cast six- and seven-year-old girls. Production assistant Sally Dennison was assigned to recruit a group of young girls from a Mobile ballet school (Dennison would go on to cast all of the extras for the film). The children would be paid $25 per day. Their teacher, Susan Helfond, was hired to be the ET choreographer and began preparing the girls for their roles by having them practice a variety of "alien" movements and gestures.

The extraterrestrial costumes were fashioned by the *Close Encounters* wardrobe department. They were essentially seamless, skintight leotards made with four-way stretch cloth and dyed a bluish gray. Padding was created for the girls to wear under their leotards to change their shapes and make them appear less human. To create the ET masks, Steven approached the top makeup man in Hollywood, John Chambers, who had designed the brilliant ape makeups for the *Planet of the Apes* series. Unfortunately, Chambers was having health problems and could not take the assignment. He recommended that Spielberg use Frank Griffin, who had been his assistant on *A Man Called Horse* (1970) and *Embryo* (1976), instead. The brother of actress Debra Paget, Griffin had also begun his career as an actor before turning to makeup. He had worked on a number of television series (*Star Trek, Time Tunnel*) and films (*Sam Whiskey* [1969], *Electra Glide in Blue* [1973], *Westworld* [1973]) and had just finished the television movie *Sherlock Holmes* in New York when he was asked to report to The Burbank Studios in February 1976.

Griffin's first task was to come up with an acceptable design for the aliens' faces. At the start of pre-production, Joe Alves had done a series of sketches of the extraterrestrials based on the witnesses' descriptions. Steven showed these drawings to Griffin and pointed out the parts of each that he liked. The various attributes were combined into a bust created by sculptor Mike McKracken that ended up looking too insect-like. They began moving back toward the look defined in Alves's original sketches and, after almost two months of work, came up with a design they dubbed "Casper," after the cartoon character Casper the Friendly Ghost—an appealing, childlike creature with a large, bulbous head and wide, inquisitive eyes. Steven approved the design and Griffin began preparing to make the masks.

He assigned the actual fabrication work to The Burman Studio, a full-service makeup facility founded in 1973 by two brothers. Thomas R. Burman began his career in 1966 as an apprentice makeup artist at Twentieth Century-Fox. One of his first major assignments was assisting John Chambers on *Planet of the Apes* (1968) and *Beneath the Planet of the Apes* (1970), and his later films included *A Man Called Horse* (1970), *The Thing with Two Heads* (1972), and *The Boy Who Cried Werewolf* (1973).

Ellis "Sonny" Burman Jr. had won an Emmy for his work on *Gargoyles* (1972) and had also worked on *The Devil's Rain* (1975) and *The Man Who Fell to Earth* (1976). The Burmans specialized in what Tom called "special makeup effects"—the integration of mechanical and other physical effects techniques with advanced approaches to makeup in order to produced more effective and believable gags and creatures. For *Close Encounters*, the Burmans were actually going to have to make two different kinds of masks. Steven wanted to be able to shoot close-ups of the ETs and show them making facial expressions, which required the production of five articulated masks—masks fitted with mechanical devices that would allow their features to move in a realistic manner. The rest of the masks would be nonarticulated—they would have no mechanisms and their features would not move. The nonarticulated masks would be used for wider shots in which no facial expressions could be discerned.

The first step in creating the articulated masks was to make a mold of the face of each child that was going to wear one. Because the articulated masks were going to be heavy (due to the weight of the mechanics), Frank Griffin decided that they should have little boys don them rather than little girls, on the theory that boys were stronger and would be better able to hold their heads up straight while wearing them. Sally Dennison recruited five Alabaman boys, and Griffin and Tom Burman flew down to Mobile to make the molds, which were then used to produce a plaster bust of each boy.

The Burmans and their associate David Ayres then used clay to sculpt alien faces over each of these busts. Molds were made of the sculptures and a thin layer of clay was placed inside each one to create a bumper. The molds were then used to produce busts of the alien heads, which were called cores. A layer of fiberglass approximately one-sixteenth of an inch thick was applied to each core, dried, and removed. The results—hardened fiberglass shells in the shape of the alien heads—were called skulls. Another layer of fiberglass was then applied to the top and sides of each of the original busts of the boys. This process produced more shells—fiberglass helmets in the exact shapes of the boys' heads that were called sub-skulls. The sub-skulls were attached to the skulls to create a set of five fiberglass alien heads that would fit snugly onto the noggins of the young performers without slipping around (elastic chin straps would also help hold the heads in place).

Veteran mechanical effects man Dell Rheaume (*Smile* [1975], *The White Buffalo* [1976]) was brought in to create the mechanical devices (consisting of servo motors and actuators) that would push and pull the surfaces of the masks in all of the ways required to create the desired expressions (all of the mechanics were incorporated into the fiberglass alien heads in the narrow gap between the skulls and the sub-skulls). The primary areas of articulation in the ET masks were the mouths and the eyes. For Rheaume, the mouths proved fairly easy to rig, but the eyes were a challenge—he needed to create a device that locked each pair of vacuform plastic eyeballs together and allowed them to move in unison. Normally, the mechanical devices in an articulated mask are triggered by the performer wearing the mask, using a series of built-in controls, but since he wasn't sure that the little boys would be able to operate the controls successfully, Rheaume designed the mechanisms in the ET masks to be activated by remote control, using the same type of radio unit that is used to fly model airplanes.

The final step in the process was to create the skins—the outer surface of each mask. To create a skin, a core was placed inside its corresponding alien head mold and then liquid foam latex was injected into the gap (created by the clay bumper) between the two. The latex was cured in a special oven at a temperature of approximately two hundred degrees, and the resulting foam rubber alien face was then coated with clear polyurethane (to give it a shiny texture) and painted to match the color of the leotards. Once all five skins had been produced, they were fitted over the fiberglass skulls and connected to the articulation devices.

The nonarticulated masks were much easier to produce. Three different sizes of alien heads (small, medium, and large, to accommodate three different sizes of children) were sculpted out of wax. Molds were made of these sculptures, filled with slip rubber, and cured. Once cooled, they were covered with clear polyurethane, painted, and then fitted with vacuform plastic eyes.

Since the extraterrestrials were supposed to have long, spindly fingers, all of the performers had to wear specially designed gloves to cover their human hands and make them look as alien as possible. Steven originally wanted the ET hands to be articulated so that the aliens could perform all of the actions called for in the script (e.g., picking up objects, touching humans, opening cans of soda, etc.), so a company called Show Craft was commissioned to design an articulated glove. It came up with a device that would allow the fingers to do everything that was required, but at $600 a pair, they were much too expensive. Frank Griffin and Tom Burman then devised some articulated finger extensions that could be operated by strings and levers built into each glove. Unfortunately, the mechanisms required a lot of strength to operate—more than most of the little girls could muster—so that approach was abandoned as well. Ultimately, the decision was made to go with a simple, non-articulated rubber glove, and an articulated model hand was created for use in close-ups.

Once several prototype ET suits had been completed, Frank Griffin shot a series of tests to see how they would look on film. After seeing the tests, Steven requested a few changes and then approved the outfits. At this point, Griffin had to leave the project. When he was hired, the ET scenes had been slated to be filmed in June, but when the start of production was pushed back from April to May, the alien scenes were postponed until July. Griffin had previously committed to start work on Robert Wise's film *Audrey Rose* (1977) in July, so he had to bow out of *Close Encounters*. Luckily, most of his work had been finished. Jim Linn's department would complete all of the necessary body stockings and padding, while the Burmans would finish the rest of the masks and gloves and deliver them to Mobile.

On March 29, 1976, the 48th Annual Academy Award ceremony was held at the Dorothy Chandler Pavilion in Los Angeles. *Jaws* won three out of the four awards it was nominated for: Best Sound (Robert L. Hoyt, Roger Heman Jr., Earl Madery, and John R. Carter), Best Film Editing (Verna Fields), and Best Original Score (John Williams). By the time Williams collected his golden statue, he was already hard at work on *Close Encounters*. Spielberg had approached John during the early stages of pre-production and asked him to come up with an appropriate combination of five musical tones that the humans and aliens could use to communicate with one another. Williams asked if he could use seven tones instead of five, feeling that it would be easier to develop a melody if he could use more notes, but Steven said no. He didn't want a melody, he wanted a signal—in his words, "a doorbell." Finding that doorbell proved to be a challenge. Together, Williams and Spielberg made a list of approximately three hundred five-note combinations and circled the ones they liked best. As they reviewed the finalists, they kept coming back to one particular combination: D-E-C-C'-G (or Re-Mi-Do-low Do-Sol in solfège). Since they liked this one the best, they finally decided to go with it. One of the things that appealed to Williams about this sequence of tones was that it ended on Sol, the fifth note of the musical scale. Sol is a dominant note—the one from which a resolution takes place. By leaving the sequence unresolved, they created great anticipation in the audience as they left it hanging, waiting for a response.

Having settled on the tones, John then began composing music for the "jam session" between the Moog synthesizer and the Mothership (the soundtrack needed to be produced ahead of time so that it could be played on the set during shooting and permit the lightboard operators and the actor playing Jean-Paul to synchronize their actions with the music). The human side of the "duel" was created with synthesizers, but Williams wanted to use real instruments for the Mothership's response. He chose a tuba and an oboe to be the "voice" of the Mothership, wanting the breathing of the wind players to give the impression of effort and make the Mothership seem "alive." The music was recorded at the Twentieth Century-Fox and a tape of it was sent to Mobile.

In April 1976, the screenplay underwent another rewrite. After Steven had finished the February revision with Jerry Belson, he sent a copy to Hal Barwood and Matthew Robbins to review. He had done the same thing with the John Hill draft, which neither Barwood nor Robbins had liked (Barwood had dismissed it as "a CIA spook movie—too hard and too cold"). They were very excited, however, by Steven's new approach to the story, which they felt was a complete "revolution" from what had come before—totally different in both focus and spirit. Still, they didn't think the script was perfect—there were holes in the plot, and certain aspects of the story needed to be much better developed. Hal and Matthew called Steven from northern California (where they had moved with their families in 1975) and congratulated him on turning the project around. Then they gave him a sharp, detailed critique of the piece and offered a number of suggestions for improving it. Steven loved their ideas and wanted to incorporate them into the script immediately. With the start of production just around the corner, time was of the essence, so Steven asked Hal and Matthew if they would come down to Los Angeles so that they could work on the changes together.

A few days later, Barwood and Robbins flew to Southern California, moved into Steven's house, and began a marathon rewrite session. Hal Barwood describes the process: "We wrote all day and all night. Every few hours we'd come out and would consult with Steven and with [Richard] Dreyfuss, who was hanging around. We'd have lunch together, brainstorm a few things and then go back in and do more writing." Barwood characterizes their role as that of "mechanics"—taking the ideas that Steven had laid out in his original drafts and "making them work...in a [more] dramatic way." As the revision progressed, many of the script's elements were significantly enhanced:

- The already-shot air traffic control scene, which originally came after the police car chase, was moved to the front of the script and became the opening scene of the movie. This allowed the story to begin on an eerie note of mystery and suspense.

- Many scenes were added that reinforced Roy's obsession with Devils Tower, including a bit in which he tries to sculpt the mountain out of a mound of shaving cream and another in which he scares his family by trying to do the same thing with the food on his dinner plate. As originally scripted, Roy used salmon croquets and corn niblets to shape the Tower, but this was later changed to a large pile of mashed potatoes.

- The sequence in which Roy constructs a replica of Devils Tower atop his model railroad landscape was also expanded. In the original drafts, the script showed Norman/Roy conceiving the idea to build the replica and then jumped ahead to the point where it was already finished. In the new draft, scenes were added that showed Roy manically digging up his yard and the yards of his neighbors (including Mrs. Harris) in order to collect the dirt, plants, and garden materials he needs to build the model and then tossing it all into the house through his kitchen window.

- The Crescendo Summit scenes were beefed up and the eccentric old farmer was given a speech that explained the three different categories of close encounters.

- A scene from the original draft in which Norman Greenhouse goes to an Air Force base to report his sighting, only to have his account debunked by a Project Blue Book representative, was revised and expanded. In the new version, an embarrassed Ronnie accompanies Roy to attend a mass debunking attended by many of the Crescendo Summit true believers, including the eccentric old farmer, who makes them all look ridiculous when he claims that, in addition to seeing UFOs, he has also seen Bigfoot. The characters of the Blue Book officers were revised to make them less adversarial and more sympathetic (with one of them even expressing a desire to see a UFO for himself), which emphasized the notion that *Close Encounters* was going to be a movie without any real villains.

- Some tweaks were made to the UFOs as well: in a Disney-esque touch, a straggler was added to the group of flying saucers that buzzes the highways in the beginning of the story. Considerably smaller than the others, this little UFO was depicted as always struggling to catch up to his big brothers. The description of the Mothership was changed too—from a whimsical, Dr. Seuss-like creation to a mysterious black shape that was so big that it literally blocked out the stars.

While most of the rewrite was devoted to augmenting ideas that were already present in the script, Barwood and Robbins made a significant addition to the story as well. When Hal and Matthew first read the script, one of their concerns had been that the ending, while packed with spectacle, didn't have enough human moments in it. They also felt that the character of Jillian Guiler was significantly underdeveloped—that she didn't have much purpose in the script other than to serve as a sounding board for Roy and to take pictures of the aliens at the end. Finally, they were very dissatisfied with the character of Barry Guiler, who served no purpose in the script at all. They toyed briefly with the idea of cutting him, but then they came up with an idea that solved all three of their problems at the same time.

Using the scene that Jerry Belson had devised in which the aliens attempt to gain entry to Jillian's house as a jumping-off point, Barwood and Robbins suggested that the extraterrestrials should go a step further and actually abduct Barry. This would give Jillian a much stronger reason to travel to Devils Tower and give the film an incredible emotional kick in the final sequence when Barry emerges from the Mothership along with the rest of the returnees and mother and child have a tear-filled reunion. Steven loved the idea and together the three of them integrated it into the story. As they did, Jillian's part became considerably larger and more important: she was given several scenes in which she faced off against the Air Force and the press in the aftermath of Barry's abduction, and she teamed up with Roy much earlier in the story (at the evacuation center rather than at the base camp) and joined him in his Act III trek across the Wyoming countryside to Devils Tower.

Although they were working under tremendous pressure due to the approaching start date, the collaboration between Steven, Hal, and Matthew was a happy one. Spielberg enjoyed working with his old friends in a format that invigorated him: "I'd much rather collaborate," he has said. "I need fresh ideas coming to me, because I can't send ideas out into space and expect them to return, I need them to bounce off something."

At the beginning of May, Verna Fields left the production. No reason for her departure was given, although there were rumors that Steven was upset with her for giving the impression in several interviews that she had "saved" *Jaws* in the editing room, which implied that Spielberg had somehow botched it during production. Whether that was the reason or not, Steven was now in need of an editor. His friends, director Irvin Kershener and cinematographer Owen Roizman, had just finished working on a picture called *The Return of a Man Called Horse* (1976), and they recommended that he consider one of that film's editors, Michael Kahn.

Born in New York on December 8, 1935, Kahn (who, like Spielberg, had once been an Eagle Scout) began his career as a messenger boy for a Manhattan advertising agency. The agency sent him to Hollywood to work on some commercials it was producing, and when the job was over Michael decided to stay. He got a job at Desilu Studios as an executive assistant to editorial supervisor Dann Cahn and was eventually hired as an assistant editor on a television series called *The Adventures of Jim Bowie*. Kahn assisted on a number of other television shows and was eventually promoted to full editor while working on *Hogan's Heroes*. Michael's first feature was an independent film called *The Activist* (1969), and, after coediting *A Man Called Horse* with Phillip W. Anderson, he landed his first solo studio assignment when George C. Scott (a *Hogan's Heroes* fan who admired Kahn's work on the show) hired him to edit a film he was directing called *Rage* (1972). Following *Rage*, Kahn edited *Trouble Man* (1972), *Black Belt Jones* (1974), *The Trial of Billy Jack* (1974), *The Savage Is Loose* (1974), *The Devil's Rain* (1975), and *Zebra Force* (1976). Based on Kershener's and Roizman's recommendations, Steven called Michael in for an interview. As Kahn recalled: "I went in and he said, 'Are you a good editor?' And I said, 'I don't know. How can I tell you if I'm a good editor? All I know is whoever hires me wants me back.' He said, 'Do you always wear jeans?' I said, 'Yes.' He said, 'Okay, I'll let you know.' The next thing I knew I was hired."

The last week of pre-production was a busy one. As all of the departments made their final preparations, Jerry Belson came back to do another quick polish on the script and then, four days before shooting was scheduled to begin, Steven finally found his Jillian. He had been auditioning actresses (including *Carrie* costar Amy Irving, whom he had just begun dating) throughout pre-production and had even offered the part to a few who declined it. Now, with less than eighty hours to go, Steven was starting to get desperate. He was on the verge of postponing Jillian's scenes when he got a call from director Hal Ashby, who was currently editing *Bound for Glory*. Ashby had heard about Spielberg's plight and told Steven that he had just directed an actress who he thought might be a good candidate for the role. Her name was Melinda Dillon.

Born in Hope, Arkansas on October 13, 1939, Dillon had begun her career in improvisational comedy at Chicago's famed Second City and then studied acting at the Goodman Theatre School in Chicago and at the Actors Studio in New York City. She was nominated for a Tony Award as Best Supporting or Featured Actress for her Broadway debut as Honey in the original 1962 Broadway production of Edward Albee's *Who's Afraid of Virgina Woolf?* After *Woolf*, Dillon appeared on stage in *You Know I Can't Hear You When the Water's Running* (1967), *A Way of Life* (1969), and *Paul Sills' Story Theatre* (1971), and on television in episodes of *The Defenders*, *East Side/West Side*, *Bonanza*, *Storefront Lawyers*, *The Jeffersons*, and *Sara*. Melinda made her film debut in 1969's *The April Fools*. She followed this with a role in *Un Hombre solo* (1969) and then landed two parts in *Bound for Glory*—as Woody Guthrie's wife, Mary, and as his singing partner, Memphis Sue. Ashby assembled a reel of Melinda's scenes and sent them over to Steven. Spielberg loved Dillon's performances and promptly called her agent and offered her the role. Having no interest in appearing in a science fiction movie, she hesitated until she read the last scene of the script—the one in which Jillian takes the pictures of the aliens. Charmed and intrigued, Dillon read the rest of the script, decided that she wanted to be in a space movie after all, and accepted Steven's offer.

With the cast fully assembled and all preparations complete, filming was finally ready to begin.

CHAPTER 15 | **Wyoming**

On Sunday, May 16, 1976, the 114-member cast and crew of *Close Encounters* boarded a chartered plane and flew from Los Angeles to Rapid City, South Dakota. From there, the company headed west in a caravan of rented buses, driving two hours through countryside dotted with mule deer, pronghorn antelopes, and buffalo to the small mining town of Gillette, Wyoming (1976 population 3,000), and checked into the tiny hamlet's most luxurious hostelry—a Super 8 motel. Filming was set to begin the next day. As he prepared to bring his dream project to life, Steven Spielberg found himself gripped by anxiety: "Every time I make a movie, it's like starting over again.... it's the same knot in the stomach, the nausea when I wake up in the morning, the sense of responsibility of spending somebody else's money." Truth be told, Steven didn't much enjoy the process of shooting a movie. "The conception of the story is the most exciting part of making a picture for me," he told *Take One* magazine. "The second most exciting part is assembling the film. The most nerve-wracking part of the movie, the process that I most dislike, is the actual shooting and directing of the picture."

The cast, crew, and two hundred extras rose early on Monday morning and drove sixty-two miles from Gillette to Devils Tower. Not everyone had to make the seventy-five-minute journey: to avoid the trip, Steven, Richard Dreyfuss, and Melinda Dillon stayed in Winnebagos parked at the Tower (François Truffaut had been given one as well, but he didn't like staying out in the wild so he took a room back at the Super 8). A short time later, shooting commenced on a portion of Wyoming's State Highway 24 for the first scene on the schedule: Roy Neary's drive against traffic as he tries to make his way to the Tower while hundreds of terrified locals flee the alleged toxic gas leak. Vilmos Zsigmond shot this scene (and all of those that followed) on Eastman Kodak's brand new 5247 fine-grain film stock using the Panaflex camera, a lightweight (and therefore easily and quickly deployed) 35mm motion picture camera manufactured by Panavision that had been introduced just a few years before (Vilmos had been one of the first cinematographers to use the Panaflex when he chose it to shoot *The Sugarland Express* back in 1973).

Filming continued the next day with the scene in which Roy and Jillian see Devils Tower for the first time. After that, production shifted to the Base Camp set—a compound erected in the park at the foot of the mountain that consisted of a series of portable trailers and crates arranged around a helipad. Joe Alves and his team had begun constructing the camp several months earlier in the freezing cold of the Wyoming winter, when the temperature could sometimes go as low as fifty degrees below zero. The weather wasn't the only hassle: Alves's design called for the compound to be surrounded by a chain-link fence. Local ordinances prohibited the building of fences, and area cattlemen and ranchers (who had often been denied permission to construct their own barriers) complained to the authorities that the Base Camp fence was illegal and insisted that it be torn down. Joe told them that the fence was only temporary, but his explanation fell on deaf ears. Eventually, a compromise was worked out that allowed the company to erect a fence around a smaller area than originally planned for. Later, when Alves tried to hang a "closed" sign at the entrance of the park for a single shot, one of the park rangers told him that he wasn't allowed to close the park. Joe explained that he wasn't closing the park, just putting up a sign that would be taken down as soon as the shot was finished, but the ranger said that if the sign read "closed" then that meant that the park was closed, and he wasn't allowed to close the park. They went around like this several times before Alves finally threw in the towel. Alves later said that it sometimes seemed that the Wyoming locals were going out of their way to make things difficult for the production.

On May 19, François Truffaut filmed his first scene—one in which Roy Neary is escorted to an evacuation helicopter and placed on board. Lacombe only played a small part in the scene—he had to ask the chopper pilot to hold for five minutes so that he could go and ask Major Walsh to allow the pilgrims to stay—which allowed Truffaut to ease into his role. It took Truffaut a while to adjust to life on the *Close Encounters* set. Film actors often have to wait for hours (and sometimes entire days) for the crew to prepare a shot. As both a producer and a director, Truffaut was used to being in constant motion on the sets of his own films and so found all of this relative inactivity to be incredibly tedious. Although Truffaut loved America, he found the local culture in Wyoming (and later Mobile) difficult to relate to, and, with his shaky command of English (and a mild hearing problem), he had difficulty connecting with the other members of the cast and crew. He did make one good friend, however: his acting partner Bob Balaban, the only other person on the set (besides Truffaut's translator, a young woman named Françoise Forget) who spoke French. The two had met a few days earlier in the lobby of the Super 8 motel (Truffaut had come to Wyoming from Los Angeles with the rest of the company. Balaban flew in from New York, where he had been starring in a play). Balaban had been extremely nervous about meeting Truffaut, but the two hit it off almost immediately and spent much of their down time discussing movies, exploring the local scene, and telling each other jokes (which, due to their rather wide culture gap, didn't always translate).

For Steven Spielberg, the prospect of directing his hero was a daunting one, and for the first few days he was overly deferential until Truffaut insisted that Steven call him "François." The two men soon bonded over their shared passion for the cinema and for directors John Ford, Alfred Hitchcock, and Howard Hawks. Truffaut liked Spielberg, whom he found to be charming and unpretentious. He admired the fact that Steven had gone to such great lengths to realize his childhood dream by making this "film of flying saucers" and marveled at the calm and self confidence that Spielberg displayed as he went about the business of directing such a massive and technically complicated production.

For his part, Steven found François to be very encouraging: "He was very curious about the way I set up shots. If he liked my setup he would tap me gently on the back, nod his head, and smile. One tap on the back from Truffaut was enough to convince me I should never change the shot." Spielberg also admired François's performance, which he thought was "superb."

On May 20, Truffaut shot his first extended dialogue scene—one in which Lacombe confronts Major Walsh and insists that Neary and the other "gatecrashers" be allowed to stay because it appears that the aliens have invited them to the meeting. Major Walsh dismisses Lacombe's argument and walks away from him. The scene ends with Lacombe quietly saying [in English], "They belong here more than we." During the first take Truffaut's accent was so thick that Spielberg initially thought that he was speaking French and asked him to repeat the line in English. Stunt coordinator Buddy Joe Hooker was so tickled by Truffaut's pronunciation—which to him sounded like "Zay bee-long 'ere Mozambique"—that he had T-shirts made up with the nonsensical line printed on them and distributed them to the crew. Although Truffaut usually didn't like being teased about his English, he got a kick out of Hooker's gag.

From May 19 until May 24, the production divided its day into two parts. The company would spend a good portion of the morning and afternoon filming scenes in the Base Camp set or in the area around Devils Tower (including the sequence in which Roy and Jillian crash their rented station wagon through several fences as they make their way across the Wyoming countryside, and another in which they are captured by a group of mysterious men in hazmat suits) and then at 4:00 p.m. it would move up onto Devils Tower itself to shoot the scene in which Roy, Jillian, and Larry Butler scale the mountain while being pursued by Major Walsh's troops. In the script, the chase begins during the late afternoon and ends at night, so it was necessary to shoot the majority of the sequence at twilight—the time between sunset and nightfall in which the light has a subdued and ethereal quality to it (which is why many cinematographers refer to it as "magic hour"). Since the gloaming only lasted about an hour, the filming of the scene had to be spread out over several days. There were no roads on Devils Tower, so the crew usually had to haul all of the equipment up onto the mountain by helicopter or on foot. It would take several hours to get personnel and equipment into position and prepare the scene for filming, a task made more complicated by the unevenness of the rocky terrain and the abundance of rattlesnakes in the area. Shooting would usually start around 8 P.M. and continue until the light finally faded at around 9:15 P.M. The unit then had to get back down the mountain, hopefully before it was too dark to see.

The production faced several other challenges as well. To begin with, the unit was under a lot of pressure to move quickly because the rangers insisted they be out of the park before the Memorial Day weekend, when a

large number of tourists were due to arrive. The weather was also a problem. At the beginning of the shoot, the sky was filled with massive cloud
formations that looked spectacular on film, but then it rained on and off
for several days. Eventually the storms passed, but so did the clouds. The
constantly changing conditions made it very hard to match both the backgrounds and the lighting from shot to shot. Vilmos Zsigmond met the
challenge by skillfully employing artificial illumination to give the impression that the sun was shining even on overcast days. When the sun
did shine, many members of the company got sunburned, even in cool
weather, due to the high altitude.

Despite these challenges, the Wyoming shoot went very smoothly.
Zsigmond attributed this to the high caliber of the crew, whose skill and
experience allowed them to move quickly without compromising quality,
even when executing a large number of extremely complex shots, including a great many that featured people moving and talking in the foreground while numerous helicopters performed complicated maneuvers
in the sky behind them. (All of the helicopters featured in the Wyoming
sequence were leased civilian helicopters that were painted U.S. Army
green.) First assistant director Chuck Meyers and second assistant director Jim Bloom received high praise from all for their ability to organize
and execute these shots (many of which Steven devised on the spot) in
record time.

The days were long ones, but for the most part the company didn't
mind because work kept everyone occupied. Apart from observing the
inhabitants of a nearby prairie dog town, there wasn't much to do at Devils
Tower except visit the souvenir stand or have a root beer float at the snack
bar. One day François Truffaut and some local kids got so bored that they
made up a game that involved throwing rocks at an empty candy bar wrap-
per. Gillette wasn't much better. The town could boast a few country-and-
western bars and mediocre restaurants, but that was about it. On the one
Sunday the company had off, a few people made the several-hour drive to
Mount Rushmore, but most of the rest just hung out. Steven Spielberg
staved off boredom by screening movies (including 2001) every night in
his Winnebago. Everyone got a big boost on the evening of Saturday, May
22, when the dailies from the first several days of shooting were screened.
Steven's assistant, Rick Fields, set up a projector in an auditorium located
in the recreation center of a church in the town of Moorcroft, Wyoming,

which was about halfway between Gillette and Devils Tower. The footage looked wonderful and left everyone feeling that they were working on a movie that had the potential to be really great.

Unfortunately, there was one person who didn't share that assessment: Columbia production chief Stanley Jaffe. When Jaffe read the final version of the screenplay—the one that included the changes that Steven, Hal Barwood, and Matthew Robbins had made during their intensive four-day rewrite—he was extremely upset. Jaffe didn't like a lot of the new material—especially the subplot in which the aliens kidnap little Barry Guiler, which he felt was disturbing and unpleasant and would turn audiences off. Stanley was so upset that he flew to Wyoming to voice his complaints to Steven and Julia. "What the hell is this?" he reportedly said. "This is not the movie I bought." Jaffe insisted that they drop the kidnapping subplot. Steven and Julia refused. The argument went back and forth, growing more and more heated until Jaffe actually canceled the movie.

The cancellation only lasted a few hours, until Julia suggested that they film the kidnapping scene two different ways—as scripted and then in another version that showed Jillian pulling Barry away from the aliens at the very last second—and postpone the final decision until post-production. Jaffe agreed to go along with this idea. Steven was resistant, but Julia took him aside and persuaded him to play along so that they could get the movie restarted. She promised to work on Stanley to convince him to change his mind before the time came to make the cut. Steven finally agreed and Jaffe restarted the movie. (When Hal Barwood and Matthew Robbins heard what had happened, they were distressed that their idea had put the movie in jeopardy, but Steven told them not to worry. He loved the idea and had no intention of cutting it).

On May 27, the unit filmed the final scene on the Wyoming schedule—a tense exchange in which David Laughlin translates as Lacombe tries to convince Major Walsh that the arrival of so many strangers at Devils Tower on the eve of first contact is an "event sociologique." Filming took place inside one of the Base Camp trailers. It was a small, enclosed space with little ventilation, and the temperature inside quickly rose to over one hundred degrees. This was Truffaut's biggest scene in the film, and he became very anxious about it. Worried that he would forget his lines, he wrote them down on manila envelopes and taped them up all over the set (even on actor Warren Kemmerling's chest).

On May 28 the company left Gillette, traveled back to the Rapid City airport, and boarded another chartered 727. Spirits on board were high and went higher when one of the stewardesses announced that *Taxi Driver* had just won the Palme d'Or for Best Picture at the Cannes film festival. Champagne was served as the *Close Encounters* team headed for Mobile, Alabama.

CHAPTER 16 | Mobile, Part I

WHEN THE MEMBERS of the company got off the plane in Mobile, they were in for a big surprise. The weather in Wyoming had been cool, but Alabama was sweltering and incredibly humid—conditions that would remain constant for the next three months. It also smelled; at the time, one of Mobile's major industries was paper manufacturing, an activity that produces a foul odor that tends to linger. Although most of the cast and crew stayed in area hotels and motels, including the downtown Holiday Inn and the Mobile Sheraton, Steven moved into a rented house with Rick Fields and Michael Kahn, who transformed the house's screened-in porch into an editing room.

The Mobile portion of the shoot began on Monday, May 31, 1976 at a Holiday Inn twenty miles outside the city, with a scene in which the members of the Mayflower Project receive word that the rendezvous with the aliens has been set. (This scene was later cut from the film.) The next major bit to be filmed was Roy's initial close encounter, which was shot over the course of several evenings at a real railroad crossing. This was not a comfortable location—there was a thunderstorm almost every night, after which large mosquitoes would swarm the area. The company also had to accommodate the freight trains that rolled through the crossing every two hours. A railroad official would notify the crew whenever a train was approaching, and they would then have fifteen minutes to move all of the lights and equipment out of the way. Once the train had passed, everything would need to be put back into position. Approximately forty-five minutes were lost to each train.

After shooting the Air Force debriefing scene in a local Mobile office building, the unit traveled thirty miles east of the city to Bay Minette. This small Alabama town was dressed to look like a small Wyoming town and then used to stage the evacuation sequence in which Roy and Jillian are reunited at a railroad depot as thousands of people attempt to flee from the alleged poison gas leak. Two thousand locals were hired to appear as extras in the sequence alongside two hundred head of cattle, one hundred sheep, and numerous cars and trucks. Because all of these elements had to be put through their paces at the same time, second assistant director Jim Bloom remembers this as being one of the most complicated and difficult scenes in the entire picture to shoot.

When the evacuation scene was finished, the company returned to Mobile and spent the next two weeks at 1613 Carlisle Drive East, filming all of the scenes set in and around the Neary home. Carlisle Drive was located in one of the city's brand new suburban subdivisions. Most of the houses on the street had just been built and were not as yet occupied. The initial plan had been to rent 1613 from the developer, but Joe Alves and Clark Paylow thought that it would be more cost-effective for Columbia to buy the house outright for the company to use as needed, and then sell it at the end of the production. This would allow the studio to recoup all of the money it would have to spend on the site and maybe even turn a profit. However, when Alves and Paylow suggested doing this, the executives at Columbia told them they were crazy and instructed them to go ahead with the rental plan. At this point, Alves and Paylow decided that they would buy 1613, lease it to the studio, and keep the proceeds for themselves. However, when they informed Columbia that they were going to do this, the executives changed their minds and decided to buy the house after all. The studio purchased 1613 for $35,000 and sold it several months later for $50,000.

On June 26, the production shifted over to Hangar 1 at Brookley Field, where a crew of film industry professionals and local laborers led by construction coordinator Bill Parks—a Hollywood veteran who had once worked with Cecil B. DeMille—had just finished building the Box Canyon set. The first step in this massive undertaking had been to extend the 300-foot-long hangar to accommodate the 450-foot-long set. To do this, a team of grips led by Dickie Deets pushed back the doors at one end of the hangar and then erected a scaffold made of tubular steel that was 150

feet long and eight stories tall on each side of the opening. The scaffold
was then covered with a large tarp that was black on the inside (in order
to provide the necessary darkness on the set) and beige on the outside (to
reflect the sunlight and keep the interior cool). To anchor it, Parks and his
team dug a trench in the tarmac 12 feet deep, 2 feet wide, and 180 feet
long. Huge cement beams were then sunk into the trench and used to
anchor the ties for the tarp.

Once the covering was in place, work began on the set itself. The eigh-
teen-inch-thick concrete floor of the hangar (built to support the weight
of the airplanes that were once stored there) was used as the floor of the
landing zone, allegedly installed in Box Canyon by the Mayflower Project's
crack construction team. The additional levels of the set were built up using red clay that was then covered with three-inch-thick concrete slabs. A
100-foot-long runway that ran from the center of the base of operations to
the far end of the tarp was constructed in forced perspective (which means
that the section farthest from the camera was built at a smaller scale than
the section closest to the camera to make it look further away then it really was). This made the runway appear to be 1,000 feet long. To create
the walls of the canyon, scaffolding was erected on three sides of the set
and then covered with six thousand artificial rocks. The rocks were made
from fiberglass (from molds created back in Hollywood by fiberglass expert George Sampson) and painted to match those found at the base of
Devils Tower. (So that they would have an accurate model to work from,
set painter Roy Ward swiped a rock from Devils Tower and brought it to
Mobile in his carry-on bag, which prompted a lot of curious looks when
he passed through the security checkpoint at the Rapid City airport.) The
rocks came in twelve shapes and sizes and two different varieties: "hard"
(rocks made from extra thick fiberglass that could support the weight of a
human being), which were placed wherever the actors were going to walk,
and "soft" (rocks that were thinner and less supportive, but much cheaper
to produce), which were placed everywhere else.

When Joe Alves first began designing the landing zone, he consulted
with a number of scientists at NASA and other organizations and asked
what sort of equipment they would utilize if they knew they were actually
going to meet with beings from another world. The scientists gave him a
list of instruments, including cameras, laser spectrographs, and devices
that could measure volume, heat intensity, and object mass. Set decorator

Phil Abramson was sent out to obtain these items and ended up renting over $100 million worth of highly advanced technology, including four consoles from the Space Center in Houston. To keep the base tethered to present-day reality, Joe Alves mixed a few Port-a-Potties and Coke machines in with the futuristic gadgets and gizmos. All of the equipment on the set was practical (i.e., working) and run by electricity obtained from working outlets that had been built into the set (when the movie lights were added in, it took approximately 4,200,000 kilowatts of electricity to run what was quickly nicknamed the Big Set—so much that city of Mobile experienced several brownouts during filming. The city eventually installed new transformers around Brookley Field in order to feed more power to the facility and ease the burden on the rest of the city). Knowing that the base of operations needed to be portable, Alves decided to house all of its components in a series of trailers and cubicles designed to look as if they could be hauled around by container trucks or helicopters. The cubicles were made from fiberglass (initial versions were made out of vacuform plastic, but the heat from the movie lights caused the plastic to melt) and equipped with video monitors, all of which featured readouts and displays recorded in advance on videotape and played back during filming under the supervision of the unit's video technician, "Fast" Eddie Mahler.

It took three months to build Box Canyon—the biggest indoor motion picture set ever constructed at that time. The final cost was $700,000 (if a comparable facility had been built for real, it would have cost $400 million). Once the set was complete, it was wrapped in the mile of custom-made black backing (the very same backing that was responsible for getting the film greenlit), and a sign reading "Ready When You Are..." was hung from the catwalks to welcome the filmmakers. Steven didn't want anyone outside of the production to see the "Big Set" until the movie was released, so security surrounding Hangar 1 was incredibly tight. In addition to having to pass through a sentry checkpoint at the entrance to Brookley Field, all personnel had to be cleared by a guard posted at the hangar door. Everyone working on the Big Set had to wear a photo ID at all times (Richard Dreyfuss was allegedly kicked off the set more than once when he forgot to wear his). Some members of the press complained about the veil of secrecy Steven had thrown over the production and accused him of overkill, but Spielberg staunchly defended his decision: "I didn't clamp the lid down because of egocentric reasons.... I wanted to surprise. And the only way to do that is by keeping quiet."

Lighting the Big Set proved to be an enormous challenge. Back when the landing zone was first being designed, the plan was still to shoot the film in gritty documentary fashion using available light. With this in mind, the suggestion was made to incorporate a series of stadium lights into the base of operations and use the illumination they provided to light the set. The hope was that this would make the base look like a real place and the movie look as if it had been filmed on a real location. To determine if the stadium lights would be strong enough to shoot with (motion picture film is considerably less sensitive than the human eye—it takes much more light to take a picture than it does to see), Vilmos Zsigmond and Joe Alves went out to the Rose Bowl in Pasadena one night during pre-production to make some tests. Alves laid out a schematic of the landing zone on the field, and Zsigmond used a light meter to measure the illumination coming from the Bowl's numerous stanchion lights. The levels proved sufficient, so the stadium light plan was adopted. It remained in place until the company arrived in Mobile and Vilmos saw Box Canyon for the first time. At that point, he realized that there was no way to do such a magnificent set justice using just the stadium lights, which illuminated the Big Set in a very flat and even way that Doug Trumbull reports made it look "just horrible." By then, the documentary approach had been abandoned and the look of the film had become much grander.

Sharing the feeling of many of the cast and crew that *Close Encounters* had the potential to be a really great film (a feeling that continued to grow as the production went on), Vilmos thought that they needed to make it grander still. He wanted to illuminate the base of operations in a much more stylized fashion, using pools of light (allegedly coming from the stanchions) and shadow to give the Big Set more richness, more depth, and more character. Zsigmond felt that taking this approach would make *Close Encounters* look "like a movie—a *movie* movie." Steven liked Vilmos's idea and asked what he would need to make it happen. "More light," was Zsigmond's reply.

Since the company didn't have enough units on hand to do the job properly, calls were placed to motion picture equipment rental houses around the country, and before long dozens of additional lights were shipped to Mobile, including almost fifty "Brutes"—large, powerful carbon arc lamps, most of which were mounted on a ring of catwalks that had been erected over the set. As big and powerful as the Brutes were, they were so high up (approximately sixty feet in the air) that the only way to significantly increase the quantity and quality of the light down on the floor was to aim three of them at the same spot at the same time. Even then, the overall light level was so low that in order to get the look they wanted, Vilmos had to shoot with the camera lens opened up as wide as possible. This allowed enough light to reach the film, but greatly reduced the depth of field (area of focus) in each shot, which meant that both the camera and the actors had to hit and hold rigid marks in order to maintain the sharpness of the image.

Many members of the production referred to the final section of *Close Encounters*—the last thirty-six minutes of the film in which the UFOs arrive at Devils Tower and the meeting between humans and extraterrestrials takes place—as "The Experience" (a phrase coined by Verna Fields). The filming of The Experience was divided into two parts. The first included all of the scenes leading up to the arrival of the Mothership, and the second encompassed the arrival itself and all of the scenes that followed. The first part of The Experience was filmed in its entirety from three different positions: from a platform situated high up near the roof of the hangar (to simulate Roy and Jillian's perspective as they look down on the landing zone from a notch near the top of Devils Tower); from a second platform located about fifty feet above the set (to simulate their perspective when they climb down to a lower point); and finally from the floor of the set (to capture the actions of the Mayflower group as they experience The Experience). Since Steven planned to intercut shots taken from all three vantage points, it was important that all of the performers make exactly the same moves at exactly the same time in each version of the sequence.

The actions of the principal cast were clearly spelled out by the script and the storyboards, but the behavior of the background performers was not. To rectify this, first assistant director Chuck Meyers wrote a script for each of the approximately one hundred local extras that Sally Dennison had recruited to play the base of operation's scientists and technicians. Each script created a basic character for the extra to portray, described that character's job, function, and attitude, and indicated every move that he or she was supposed to make during the sequence. Meyers gave each character a nickname and even included a complete set of operating instructions for each piece of equipment that he or she would be seen handling. (During the filming of these scenes, Meyers spent most of his time directing the extras and turned the rest of his assistant directing chores over to Jim Bloom.)

Each version of the sequence was filmed in order, beginning with the scene in which a group of UFOs, flying in formation, imitates the Big Dipper. This was followed by the scene in which the three scout saucers and their straggler buddy fly down to the landing zone and respond to the humans' overtures by playing the five tones. Next up was a portion of the story known as the "cuboid sequence," during which a swarm of small, box-shaped UFOs was supposed to emerge from the three scout saucers, zoom around the landing zone, and then link up to create a series of incredible geometric shapes in the air above Box Canyon. At the conclusion of the performance, the cuboids were to emit thousands of smaller, pinpoint-sized cubes that would settle over the landing zone workers like fairy dust. The micro-cuboids—which were apparently meant to be little probes—would then melt into the humans' skin and enter their bloodstream, briefly lighting up their veins before fading away into nothingness. Meanwhile, the large cuboids were to form a cordon around the landing zone and hold their position until the Mothership arrived, at which point they would zoom up and surround the giant spacecraft, ferry it down to the runway, and bring it in for a soft landing.

As exciting as this sequence was on paper, the production team had not been able to figure out how to bring the cuboids to life. During pre-production, Roy Arbogast and his team constructed several dozen practical cubes—five-inch-square boxes made from plywood and rice paper, each containing a five-hundred-watt light bulb. The boxes were strung together in groups and flown around the set on wires as the actors reacted with varying degrees of awe, fear, and confusion. Since the practical cuboids could only travel in a straight line, they were only going to be used in brief snippets. Doug Trumbull intended to create the rest of the acrobatic objects using an early computer graphics program developed by the Mathematics Applications Group, Inc. (MAGI), called SynthaVision. As soon as filming began, however, it became clear that the cuboids weren't going to work—the movement of the practical squares was too limited and the SynthaVision tests weren't convincing—and after filming just a few shots, Steven decided to cut the entire sequence. Although he made his acting debut in the scene (playing one of the startled technicians), Doug Trumbull felt that this was ultimately for the best, as the cuboids were the only element in Steven's script that was not based on real UFO lore.

Moving on, the company began shooting the "barnstorming" scene—an awesome sequence in which dozens of UFOs burst out of the clouds and buzz the landing zone. Days were spent filming the actors and extras running around the Big Set reacting to imaginary flying saucers. Although the spaceships themselves would be added to the scene in post-production, the light spilling from them onto the characters had to be created on the set. To do so, some of the Brutes up on the catwalks were fitted with different colored gels, then shined down upon the actors and swiveled around as necessary to simulate the movements of the soon-to-be-inserted UFOs. (When six of the lights proved to be too heavy to pan as required, Doug Trumbull came up with the idea of aiming them into mirrors, which reflected the beams down onto the floor and could be moved about easily.) So that the actors would know where to look during the scene, numbers were put on all of the lights, and Chuck Meyers and Jim Bloom spent much of their time calling out directions such as "Look at light number one. Okay, now look at light number twelve." For the shots in which the UFOs were supposed to be zipping by closer to the ground, a 350-foot-long monorail was erected across the top of the landing zone. Four large HMI mercury arc spotlights were attached to a basket, which was then run across the set on the monorail as four electricians positioned inside swiveled the lights to and fro over the actors. To simulate the effects of the static charge and reduced gravity allegedly generated by the UFOs, Roy Arbogast's team placed air jets in strategic places around the set. When the actors stood over the jets, air would shoot out and cause clothing and papers to fly up into the air. Some of the performers had personal air jets inside their costumes to make their hair stand on end.

All of these scenes were challenging for the crew, but filming went more smoothly than it might otherwise have done, thanks to the extensive preparation that had been done in pre-production. Steven's storyboards established the continuity and let everyone know just what physical and lighting effects were required for each shot, and the tests that Roy Arbogast and Vilmos Zsigmond had conducted showed them how to generate those effects with a minimum of fuss. Still, most of the shots in the sequence were so complex that it took a great deal of time to set up, rehearse, and then shoot each one. This led to some very long (twelve hours or more) working days and some perpetually exhausted crew members. The Experience wasn't easy on the actors, either. Required to restrict their movements in order to accommodate the many needs of the camera and the special effects, they sometimes felt more like puppets than actors. They also found it extremely difficult to react convincingly to things they couldn't see. To help, Steven would talk the actors through the effects shots, doing his best to describe what they were supposed to be seeing. Even with Spielberg's assistance, however, most of the actors found the experience frustrating and unsatisfying. Richard Dreyfuss was reportedly very unhappy with his performance in the finished film, feeling that had he been able to see what he was reacting to, he would have done things much, much differently.

Conditions on the Big Set made things harder for everyone. Just standing on the concrete floor for so many hours a day was hard on everyone's feet, and, thanks to Mobile's overall mugginess and the large number of lights being used on the set, the heat and humidity inside Hangar 1 were intense, with the temperature frequently climbing into the triple digits (often reaching 120 degrees Fahrenheit on the set and 140 degrees inside the cubicles). Although air conditioning had been installed in the hangar, it didn't help much. It got so hot in the rafters that several of the electricians operating the lights (who because of the steamy conditions they were working in were nicknamed "The Sweathogs") passed out. Many of them quit; then their replacements quit, too, prompting a joke to circulate that there were more electricians flying between Mobile and Los Angeles than there were on the set. To thank everyone for working in such miserable circumstances, Richard Dreyfuss once ordered a case of ice cream bars for all to share.

Although the Box Canyon had been built indoors to protect it from the elements, the weather was still an issue. It rained in Mobile for an hour or so almost every afternoon, and some of that precipitation would leak through the holes in the hangar roof and drizzle down upon the set. Hurricanes blew the tarp off the end of the hangar—twice. The tarp had been erected on the lee side of the hangar in order to shelter it from the Gulf winds, but that didn't do much good when the winds were gale-force. On the afternoon of July 16, Joe Alves was looking up from the floor of the set and saw "...a crack in the tarp. It got bigger and bigger and then suddenly it just exploded. The winds ripped the top (of the tarp) right off the scaffolding. It became a 150-foot flag—the biggest flag you ever saw—just blowing in the wind. Rain poured onto the set. It was just devastating." The company left the hangar and filmed elsewhere for a few days until the tarp was repaired. Then things were fine until August 12, when the same thing happened again.

Fog was also a problem—artificial fog, that is. In order to capture beams of light on film, they must be photographed in some sort of smoke or mist. Because Steven and Vilmos wanted the light coming from the UFOs to be visible, the set was fogged in before every shot with smoke produced by vaporizing mineral oil. Although the mist enhanced the lighting effects beautifully, it was extremely unpleasant to work in—it was hot, made it hard to breathe, irritated people's eyes and sinuses, and (because of the mineral base) caused a great deal of gastrointestinal distress.

As difficult as all of these things were, the biggest problem that arose during the filming of The Experience had nothing to do with heat, fog, or hurricanes. On the first day of shooting on the Big Set, the company finished ahead of schedule (Steven's production plan called for the unit to film four storyboards a day), but before long they began to fall behind. Since every additional day of shooting added $50,000 or more to the budget, this news was obviously not well received back in the Columbia executive suite. Worried that they might have a runaway production on their hands, David Begelman, Stanley Jaffe, Alan Hirschfield, Herbert Allen, and John Veitch decided to go down to Mobile to confront Julia Phillips and find out what was going on. Although there were several reasons for the delays—the large number of extras that needed to be positioned and rehearsed for every shot, the complex special effects, etc.—Julia laid most of the blame on Vilmos Zsigmond.

The new lighting concept had turned out to be very expensive. It cost a great deal of money to rent all of the additional lights (and the generators needed to run them), and, since each light required a union electrician to run it, this meant a lot more high-priced employees had to be put on the payroll as well. The new approach also added days to the schedule, as it took much longer to light Box Canyon with dozens of individual lamps than it did to simply switch on a bank of stadium lights. Although the results were spectacular—much better than anything they could have accomplished with the original plan—Julia didn't care. She felt that Vilmos was much too slow and meticulous, and that a lot of what he was doing was unnecessary. After seeing how long it took to prepare each shot, the Columbia executives came to share her view. Some of them felt that Zsigmond was out of his depth—that, since most of his previous features had been shot using primarily natural and available light, he lacked the experience with traditional studio lighting necessary to handle a production of this size and complexity. Several people associated with the production felt that this assessment was accurate (including gaffer Earl Gilbert, an old-timer who had a lot of definite ideas about how to light a set and little patience for some of Vilmos's concepts. It was often quite a struggle for Zsigmond to get the recalcitrant Gilbert to do things the way he wanted them done). However, others thought that it was terribly unfair: "They blamed Vilmos because he had never lit a set like this before," says one person familiar with the situation. "But nobody had ever lit a set like this before. There had never *been* a set like this before."

Zsigmond felt that neither Julia nor the Columbia executives understood what a difficult task it was to properly illuminate such an enormous space or appreciated how hard it was to create the complicated lighting effects that the film required. He also felt that Julia used him as a convenient scapegoat for a lot of things that had nothing to do with him, including her own lack of preparation. As the shoot dragged on, Julia and the Columbia executives pressured Zsigmond to use fewer lights and take less time to set them. Knowing that this would harm the quality of the final footage, Vilmos resisted. Steven supported his director of photography (as did Doug Trumbull), but when the production fell further behind schedule and the budget continued to rise, both Phillips and the executives finally insisted that Spielberg fire Zsigmond. Steven refused—he was happy with what Vilmos was doing and wanted him to continue. Julia and Columbia pressed (and even went so far as to sound out several possible replacements), but Spielberg stood his ground. The producer and the studio eventually backed down, but continued to look askance at Zsigmond for the rest of the shoot.

By the end of the executives' visit it had become obvious that the cost of *Close Encounters* was closing in on $15 million—almost $3.5 million more than the originally approved budget. The production was obviously going to need more money to keep going, something the Columbia brass was not at all happy about. After some heated exchanges with Julia, the additional funds were approved, but with conditions. To save money and pare back the schedule, several scenes deemed nonessential to the story (most significantly the return of the M.S. Sulphur Queen in the Gobi Desert) were cut from the script. In addition, John Veitch was assigned to stay behind in Mobile to keep an eye on expenditures and to help move things along.

Veitch's brief was to keep the pressure on, which he certainly did, but all in all the production could not have asked for a better watchdog. The dashing, impeccably groomed executive was extremely supportive of the project and of Steven, whom he considered a genius (Spielberg, in turn, had great admiration and respect for Veitch). John had a solid understanding of the production's complex logistics and worked closely with Steven and Julia to solve problems economically but without compromising the movie's quality. He was willing to let them spend the time and the money they needed to do things right (which occasionally landed him in hot water with some of his fellow executives, not all of whom shared Veitch's appreciation for the film's artistic aspirations) but he was no pushover. John refused to approve expenditures for things that he didn't think were absolutely necessary, and when he felt that Steven had spent enough time on a scene, he would politely but firmly press him to move on.

Once the filming of the first part of The Experience had been completed, the company moved off the Big Set for a few weeks so that Joe Alves and his crew could prepare it for the movie's biggest moment: the arrival of the Mothership.

CHAPTER 17 | **The Director**

IN AN ARTICLE IN *American Cinematographer* magazine about the making of *Close Encounters,* author Herb A. Lightman wrote the following about Steven Spielberg: "Much has been written about his boyish grin and childlike delight in playing with the massive toys of film production, but beneath all that Huckleberry Finn there lies a will of steel and an unshakable determination to turn out the best motion picture ever made."

Lightman's observation was right on target: *Close Encounters* was Steven's dream project. He was determined to make the movie as good as he possibly could and was willing to go to whatever lengths were necessary—including pushing the boundaries of the schedule and budget on a regular basis—to do so. He had a very clear vision of what he wanted the film to be and worked tirelessly to achieve it. As Richard Dreyfuss observed at the time: "He [Steven] shoots scenes again and again, until he gets exactly what he wants.... From the time Spielberg starts a film until it's released in the theaters he works day and night to get it perfectly in tune with his intentions." Steven's friend John Milius echoed this sentiment: "He has unlimited patience and the integrity not to cut corners under pressure. He sticks with a shot no matter how long it takes to get the damned thing right." Spielberg's intense focus on the job at hand could sometimes cause him to be a little brusque. "I don't have the best sense of humor when I'm making a film," Spielberg has said. "I'm usually the first person who loses his temper or gets a little pushy, because I run blind sometimes when I direct. I only see the work, and sometimes I forget that there are a lot of human people who are trying to contribute to your vision."

In addition, Steven's overwhelming commitment to his vision did not always make him the easiest person to collaborate with, as he himself acknowledged: "I'm not the most fun to work with unless the people I hire can sit on their egos. Spielberg was definitely open to suggestions from other members of the company and accepted many of them, but in the end he made it clear that "I'm a real stickler for having things my way." Some members of the company felt that Spielberg's desire to have things his way stifled their own ability to contribute to the film—Vilmos Zsigmond has said that working on *Close Encounters* was sometimes frustrating for him because Steven would often tell him what to do rather than work in concert with him as he had done on *The Sugarland Express*. Zsigmond attributed this change of approach to the tremendous confidence that Spielberg had gained while working on *Jaws*. "He didn't need my help anymore."

Despite the occasional rough patch, the members of the crew generally liked working with Steven. They admired his enormous creative talent and strong technical expertise and appreciated the respect that Spielberg gave to each and every aspect of the filmmaking process. For example, sound is often given short shrift on a movie—camera crews and actors aren't always eager to accommodate a soundman's booms and mikes and when a director is under pressure to finish a scene, the last thing he wants is to have to do another take because the recording was off. The attitude can often be "We'll fix it in post," but production mixer Gene Cantamessa was a tireless and vocal advocate for doing the job right on the set.

Recording the sound on *Close Encounters* was frequently a challenging task. To create a greater sense of realism, Steven was fond of having his actors all talk at once—overlapping and interrupting one another, often with a lot of noise going on in the background. It required a great deal of complex miking and deft mixing to produce a high-quality recording under these circumstances, and Cantamessa appreciated the fact that Spielberg was willing to give him the time and the latitude to do what he had to in order to get good tape, even when it wasn't always convenient. Steven in turn appreciated Gene's expert work, which he characterized as being "super."

The actors also enjoyed working with Spielberg. "Steve is not what you would call an actor's director in the classical sense," said Richard Dreyfuss. "But he's relaxed and open in the way he communicates what he wants and he helps you get there."

Spielberg had confidence in his cast members and tried to approach his work with them in as collaborative a manner as possible. In highly technical or effects-oriented scenes, he would ask the actors to incorporate themselves into his preplanned shots and staging, but in scenes that focused more on character than effects, "I would rather let the actors inspire me...and begin making visual choices after I've watched a rehearsal. After...the actors move where they feel they should move...Then [I] introduce the camera and film it." Teri Garr appreciated this respect for actors and the acting process, as well as the fact that Steven allowed the performers to participate in the creation of their characters and make contributions to the scenes they had appeared in (many of Ronnie Neary's lines were variations on things that Garr had heard her sister-in-law and her friends say and worked into the scenes with Steven's approval). François Truffaut was surprised by the lengths Steven was able to get him to go to in his scenes: "Steven did force me to act more than I have in my own films." Truffaut enjoyed the experience. "[Steven] pushed me farther...[and]...several times during the shooting he made me surpass myself. Thanks to that, I discovered a real pleasure as an actor."

The entire company was amazed by Spielberg's seemingly endless reserves of energy and enthusiasm, as well as by the confident way that he approached each scene. This confidence was something of an illusion. Steven has said that beneath his self-assured exterior he was "...always worried that what I planned isn't working, that there's a better way...about whether I'm making the right move." Knowing how much pressure he was under, the company was also impressed by how calm and composed Steven always appeared to be. Once again, Spielberg's placid exterior was a bit of a façade. In reality, he found the filming of *Close Encounters* to be an extremely stressful experience. Apart from all of the trouble the studio was giving him, he was frustrated by the problems they were having with the Big Set (which, because of all the difficulties they had with it, he began to refer to as "this film's shark"—a reference to the troublesome mechanical monster from *Jaws* whose constant malfunctioning caused so many headaches on that film). He was also frustrated by the fact that much of the time he felt like he was shooting in the dark, since he was directing so many scenes to match visual effects that wouldn't be created until long after filming was over and it would be too late to fix any problems. For a self-described "control junkie," this was a very tense position to be in.

Despite all of this, Steven was rather remarkably able to keep his attention focused where it needed to be—on making the best movie possible.

To this end, Spielberg was constantly coming up with new ideas—for shots, for scenes, and for bits of business—that would make the film more exciting, more emotional, and more spectacular. The inspiration for these ideas came from all sorts of places—from items that he read, from shows he saw on television, from casual conversations with friends and acquaintances, and from intriguing things that he saw or heard in passing. Many of his ideas were inspired by the dozens of movies that he watched over the course of the shoot. To incorporate these new concepts into the film, Steven brought Jerry Belson and then later Hal Barwood and Matthew Robbins down to Mobile to do more work on the script. George Jensen was also on hand to revise old storyboards and whip up new ones. Although Steven liked to prepare thoroughly, he was also willing to make changes on the spur of the moment if he thought they would improve the scene. As American Film Institute observer Seth Winston recalls, "He [Steven was] pretty improvisational. Shots were assembled and reassembled, lines were changed on the spot." The Burman Studio associate David Ayers's recollections echoed Winston's: "You'd see him [Spielberg] just kind of walking back and forth and pacing; and then he'd come up with an idea. He'd try it, and then he'd do it again—and then he'd try something different…. He had guts. He'd try anything to see if it would work on film." It was the intensive preparation that Steven had done during pre-production that allowed him to be so spontaneous during shooting: "I'm almost at my most improvisatory when I've planned most thoroughly, when my storyboards are in continuity. That gives me confidence to ad lib. Then when I improvise, I improvise around the planned stuff."

Steven's constant addition of new shots and scenes sometimes caused the production to fall behind (prompting Earl Gilbert to tell Spielberg that "If you would stop watching those fucking movies every night, we would be on schedule"), but it also enhanced the film in many important and valuable ways. For example:

- It solidified Neary's obsession with Devils Tower as Steven incorporated more and more objects into the story that could remind Roy of the mountain, including a mound of shaving cream, a Jello mold, a pillow, and several items cut from the finished film (a supermarket soft drink display, a miniature golf attraction, and the curve of his wife's breasts). Some critics later accused Steven of overkill, saying that he emphasized Neary's obsession too much, but Spielberg didn't agree—he felt it would take a lot more than one or two moments of recognition to pull Roy out of his placid suburban existence. In some interviews Steven said he felt he should have gone further and emphasized Neary's obsession even more.

- It landed one non-actor a role in the film. When technician Phil Dodds came to Mobile to install the ARP 2500 synthesizer (which the production had decided to use in place of the Moog synthesizer indicated in the script) on the Big Set, Steven invited him to play the part of Jean-Claude, the Mayflower Project's keyboard artist. Excited by the chance to appear in the movie, Dodds said yes. (He was much less excited a month later when he had gone two weeks over his two-week vacation and his boss was hounding him to return to work.) For some unknown reason, he ended up being mentioned twice in the film's end credits: once as "Jean-Claude" (where he was billed at Philip Dodds) and a second time as "ARP Musician" (where he is billed as Phil Dodds), even though Jean-Claude *is* the ARP musician.

- It enhanced the parts of two actors already cast in the film. Originally, the character of "Texas," the Mayflower Project's leader, only appeared in one scene in the script: the auditorium conference in which Project members are introduced to the five musical tones. To play the role, Steven engaged Merrill Connally. The brother of former Texas governor John Connally, Merrill was a real-life cattle rancher from Floresville, Texas, He had also been Lyndon Baines Johnson's former campaign manager, had played the part of Baby Langston's foster father for Spielberg in *The Sugarland Express*, and claimed to have once chased a flying saucer down a dark Texas road. A distinguished, authoritative-looking man, the six-foot-six, white-haired Connally was completely convincing as the head of a top-secret government project.

Steven was so enamored of Merrill that he decided to include him in The Experience. Spielberg did this primarily by taking lines away from other actors and giving them to Connally (including "Einstein was probably one of them," which had originally been assigned to Claude Lacombe). Due to Connally's regal appearance, "Texas" was renamed "American Eagle" on the daily call sheets and then finally identified as "Team Leader" in the credits of the finished film.

• Steven did something similar for J. Patrick McNamara. An experienced stage actor who was the producer/director of his own theater company in New Orleans, McNamara had originally been cast in the small part of "Shakespeare" (even though he didn't look anything like the Bard)—the Mayflower Project official who appears in the auditorium scene to explain what the five tones mean (each tone is supposed to represent a single word in a greeting). McNamara was originally hesitant to take the role, because it was only one day's work and he had already accepted an offer to direct a play in Los Angeles. Steven really liked McNamara and wanted him in the movie, so he promised that if Pat took the role, he would enlarge it as they went along. McNamara agreed, and when production moved onto the Big Set Steven began giving McNamara small bits of business and snippets of dialogue to perform, encouraging him to come up with his own material as well. Adopting the persona of an anxious bureaucrat, McNamara improvised a speech in which his character begins screening Roy Neary for his interstellar journey by asking about his medical history. McNamara later wrote a humorous scene (which Steven shot but ultimately cut) in which his character tries to get Neary to sign a release form that absolves the Mayflower Project of any and all liability should he not return from space. McNamara became such a strong presence in the film that his character was eventually given the title of "Project Leader."

• Steven's improvisations provided opportunities for members of the crew as well. In the 1970s there were three camera unions in the United States, one for each region of the country (East, Central, and West). Union rules required that a production shooting in a particular region hire a cinematographer from that region, even if it already had one. Since Vilmos Zsigmond was a member of the western union and Mobile was located in the middle of the country, *Close Encounters* was obligated to hire a member from the central union. Chicago-based (and central union member) Steven Poster was a veteran of numerous commercials and documentaries who had worked with Vilmos several years earlier on a car commercial. When Poster heard that *Close Encounters* was going to be shooting in Mobile, he contacted Zsigmond, who hired him to be the unit's "standby" cameraman. After a few weeks of standing by, Steven Poster began receiving assignments from Steven Spielberg to film inserts and additional shots—many of which were directed by Matthew Robbins—that Steven had devised but didn't have time to shoot himself. Poster was soon asked to man a second camera on the Big Set and to form a second unit and shoot a few complete sequences on his own. By the end of the production he had earned a credit as Second Unit Director of Photography.

- Perhaps Steven's greatest last-minute addition was the Kodály Hand Signs, no mention of which exists in any draft of the *Close Encounters* screenplay. Zoltán Kodály (1882–1967) was a Hungarian composer and educator who believed that everyone, not just the musically gifted, had the right to a musical education. His philosophies inspired Hungarian educators to develop a multifaceted approach to teaching music, which they named after Kodály. One component of the Kodály Method is the use of a specific set of hand gestures—originally developed by the English minister and music teacher John Curwen (1816–1880)—to teach the solfège syllables for each note in the musical scale. Doug Trumbull told Steven about the Kodály signs one day on the set in Mobile, and the director, thinking that they would be a terrific way to further visualize the communication process between humans and aliens, decided to work them into the movie. Julia Phillips's assistant, Kendall Cooper, contacted the Kodály Institute and received permission for the production to use the signs and related printed materials in the movie in exchange for a donation. This spur-of-the-moment decision led to the creation of one of the film's most joyous moments: the climactic greeting between Lacombe and the lead extraterrestrial at the end of the movie.

While Steven's methods were sometimes unconventional, there was no denying the quality of the results, which everyone agreed were spectacular. Seth Winston echoed the feelings of most members of the production when he says that he was continually astounded by the images that Steven put on film: "He really goes for the home run, the amazing thing.... Each shot has to be a three-ring circus." Michael Phillips concurred: "Spielberg gives you all you can imagine and then gives you *his* imagination as a topper."

CHAPTER 18 | **Mobile, Part II**

WHILE WAITING for the Mothership to arrive, the main unit moved to an old farmhouse located on the outskirts of the small town of Fairhope, Alabama, to film the scenes set in and around Jillian's house. Joe Alves had come across the place during one of his pre-production location scouting trips. It was in very bad shape, so Alves and his crew gutted the interior and remodeled it to meet the needs of the production. The first scene shot there was the one in which little Barry Guiler comes downstairs in the middle of the night and discovers several offscreen aliens ransacking the kitchen. As planned, Steven used the filming of this scene as the final audition for Zachariah and Cary, the two finalists for the role of Barry. The boys were as different as night and day: Zachariah was a willful, rambunctious tot who refused to do anything anyone told him to. In contrast, Cary was (in the words of Melinda Dillon) "this wondrous, quiet, soft, attentive, *listening* child." Although Steven liked both boys, he responded more strongly to Cary's ethereal qualities and decided to give him the part.

Cary Guffey was born in 1972 in Douglasville, Georgia, a suburb of Atlanta. *Close Encounters* casting director Shari Rhodes first spotted him when she came to his preschool to pick up her niece, who was one of Cary's classmates. She then contacted his parents, who were quite surprised to learn that Hollywood was interested in their son. They agreed to let the four-year-old do a videotaped screen test and before long he was on his way to Mobile.

Steven and Cary became instant pals, and their bond had a powerful impact on the work they did together. Steven took care to explain everything to Cary in great detail so that he would understand what was going on and not get scared. To elicit the proper reactions in certain scenes, Steven would sometimes employ off-camera manipulation techniques such as opening elaborately wrapped presents as Cary watched with eager anticipation to see what was inside or dress crew members up in silly costumes to evoke surprise or laughter. A camera trained on young Guffey's face would capture his expressions, which would later be spliced into the appropriate point in the scene. Sometimes Spielberg would just describe what it was Barry was supposed to be seeing and let Guffey's four-year-old imagination take over from there. The result of all of these approaches was a wonderfully real and natural performance that lit up the screen and touched audiences everywhere. Years later, Spielberg recalled that when François Truffaut saw how well he worked with young Guffey, the great French director told him that he needed to stop making big movies and to instead make a movie about kids (or, as Truffaut pronounced it, "keeds"), a directive Spielberg would fulfill five years later when he made *E.T.:The Extra-Terrestrial*.

Once Cary had been cast, the company moved on to film the scenes in which Barry's toys come to life in the middle of the night, Jillian is awakened by her son's laughter as he chases after his new friends, and the extraterrestrials lay siege to the farmhouse and kidnap Barry (which, despite the agreement he and Julia had made with Stanley Jaffe, Steven did not film with an alternate ending). Most of these scenes were filmed at night, which the team enjoyed because Alabama summer nights are a lot cooler than Alabama summer days. After finishing in Fairhope, the main unit traveled back to Brookley Field and stayed there for the balance of the time that the production remained in Alabama, although every once in a while they would take a break to film short scenes at other locations in the Mobile area.

When the company returned to Hangar 1, it found a seventy-foot-long, black, trapezoidal object sitting in the middle of the Big Set. This was the Mothership—or part of it, anyway. The complete spacecraft would later be built in miniature and matted in over the live-action footage, but a full-size version of the ship's hatch was constructed for use in the scenes in which the returnees (the dozens of people whom the aliens had kidnapped over the years and were now bringing back) and then the aliens emerge from inside the craft. Joe Alves describes how the design for the hatch was originally conceived: "I was working nights, drinking a little scotch at the time, and I took my conical-shaped drawing lamp, put it on my board, turned off the lights, and lifted [the edge] up. [This produced]...a surgical sliver of light. I said 'That's interesting....' So, the next day, I brought Steven in, turned the lights off, put on the music for *2001*...and I said, 'Look at this....' And he said, 'Wow!'" Based on this offbeat inspiration, Alves designed a round hatch that would emit a slash of blinding light as it opened. A hydraulic ramp would then lower to the ground to allow the occupants to exit. Ultimately, there wasn't enough room on the Big Set to build a conical hatch, so Alves opted for a wedge-shaped one instead. The hatch had to be rock steady, because any movement would blur the matte line that joined it to the miniature Mothership in the visual effects shots. For this reason, Alves decided to construct the hatch using steel beams rather than the usual wood, which had a tendency to warp and wobble. The finished structure was covered in black velvet and weighed an incredible forty thousand pounds.

The filming of the second part of The Experience began with the live-action portion of the scene in which the Mothership rises up from behind Devils Tower and moves into position over Box Canyon. According to the final draft of the script, the Mothership was supposed to be a big, black shape that blocked out the light of the stars, so a number of shots were made that showed an ominous dark shadow falling over the landing zone. For the scene in which the Mothership actually lands, the hatch was lifted into the air by two cranes and then lowered back down to the stage floor as the cameras rolled. The process was reversed to film the shots of the Mothership lifting off at the end of the film. As originally conceived, the Mothership was supposed to generate a low-gravity zone around itself, so several shots were filmed of landing zone personnel—including a technician in a wheelchair—floating up into the air (the actors were flown on wires rigged by Roy Arbogast and his crew). A scene was storyboarded in which Roy Neary gets caught up in the zone and has to be rescued by Lacombe, who throws him a rope and pulls him back down to earth, but it was never shot.

Following the touchdown, the company shot the scene in which ARP player Jean-Claude signals the Mothership with the five tones, the Mothership responds, and then the two engage in a joyful, escalating jam session. The colorboard was featured prominently in this scene. A full-scale version of Joe Alves's innovative design had been constructed on the Big Set out of wood, metal, and plastic. Gels were added to the board's seventy-two rectangles to give them color. In the film, whenever Jean-Claude presses a key on the ARP, one of the rectangles lights up on the colorboard. In reality, the synthesizer wasn't connected to the board. In fact, it wasn't even turned on. During filming, actor Phil Dodds was simply pantomiming, making movements to match the music track that John Williams had pre-recorded for the "duel." The colorboard was activated by another keyboard player hidden inside one of the cubicles on the Big Set. He was playing a specially constructed piano that had seventy-two keys. Wires connected each key to one of the rectangles on the colorboard, and the keyboardist played the notes in sync with the music track. Whenever he pressed a key on the piano, the corresponding rectangle would light up on the board.

Once the jam session was over, it was time for the hatch to open for the very first time. To create the required sliver of light, five thousand photoflood bulbs had been installed on the inside of the massive trapezoidal structure and aimed down at the ramp, which had been covered in reflective Mylar so that it could bounce the light out onto the set. However, while the photofloods certainly generated an enormous amount of illumination, they didn't provide the character of light that Steven and Vilmos were after. The storyboards showed dozens of individual rays of illumination streaming out of the open hatchway, but the photofloods gave them one great big blob of light instead. To create the multi-ray look, they needed to use directed light, so Zsigmond replaced the photofloods with six high-powered HMI spotlights and eight Brutes. Unfortunately, this didn't do the trick, either. Realizing that the smooth Mylar surface of the ramp was reflecting all of the light in the same direction, Zsigmond and his team decided to use hammers to break the Mylar up into different pieces. The individual shards reflected the rays in many directions and finally created the desired look. Zsigmond then overexposed all of the hatch shots by several stops in order to enhance the light's blinding intensity.

As soon as the hatch was open, the returnees emerged from the ship. The first out were three very confused and puzzled pilots from Flight 19. The first—Lt. J.G. Frank Taylor—was played by actor Randy Herman. The second two—Captain Harry Ward Craig and Lt. Matthew McMichaels—were played by Hal Barwood and Matthew Robbins. Barwood describes the grueling process they had to go through to land the parts: "We were working on the script when Steven poked his head into the trailer and said 'Hey, if you guys shave your beards off I'll stick you in the movie.'" The other returnees were played by a variety of people, including members of the crew and friends of the production. Even Steven's dog, Elmer, got into the act—he's the cocker spaniel seen sliding down the ramp next to Barry when the young boy emerges from the Mothership. Because of all of the lights, the interior of the hatch was incredibly hot, so the returnees could only remain inside for a few minutes at the most. To prevent them from slipping on the slick surface of the ramp, all of the returnees wore rubber on the soles of their shoes (some, including a very embarrassed Cary Guffey, wore ballet slippers). In between takes, crew members used mops and Windex to remove any scuff marks from the Mylar so that it would retain its reflective capacity.

After all of the returnees had returned, the ETs disembarked. The Burman Studio had finished the alien masks on schedule and Tom Burman brought them down to Mobile at the beginning of July. Although they had been manufactured to match the design that Steven had approved, when Spielberg saw the finished masks, he felt that they looked much too scary. (Apparently, the little girls from Susan Helfond's ballet class agreed—when they first glimpsed the masks, some of them allegedly screamed and started crying). Steven wanted the masks to be completely redesigned. Since Frank Griffin had already moved on to *Audrey Rose*, it fell to The Burman Studios to design a new look, something Tom Burman (who had only signed on to do a straight manufacturing job) was not at all happy about.

Burman returned to California to begin the redesign. In the meantime, his assistants, David Ayres and Frank Massarella, stayed in Mobile to help Susan Helfond and Kathy Poster (Steven Poster's wife, who had appeared as an extra in the film and then was hired to serve as the production's "ET wrangler") work with Helfond's ballet students to get them used to wearing and working in their ET costumes. Using the rejected masks, the team had the girls practice donning their foam rubber heads and gloves. The masks were extremely uncomfortable and so hot that they could only be worn for ten minutes or so at a time. They were not well ventilated, either, so Ayers and Massarella had to cut holes into the mouths so the children could breathe. Some of the girls had trouble seeing out of the eyeholes and had to peer out of the nostrils instead. And, since the body stockings were seamless, the bathroom was always a problem. For many of the children, none of this was much fun, and after a few days almost half of the original one hundred recruits had dropped out.

Back in Burbank, Tom and Sonny Burman had sculpted several designs for friendlier and less scary alien faces. They sent Polaroids of the new sculptures to Steven, who chose one that he liked and okayed it. The Burmans created new molds for the articulated masks, which were then used to produce new skins to fit over the old mechanized skulls. Since the non-articulated masks were only going to be seen in the background or in wide shots, they didn't need to be altered as extensively, so rather than create new molds, the Burmans simply made a few changes to the existing ones and then used them to produce a whole new batch of slip rubber masks. It took ten days of around-the-clock work to produce the revised heads, which Tom Burman promptly brought to Brookley Field. Although Steven thought the new masks were a definite improvement over the old ones, he still didn't find them convincing and instructed Vilmos Zsigmond to film the ETs using a lot of backlight so that they would appear mostly in silhouette.

Vilmos also decided to overexpose the aliens to further obscure their features. This decision sparked another conflict between Zsigmond and Julia Phillips when, on one occasion, the lab printed one of the overexposed scenes too brightly. As a result, there was almost nothing on the film when it came back from the lab. When Julia saw this, she assumed that Vilmos had screwed up and accused him of ruining a very expensive day's work. Irritated, Vilmos looked at the lab report and saw what had happened. He told Julia to tell the lab technicians to follow his original instructions and print the film darker. They did and the footage came out fine.

The first ET scenes were filmed on July 19, 1976 (the rest were shot in bits and pieces over the next month). The ETs' entrance was easy enough—the girls simply had to walk down the ramp and line up at the foot of the open hatch. Next some shots were made of several ETs flying around in the Mothership's reduced-gravity zone, with some of them doing midair backflips and other acrobatics. To achieve these shots, the little girls were flown on the same wire rigs that Roy Arbogast and his team had previously used to float the adult actors. The company then photographed

a series of vignettes that showed the curious ETs enthusiastically exploring the base of operations—fiddling with equipment, spinning around
in chairs, popping open fizzy cans of Coke, etc. Next, a scene was filmed
that showed the aliens playing with Claude Lacombe, who was depicted as
thoroughly enjoying his interaction with the extraterrestrial beings while
some of the other humans backed away in fear or aversion. The ETs also
had fun with J. Allen Hynek. Hynek had come to Mobile for a visit, and
Spielberg talked him into making a cameo appearance in the film. In his
bit, he was seen reacting with delight as the aliens removed his glasses
and yanked on his tie. One of the ETs even grabbed Hynek's trademark
pipe and tried to stick it up its nose.

Steven wanted to disguise the fact that the aliens were really just people
in costumes, so he kept trying to come up with a way to make them lo-
comote in non-human fashion. One of his first ideas was to have the ETs
make their entrance on roller skates (hidden by fake alien feet) so that it
would appear that they were gliding rather than walking down the ramp.
On another occasion, he decided that the ETs should move at a much
higher rate of speed than the humans did. To create this effect, he hired a
group of mimes to play landing zone technicians and had them perform
the scene in ultra slow motion. The little girls were told to move at normal
speed, and the scene was shot in fast motion. It was hoped that when the
film was projected at a regular frame rate, the humans would appear to
be moving normally while the ETs zipped around at super speed. Unfortunately, neither of these gimmicks worked (the ramp was too steep,
causing the roller ETs to shoot rather than glide down the ramp, and the
movements of all of the performers on the speeded-up film looked much
too herky-jerky), and Spielberg eventually gave up on the whole idea.

The filming of the ET scenes was rough on the little girls. The hours
were long, and working in the suits under the hot lights was exhausting.
(François Truffaut, always a strong champion of children, kept a paternal
eye on the girls. Steven Spielberg remembered an occasion when Truffaut saw one very tired little girl struggling to put on her alien mask. "He
broke ranks, walked over to the little girl, took the mask off her head,
escorted her over to her mother, and then very sweetly said to me: 'You
have forty-nine. You don't need fifty.'"). The girls were prone to bouts of
crankiness when they got tired (at one point, two of the girls got into a
fight that climaxed with one pulling off the other's rubber ET hand and

hitting her over the head with it). Being normal seven-year-olds, the girls had extremely limited attention spans, and as the assignment expanded from two days to eight, more and more of them dropped out, so that by the time the ET scenes wrapped on August 11, only about thirty-five of the original one hundred were left. Still, most of the girls held up pretty well—much better than the boys, who, as it turned out, had a lot less stamina than their female counterparts. In fact, the boys tuckered out so quickly that the crew ended up not using them for most of the shots that they had been hired for. Instead, when the time came to film the close-ups of the articulated masks, the crew found that it was easier to simply stick the masks on their own hands as if they were puppets.

As the rest of the shoot continued, the company would occasionally take a break from filming on the Big Set and move next door to Hangar 2, where Bill Parks and his team had constructed two additional sets: Crescendo Summit—the curved piece of roadway where the UFOs make their first appearance—and the Notch—the point high atop Devils Tower from which Roy and Jillian watch the first part of The Experience.

To create Crescendo Summit, tubular steel scaffolding was erected on a granite base and then covered with fiberglass. An inch of topsoil was spread over that, and then the set was decorated with real trees and plants (the humidity in Hangar 2 was so great that real grass grew on the artificial hilltop). The highway that ran through Crescendo Summit was a real road constructed to bear the weight of Roy Neary's truck and of the three police cruisers that sped through the set during one of the scenes. Cars usually drive at an abnormally slow pace through interior sets because there isn't enough room inside a soundstage for them to accelerate to normal speeds. For this reason, Joe Alves built the roadway so that it extended to the doors on either end of the hangar. This allowed the vehicles to get up to speed outside, enter the hangar and pass through the set at full throttle, and then exit the building before having to slow down. Crescendo Summit was an expensive set—so expensive that the price tag became a source of contention between Joe Alves and the studio. As Alves recalls, when he first showed the executives the clay model he had made of the set, "I told them it was going to cost $250,000. They said, 'You're out of your mind. You're spending too much money. You can't do this.' They only wanted to spend $75,000. And I said "Well, you don't understand—that's the square footage. [It costs] so much a square foot to build [a set]. So, if you don't want that...' and I did a very dramatic thing. I took [a piece of sheet metal] and I cut...[the model]...to pieces until it was this little thing and I said 'There—that's $75,000. Is that what you want?' [And they said] 'Oh, no, no, no, that's okay. All right, build the thing.' You sort of had to do this sometimes...." Despite the cost, the studio got its money's worth out of the set. Aside from the UFOs' first appearance, it was also used to film the scene in which Roy and Ronnie make out while Roy keeps his eyes on the sky, and the scene in which the UFO true believers gather in anticipation of a second sighting only to be scattered by a group of Air Force helicopters.

The Notch was also constructed out of steel scaffolding and fiberglass. The set was cramped and hot, and both Richard Dreyfuss and Melinda Dillon found shooting on it to be incredibly tedious and uncomfortable (Dillon recalled getting shards of fiberglass stuck in her rear end on a regular basis).

As filming continued, the difficult conditions began to wear on everyone. Tempers grew short and people got snippy (which sometimes required second assistant director Jim Bloom, who possessed a very diplomatic temperament, to step in and calm the waters). Some folks began suffering from stress-related conditions (Clark Paylow, for example, had a nasty bout with psoriasis). The slow pace of filming especially tried everyone's patience (Truffaut joked that things were going so slowly that the production had become "im-Mobile-ized"). Some people quit (toward the end, so many of the extras had left that Chuck Meyers kept having to move the remaining ones around from shot to shot so that it would still look like the base of operations was still fully staffed). The rest did what they could to relieve the tedium:

- In addition to watching the movies he screened at his house almost every night, Steven liked to play music (he had an organ in his house and an electric piano in his office) and electronic games. (He played mostly with Richard Dreyfuss. They enjoyed *Tank* and *Gunfighter*, but their favorite was *Pong*, at which Dreyfuss was an undisputed champ). Spielberg also bought a dirt bike, which he and Hal Barwood took turns riding up and down Brookley's deserted runways. And Steven began working on his next picture, inviting screenwriters

Robert Zemeckis and Bob Gale to come to Alabama to work on the script of the World War II homefront comedy *1941*.

• Besides playing electronic games, Richard Dreyfuss hosted a regular poker game at his Mobile apartment. He also involved himself in local civic affairs: the area branch of the Ku Klux Klan had been given permission to march in the city's Bicentennial Fourth of July parade. Outraged, Dreyfuss issued a statement saying that if the Klan had a right to march, then he had a right to protest their existence. Later that same day, he received a death threat. In response, Julia Phillips hired two bodyguards to protect him. (The news that Richard had been threatened worried Bob Balaban because of their close resemblance. Not wanting to end up as a fatal case of mistaken identity, Balaban requested a bodyguard for himself and was not at all pleased when he was told there wasn't enough money in the budget for one. He decided to go home until the holiday and the controversy were over.)

• François Truffaut spent much of his time in his office at Brookley Field reading, working on the script for *L'Homme qui aimait les femmes,* and writing letters to his friends back in France. Recognizing that morale was low, he threw a big party for the entire company that helped to boost everyone's spirits. And, of course, he enjoyed talking about movies. Pat McNamara, who sometimes screened foreign films at his New Orleans playhouse, peppered Truffaut with questions about *L' Histoire d'Adèle H.*, which had enjoyed a successful run at the theater, and Matthew Robbins recalls from one long conversation with François that *The Naked Jungle*, a 1954 Charlton Heston film about a South American plantation threatened by a twenty-mile-long column of army ants, absolutely fascinated the great French director.

• Julia Phillips took flying lessons and was the opening night guest of honor at a local dog track. When he wasn't fearing for his life, Bob Balaban wrote letters to his wife detailing life on *Close Encounters* set. Teri Garr visited many of Mobile's historical sites and museums, and J. Allen Hynek gave a lecture on the UFO phenomenon for interested members of the cast and crew. Many folks followed the 1976 Olympics, which were televised on the ABC television network. Cary Guffey went to the movies—the four-year-old had never seen a film before, and since he was starring in one his parents thought they should show him what all the fuss was about. They decided to get him started with a Walt Disney double-feature of *Bambi* (1942) and *Gus* (1976).

• Those who could left town. Julia Phillips flew to Los Angeles for a few days to play a cameo part of a "rich bitch" in *New York, New York* (1977)—Martin Scorsese's follow-up to *Taxi Driver*. Joe Alves took several trips to Florida to scout locations for his next project, *Jaws 2* (Alves had been signed to serve as production designer, associate producer, and second unit director on the shark sequel). Bob Balaban went home to New York whenever he could, and François Truffaut traveled to Hollywood, where he visited the Larry Edmunds Bookshop, his favorite movie bookstore, and bought a stack of books that he brought back to Mobile and handed out as gifts (each one with a personalized inscription).

• Those who couldn't leave town invited friends and family to visit them. One guest was George Lucas, who had just finished shooting *Star Wars*. Lucas was convinced that *CE3K* was going to be a bigger hit than his movie. Steven felt exactly the opposite. In a gesture of mutual support, they each agreed to give the other 2.5 percent of the profits of their respective films. Some of the other people who came to Mobile were actress Amy Irving, Lucinda Valles (Richard Dreyfuss's girlfriend), Lynne Grossman (Bob Balaban's wife), and Richie Libertini, Melinda Dillon's eight-year-old son. Unfortunately, Richie was the victim of a cruel practical joke when two men called Melinda's hotel room one day when the boy was there alone and told him that they were coming to arrest his mother and put him in a juvenile detention home. Melinda reported the incident and two more bodyguards were hired for her and her son. Thankfully, nothing ever came of the threat. Several

visitors ended up appearing in the movie, including Richard
Dreyfuss's father, Norman (who played a scientist for a few
weeks on the Big Set until he finally got fed up with all the
waiting around and went home to Pasadena), screenwriter
Willard Huyck (who played a technician), and Steven's next
door neighbor, the actor Bruce Williamson (who played one of
the Flight 19 pilots).

- A few members of the company indulged in location romances
(including one between François Truffaut and Teri Garr), while
some pursued less wholesome diversions, including drugs and
alcohol (although not the director, who was then and remains
today staunchly anti-drug).

- Inspired by the subject matter of the movie they were working
on, some folks took to stargazing. One evening, several crew
members reported seeing a UFO hovering about the hangar.
Along with many others, Steven rushed out to take a look, but
by the time he got outside, the object had gone. A few people
were scared, and Steven—having now missed seeing a UFO
for the second time in his life—was disappointed, but many
others took the sighting as a good omen and a sign that they
were on the right track. (The object was later determined to be
a satellite.)

Monday, August 16 was the production's last day on the Big Set. The
main unit filmed Roy Neary's farewell looks to Lacombe and Jillian, followed by his fateful walk up the ramp and into the Mothership. A little
later, they shot Lacombe and Laughlin's reaction to the Mothership's departure, and that was it—after almost two months, the filming of The
Experience had come to an end. After shooting wrapped for the night, the
production had a cake for Bob Balaban (it was his birthday), and the next
day he and Truffaut left Mobile. Soon after, Bill Parks and his crew began
tearing down the Big Set. The extension was removed first—the tarp was
stripped away and the scaffolding dismantled. The black backing was then
peeled away from the set and all of the scientific equipment returned to
the companies it had been rented from. Next, the cubicles, trailers, and
fiberglass rocks were removed from the hangar and the rest of the scaf-

folding was dismantled. Finally, the concrete risers and piles of dirt were scooped up by bulldozers and sold off as fill. A few of the cubicles, trailers, and fiberglass rocks were sent back to The Burbank Studios in the event that they would be needed for reshoots. Clark Paylow sold off the rest at an auction he held after production was over. All of the leftover props, costumes, and set pieces were offered for purchase. As it turned out, the fiberglass rocks were the most popular items—the big ones sold for $15, the little ones for $8.

The company spent its last two weeks in Alabama finishing up work on the Crescendo Summit and Notch scenes. At this point, the production was several weeks behind schedule. Columbia's patience was running out and John Veitch was putting a lot of pressure on Steven and Julia to finish up as soon as possible. As a result, the filming of these final scenes was rushed and some planned effects work was abandoned. At the beginning of September, the Mobile portion of the *Close Encounters* shoot finally wrapped—approximately two weeks behind schedule—and the company left Mobile just before Labor Day. While the production's departure from Wyoming had had a celebratory feel about it, the team now leaving Mobile made a weary retreat. Julia Phillips spoke for many when she said, "We were just happy to get the hell out of there."

CHAPTER 19 | **Back to Los Angeles and on to India**

UPON THEIR RETURN TO LOS ANGELES, the members of the company began focusing on the final phase of principal photography: the trip to India to shoot the scene in which Lacombe and his team first hear the five tones as they are sung by a massive crowd.

The original shooting schedule had called for filming in Alabama until the middle of August, taking a few weeks to prepare, and then traveling to the subcontinent in the middle of September. However, when the Mobile shoot ran long, the overseas expedition had to be pushed back. Steven then decided that he wanted to go to India at the beginning of October in order to attend a religious event nicknamed "The Leper Festival" that was scheduled to occur at that time. During the festival (which is held annually), thousands of pilgrims converge on the city of Benares (now known as Varanasi) so that they can bathe away their sins and ailments in the holy waters of the Ganges River. Spielberg wanted the company to go to Benares and film Lacombe and his team walking among the multitudes. This plan was abandoned when they found out that François Truffaut wasn't going to be available because his film *L'argent de poche* was opening at the New York Film Festival on October 6. As a result, the India shoot was pushed back again—this time to the end of October. Julia had already instructed the members of the company to get their shots (a smallpox inoculation was required, but most people also chose to be immunized against cholera, typhus, and yellow fever) when she found out that Truffaut couldn't go then either because he was supposed to start filming *L'Homme qui aimait les femmes* on October 19. Since Truffaut's shoot was going to last until the end of the year, Steven and Julia decided to postpone the India trip until January 1977. In the meantime, Joe Alves was sent to India to scout locations, but inasmuch as they were going to miss the Benares festival, Alves went to Bombay instead. Steven had decided that, rather than shoot the scene with pilgrims, he wanted to use hundreds of Buddhist monks, so Alves (with the help of a local production manager named Baba Shaik) found some suitably exotic locations (including several temples) and made arrangements for the production to rent a large number of saffron robes from a local manufacturer.

While Joe was busy overseas, Steven began rethinking his aliens. He had not been happy with the look of the articulated ET masks and wanted to reshoot their scenes with a more believable substitute. Working with George Jensen, Steven came up with an entirely new extraterrestrial design that was considerably different from the one he had worked on with Frank Griffin and the Burman brothers. Instead of being squat, bulbous-headed, and gray, the new creature was taller (approximately five feet) and thinner, with an extremely long neck and transparent skin through which its internal organs were visible. It had arms long enough to wrap around a human being several times, as well as the ability to project light beams out of its eyes. Rather than use an actor in a costume, Steven wanted to realize the new alien as a puppet. Doug Trumbull came up with a design for a rod puppet that could be attached to a computer-controlled mechanical device. The device would operate the rods and could be programmed to allow the puppet to make a series of elaborate moves and gestures. Unfortunately, the cost of the system was approximately $100,000, which was more than the production could afford at that point, so they didn't proceed with it.

Steven then considered bringing the alien to life as a sophisticated hand puppet. He contacted Muppet maestro Jim Henson and asked him to build the creature, but Henson wasn't interested. Finally, Steven decided to approach Bob Baker. Baker had begun his career as a puppet maker and animator on producer George Pal's *Puppetoon* shorts in the 1940s. Baker went on to do puppet-oriented creature effects for films such as *Monster from the Ocean Floor* (1954), *Angry Red Planet* (1960), *Tom Thumb* (1958), and *Bedknobs and Broomsticks* (1971), and the television series *Star Trek, Voyage to the Bottom of the Sea,* and *Wild Wild West.* In 1961, Baker opened his own theater in downtown Los Angeles, where he staged elaborate shows featuring a cast of superbly crafted marionettes. Spielberg commissioned Baker to create a prototype for a marionette version of the new extraterrestrial. If it proved successful, then Baker would be commissioned to produce seven more of the string-operated creatures. Since it was going to take Baker several months to fabricate the prototype, Spielberg decided to shoot the new ET scenes after he got back from India. As filming was now going to last until at least the end of January 1977, it was obvious that *Close Encounters* was not going to be ready by Easter, so Columbia decided to push the film's release back to the summer.

With several months to kill before the final scenes of the film could be shot, the production moved forward in other areas. Editing and special effects work got under way, and a small second unit was sent to Washington, D.C., to film ABC News anchorman Howard K. Smith's portion of the Devils Tower newscast. Unfortunately, what should have been a quiet autumn was upset by a rash of bad publicity surrounding Julia. Phillips had proven to be a controversial member of the production. Smart, sharp, and savvy, with good taste, a great eye for talent and material, strong business and negotiating skills, and relentless zeal when it came to pursuing her goals, Julia was considered by many to be an excellent producer. She believed passionately in *Close Encounters* and was a tireless fighter for the film. During the project's long gestation period, she continued to push its development, even when others involved were ready to give up.

During the shoot she went to great lengths (including returning repeatedly to the studio to ask for more money) to provide Steven and the rest of the creative team with the resources they needed to make the film the way they saw fit. She also served as a strong liaison to Columbia and kept the executives focused on the film's potential whenever the rising costs and elastic schedule prompted them to panic and contemplate pulling the plug. In addition to her considerable talents, Julia had a very forceful personality. She was fiercely opinionated and extremely blunt—she was not afraid to ask pointed questions, did not mince words, and called things as she saw them, often using language laced with a level of profanity that John Landis once described as "satanic." In no way demure (she once tried to have a script meeting with John Hill while she was sunbathing topless, but he insisted, much to her annoyance, that she get dressed first), she had a ribald sense of humor, threw great parties, and could be great fun to be around.

Unfortunately, she could also be very difficult to be around. Julia's blunt manner, while refreshing to some, was upsetting and offensive to others. She had a short fuse and would berate people when she got angry, even for things that were not their fault (Joe Alves recalls a time when Julia screamed at him at length about a problem with the lighting on the Big Set, which was not Joe's area of responsibility. When he pointed this out to her, she screamed even louder. These actions alienated a lot of people who worked on the film, including François Truffaut, who did not care for the rough way Phillips treated many members of the company, especially Vilmos Zsigmond, with whom he was close. Truffaut also felt that many of the problems and delays on the film were due to the fact that Julia was disorganized and unprepared.

As time went on, Julia's moods became increasingly erratic (a few members of the production recall watching her go from ranting and raving to sobbing uncontrollably in a matter of moments), and there were times when the people around her were convinced that she was having a nervous breakdown. Although some felt that Julia's difficult and odd behavior was a reaction to all of the incredible stress and pressure she was under, most attributed it to her drug use, which, as she herself later admitted, had begun to get seriously out of hand in Mobile. By the time the production returned to Los Angeles, Julia was in the grip of a full-blown addiction to cocaine, and rumors about her involvement with drugs began to spread around Hollywood.

The negative publicity began in October when François Truffaut bad-mouthed Julia in the pages of the *New York Times*. In an interview given to promote the opening of *L'argent de poche*, Truffaut said of Phillips: "She is incompetent. Unprofessional. You can write that. She knows I feel this way." Actually, Julia did not know that Truffaut felt that way and only discovered it along with the rest of entertainment community in New York and Hollywood when she read it in the paper. Hoping to repair the damage, both Julia and the studio asked Steven to write a letter to the *Times* expressing support for her. Steven agreed and composed a missive that characterized Truffaut's remarks as "rather unkind," adding that "knowing him as I do, it is hard for me to believe that he said these things. I have never had such constructive and consistent support from a producer as I have had from Julia Phillips, and I know that Columbia Pictures concurs." (Julia later complained that Steven's statement of support had not been as strong as she had hoped it would be. Some members of the production have suggested that if Spielberg's response was a bit lukewarm, it may have been because Julia's behavior was become increasingly difficult for him to deal with—he had to spend a lot of time smoothing the feathers that she had ruffled and her antics were starting to interfere with the movie's progress.)

The *Times* published Spielberg's letter in November, by which time the damage had already been done. Bad turned to worse a few weeks later when Julia was stopped by the police for driving erratically. When the two officers who pulled her over smelled marijuana smoke in the car, they searched the vehicle and discovered a small vial of cocaine. Julia was arrested for driving under the influence and drug possession. Since she had not actually been smoking while in the car (the smell was on her clothes) and because the vial was empty except for a small bit of coke dust, Julia's lawyer was able to get the charges dropped and have the arrest expunged. However, the incident was reported by Hollywood gossip columnist Rona Barrett on ABC's *Good Morning America* program a few days later, giving the production yet another black eye.

The production had one more unpleasant moment in December, although this one had nothing to do with Julia. The script of *Close Encounters* included a sequence in which Roy Neary joins three police cruisers as they chase after the trio of scout UFOs following the Crescendo Summit encounter. Neary and the cops chase the saucers through a tollbooth and then follow them to the edge of a cliff. The UFOs sail off into the sky as one of the police cars—whose driver has his eyes on the spaceship instead of the road—crashes through a guardrail and goes over the cliff. The sequence ends with Roy and the two other policemen screeching to a halt at the edge of the cliff and watching with mouth agape as the UFOs vanish into the clouds. The beginning and the end of the chase had been shot on the Crescendo Summit set in Hangar 2 at Brookley during the summer. A few weeks before Christmas, the main unit reassembled in San Pedro, California (just south of Los Angeles), to film the rest of the sequence.

When it did, a key member of the team was missing—Vilmos Zsigmond. After all of the trouble in Mobile, Vilmos wasn't sure he was going to be asked back to finish the rest of the movie, but Steven assured him that he would be (and in fact sent Zsigmond to get his shots for the India trip). When the time came to film the chase scene, however, noted cinematographer John A. Alonzo (*Harold and Maude* [1971], *Chinatown* [1974], *The Bad News Bears* [1976]) was hired to do the job instead. Vilmos was never told why he was not asked to return, but he suspects that Julia and Columbia simply refused to let Spielberg rehire him. Unfortunately, no one notified Zsigmond that he was off the picture, and when Vilmos heard that another cinematographer had been hired to replace him, he was extremely hurt.

The tollbooth scene was filmed at the Vincent Thomas Bridge in San Pedro. The next night, the company filmed the scene in which one of the police cruisers crashes through a guardrail and goes over the cliff. It took several days to prepare the stunt, which, as designed, was supposed to end with the police car landing on the embankment below the cliff and then barreling down the hillside until it skidded to a stop in a gully at the bottom. In order to launch the police cruiser at an angle that would allow it to sail smoothly off the road and touch down safely on the hill, stunt coordinator Buddy Joe Hooker asked Joe Alves to have his team construct a ramp with a two-foot elevation, which Alves did. Stunt man Craig R. Baxley was brought in to do the actual jump. There are differing accounts as to what happened next.

Some people associated with the production claim that John Alonzo requested that the ramp be raised because he wanted to have the police car make a higher arc when it left the cliff in order to produce a more dramatic image for each of the five cameras he was using to cover the stunt. Others claim that the ramp wasn't raised, but that when the time came for Baxley to drive off of it, he went much faster than he was supposed to. Still others assert that both are true: Alonzo asked that the ramp be raised, and Baxley drove off of it too fast. No matter what happened beforehand, all agree that when the police car drove off the cliff, it arced too high, overshot its mark, and slammed down onto the hillside. The impact destroyed the car, and all of those watching felt certain that Baxley had been killed. As it turned out, he survived and was rushed to the hospital, where it was discovered that he had sustained a concussion, damaged his back and legs, and crushed his heel. Luckily, he recovered, and the stunt ultimately stayed in the film.

In mid-December, not long after the San Pedro shoot concluded, Joe Alves left the production and reported to Universal to begin work on *Jaws 2*. A short time later, Steven found another solution to his ET dilemma.

Attending a screening of producer Dino De Laurentiis' remake of *King Kong*, Spielberg was impressed by the incredible articulated masks that had been used to bring Kong '76 to life. The masks had been designed and fabricated by makeup artist Rick Baker (who wore the masks and played Kong in the film) and mechanized by Italian artist and special effects technician Carlo Rambaldi, although only Rambaldi had received credit for the work. Born in Vigarano, Italy in 1925, Rambaldi attended the Academy of Fine Arts of Bologna and went on to win many awards for his dramatic paintings and drawings. He entered the Italian film industry in the early 1960s as a prop maker and worked on a string of films including *Barrabas* (1961) and *The Bible* (1966). In 1968, Rambaldi worked with special effects director Gerard Cogan on *Barbarella*. Cogan was a toy maker and special effects artist who had devised innovative ways of using cable-controlled mechanical devices to animate toys and props. On *Barbarella*, he used his innovations to bring the vicious mechanical dolls that attack Jane Fonda to life.

Rambaldi improved upon Cogan's techniques in subsequent projects, and earned a reputation as an expert creator of cable-controlled articulated props (his proudest achievement was a life-size wooden Pinocchio that he created for an Italian television special). De Laurentiis was a great admirer of Rambaldi and brought him to America to work with Baker on *Kong*. In the early part of January 1977, Spielberg called Rambaldi at his studio in Rome and asked him to create an articulated ET puppet for *Close Encounters*. Returning to his original concept, Steven wanted Rambaldi to design a creature that was four feet tall with a large head and slender arms and legs. Rambaldi developed a concept that met with Steven's approval and then set to work building the puppet, a task that would take him several months.

At this point, the company was supposed to leave for India, but at the last minute the trip was pushed back once again—this time to the end of February. This additional delay meant that the inoculations people had received back in October were no longer valid, so anyone going to India had to be immunized all over again. Not wanting to have to get a third round of injections should the trip be postponed yet again, Bob Balaban refused to get any more shots until he was actually holding his plane ticket in his hand. As it turned out, a third round wasn't going to be necessary, because this time they were really going. However, it was decided that, apart from the actors, the only members of the main unit who would travel to India would be Steven, Julia, and Jim Bloom (Chuck Meyers had gone on to another film, so Spielberg asked Bloom to replace Meyers as his first assistant director). The camera and sound teams would be hired out of London, and the rest of the crew would be recruited in India and paid with Columbia's frozen rupees (India has a large indigenous motion picture industry, so there were plenty of experienced film workers available).

To photograph the Indian sequence, Steven hired renowned British cinematographer Douglas Slocombe. Born on February 10, 1913, Slocombe began his career as a journalist. He starting taking pictures to illustrate his stories and soon was selling his photographs to newspapers, magazines, and wire services. He moved into motion pictures when he shot some footage of the Nazi domination of Danzig and the German invasion of Poland for a documentary called *Lights Out in Europe* (1940). During World War II, Slocombe was based at Ealing Studios and assigned to shoot footage for combat documentaries and propaganda films.

After the war, Slocombe began working full time at Ealing, serving as the director of photography on many of that studio's classic postwar comedies, including *Kind Hearts and Coronets* (1949), *The Man in the White Suit* (1951), and *The Lavender Hill Mob* (1951). After seventeen years and thirty-five films, Slocombe left the Ealing studio and began working freelance on dozens of British and American productions such as *Freud* (1962), *The L-Shaped Room* (1962), *The Blue Max* (1966), *The Fearless Vampire Killers* (1967), *The Music Lovers* (1970), *Jesus Christ Superstar* (1973), and *Rollerball* (1975). He was nominated for an Academy Award for his work on *Travels with My Aunt* (1973) and won a BAFTA award for Best Cinematography for *The Servant* (1963) and *The Great Gatsby* (1974). A big fan of Slocombe's work, Steven contacted him early in 1977 and asked him to photograph the Indian portion of *Close Encounters*. Having just finished work on Fred Zinneman's *Julia* (1977), Slocombe was available and happily agreed.

Steven, Julia, and Jim left California on February 19, 1977. They flew to New York and then to London, where they met up with Douglas Slocombe and his crew—camera operator Chick Waterston and camera assistant Robin Vidgeon—and with veteran British sound mixer John Mitchell (*Hamlet* [1948], *The African Queen* [1951], *The Bridge on the River Kwai* [1957], and many James Bond movies), who had been engaged to record the location sound. From there the company flew to Bombay (now Mumbai). They arrived at three o'clock in the morning on February 21, 1977 and checked into the Hotel Taj Mahal, a luxurious palace that was an exact replica of the real Taj Mahal. There they met up with production manager Baba Shaik, who had been busy putting together the Indian crew and working out the logistics of the shoot. The Westerners had a hard time adjusting to India. They were troubled by the incredible poverty and squalor that they saw all around them and were extremely suspicious of the food and water. Still, there were so many exotic sights, sounds, and smells to take in that Jim Bloom called the country "an invasion of the senses."

On February 22 the production team traveled out to the primary location to prepare for filming. Although Joe Alves had found many wonderful places to film during his scouting trip a few months earlier, ultimately none of them were used. Instead, the concept for the scene was simplified and the decision was made to film the sequence on a desolate hillside on the outskirts of Hal, a small, impoverished village thirty-five miles from Bombay. When the team returned to the hotel that evening, they met up with François Truffaut, Bob Balaban, and Lance Henriksen, who had arrived in the country that day. (Still in the midst of their feud, François and Julia made it a point to stay as far away from one another as possible.) That night, Columbia held a big press conference during which the company answered questions posed by members of the Indian media. Much of the next day was spent trying to free the unit's cameras and film from the clutches of the Indian customs agents who had impounded the equipment because they said they were concerned that the company planned to sell it (which was illegal) rather that use it to film a movie. It took Baba Shaik many hours (and allegedly a few payoffs) to convince them otherwise.

Filming began on February 24. The sequence was fairly simple: Lacombe and his team arrive in Hal and find the villagers gathered on a hillside singing the five tones. As Mayflower Project sound technicians record their voices, a local holy man—at Lacombe's request—asks the villagers where the sounds came from. In response, they all point to the sky in unison. As simple as the scene was, the three-day shoot was not an easy one. To begin with, the conditions in Hal were difficult: it was extremely hot and humid (the average temperature was 100 degrees), and amenities were scarce—there were no trailers for the members of the company to repair to between shots (they had to sit on empty camera boxes instead), the only bathrooms were outhouses, and the food left much to be desired. Making matters worse, on the first day of filming several members of the company, including François Truffaut and Jim Bloom, collapsed from heat exhaustion. Truffaut recovered in a few hours, but Bloom became so ill that he missed the rest of the shoot. Later that afternoon, Chick Waterston fell and cut a deep gash into his forehead.

Baba Shaik had recruited two thousand locals to serve as extras in the scene and working with them wasn't easy, either:

- Early in the sequence, there is a shot in which hundreds of villagers run across a field toward the hill. Rehearsals went well, but when the cameras started turning, a large majority of the locals ran off in the opposite direction. It turned out that a rabbit had run across the field and the locals had gone chasing after it, hoping to catch a tasty dinner.

- It took several hours to get the villagers situated for the big hillside scene. Once they were set, it was time for lunch, so the crew put markers down on the ground so that everyone would know just what position to take when they returned from the break. Unfortunately, most of the villagers picked up their marks and took them with them when they went to get their food. As a result, the entire scene needed to be reset.

- The Indian choral leader who had been hired to lead the villagers in the singing of the five tones kept getting the notes wrong, so the extras spent take after take happily singing the incorrect music.

- When it came time for the villagers to point to the sky, it took hours to get them all to point in the same direction at the same time and not to lower their hands before the take was over.

Despite these difficulties, the shoot yielded some pleasant surprises. Spielberg was thrilled with the work of the British technicians. Steven had initially been reluctant to use an English crew, because in those days U.K. film workers had a reputation for being more interested in drinking tea than they were in working hard, but he quickly found out that this was not the case at all. The Englishmen were incredibly hard and fast workers, and the quality of their work was superb. Steven was so pleased with Slocombe and his team that he ended up using them on all three of his Indiana Jones movies. The Brits enjoyed working with Spielberg as well. "I found it extremely easy to get on with [Steven]," Douglas Slocombe recalls. "I found him very inventive and a wonderful charmer and I enjoyed it immensely talking to him. He was very open to suggestions. If I felt that I would have liked to have had something different or to do something he was completely open. He would change things if necessary, but generally I just found him tremendously competent and one knew that he knew exactly what he wanted." Spielberg was also pleased with the work of Baba Shaik, who by all accounts did an expert job of organizing the shoot.

Filming ended on February 26 and the company left India late that night. Although there were a few minor inserts and pickup shots that still needed to be completed, principal photography on *Close Encounters of the Third Kind* had officially come to an end.

CHAPTER 20 | Special Photographic Effects, Part I: Clouds, Miniatures, and Matte Paintings

THE CREATION OF *Close Encounters'* special photographic effects ran parallel to the production of the live-action portions of the film. As soon as Douglas Trumbull signed on to the project in January 1976, he and Richard Yuricich began putting together a state-of-the-art photographic effects workshop. Yuricich began by acquiring a number of pieces of 65mm motion picture equipment, including three Mitchell cameras, four Todd-AO cameras, two Houston Fearless cameras, an editing machine, and an optical printer. Because the 65mm format was no longer in wide use, he was able to purchase the lot for the bargain price of just $75,000. Richard also bought, in just one day, $30,000 worth of lights and grip equipment. To house these acquisitions, Future General leased a 13,500-square-foot warehouse located at 4094 Glencoe Avenue in Marina Del Rey, just around the corner from the company's main office, and with the help of Robert Shepherd— an experienced production manager who had just finished setting up the original Industrial Light & Magic facility for the *Star Wars* photographic effects team headed by John Dykstra—Richard began converting it into a production workshop. Yuricich and Shepherd supervised the construction of a warren of rooms in which to do the effects photography and the optical processing. They also set up a machine shop (run by George Polkinghorne) and a model shop and installed a black-and-white film processor (for developing film tests in-house) and a power generator. In need of more room, they rented another building a few doors down from the main workshop. Nicknamed "the Annex," this second space housed the animation department and contained a projection room for screening dailies.

To staff the facility, Trumbull and Yuricich hired an eclectic mix of seasoned professionals and eager young novices. Doug was the team's leader—he developed the creative concepts, determined the technical approach that they would take to realize each shot, and then directed the overall work. Richard was the day-to-day supervisor—in addition to his photographic duties, he marshaled the staff, tracked the progress of every element of every shot as they all made their way through the production process, and planned and oversaw their final compositing. Both men were ideally suited for their jobs. Trumbull's prodigious combination of mechanical and creative talents made him uniquely suited to head an effort that used technology to produce art. When asked to identify the single most important factor in the success of *CE3K*'s effects, Yuricich said it was "the creative lead supplied by Douglas. Without his ideas, his innovations, and his vision we would have had nothing." Meanwhile, Yuricich, whom Trumbull described at the time as being "the most gifted photographer working today," had an unparalleled understanding of the science and craft of cinematography and an exact attention to detail without which, Trumbull said, "*Close Encounters* would have been impossible." The duo's goal was to produce high-quality effects that were down-to-earth realistic and out-of-this-world spectacular at the same time.

Front Projection

Future General's first task was to develop a 65mm front-projection system that could be used to film the Crescendo Summit scenes. Since Crescendo Summit had been built as an interior, a background depicting the Indiana countryside at night needed to be added to the set. Rather than use a painted scenic backdrop, Trumbull wanted to utilize a process background—moving images (called "plates") projected onto a screen positioned behind the set—to create a more realistic image. There are two main forms of process photography: rear projection, in which the plates are projected onto a translucent screen from behind, and front projection, in which the plates are thrown from a forward position onto a screen made of Scotchlite, a highly reflective material manufactured by the 3M Company. Covered with millions of microscopic glass beads, Scotchlite is capable of reflecting any light projected onto it back to the source in a straight line at almost a thousand times its original intensity. This allows the background plate and any object placed in front of the screen to be photographed together in an almost perfect composite. The only catch is that, since the background plate is beamed directly back at its source, the camera and the projector have to occupy exactly the same physical space in order for the process to work.

As this isn't possible, the camera is set up directly in front of the screen and the projector is placed at a ninety-degree angle to the camera. The background plate is then projected onto the screen through a beam-splitter—a half-silvered mirror positioned at a forty-five-degree angle in front of the camera lens. The mirror reflects the light from the projector onto the screen, which in turn bounces it back at the camera. The light used to illuminate the foreground object washes out any part of the projection that might appear on it, and, since the foreground object is between the camera and the screen, it blocks its own shadow and prevents that shadow from being photographed. Front projection has its challenges—it takes a long time to set up a shot, and the camera can be panned and tilted only minimally. Done properly, however, it provides a result that is far superior to other forms of process photography. Trumbull was a big proponent of front projection, having used it extensively and successfully on both 2001 and Silent Running.

To create the system, the camera technicians used the movement (the internal mechanics that move film past the lens) from one of the 65mm cameras to construct a projector. Doug's father Don "Pappy" Trumbull, who engineered a number of special pieces of equipment for the production (John Russell and Fries Engineering also did some engineering work on the project), then developed a mechanism that connected the projector to a 35mm movie camera so that they would run together in interlock (this would prevent image flicker). Some years earlier, Future General had developed a slide projector that could front-project eight-by-ten still-frame images. So that they would have a backup system in place in case the moving-image front-projection system didn't work, Richard Yuricich asked Don to modify the slide projector—which had been designed to have a 35mm movie camera mounted to it—so that it could accommodate a 65mm movie camera. Meanwhile, Robert Shepherd supervised the creation of a large (one hundred feet wide and thirty-seven feet tall) front-projection screen. A frame was constructed out of tubular steel, and then a giant sheet of Scotchlite was stretched across it. Once the screen was finished, it was shipped to Alabama and set up in Hangar 2. To extend the backing further, a second screen (thirty-seven by thirty-seven feet) was set up alongside the first, with a strip of Scotchlite placed over them to hide the join.

Because it wasn't possible to photograph a sufficiently detailed image of the Indiana countryside at night, the Future General team decided to create the background plates by photographing a twelve-foot-by-five-foot model of the Midwestern landscape instead. As all of the miniatures featured in the film would be, this landscape was created by a model-making team headed by Gregory Jein. Having earned a degree in fine arts from the Los Angeles State College of Applied Arts and Sciences, Jein began his career working in public relations and then got a job fabricating fiberglass props for the *Chicken of the Sea* show at Sea World of San Diego. Following that, he built models for the low-budget features *Flesh Gordon* (1974) and *Dark Star* (1974), then went to work for Cascade Pictures creating miniatures for numerous television commercials. Doug Trumbull saw a spaceship model that Jein had built for *Dark Star* on display at a science fiction convention and hired him soon afterward to work on a test reel he was making for *Journey of the Oceanauts*. When that project stalled, Greg went to work for Magicam, a company set up by Paramount Pictures to make use of Doug's innovative video compositing system, where he built models for a number of projects (including an invisible plane for the *Wonder Woman* television pilot and a UFO for a 1975 TV movie about alien abduction called *The UFO Incident*) before going back to commercials. Jein was working on a Hunt's Tomato Catsup ad when Bob Shepherd called and invited him to work on *Close Encounters*. Accepting the invitation, Jein headed up a team that included J. Richard Dow, Kenneth Swenson, Michael McMillen, Jor Van Kline, Robert Worthington, Lorne Peterson, John Erlund, and consultant Peter Anderson. Jein and company would eventually create a series of miniature landscapes for *Close Encounters*, as well as a miniature Devils Tower, a selection of UFOs, and even a fully operational miniature helicopter.

To construct the Crescent Summit miniature, Jein first made a slide out of a black-and-white drawing of the landscape by production illustrator Dan Goozeē. The slide was projected (from the same angle that the 65mm camera would later use to photograph it) onto a large table, the surface of which had been painted white. A tracing of Goozeē's drawing was made on the tabletop and used as the foundation for a forced-perspective model fabricated from plaster and papier-mâché and detailed with real plants and dirt. When the model was completed, Richard Yuricich photographed it on 65mm motion picture film from nine different angles to produce plates that would be compatible with any angle the main unit chose to shoot from. After Yuricich was finished, photographer Marcia Reid shot the model from the same nine angles using an eight-by-ten still camera. Color enlargements made from these stills were retouched by airbrush artist Cy Didjurgis to add horizon haze, stars, and distant lights to the images. The enhanced eight-by-tens were then rephotographed onto Ektachrome transparency film so that they could be projected.

The Clouds

The team's next major challenge was to develop a method for creating the cloudbanks that the UFOs use for cover in several scenes in the movie. Although movie special effects experts had been producing artificial cloud formations on screen for years, Doug was stumped as to how to create the self-generating ones called for in the *Close Encounters* script and storyboards until one morning during pre-production when he poured cream into his coffee and noticed that it billowed out into the java exactly as he wanted the clouds to billow out into the sky. To find out if it would be possible to generate the same effect on a larger scale, a number of different liquids would have to be tested in a number of different combinations. Busy preparing for the start of shooting, Trumbull didn't have time to experiment, so he handed the assignment to his assistant—a nineteen-year-old from Monticello, Indiana, named Scott Squires.

When the Glencoe Avenue workshop was first gearing up, Bob Shepherd hired two young men to work for the company as "gofers" (production assistants). The first, a twenty-five-year-old UCLA film school graduate named Glenn Erickson, would go on to do several jobs on the film, including projecting dailies, serving as an interim special effects editorial clerk, taking behind-the-scenes photographs, production managing an insert shoot, and assisting Greg Jein's modelmaking team. The second was Squires, a fantasy and special effects film fan who began making his own animated movies in the tenth grade. After graduating from high school, Scott came to California to take the entrance exam for a movie industry–sponsored program designed to train participants to be assistant cameramen. Squires wasn't accepted, so he began knocking on the doors of various production companies looking for work. Aware that Douglas Trumbull was about to begin a new project, David Allen and Bill Hedges at Cascade Productions referred Scott to Future General, where he was hired to be Doug's assistant. He was given the cloud-testing assignment on his very first day on the job.

Armed with twenty dollars from petty cash, Squires went to a grocery store and bought a variety of liquids, including milk, cream, rubbing alcohol, and paint, which he then began to mix together in a small twenty-gallon aquarium. After much experimentation, he came up with an approach that involved injecting white tempera paint (made by mixing powdered tempera with fresh water) into a tank filled with a layer of salt water and a layer of fresh water. Squires explains, "The bottom layer was salt water and the top layer was fresh water. Salt water is heavier than fresh water so it stays on the bottom. The two layers were invisible to the camera, [although] you could sometimes see the layer edge by eye if you got in just the right position. When the tempera paint was injected into the fresh water it would look like cream in your coffee, but the salt water layer would prevent it from going any lower into the tank [because it was heavier than the paint], so that meant the clouds would rest or 'float' half way down. This created the same [look that you see]...when clouds form at a specific altitude."

Trumbull approved Scott's approach and decided to move forward with it. A San Diego company that built many of the tanks for Marineland was commissioned to build a seven-foot-by-five-foot, two-thousand-gallon glass tank. The tank was backed with black velvet and outfitted with a paint injector made from a modified pressure cooker. A compressor was attached to the cooker to create the pressure. An aquarium hose connected the cooker to an electronic valve, which itself was linked to another hose that was tipped with a narrow, L-shaped, brass tube. This was the paint jet. The jet was held by a mechanical arm of the sort used in laboratories and atomic energy plants to handle contaminated substances (Trumbull had seen a similar arm used in a scene in *The Andromeda Strain* and had become fascinated with its possible applications for effects work). Two large (six feet tall and six feet in diameter) redwood hot tubs were set up nearby to store the water that would be used to fill the tank. One of the tanks held fresh water and the other salt water (made by mixing large bags of pure salt with fresh tap water). The water in both tanks was filtered for a minimum of twenty-four hours to strain out impurities.

Scott Squires describes what would happen when it came time to make a shot: "We'd fill the tank half full of salt water. Next a sheet of thin black plastic tarp was placed on top of the water and then we'd slowly fill the rest of the tank with fresh water. When it was filled, we'd slowly remove the plastic by pulling it up around a horizontal pipe in the water (this way it would glide out sideways and not disturb the two layers much). The idea was not to mix the water together, otherwise the paint would just swirl and drop to the bottom. We then mixed the paint right before photography in a blender [because we found that premixed liquid tempera didn't work as well]...and poured it into [the] pressure cooker." Doug Trumbull would stand in front of the tank next to the camera, use the mechanical arm to move the jet into position, and press a button on the arm's pistol grip that activated the valve and released the paint. Trumbull would then move the jet around in a variety of patterns to make the clouds while Richard Yuricich photographed them. For some shots, Squires or another technician would use a large hand syringe to inject paint into the back of the tank (an area that the mechanical arm couldn't reach) to create small clouds behind the big ones, thus generating a forced-perspective look that made it seem as if the banks were stretching far out to the horizon.

Lights were suspended (by veteran grip Ray Rich and effects electrician David Gold) above the tank to simulate the light of the moon and flickered to create heat lightning. For shots in which the lights of the UFOs were to be seen moving around inside the clouds, fiber optics were threaded down through the injector tube and pushed out the end of the jet. (A fiber optic is an extremely thin, flexible glass tube that transmits light. One end of the tube is placed in front of a light source—a bulb, a lamp, etc. The light from the source travels through the tube and illuminates the far end. Fiber optics are often used to create tiny practical lights in miniatures.) On other occasions, light bulbs would be placed on the ends of metal tubes (through which electrical wires would be threaded), stuck into the water, and moved around in the tempera. The clouds were filmed at various speeds, depending on how fast they needed to move through a scene. Sometimes shots of separate groups of clouds were superimposed over one another in order to create more complex formations. By the time a shot was finished, the tank would be filled with paint, at which point it would be drained, scrubbed clean, and refilled with water. This was a very time-consuming process, so the team could only make an average of two cloud shots a day. It took approximately two months of on-again, off-again filming to complete them all.

The screening of the initial cloud tank shots for Steven Spielberg and Julia Phillips—the first photographic effects footage that either of them saw—was a triumphant event for Doug Trumbull and Future General. Trumbull believes that until that point Spielberg and Phillips weren't completely confident that he and his team were going to be able to deliver the high quality of photographic effects that they had promised. This lack of confidence appeared to be justified as the film began and the audience was faced with nothing but a black screen. "Where are they?" Julia called out. All of a sudden, a single cloud appeared in the distance and began billowing outward in a truly spectacular display. From that moment, with the entire audience amazed, Doug felt that Steven and Julia finally began to trust him. "That was," he recalls, "one of the most fun moments for me."

Going Mobile

In May 1976, as the rest of the team scrambled to get Future General up and running, Trumbull and Yuricich traveled to Wyoming with the main unit. While there, they filmed a series of 65mm shots—including several of Devils Tower—to which visual effects would later be added. The duo then followed the company to Mobile, where they supervised all of the 65mm photography (including the high-angle views of the base camp, which were filmed from positions they had selected). Doug and Richard also worked with Steven, Vilmos Zsigmond, Earl Gilbert, and Roy Arbogast to develop the interactive lighting and mechanical effects for the various UFO shots, and were integrally involved in the filming of the Crescendo Summit scenes, most of which required the use of the 65mm front-projection system.

Unfortunately, the 65mm motion-picture projector didn't work as well as they had hoped it would—the machine was very noisy, and the interlock between the camera and the projector turned out to be unreliable. It also proved to be extremely difficult to balance the foreground lighting with all of the incredibly brilliant light coming off of the Scotchlite screen. In Trumbull's view, all of these bugs could have been worked out, but he was unable to get Julia and Clark Paylow to give him the crew, the lights, and the stage time he needed to set up the shots and solve the problems in advance of shooting. The bulk of the Crescendo Summit scenes had been slated for the end of the Mobile shoot, and when the time came to film them, the production was behind schedule and over budget. The studio was pressing the company to wrap things up as quickly as possible, so the team decided to abandon the moving plates and to use the eight-by-ten transparencies—which were much simpler and therefore much faster to set up—instead. In contrast to the 65mm moving picture unit, the slide projector worked perfectly. Because the front-projection system generated intense light, it also generated intense heat. As a result, most of the Crescendo Summit scenes were filmed at night, when the ambient temperature was a bit cooler.

When principal photography wrapped in September 1976, Trumbull and Yuricich returned to Marina Del Rey to begin work on the balance of the special photographic effects shots.

Matte Paintings

Before they left for Mobile, Doug and Richard had hired a matte painter. A matte painting is a painted image that is optically combined with live-action footage in order to enhance existing sets and landscapes. To produce a matte painting, a clip of the live-action shot is projected onto a large sheet of glass or Masonite that has been painted white. An outline of the portion of the live-action scene that will be used in the final composite is traced onto the white surface. The matte artist then paints the rest of the image around that outline, taking great care to match the elements (architecture, topography, etc.) in the live-action image with those in the painting. Eventually, the live-action material and the painting are composited together on the same piece of film to create a single unified image.

Originally, there had been no plans to use matte paintings in *Close Encounters*—all of the artificial environments were going to be created in miniature and composited with the live-action scenes using front projection. Thinking it would be a good idea to have an insurance policy in case the 65mm front-projection system didn't work out, Richard Yuricich had suggested that they bring his brother, Matthew, on board as a backup. Born on January 19, 1923, Matthew Yuricich had earned a Bachelor's degree in fine arts from Miami University in Oxford, Ohio before entering the film industry in the early 1950s. Matthew worked on films such as *The*

Day the Earth Stood Still, Forbidden Planet, Ben Hur, North by Northwest, Mutiny on the Bounty (1962), *The Greatest Story Ever Told, Ice Station Zebra* (1968), *Soylent Green* (1973), and *Young Frankenstein* (1974). With L.B. Abbot and Glen Robinson, he won a Special Achievement Academy Award for his work on *Logan's Run* (1976). When the 65mm front-projection system didn't work out, Matthew was pressed into service. For Richard Yuricich, it was a thrill to be able to work with his big brother—his self-described "best buddy."

Ultimately, over 100 shots in *Close Encounters* utilized matte paintings. Some were complete works, and others were just tiny bits and pieces that were used to tie together all of the various elements in the effects shots. The 6½' x 3' paintings were all done in oil—some on glass, most on Masonite. Matthew, who loved to paint while listening to polka music, used a loose, informal style to execute his work because he felt that if a picture was too detailed it tended to look like a painting when it was photographed, but that if the particulars were kept loose and were a bit indistinct, the result looked more like the images that are seen by the human eye. Yuricich's "informal" paintings were so successful that most of them are almost impossible to detect in the finished film, which is just the way he wanted it. As he told *Cinefantastique* magazine, "When you do it well enough, and everybody else does their job well enough, you can't tell. That's the ultimate objective."

Matthew was assisted in his efforts by a young man just out of high school named Rocco Gioffre. Born and raised in Lorain, Ohio, the hometown of the Yuricich brothers, Rocco was a talented painter, and sculptor who—like Scott Squires—was also a big fan of fantasy and special effects films. Inspired by the original 1933 *King Kong* (his favorite film), Gioffre began making his own stop-motion animation films as a teenager, for which he created a number of foreground and background paintings to use as scenery. After reading an article on Matthew Yuricich in a local paper in the spring of 1976, Rocco wrote Yuricich a letter of introduction in which he enclosed some samples of his artwork. Matthew wrote him back (sending along a roll of Scotchlite as a gift), and the two arranged to meet in person that summer when Yuricich came to Ohio for a visit. After Matthew returned to Los Angeles, he was hired to work on *Close Encounters* and, in need of an assistant, told Richard Yuricich that he wanted to hire Rocco. Richard reviewed Gioffre's letters and samples and agreed that he would be an excellent choice. In October 1976, Gioffre flew out to Los Angeles (Future General paid for the plane ticket with the proviso that Rocco reimburse the company when he began getting paid) and went to work as Matthew's apprentice—cleaning brushes, preparing matte surfaces, and tracing the live-action elements. Gioffre attended to his duties with energy and dedication and quickly became an invaluable member of the Future General team.

| ## Special Photographic Effects, Part II: Making Saucers Fly

WHEN PRE-PRODUCTION BEGAN on *Close Encounters,* no one on the creative team had a clear idea of how they were going to realize the flying saucers. Larry Butler introduced them to methods that had been used in the past, including stop-motion animation (*Earth Versus the Flying Saucers*) and suspending model spacecraft from wires and moving them along an overhead track (*War of the Worlds*). Some consideration was even given to building full-size UFOs and swinging them around on cranes, but ultimately the production team decided that none of these techniques would provide sufficiently realistic results. As previously mentioned, Steven's desire for a more convincing approach led him to briefly consider Colin Cantwell's proposal to conjure up the saucers digitally, but when that proved to be impractical, he opted for the models-on-wires technique. Several three-foot-long flying saucer models were constructed and flown from one end of a Burbank Studios soundstage to another as cameras rolled. These tests were in progress when Doug Trumbull came aboard, and he was not alone in the opinion that they looked "terrible."

Like Colin Cantwell, Trumbull initially wanted to explore the idea of using computer graphics to create the UFOs. To this end, he commissioned Gary Demos and John Whitney Jr. of Information International, Inc., a computer technology company that used a Cray computer to create graphic effects for motion pictures (including 1973's *Westworld* and 1976's *Futureworld*), to produce several tests. They did, but, as with Cantwell's attempt, the results were disappointing. "The technology just wasn't ready," Doug recalls. At this point, Trumbull conceded that they were going to have to use models, but he didn't want to fly them on wires. Instead, he wanted to use a new computerized process called *motion control.*

Motion Control

One of the drawbacks of wirework in making a model fly is that the wires themselves (along with the rigid overhead track they hang from) severely limit the model's range of motion. The result is stiff, clumsy movement that is nothing at all like the graceful motion characteristic of actual flight. Over the years, special effects cameramen began to realize that they could create smoother and more believable flight by mounting a model on a stationary support in front of a neutral background and pushing a dolly-mounted camera toward, past, or away from it. When film shot using this technique is projected, it is the model that appears to be moving toward, past, or away from the camera. If the camera is also panned (moved horizontally) or tilted during the dolly move, the model can be made to appear to bank, turn, climb, or dive as well. The addition of an appropriate background (via rear or front projection or a matting process) can make the model look as if it is soaring through the skies or zooming through space. Another advantage of this approach is that, since the model itself doesn't have to move, it can be built on a much larger scale and with much greater detail, which makes it look more realistic.

This realism can be enhanced through the use of dramatic lighting effects—e.g., model lighting cast onto a miniature from an outside source, and small-scale practical bulbs built in—which, when properly employed, can give a model a tremendous sense of scale and believability. However, for a lighting effect to work, it must be photographed at a level of exposure that is correct for that particular effect. This can be difficult to do when, as is frequently the case, several different effects—each with its own specific exposure requirements—are used on the same model at the same time, because the ideal level of exposure for one effect might over- or underexpose another. When faced with this situation it is best to photograph each effect separately by filming the model with one effect activated, then rewinding the film and shooting another pass, this time with another effect activated, and then repeating the process until all of the different lighting effects have been photographed. Each new pass is superimposed over the previous ones until the desired result has been achieved.

In order for the technique to work, all of the passes have to line up perfectly, one on top of the other, so that only a single image of the model is produced. If any of the passes are off, then multiple images of the model will appear on the film and the shot will be ruined. This sort of precision is difficult to achieve when both the model and the camera are completely static. It is impossible when the camera is moving, because human operators are simply not capable of reproducing their movements with that degree of accuracy. For this reason, visual effects cameramen began looking for ways to automate cameras, dollies, and camera heads (a camera head is the mount used to attach a camera to a support base such as a tripod, a dolly, or a crane. It contains gears that enable it to pan and tilt the camera) so that they could be run hands-free and their moves could be repeated exactly. A very simple automated system was used to photograph the spaceships in *2001*—the camera was mounted on a dolly that was pushed along a 150-foot-long track in precise increments past the models by a motor-driven worm gear (a cylinder with a spiral groove mounted on the shaft). The gearing could be reversed to return the dolly to its starting point so that the move could be done again. Although this system worked very well, its range was extremely narrow—it could only move the camera in one direction at a single constant speed, which meant that complex moves incorporating pans and tilts were not possible. As a result, the models could only glide across the screen on a single axis at a very measured pace.

In the years after *2001*, Doug Trumbull experimented with several systems that would allow him to create repeatable camera moves that were more complex. In the early 1970s, he commissioned Alvah J. Miller and Jerry L. Jeffress of Interface Systems in Berkeley, California, to develop a device called a Mini-Scan—a drive speed regulator that was run by a set of digital timers and frame counters, which could be programmed to drive up to four pulse motors simultaneously. One of these motors was dedicated to the camera's drive shaft. The other three could be attached to other parts of the camera rig, including the head and dolly, and used to create multi-axis moves (shot one frame at a time in the same manner as stop motion animation) that included panning, tilting, and trucking. Because the system was run digitally, the moves could be repeated precisely each and every time. Trumbull used the Mini-Scan to produce effects for a series of commercials. It was an effective tool, but it had some severe limitations—the primary one being that all of the motors had to run at the same continuous speed, which meant that, while a model's onscreen motion could now be more complex, its pace remained quite deliberate.

When the time came to make *Close Encounters*, Doug wanted something far more sophisticated and flexible. To begin with, he wanted to be able to add more motors to the system, so that he could control not just the camera, head, and dolly, but also the focus ring on the camera's lens (which would allow it to be continually adjusted to keep a model in crisp focus throughout a shot) and an articulated rig for holding the UFOs that could pan, tilt, and rotate them a full 360 degrees (which would allow the UFOs' attitudes to be adjusted during filming and let them move more nimbly onscreen). Trumbull also wanted the ability to run all of these motors at different speeds simultaneously. This would allow the velocity of the camera movements to be changed during a take, which would give them the appearance of speeding up or slowing down while in flight.

Miller and Jeffress had recently developed a system with all of these capabilities for John Dykstra to use on *Star Wars*, so Doug asked them to create a similar one for *Close Encounters* that could do a few other things as well. The system—which Miller and Jeffress called the Electronic Motion Control System (EMS) and which Trumbull dubbed the MTS (for Motion Tracking System)—was run by a joystick controller. When the joystick was moved, it generated a series of electrical pulses that turned the shafts on stepper motors, which would run the camera and move the head, the dolly (which ran on a forty-two-foot-long track), and the model rig. While running the motors, the joystick would also run a counter that would add up the number of pulses sent to each motor. These counts were recorded on magnetic (cassette) tape by a high-precision digital recorder. When the tape was played back, the counts would be repeated, sending precisely the same number of pulses back to the motors and thus causing them to repeat their original moves exactly. The digital recorder had eight channels, which meant that the system could run up to eight motors at a time. (The recorder had two tape heads—one to record the pulse signals and the other to make a simultaneous back-up copy. The heads had a tendency to eat the tapes, prompting the Future General team to nickname them Jaws 1 and Jaws 2.) Unlike the Mini-Scan, which only worked frame by frame, the MTS could photograph a scene in real time. This provided the natural motion blur common to regular cinematography and thus eliminated the strobing common to frame-by-frame shooting (i.e., the "herky-jerky" motion that frequently characterizes stop-motion animation).

One of the MTS's key capabilities (one the *Star Wars* system didn't have) was that it could record the pans, tilts, and trucks made by a human camera operator. When the operator turned the wheels or levers that moved the rig, a series of optical encoders attached to the rotating shafts of the motors and/or gears of the camera, head, dolly, or model stand would transform the spinning of the motor shafts into digital signals that were then fed into the counter and recorded for later playback. The MTS system could scale the moves up or down proportionately, which allowed moves made while filming live-action shots on the set to be repeated exactly in miniature during the filming of the models. By utilizing this function, the Future General team was able to integrate moving shots of the UFO models and other miniatures into moving live-action shots (e.g., the shot in The Experience of Lacombe walking out of one of the landing zone cubicles and crossing the tarmac to confront the three scout saucers hovering above it), something that previously had not been possible. Prior to *Close Encounters*, model effects and live-action scenes could only be joined in static, split-screen shots, with the models confined to one part of the frame and the live-action to another (the rigidity of the frame was always a tip-off to the audience that an effects shot was coming, which of course helped destroy the illusion). Allowing the two to mix together freely enhanced the effect's believability tremendously.

Miller and Jeffress built the MTS from scratch in just ninety days. They finished it in July 1976 and bought it to Mobile, where it was used to film a number of live-action shots to which UFOs would later be added. Following the completion of principal photography, the system was packed up and sent to Marina Del Rey so that it could be used to photograph the saucers.

The Saucers

Before the UFOs could be filmed, the filmmakers first had to decide what they were going to look like. Concept work on the saucers had been going on since pre-production. Steven had a lot of ideas for spacecraft design. Joe Alves did a bunch of sketches, and George Jensen did dozens more. The initial thought had been to make them look like traditional 1950s flying saucers, but as time went on, the designs grew more exotic.

For a while they played around with a notion of Steven's that the aliens would try to make the people of the earth feel comfortable by disguising their ships to look like familiar objects such as the McDonald's golden arches and the Chevron gas station logo. Doug Trumbull then came up with an idea to project abstract light patterns onto the hulls of the UFOs. Finally, inspired by the many eyewitness accounts that emphasized the saucers' brilliant lights, Steven decided that they should look like the landing lights of a 747—in other words, like blindingly bright colored lights, with the ships themselves appearing only dimly behind the brilliant glow. (There may have been more than just artistic considerations behind this choice—Julia Phillips wrote that Steven initially wanted the glare from the spaceships to be really bright in order to obscure the models in case they didn't look realistic.)

To create the UFOs, Future General developed a "saucer kit," the primary component of which was a metal disc eighteen inches in diameter that could be connected to the motion-controlled model rig. A variety of spherical, ellipsoid, conical, and disc-shaped "shrouds"—hollow shells made of white vacuform plastic with flat circular bases that were also eighteen inches in diameter—were attached to the top and bottom of the metal disc in different combinations in order to create a wide variety of saucers. Once the basic shape of a saucer had been determined, both the top and the bottom shrouds were painted black. Neon and xenon lights were then installed inside each shroud, and holes were cut into the shells and covered with filters to allow the neon and xenon to shine out as if the saucer was an extraterrestrial jack o' lantern. These holes were cut in specific patterns in order to give each UFO a unique look. Steven asked that the patterns be arranged in ways that would allow them, from certain angles, to resemble human faces.

As Douglas Trumbull explains, "We wanted to project a feeling of involvement with some being—not just a piece of hardware sailing by two feet off the ground." After the interior lighting had been installed, fiber optics and tiny "grain of wheat" bulbs were mounted on the exteriors of the shrouds. Post scanners—miniature searchlights that could be aimed directly into the camera to create a lens flare—were also mounted on some of the ships.

Although most of the UFOs were created using the saucer kit, there were a few exceptions: Saucer H—the UFO that Roy Neary sees hovering over his truck after his initial close encounter and that Lacombe later reaches up and touches during the barnstorming sequence—was a detailed model created by Greg Jein based on one of Steven's designs. The "Red Whoosh"—the tiny straggler UFO that is constantly chasing after the three scout saucers—was originally intended to be one of the cuboids, but was reconceived as a more amorphous shape after the luminous squares were cut from the film. No model was built for the whoosh—it was simply a red light bulb attached to a stick that was then mounted on the model rig.

So that the saucers' light effects would be visible on film, Trumbull decided that they should be photographed in a fog-filled environment. To this end, a "smoke room" was constructed in the Glencoe Avenue facility. The room—which was fifty-four and a half feet long, twenty-five feet wide, and twelve feet high—was covered in black velvet and outfitted with a closed-air circulation system. A Mole-Richardson smoke machine was incorporated into the system and used to pump "bee smoke"—a fine mist made by vaporizing low-grade diesel oil—into the room. (The mist left a shiny residue over all of the equipment, and anyone working in the smoke room was required to wear a surgical mask in order to avoid breathing in the nasty vapors.) Since the smoke was being used as a photographic filter, it was vital that its density remain consistent throughout the length of the shot. To ensure this, an optical sensor was installed in the smoke room. The sensor would shoot infrared light beams across the room to receiver units. If the smoke level in the room dropped below an acceptable level, the Mole-Richardson machine would be signaled to pump more smoke into the room. The motorized camera, dolly, and model rig were set up on the floor of the smoke room, and the digital recorder was placed in an air-conditioned booth built into the corner.

The first step in producing a UFO shot was to blow up a single frame of the live-action plate that the model was going to be composited with. A clear acetate cel was laid on top of the enlargement, and Steven and Doug used grease pencils on the cel to plot the saucer's journey through the frame. Once the shot had been designed, the camera operator would mount an all-white duplicate of the saucer being filmed (made from duplicate, unpainted shrouds) onto the model rig (the white saucers were used because they showed up better against the black velvet walls of the smoke room, which made plotting the moves easier). The camera operator would then program the various dolly and camera moves required to create the planned-for action into the MTS. First, he used the joystick controller to drive the dolly along its track at the required speed. The pulse count produced by the dolly move would be taped by the MTS on one of its eight channels. The tape would then be played backward, which would reverse the motor and return the dolly to its starting position. After that, the tape would be rolled forward, and as the dolly repeated its trip the operator would use the joystick to add the next piece of the overall move (e.g., a camera pan or tilt), which would be recorded on another one of the MTS's channels. This process was repeated until all parts of the integrated move had been recorded.

While composing the moves, the operator had to keep several factors in mind. The first was that the perspective and the size relationships between all of the elements in the shot needed to remain constant so that the saucers would always appear to be the same size (they were each meant to be approximately twenty feet across). To ensure that they would, a clip of the live-action plate would be traced to create a line drawing indicating where all of the major elements in the shot (roads, hillsides, trees, buildings, etc.) were located. The line drawing would then be inserted into the viewfinder of the camera for the operator to use as a guide. (This technique was used for static shots. When the UFOs were being incorporated into moving shots, test footage of the saucers would be superimposed over a copy of the live-action scene to make sure all of the elements lined up properly.) The operator also had to vary the speed of the UFOs (by varying the speed of the camera) to create what Doug Trumbull referred to as "compensated moves"—if the saucers zipped through the frame at a single continuous speed, they would appear unrealistically lightweight, but slowing them down as they neared the camera gave them a tremendous sense of scale, weight, and mass.

Once every component of the move had been programmed, a test shot would be filmed on high-contrast black-and-white film and then screened in the Annex projection area. If any problems were detected, the offending section of the move would be reprogrammed. When everything was set, the white saucer would be replaced with the tricked-out black one and the real shot would then be filmed, with separate passes being made for each lighting effect. Depending on the overall look they were trying to achieve, some of these passes (e.g., any featuring the air glow or beams of light) would be shot in smoke and others would be shot without smoke (the flares had to be filmed in a smokeless atmosphere to maintain a sharp, crisp look). Each pass was filmed one frame at a time. The exposure time per frame for each pass varied, depending on the intended look (longer exposures produce an increased glow from static objects and can cause moving ones to streak). The average exposure for a regular frame of live-action film is one-forty-eighth of a second. The exposure time on the saucer shots ranged from six seconds to almost three hours per frame (all with the camera moving at a speed that would maintain an appropriate blur). Since each saucer required from five to nine passes, a complete shot could take hours and sometimes even days to film. No more than one saucer was shot at a time. For shots featuring multiple UFOs, each ship was shot separately (pass by pass) on the same piece of film.

Richard Yuricich and Douglas Trumbull did the initial motion-control model shots, but the bulk of the work was turned over to veteran animation cameraman David K. Stewart, another Dickson-Vasu alumnus. Everyone who worked with the then forty-year-old Stewart describes him the same way—as an extraordinary cinematographer and wonderfully larger-than-life personality who was gruff on the outside (his nickname was "Grumpy") and a sweetheart on the inside. A driven perfectionist, Dave took his work very seriously and was revered for his tremendous dedication, his exacting standards, and his incredible attention to detail. With the help of assistant cameraman Dave Hardberger, Stewart started shooting the saucer footage in December 1976, while elsewhere in the facility work began on the biggest UFO of all.

The Mothership

Like the saucers, the design of the Mothership evolved considerably throughout the life of the project. In the original drafts of Steven's script (the ones credited to Sam Irvin), it is described as "an oddball type of machine that...Dr. Zeuss [Seuss] could have designed, for all of its colorful eccentricities.... Light beams stab dozens of yards in every direction from a thousand port-like openings. Party lights revolve around its Dutch perimeters. Dozens of strobe devices sting the eyes. It's such a tasteless, bizarre and impossible device that it doesn't seem like it should be real, let alone capable of flying." As pre-production design work got under way, the "oddball machine" was reconceived as a large cylinder along the lines of the cigar-shaped craft reportedly seen over Germany in the sixteenth century and over the United States in the nineteenth century. Eventually this idea was discarded in favor of a vision of the Mothership as an ominous black wedge that was so massive it would blot out the stars as it passed over the landing zone. The wedge would have a hemispheric bottom that would light up as the ship landed. This concept was written into the final drafts of the script and remained in place throughout production (which is why so many shots in The Experience feature a large shadow falling over the landing zone). At the start of the photographic effects work, two different Mothership models were constructed: a four-foot-long version of the complete craft for use in the long shots of the ship appearing over Devils Tower, and a separate five-foot version of the hemispheric underbelly for use in the closer shots that take place after the Mothership has touched down. The underbelly model would be matted into the live-action footage over the full-scale hatch that had been filmed on the Big Set in Mobile.

In refining the design of the underbelly, Doug Trumbull suggested that—since it was, after all, part of a *Mother*ship— they make it look like a giant breast (with the hatchway representing the nipple). Inspired by the sight of L.A.'s San Fernando Valley at night, Steven suggested that they cover the hull with thousands of sparkling lights. The underbelly model was made out of blown Plexiglas, reinforced with wood and steel, and painted white. It had a circular cutout in the center from which the hatch would descend. Trumbull came up with a novel way of creating Spielberg's "San Fernando Valley" look. Rather than mounting thousands of tiny practical lights on the surface or drilling holes into the Plexiglas to allow light from an interior source to shine out, he decided instead to project circular patterns made up of thousands of tiny dots onto the surface. Several different patterns would be projected on top of one another at the same time and filmed with very long exposures so that they would glow and streak.

The task of creating these patterns fell to Future General's animation team, headed by Robert Swarthe. While earning a master's degree in motion pictures from UCLA, Swarthe had worked at Graphic Films, where he met Doug Trumbull, and later at Dickson-Vasu, where he met Richard Yuricich. After graduating, Swarthe became a staff director of animated and live-action commercials at the Haboush Company. He also worked on his own projects: *K-9000: A Space Oddity* (1969), an animated spoof of *2001* (co-directed with Bob Mitchell); *Radio Rocket Boy* (1973), a live-action spoof of old-time movie serials (codirected with John Mayer); and *Kick Me* (1975), his own animated film that earned Swarthe an Academy Award nomination for Best Animated Short Subject in 1975. In need of an animation supervisor for *Close Encounters*, Yuricich contacted Swarthe. Although he knew that he would not be in the prime creative position on *Close Encounters* and that his work would be primarily supportive, Swarthe welcomed the rare opportunity to work on a serious, big-budget science fiction movie and accepted the position. He joined the project in May 1976.

Swarthe had animator Harry Moreau draw three extremely intricate patterns. Since time was short, Moreau only drew a twelve-degree slice of each pattern. Copies were then made of the wedges and pasted together to form complete circles. The circles were photographed onto eight-by-ten black-and-white transparencies and mounted between two panes of Pyrex. Because the smoke room was being used to film the saucers, the underbelly shots were filmed in a small (fifteen feet by thirty feet), black velvet–covered room in the Annex. To make it easier to set up the camera at the correct angle, the underbelly was mounted on its side (for tighter shots, a notch was cut in the hull that allowed the camera to move in closer). The dot patterns were projected onto the underbelly using a motorized projector that could hold two slides at a time, rotating one while the other remained fixed. Gels were placed over the projector's lenses to add color to the black-and-white dots. Several different combination patterns were used in each shot. Each combination was filmed in a separate pass using exposures that ranged from twelve seconds to seven minutes per frame.

Another important lighting effect on the underbelly was the scanner—a series of white lights that rotate around the circular cutout from which the hatch emerges. To create the scanner, a piece of fiber-optic cable was attached to a tiny motorized arm that circled around the cutout at the rate of one revolution per frame. The cable was threaded down through the underbelly and attached to a motorized grip that moved back and forth on a track set up in front of a very bright light source. Robert Swarthe cut several zigzag patterns out of pieces of shiny black paper, which were then mounted in glass and placed between the light source and the motorized grip. During filming, the grip would move past the patterns. The black paper would block the light coming from the source, but when the grip moved over an open area in the pattern, the light would shine through and the fiber optic would transmit it to the scanner arm. This on-again, off-again pattern broke the scanner line into segments. The long exposures employed to shoot each frame caused the lights to streak a bit. As a result, some of the scanner lights appeared to expand and contract, while others appeared to merge with and separate from one another. Like the other light patterns, the scanner effect was filmed in its own separate pass.

Although the scanner lights were white, during the musical jam session they pulsated with brilliant bursts of color. These pulses were created in the animation department using "slot gags." To create the gags, Bob Swarthe cut a series of small rectangular boxes ("slots") into a piece of black paper in a pattern that matched the arrangement of the scanner lights in a particular shot. The black paper was placed on the Oxberry (an animation stand consisting of a 65mm camera, rigged for single-frame shooting, mounted on a vertical column above a flat bed upon which artwork is placed), lit from below, and photographed. During the course of the shot, pieces of black paper were moved frame by frame over the slots to open and close them in sync with the notes being played by the Mothership on the soundtrack. Color was added to the slots by placing gels over the camera lens. (No attempt was made to match the colors of the slots with the hues on the colorboard. The slot colors were chosen based solely on what Bob Swarthe felt would look good.) The "slot gags" were not photographed during the main shoot—they were burned into (superimposed upon) the shots after filming was over. Fog filters were used to take the crisp edges off of the slots so that they would better match the softer look of the underbelly footage.

The animation department was also responsible for the "solar explosions"—brilliant bursts of light that appeared on the underbelly during the jam session. To create these bursts, a high-intensity slide projector light was aimed directly into the lens of a camera through .045-inch holes drilled in thin metal plates. Doug Trumbull wanted the explosions to pop onto the screen and then slowly fade away, so the animators would start shooting with the iris in the camera lens closed down all the way, allowing the least amount of light possible through to the film. During the course of the shot, the iris would be quickly opened up to create the "pop," and then gradually closed down again to create the fade. If multiple explosions appeared in a single shot, then each one was photographed separately. Like the scanner colors, the solar explosions were shot on the Oxberry after the main shoot was over and burned into the underbelly footage.

Because of the complex elements and passes required, each underbelly shot took many hours to complete. Richard Yuricich photographed the first one himself, but with all of his other responsibilities, he didn't have time to shoot them all. Since Dave Stewart was busy filming the saucers, the decision was made to hire another cameraman to supervise all of the Mothership photography.

Dennis Muren was born in the Los Angeles suburb of Glendale, California, on November 1, 1946 and was raised in nearby La Canada. A fan of the work of Ray Harryhausen, Muren began making his own stop-motion and special effects films as a boy. During his first year at Pasadena City College, he joined with his friends David Allen and Mark McGee to make a low-budget 16mm monster movie called *The Equinox...A Journey into the Supernatural*. Dennis directed the film and helped create its effects. The seventy-one-minute finished product was sold to producer Jack H. Harris (*The Blob*), who brought in veteran editor Jack Woods to rework the movie by writing and directing a series of new scenes and removing many of the old ones. Blown up to 35mm, the revised *Equinox* was released in 1970, with Muren receiving credit as an associate producer and cocreator of the special effects. After leaving college, Dennis began working as an animator and photographic effects cameraman on commercials, documentaries, and the feature films *Willy Wonka and the Chocolate Factory* (1971) and *Flesh Gordon* (1974). In 1976, he was hired as an effects cameraman on *Star Wars*. As that film was winding down, Muren heard that Future General was looking for another cinematographer for *Close Encounters*. Figuring that it would be neat to work on two big visual effects films back to back, he got in touch with Trumbull, who hired him. Muren joined Future General in February 1977, just four days after he finished work on *Star Wars*. Richard Yuricich felt very lucky to have a cinematographer of Muren's talent working on the project.

Since all of the Mothership shots had already been designed by Doug Trumbull and Richard Yuricich, Muren described his role on the production as largely that of a "babysitter" whose job it was to execute the already-determined shooting plan, although he did do what he could to identify interesting patterns in the dot projections. Muren and Scott Squires, who had been assigned to assist him, would set up the shots, activate the machinery, and then monitor the system to make sure that everything was going smoothly. Since it often took more than one working day to complete a shot, a young UCLA student with an affinity for visual effects named Hoyt Yeatman was hired to monitor the system at night. (Yeatman had been recommended by Glenn Erickson, who had worked with him on several student films.)

As the underbelly shots were being filmed, Steven and Doug began casting around for a new look for the rest of the Mothership. Both had become disenchanted with the black wedge concept—Trumbull didn't think the design was all that interesting, and Spielberg wanted something that was more colorful and visually exciting. In an oft-told tale, Steven has said that the inspiration for the final look of the Mothership came from the chaotic yet beautiful appearance of an oil refinery—a massive, ramshackle assemblage of pipes and towers illuminated by thousands and thousands of tiny light bulbs—that he drove past while filming in India, although Joe Alves recalls discussing the idea with Spielberg even earlier, after they spotted a refinery in the American heartland while on a pre-production location scouting trip. Whichever sighting inspired the idea, Steven decided that he now wanted the Mothership to look like a "city of lights." Trumbull loved the idea and suggested that they put structures on top that resembled the Manhattan skyline in order to give the model a sufficient sense of scale and recognition. The curved underbelly would be retained in order to accommodate the scenes that were already in production.

To flesh out the concept, they brought in Ralph McQuarrie, a veteran illustrator (and another Graphic Films alumni) who had done a series of striking conceptual paintings for Star Wars that had helped convince Twentieth Century-Fox to go ahead with that film. McQuarrie did six or seven sketches of the Mothership, all of them incorporating the oil refinery concept, the Manhattan skyline idea, and the curved underbelly. Feeling that the design needed another element to balance it, Ralph added a series of spiky arms jutting out from the sides of the ship, theorizing that they would be used to retrieve the saucers when they returned home. McQuarrie selected one of the sketches and used it to create a ten-inch-by-eighteen-inch painting. Steven and Doug both loved the finished piece and gave it to Greg Jein, who fashioned a small model, made of wood and metal, based on the painting to use as a construction guide.

Jein and his team began building the new Mothership model by fabricating a second (smaller) Plexiglas underbelly, over which several levels of round platforms were constructed. To create these platforms, Greg modeled a quarter section of each one in clay, replicated it four times over in fiberglass, and then pieced them together. Aluminum tubes of various lengths and diameters (not cigar tubes as has frequently been reported) were erected on top of the platforms. Neon artist Larry Albright was hired to custom-bend a series of neon tubes to fit inside the aluminum cylinders. Two drill presses were employed to drill thousands of tiny holes into the aluminum to let the brilliant light shine through (so many holes were required that just about every member of the team—including Steven—was tapped to do drilling duty at one time or another). The holes were drilled in horizontal and vertical patterns in order to make the tubes look like architectural structures, and colored gels were placed inside the cylinders in order to add hue to the light. The rest of the ship was outfitted with thousands of feet of fiber optics, as well as many "grain of wheat" and "grain of rice" bulbs. Once the lighting was finished, the entire model was painted black and detailed.

The model was detailed in sections, each named for one of the five boroughs of New York City (there was a Manhattan area, a Brooklyn area, and so on). Although most of the detailing consisted of custom-made bits and pieces cut from sheets of plastic, the cranes were from the Revell model kit of Jacques Cousteau's famous ship *Calypso* (the Revell company was located directly across the street from Future General's Glencoe workshop); the tracks on the underbelly were couplings from an HO railroad set; and the spiky arms jutting out from the side were telescoping metal rods bought in a local store. A neon ring was inserted into the cutout at the bottom of the underbelly to substitute for the scanner. To amuse themselves, the model makers incorporated a series of gags into the body of the Mothership, including a miniature R2-D2 and TIE fighter (a lot of the people working on *Close Encounters* had also worked on *Star Wars*), a mailbox, a Volkswagen microbus, several WWII fighter planes, and a cemetery. There were little people hanging off some of the rods, and silhouettes of Mickey Mouse and other iconic figures were visible in the windows in some of the globes. In a more macabre vein, some dead mice and a few random bug parts were tossed into the mix as well. Working twelve hours a day, six and seven days a week, it took the model makers eight and a half weeks to finish the Mothership (the job was originally scheduled for five). The final product was approximately four feet in diameter (six feet including the spiky arms), approximately three and a half feet high, and weighed several hundred pounds.

The full Mothership scenes were filmed after work on the underbelly shots had been completed and after Dennis Muren returned from a five-week sick leave (he had come down with pneumonia at the end of the underbelly shoot). To prepare the model for filming, it was mounted on its side (to make it easier to position the camera) on a two-inch pipe that fit into a hole drilled in the underbelly. The pipe was connected to a motorized rotor that would turn the Mothership slowly during the shot. The model was so heavy that the support rig had to be counterbalanced so that it wouldn't tip over.

As the motion-control system was already being used to shoot the saucers, the Mini-Scan was taken out of mothballs to film the Mothership (this ended up working out well, as the slow, stately moves the Mini-Scan produced were perfectly suited for the giant craft). As with the saucers, the Mothership was to be shot in bee smoke, so the tiny Annex stage was converted into a makeshift smoke room by putting tape over the cracks in the windows and doors (the Mini-Scan was placed in a sealed booth, in which Muren and Squires could also sit). Since there was no forced air system in the Annex, the smoke from the Mole-Richardson machine had to be pumped into the room by hand. The Annex didn't have an optical smoke sensor, either, so Muren and Squires had to monitor the smoke levels (approximately every three minutes) by eye. They did their best, but without the high-tech monitors, the smoke levels fluctuated more than they did in the main smoke room. Because the atmospheric density was changing frame by frame, the glow around the Mothership appeared to "pulse" in some of the film's final shots. Luckily, much of the pulsing matched the beats of John Williams's score, which made it look as if the Mothership was keeping time with the music. The Mothership shots required multiple passes, but because the intensity of the lighting on the model was fairly uniform, most required only a few (some required only two—a "beauty pass" to photograph the model itself and another to photograph the glow). Exposure times ranged from twenty to eighty seconds per frame, and many of the shots took between eight and ten hours to film.

The movie was originally intended to end with the wide shot of the Mothership lifting off from the base camp and rising up out of the frame until it vanished from sight—a shot that, because it required the moiré patterns to be projected on the full Mothership model (as opposed to the more manageable underbelly) while it was moving, Dennis Muren described as being the "hardest" shot in the movie for him to film—after which the credits were supposed to play over a montage of Jillian's snapshots. However, Steven was so happy with the look of the Mothership that he decided to include more images of it flying off into the heavens as the final credits rolled. To give the shots a chance to play, Steven decided to list the names of just about everyone who had worked on the movie. At the time, this was a rather unusual thing to do. Prior to 1977, the standard film industry practice had been to run only the names of the department heads, but George Lucas had broken that tradition when he recognized the entire company at the end of *Star Wars*. Once Steven had done it as well, the whole industry followed suit, leading to the lengthy credit rolls seen on most movies today. Needless to say, all at Future General (and in the rest of the film's departments) appreciated the gesture and enjoyed seeing their names appear up on the big screen.

As none of these additional bits had been planned for or storyboarded, Dennis was given a free hand to design them himself. Rising to the challenge, he created a series of shots in which the Mothership drifts gracefully toward, past, and away from the camera. A snorkel lens—a special lens set in a tube that extends out from the body of the camera, allowing it to snake into tight places where the bulky camera couldn't go—enabled him to get so close to the model that some of the ship's spires appear to practically scrape by the camera. When it came time to film the final shots of the sequence, in which the Mothership is seen floating far off in the distance, Muren and Squires found that the room they were working in was too small and they were unable to move the camera back far enough to frame the shot properly. They were stymied until Scott came up with the idea of bringing in a concave mirror and filming the reduced reflection of the model instead. Squires' idea worked perfectly, and the shots were captured. The end credit sequence took six weeks to film.

CHAPTER 22

Special Photographic Effects, Part III: Putting It All Together

ONCE ALL OF THE ELEMENTS for each visual effects shot had been created, the next step was to composite them all on the same piece of film. This work was done on an optical printer (called an optical camera by the Future General photographic team)—a piece of equipment that consisted of a motion picture camera (called a taking camera) attached to a base facing a projector head. Light from a lamphouse illuminated images from strips of film that ran through the projector head. The images were then photographed one frame at a time by the taking camera onto a new piece of film negative (called a duplicate or "dupe" negative). The optical printer was a very versatile machine. Through the use of various techniques, it would be used to enlarge or reduce an image; create fades, wipes, dissolves, and flips; and to convert film from one format to another. It could also be used to create composites by photographing separately shot images onto a single dupe negative.

Making Mattes

To make a composite, the images cannot simply be rephotographed onto the same dupe negative. If they were, the result would resemble a collection of double exposures—lots of semi-transparent images piled on top of one another, each showing through the other. In order to combine a number of different images together on the same dupe and have each remain solid, mattes must be employed. Simply put, a matte is a mask—an opaque or semi-opaque piece of celluloid whose purpose is to prevent a specific portion of a frame of film from being exposed.

The process worked as follows: When two images were going to be composited, one was designated the foreground image and the other the background plate. Through one of a number of processes, a high-contrast black-and-white copy of the foreground image was generated, resulting in a strip of film that contained a black silhouette of the foreground subject against a stark white background. This was called a holdout matte. A reverse print of the holdout matte was then made, resulting in a second strip of film containing a white silhouette of the foreground subject against a black background. This was called a cover matte.

Once the mattes had been completed, a positive print of the background plate (called an interpositive) was placed in the projector head along with the holdout matte (this process is called bi-packing) and re-photographed by the taking camera onto a dupe. The holdout matte blocked the projector light and prevented an area in the exact shape of the foreground subject from being exposed on the dupe. (If the dupe had been developed at that point, the result would have been a copy of the background plate containing a "hole"—a black area where no light had exposed the negative—in the shape of the foreground image.) Without being processed, the dupe negative was rewound and an interpositive of the foreground subject was then bi-packed into the projector with the cover matte and photographed onto the dupe neg. The cover matte prevented the projector light from striking the area of the dupe negative that now contained the latent image of the plate, but allowed the foreground image through to be exposed onto the "hole" in the dupe. If all went well, the foreground and background images fit together seamlessly to create a single composite image.

For static shots (such as many of those involving Devils Tower), stationary glass mattes were used. Glass mattes were created on the matte camera stand. A matte camera is a combination camera/projector that can project images as well as take them. At Future General, the matte camera was mounted on a steel beam (to insure that it would always remain rock steady) in front of two wooden frames (wood was used instead of metal so that the intense heat from the lights would not cause the frames to expand and warp) that were also sturdily mounted. Don Jarel, an alumnus of the MGM optical department, was in charge of all photography done on the matte camera.

To create a stationary matte, a six-foot-by-three-foot piece of glass was painted white and placed on one of the frames. The foreground image was projected onto the glass and its silhouette was then traced on the white paint. All of the paint outside of the silhouette would be scraped away until all that was left was a clear piece of glass with an opaque white silhouette of the foreground image on it. To create the cover matte, a piece of black velvet was hung behind the glass and the silhouette was illuminated from the front (so that it would appear as a white image against a black background) and then photographed. A reverse contact print of the cover matte was then made (resulting in a black image against a white background) to produce the holdout matte.

Shots containing moving objects (such as the UFOs) utilized traveling mattes, in which the silhouette of a moving foreground image traveled through the frame as the shot progressed—either as a black image running across a white background (the holdout matte) or a white image moving across a black background (the cover matte). There were several techniques that could be used to produce a traveling matte. Future General's approach was to use the model saucers to create their own mattes.

Once all of the passes had been completed on a particular shot, the black model would be removed from the motion-control rig and replaced with its white duplicate. The white saucer was lit and shot against the black velvet on a piece of color negative. To create the cover matte, the color negative was printed on high-contrast black-and-white film. A reverse print was then made of that to create the holdout matte. Some of the heavily detailed models (such as the Mothership and Saucer H) didn't have duplicates—their contours were too complicated to easily copy. In that case, a white card or sheet was held up behind the actual model and lit, throwing the model (which was not lit) into silhouette. This image was photographed and printed onto high-contrast black-and-white film to create the holdout matte and then reverse printed to generate the cover matte.

One of the biggest challenges in creating traveling mattes for the *Close Encounters* UFOs was their distinctive glows and flares. Traveling mattes are designed to work with solid objects that have hard, sharply defined edges. The glows and flares, however, had a variety of densities (thicknesses) ranging from solid to transparent, with edges that were soft and amorphous. To deal with this challenge, Richard Yuricich came up with a way to make a soft-edged traveling matte that could accommodate these qualities.

To create these soft-edged mattes, a pass of each model lit to feature only the glow or the flare was shot on a new piece of negative—one that was separate from the negative upon which all of the other passes of the model had been made. A 70mm color motion-picture print of the glow or flare was made from this negative. A holdout matte for the glow/flare was generated on panchromatic, black-and-white print film (the black surrounding the glow/flare on the 70mm color print allowed the print to serve as its own cover matte). This soft-edged, low-contrast matte of the glow/flare was then combined with a sharp-edged, high-contrast matte of the model to create what was called a pre-comp composite matte. When the final composite of the entire shot was made, the pre-comp composite matte was used to completely hold back the body of the UFO and most of the glow/flare while the other elements of the shot were being printed on the dupe neg. When the time came to add the saucer and the glow/flare to the final composite, an interpositive of the saucer footage would be placed in the optical printer and used to fill in the saucer-shaped "hole" in the image on the dupe negative. In a separate pass, the color 70mm print of the glow/flare would then be used to burn the glow/flare into the final composite. (Since the camera could only accommodate 65mm film, 2.5mm on each side of the 70mm print had to be stripped off before it could be placed in the camera.)

Other types of mattes were used as well. For shots featuring the self-generating clouds, hand-drawn mattes called roto-mattes were created by animation department staffers Eleanor Dahlen, Carol Boardman, and Connie Morgan. To create the roto-mattes, a print of the 65mm cloud footage would be placed in the Oxberry camera and projected down onto the bed one frame at a time. The outline of the clouds would be traced (rotoscoped) frame by frame onto individual pieces of paper. A clear acetate cel would be then be placed over each sheet of paper, and the outline of the clouds would be traced onto the cel and later filled in with black paint. These individual hand-painted cels were put back onto the Oxberry and photographed one at a time to create a traveling matte of the clouds. This labor-intensive process had to be employed because, unlike the saucers, the clouds had soft edges that were constantly changing, so the motion-control techniques used to generate the saucer mattes could not be used here. Roto-mattes called garbage mattes were also used to remove unwanted items (such as model supports or light stands) from certain shots.

Some of the garbage mattes were made by Bob's Swarthe's friend Tom Koester, a cameraman/sound mixer who worked on the film in the early weeks of production, doing a number of odd jobs for the animation department before leaving to go on an around-the-world documentary shoot.

Making Composites

When the mattes were completed, they were sent to the optical effects editorial department, where they would be catalogued along with the rest of the elements and the compositing process would begin.

The first step in this process was to determine where each element would be positioned in the shot and how big or small it would appear in the frame. To help figure this out, Richard Yuricich came up with the idea of making still frame blowups of each of the elements in various sizes. He would cut out the photos and lay them on a twenty-four-inch-wide graph called a field chart, and then Doug and Steven would play around with them, arranging the elements until they had a composition that they liked. Once this was done, the pieces would be pasted down and photographed. One of the major size decisions concerned the base of operations. All of the base shots made in Mobile had been filmed full frame, but needed to be reduced in size so that they could be composited into certain shots along with images of Roy and Jillian huddled in the Notch to make it appear as if the two of them were looking down at the landing zone. After Steven and Doug determined how big the base was going to be, the original footage would be placed into the optical printer and photographed onto a dupe negative at the appropriate size. A positive print would then be made of the dupe for use in the final compositing process.

Once all of the pasteups had been prepared, Richard Yuricich would create a line-up plan—a written set of instructions for each shot indicating the elements that were to be used, the order in which they were to be composited, and whether they were to be placed in the optical projector or the optical camera. The plan would also dictate which elements were to be bi-packed, the size each element was to appear in the frame, and which lenses, films speeds, exposure times, and exposure levels were to be used to make the composite. Optical line-up technicians would then assemble, clean, and mark (starting and end points in accordance with the line-up plan) the elements required for each composite. The pasteup, the line-up plan, and the elements would then be handed over to optical cameraman Robert Hall—

another MGM alumnus—who would place the pasteup in the viewfinder of the optical camera to use as a visual guide for setting up the composite and then, following the line-up plan, begin putting the shot together.

Future General's approach to optical compositing was a bit unorthodox. Normally, each element in a composite (live-action footage, a model or matte painting shot, an animation effect, etc.) is photographed separately and then printed onto its own individual piece of intermediate stock—a fine-grain film designed especially for duplication. This print is called an interpositive. The interpositives for all of a shot's elements would then be placed in the optical printer (along with their mattes) and rephotographed onto the duplicate negative (which is also made of the fine-grain intermediate stock) to create the composite. However, *Close Encounters* presented some special challenges that required the optical team to make a few innovative adaptations to this process. To begin with, each *CE3K* visual effects shot was made up of a large number of elements (some shots consisted of as many as fifteen separate pieces). This presented a problem, because every time an element is printed onto a dupe negative, there is a risk of contamination—unwanted excess light striking the negative and overexposing it. To prevent this from happening, optical cameramen prefer to print as many images as possible onto the dupe negative at the same time in order to limit the number of exposures that it is subjected to.

Had Future General produced its effects in 35mm, this would have been relatively easy to do. The optical team could have used an optical printer with multiple projector heads, which would have allowed a number of different elements to be projected into the taking camera simultaneously (double- and quadruple-headed 35mm printers were fairly common pieces of equipment at that time). However, because they were working in 65mm, Yuricich and Hall had to make do with a single-headed 65mm optical printer that Yuricich had obtained from Twentieth Century-Fox (the studio built the machine in the late 1960s for use on *Hello, Dolly*)— the only optical printer available that could accommodate this no longer fashionable format. This meant that they could only print a few elements at a time (four if both the camera and the projector were bi-packed—three interpositives or mattes and the dupe negative), which greatly increased the possibility of contamination.

One way to prevent excess exposure when working with a single-headed printer was to create pre-comps (pre-composite composites). A pre-comp was made by breaking down the overall number of elements required to make a shot into smaller groups. Each group was composited onto its own dupe negative. Interpositives made from these dupes were then used to make the final composite. Reducing fifteen elements to five greatly decreased the number of times the final dupe negative needed to be exposed. The problem with the pre-comp process was that it required that the original elements be photographed many more times than usual, which degraded the quality of the images.

Since they didn't want this to happen, the Future General team decided not to make pre-comps, but to instead print the elements onto the dupe negative one or two at a time. To prevent contamination, they would use "density" mattes. The first was used primarily with the base-of-operations reductions. When the original full-frame shots were reduced, the result was a small image of the base in the middle of an otherwise clear frame of 65mm film, through which light could leak onto the dupe negative. As a countermeasure, Richard Yuricich and Rocco Gioffre would use the matte camera to project the reduction shot onto a white Masonite board. They would then trace the outline of the image onto the Masonite and use an airbrush to paint the rest of the board black. This matte was then burned into a new interpositive along with the reduction. The final result was a small image of the base of operations surrounded by an otherwise black frame of film. When this new interpositive was printed onto the dupe negative, the base would print through onto the dupe and the black area would darken the rest of the frame and dampen any overexposure. For shots featuring the glows and flares, the black area surrounding the glow/flare on its interpositive would serve the same purpose. For other shots, Don Jarel used an adjustable template that fit inside the optical printer to mask select areas of the frame.

To further protect against image degradation, the team decided not to make interpositives of the animation elements and the matte paintings, but rather to burn them directly onto the dupe negative, meaning that those elements would all be pristine first-generation photography. One problem with this approach was that internegative stock was designed for duplication photography, not original photography. The pigments in the emulsion of the stock tended to skew the colors in the matte paintings. To compensate, Matthew Yuricich needed to create his paintings using a palette that was compatible with the intermediate stock so that the colors would skew back to the correct hues in the final print (for example, he had to paint the rocks at the base of Devils Tower in vivid shades of yellow and red so that they would appear grayish blue in the finished movie).

Although the exact order in which the elements were composited was different for each shot, the basic procedure was as follows: Following Richard Yuricich's line-up plan, Robert Hall would place an interpositive of one of the previously photographed elements (either a live-action plate, a base-of-operations reduction, a model shot, or some cloud footage) into the optical printer (along with its matte) and photograph it onto the dupe negative. Once the take was finished, the interpositive was removed from the projector and the dupe would be wound back to the beginning. Another interpositive would then be placed in the projector and filmed. This process would be repeated until all of the elements had been printed onto the dupe.

It was not always a straightforward process. In many cases, the elements had to be finessed during the optical photography. For example, sometimes the density (opacity) of the traveling mattes had to be adjusted in the course of a shot. It was discovered that in shots in which a UFO approached the camera from a distance, the saucer needed to appear very solid when it was far away, but that if it maintained that same level of solidity as it neared the camera, it tended to look like a cardboard cutout that had been pasted over the shot. To solve this problem, the regular traveling matte was replaced with a lower-density matte as the saucer grew closer. This semi-transparent matte would let some light leak through to the black "hole" in the internegative where the saucer was supposed to go. When the saucer was printed into the "hole," this light would show through the saucer a bit, softening its sharp outline enough that it wouldn't stand out. For shots in which the UFOs crossed in front of or behind solid objects (rocks, other saucers, etc.) the mattes for the various objects that appeared in the frame would have to be dissolved in or out as the shot progressed so that the wrong object would not be blocked at the wrong time.

Matting the Paintings

Once all of the interpositive elements had been printed, the unprocessed dupe negative (which was called a "held take") was removed from the optical printer. If the shot required a matte painting, it would then be sent to the matte room and put into the matte stand camera to be photographed by Don Jarel. The matte painting itself was set up in front of the camera on one of the frames. To avoid creating any unsightly matte lines (a dark, black outline that can surround an imprecisely matted element), separate masks were not used with most of the paintings. Instead, the clear portions of the Masonite were covered with a high-gloss black paint that was feathered to the edges of the painting, which allowed the painting to act as its own matte. When the painting was photographed, the black paint would prevent exposure of everything but the artwork itself, burning the painted image into the internegative with no matte lines in evidence.

The matte stand was also used to enhance the stadium lights in shots filmed on the Big Set. The lights used on the stage did not register with sufficient intensity in the original production footage, so matte paintings of the lights were created and holes drilled into the Masonite board where the lights were to appear. A series of projector bulbs was arranged on a Peg-Board positioned behind the painting so that the incredibly bright light from the bulbs would shine through the painting during photography. Extra flares were added to some of the UFO shots using a similar process.

The matte camera room, the optical camera room, and the optical line-up room were all connected to an air filtration system that was designed to keep the rooms free from dust and other particles. This is a must in all optical work, as a speck of dust on a negative can end up as a giant blob on screen.

Seeing Stars

Once all of the other elements had been composited, the internegative was sent to the animation department so that the animation effects (solar explosions, scanner effects, etc.) could be burned in. The final animation effect added to each shot was the stars. This was done because each time the stars were copied, they spread and got larger. After too many generations, they began to look like big polka dots rather than delicate pinpoints. To prevent this from happening, the stars were burned directly into the internegative just before it was sent to processing.

To position the stars in the frame, Robert Swarthe would make still frame blowups of each shot. Along with Doug and Steven, he would determine exactly where the stars would fit into the picture. Harry Moreau would then use a technique developed by Doug Trumbull during the making of 2001 to custom-make a star field for the shot by carefully airbrushing splatters of paint onto shiny black paper (Trumbull created a few of the star fields as well). Roto-mattes were generated by tracing around all of the people and objects in each frame. When the time came to film the shot, the internegative would be loaded into the animation camera and the star field placed on the Oxberry bed. The shot would be exposed frame by frame, burning the stars into the internegative. Initially, the roto-mattes were placed directly onto the star field and changed after each frame had been shot. Eventually, however, they were photographed onto high-contrast black-and-white film and the resulting traveling matte was bi-packed into the animation camera along with the internegative.

Because the internegative stock was not designed for photography, it was not very sensitive to light, so to shoot the stars the animation cameramen had to use a lot of illumination—a blinding eight thousand watts—and long exposures ranging from ten seconds to a minute or more per frame. It could often take up to eight hours to insert all of the stars into a single shot. Because stars needed to be added to almost half the shots in the movie, multiple crews worked around the clock making and filming star fields and mattes. It got so busy that Richard Yuricich had a second animation stand built out of pipes that was used just for the stars. Since the main animation stand was called the Oxberry, this new contraption was dubbed the "Pipeberry." Alan Harding was the production's primary animation cameraman, but when the workload increased, veteran Disney animation photographer Maxwell Morgan (*Snow White*), who at the time was almost eighty, came in to help out. Bill Millar was the night shift cameraman, and the seemingly ubiquitous Scott Squires was also occasionally roped into evening duty.

Bob Swarthe reports that the stars looked spectacular in the 65mm dailies. However, many of them were lost when the shots were reduced to 35mm, and even more were lost when the release prints were made. They were still so convincing, however, that many viewers never realized that the stars were an effect. Instead, they thought that the filmmakers had taken their camera outside and simply photographed the night sky.

Finishing Up

Once the stars had all been inserted, the dupe negative was sent to MGM for developing (Special Visual Effects Coordinator Larry Robinson was Future General's liaison with the MGM lab, where all of the dailies, interpositives, and composites were processed). The finished composite was then screened at the Annex. If Doug Trumbull and Steven Spielberg approved it, then a 65mm interpositive would be made from the dupe negative and used to create a 35mm reduction negative of the shot. The 35mm reduction negative was sent to Michael Kahn's editorial department, where it could be used to make workprints for the editing process and then eventually cut in with the rest of the 35mm negative when the film was finished. If Steven and Doug didn't approve the shot, then it would have to be redone. (On one occasion, Spielberg and Trumbull had both signed off on a shot when Rocco Gioffre pointed out a minor flaw that no one else had noticed. Steven immediately ordered that the shot be redone, a task that required considerable time and effort. Following this incident, the Future General team made Rocco a muzzle out of gaffer's tape as a joke, and John Veitch decreed that no screening could start until Rocco put it on, which Gioffre, with tongue good-naturedly in cheek, would cheerfully do.) This didn't happen very often, however. Because the optical compositing process was so extraordinarily complex and delicate, each visual effects shot was subjected to an intensive amount of testing, checking, fixing, and tweaking at every step of the way to ensure that everything would come out correctly. All of this time and effort paid off because approximately ninety percent of all the effects shots that appear in the final film were first takes. Only a very few of them had to be redone.

Death Burgers and Deadlines

Steven spent a lot of time at Future General. Throughout the entire post-production period he came by the facility three or four days a week to view rushes, consult with Doug and Richard on the work in progress, and check out the general goings-on. Spielberg took an active interest in every aspect of the process, and his boundless energy and enthusiasm served as a great motivator and morale booster. He enjoyed working with Doug Trumbull—whom he described as "the next Walt Disney"—and described their collaboration as being "a turn-on.... I would give Doug an idea, and then he would give me an idea; and we'd just kind of bounce things of each other until a new idea grew out of an old one." Steven also had great respect for Richard Yuricich, whom he described as "a creative collaborator... without whom I would have lost my head more than once." Steven also had a good time working with the rest of the team, including Bob Swarthe and Dennis Muren. He was especially close to Dave Stewart, and the two of them would work closely together planning the saucer shots.

As he had done during principal photography, Steven was constantly coming up with notions to enhance, improve, and augment the existing visual effects shots. As he saw the quality of work that Future General was turning out and his confidence in the team's ability to bring the impossible to life increased, he began dreaming up new shots as well. These additional bits were terrifically exciting, but they did cause the effects shoot to run over schedule and over budget. This exacerbated an already tense situation, because by this point Julia had begun asking Columbia for the additional $2 million required to complete the photographic effects work, and, needless to say, the studio was not happy. Having originally been told that the effects would cost $1 million and then learning out they were actually going to cost $3 million (as well as finding out that their producer had misled them—by now, Julia had admitted her initial deception), the executives were in no mood to spend any more money.

The apparently slow process of the work did little to cheer them. Since all of the elements for each shot needed to be produced before the composites could be done, very few visual effects shots were completed until production was almost over. From Columbia's perspective, it appeared that the studio was spending enormous amounts of money and not getting anything in return. Because of this, Richard Yuricich feels that the studio "...thought we were out of control. We looked it, but we weren't. We were always under control." Hoping to speed things up, the studio brought Larry Butler out of retirement once again and sent him down to Future General. When he arrived on Glencoe Avenue, Butler told Yuricich that he had been "crowned" with the authority to move them along. Richard's response was to go home until Butler's crown was removed, which took less than a day.

The Columbia executives eventually approved the additional funds, but they remained extremely concerned. John Veitch began spending part of almost every day at Marina Del Rey to keep an eye on things. As he had been in Mobile, Veitch—whom Richard Yuricich describes as being "a very positive presence"—was extremely supportive of the effects team and their efforts, although he still did his best to hurry things up and keep a lid on costs, which wasn't easy to do when Steven was continually adding new shots. To corral him, Veitch would occasionally decree that all work on the effects would need to stop by a certain "inflexible" date, but most of those deadlines came and went without notice. Outwardly, Veitch remained un-ruffled, although Rocco Gioffre is sure that "John had a room somewhere where he could go and scream."

The intensive workload was hard on the Future General staff. Everyone worked long hours, often six or seven days a week. As time went on, the facility began operating on a twenty-four-hour-a-day basis and additional workers were brought on to help out (the staff eventually topped out at about thirty-five). Fortunately, there was a great sense of camaraderie and sense of purpose among the staff—most everyone liked each other and all were extremely dedicated to the task at hand—that helped get them through. To sustain them in their labors, they would send out for guaca-mole and chips or pop down to a local diner to consume a potent fast food concoction they dubbed the Death Burger, a favorite of Steven's (at the time Spielberg was apparently something of a junk food connoisseur—he was also reportedly quite partial to Slurpees). On occasion, the Future Generalists would visit their friends at Industrial Light & Magic and watch footage from *Star Wars*.

The saucer and Mothership model photography wrapped toward the end of August 1977, and over the next five or six weeks the finished com-posites began rolling out at a rapid rate. The quality of the work was spec-tacular and Steven was thrilled—Trumbull and his team had literally made his dreams come true (at the time of the film's release, Spielberg stated several times that Future General had given him only seventy-five percent of what he wanted, but fifty percent more than he had ever thought would be possible). The final cost of the effects was approximately $3.5 million, only a modest percentage over the initial $3 million estimate, which was remarkable considering how many shots had been added in the mean-time.

Future General finished work on *Close Encounters* in October 1977. The entire crew was exhausted but extremely satisfied with their efforts (Doug Trumbull described the experience as being "very rewarding" and was pleased that they were able to create extremely beautiful and realistic illusions that had even experienced professionals asking "How did they do that?"). When asked by Julia Phillips how he came to know all that he did about visual effects, Richard Yuricich—referring to the many months he had spent working on Stanley Kubrick's space epic—quipped that he was a member of "the Class of 2001." Inspired by Yuricich's comment, Julia had dozens of diplomas made up and handed them out to all of the members of the visual effects staff. Signed by Steven, Doug, Julia, Michael Phillips, and John Veitch, the diplomas certified that the recipients had "successfully completed creative activities and requirements for graduation" and that they were all now proud members of "the Class of CE3K." This pride was justified—the team had toiled long and hard and in the end had produced what *American Cinematographer* characterized as "the most believable and sophisticated visual effects ever put on film."

CHAPTER 23 | **Post-Production**

THE EDITING OF *Close Encounters* began at the same time that principal photography did. Some directors prefer to wait until production has wrapped to begin putting a film together, but Spielberg liked to cut as he shot, because it allowed him to see how the movie was shaping up and gave him the option to reshoot or add additional material if necessary. Film editor Michael Kahn worked in the makeshift cutting room that he had set up on the screened-in porch of the house he shared with Steven in Mobile, assembling preliminary versions of each scene. Kahn made so much progress that he had a rough cut of the entire movie ready just two weeks after the company returned to Los Angeles in September 1976. Kahn and Spielberg refined the rough cut throughout the fall and winter in a second editing room that was established in a rented apartment in a gated complex in Marina Del Rey. This location was chosen because it was close to Future General. Since Steven needed to split the majority of his post-production time between editing and the visual effects work, he wanted to cut the film in a place that would allow him to get to Glencoe Avenue without having to waste a lot of time traveling (The Burbank Studios, where most Columbia pictures were edited, was a thirty to forty-five minute drive away from the Marina). Spielberg had originally wanted to edit at Future General, but there wasn't enough room.

One of Michael Kahn's major challenges was to effectively interweave the film's three major plotlines: Roy's odyssey, Lacombe's investigation, and the scenes devoted to Jillian and Barry. To achieve a proper balance, bits and pieces were cut from each. As the editing process progressed,

Neary's story suffered the most—a number of scenes showcasing Ronnie and the kids, Roy at work, and his interactions with UFO true believers at Crescendo Summit were dropped. Lacombe's story only lost one major scene—one in which the Mayflower team boards Air East 31 (one of the planes involved in the UFO encounter monitored by the air traffic controllers at the beginning of the film), tells the passengers that they flew through restricted military airspace while some top secret weapons were being tested, and confiscates their cameras and film. Only a few minor bits were trimmed from Jillian's story, which was the least extensive of the three to begin with.

Kahn's other big challenge was The Experience. An astounding one hundred thousand feet of film (enough for seven or eight full-length features) had been shot for the sequence—so many scenes, incidents, and vignettes that assembling them into a coherent whole proved to be enormously difficult (especially since most of the visual effects weren't available until the very end of the process). For a long time, the sequence refused to jell until one evening in late February or early March 1977 when Michael pulled an all-nighter in which "the images came fast and furious." The next morning, Kahn showed Spielberg what he had done. Steven approved it and, although changes continued to be made, the version of The Experience that Michael put together that evening was essentially the one that ended up in the finished film. By the time it was completed, most of the ET footage—including the extraterrestrials' midair acrobatics, their explorations of the base of operations, and their interactions with Lacombe and Hynek—had been cut. Steven removed these bits because he was dissatisfied with the appearance of the aliens and was worried that audiences would find these vignettes comical.

Spielberg loved working with Kahn, whom he described as being "irrepressible…. His enthusiasm for this project bordered on the ridiculous and occasionally it dwarfed my own. He would recut a scene twenty times if it meant discovering something fresh—an extra laugh, three more seconds of tension, a better reading." Kahn got so caught up in his work that he found that his perspective was becoming skewed. "We got so paranoid after a while," Kahn recalled in *The Making of Close Encounters of the Third Kind*, a 1999 documentary. "We'd run outside and see a cloud and say, 'Let's get this picture done before the Mothership comes down.' You started really believing this stuff."

Even as they were cutting things out of the movie, Steven was busy shooting new bits to put into it. Throughout post-production, Spielberg filmed a number of inserts that were spliced into existing scenes to clarify or enhance them. The scene that had the most new material added to it was the one in which the aliens descend on Jillian's farmhouse and kidnap Barry. Feeling that it wasn't intense enough, Steven augmented a brief bit in which Jillian shuts the fireplace flue to keep the aliens from entering the house through the chimney and turned it into a suspenseful sequence in which she struggles to close the flue as the unseen creatures (represented by an eerie POV shot) come racing down the chute. Spielberg then added another interlude in which Jillian blocks the ETs' attempt to climb up through a vent in the floor by pulling a rug over it and anchoring it with a piece of furniture. These new bits were filmed on the small stage at the Future General Annex by cinematographer John Alonzo. Cary Guffey wasn't available, so a double was brought in to work with Melinda Dillon. When Guffey did become available some time later, a second shoot was scheduled to film close-ups of Cary and Melinda, which were photographed by veteran cinematographer Laszló Kovács (*Easy Rider, Steelyard Blues, Five Easy Pieces, Paper Moon, Shampoo*). Kovács was a close friend of Vilmos Zsigmond—the two men had gone to film school together in Hungary and Kovács had helped Zsigmond shoot the footage of the revolution and escape with it to the west.

While Michael Kahn was editing the picture, Frank Warner was editing the sound. Usually the only audio recorded for a movie is the dialogue. All other sounds are put in later by the sound editor. Warner had worked on a long list of films, including *Hell in the Pacific* (1968), *Little Big Man* (1970), *Harold and Maude* (1971), *Paper Moon* (1973), *Shampoo* (1975), and *Taxi Driver* (1976). He was finishing *Bound for Glory* in the summer of 1976 when Steven invited him down to Alabama for a job interview. The two men hit it off and Warner was hired.

Frank began his assignment by asking Gene Cantamessa to record certain sounds that were unique to the Big Set (including many of the noises made by the scientific equipment), since these would be impossible to recreate later. He then spent some time selecting pre-recorded sounds from his own personal library. What he couldn't find, he would record. When an unusual or otherworldly sound was required, Warner would create it by recording existing sounds (Steven and Frank wanted all of the audio in *Close Encounters* to be "real," so they had agreed not to use anything electronic or synthesized) and manipulating them—by slowing the recordings down, speeding them up, playing them backward, changing their equalization, or blending them with other recordings. Warner's biggest creative challenge was to create a "sound" for the UFOs. Spielberg wanted the saucers to have a "presence" of some sort, even when they weren't on screen, so he and Frank decided to have all natural sounds (dogs, crickets, birds, etc.) cease just before the UFOs appeared. When the saucers finally arrived, they would emit a low roar as they flew through a shot. The natural sounds would resume a few beats after they had gone. The Mothership required a number of different sounds to bring it to life. The ominous rumbling heard as it appears over Devils Tower was a slow-speed mixture of low-end noises, deep musical notes played by an orchestra, and a chorus of human voices. The continuous throbbing that it makes after it touches down (which was developed in response to Steven's desire for the Mothership to sound like a factory or a refinery) consisted of a slow-speed recording of Marines on the march mixed in with a steel girder twisting and other metallic sounds. Because the visual effects were often not available, Frank, like Michael Kahn, often found himself working blind—creating sounds for images he couldn't see.

Warner liked working with Spielberg because he felt that, unlike many directors, Steven respected creative sound work and considered it to be just as important to the success of a film as the cinematography, editing, and special effects. He also liked that Spielberg was willing to experiment and try just about anything to see if it would work. (As a result of one of these experiments, Steven and Warner decided to record certain sounds in a lower register so that they would move the air in the theater when they emerged from the speakers, allowing the sound to impact the audience in a very physical way.)

By March 1977, Spielberg and Michael Kahn had completed a solid first cut (the cinematic version of a first draft) of the movie. Doug Trumbull asked Steven if he would show it to the Future General effects team, since none of them had seen any part of the film other than the shots that they were working on. Steven agreed, and a screening was held on Monday, March 14. The reaction was decidedly lukewarm. One of the main complaints was that some parts of the story were hard to follow—specifically, people had a hard time understanding how Lacombe and his team know to rendezvous with the aliens at Devils Tower (in the script, this point is never explained—the meeting has apparently been arranged before the story begins). Many people also didn't understand the subplot involving the Mayflower Project's nerve gas hoax (in the script, we only learn that it is a hoax by implication, when Roy takes off his gas mask and doesn't die. Up until that point, there is no indication that the spill is a put-on. This ultimately proved to be too subtle and after-the-fact for the audience to clearly grasp). There was also some confusion as to the identity of the Navy pilots who come off the Mothership first. Following the screening, Spielberg decided that he needed to restructure some of the plot and shoot some additional scenes that would clarify these confusing story points.

These were not the only new scenes that needed to be filmed. By now, both Bob Baker and Carlo Rambaldi had finished their ET puppets. Since most of the alien action had been cut, Steven decided not to go forward with Baker's marionette, but he did want to use Rambaldi's animatronic extraterrestrial to reshoot the farewell exchange of Kodály hand signals between Lacombe and the lead alien (a bit that had originally been filmed in Mobile with one of the ballet students wearing a rubber ET glove that crinkled visibly when she made the signs). Feeling that the air traffic control scene was a weak way to begin the movie, Spielberg also wanted to create a new opening for the film.

These additions were obviously going to cost money, which meant that again Julia Phillips had to go back to Columbia to ask for more funds. This time she would be dealing with the studio's new head of production. Stanley Jaffe had resigned and been replaced by Daniel Melnick, a former stage, screen, and television producer (*Get Smart*, *Straw Dogs*) and head of production at MGM (where he was responsible for greenlighting films such as *That's Entertainment* (1974), *That's Entertainment Part II* [1976], and *Network* [1976]) who joined Columbia in February 1977. Fortunately, Melnick was extremely enthusiastic about *Close Encounters*, and he and David Begelman were willing to invest more money in the film. To write the new scenes, Steven once again turned to Hal Barwood and Matthew Robbins, who were currently at MGM preparing to produce and direct a film that they had written called *Stingray*. Answering Spielberg's call, they put their movie aside for a few days and returned to *CE3K*.

To give the film a more exciting opening and to explain the identity of the Navy pilots, Steven wanted to resurrect a scene that had been in the early drafts of the script but had been cut for budgetary reasons: the return of the planes from Flight 19. The original Flight 19 scene had been set in Brazil, but when a trip to South America proved to be too costly, Steven, Hal, and Matthew batted around some cheaper variations, including having the planes reappear inside an aviation hangar or on an abandoned freeway. Finally, the trio decided that Flight 19 would be discovered in the middle of a raging sandstorm in Mexico's Sonora Desert. To explain how Lacombe and company know to meet the aliens at Devils Tower, Barwood and Robbins wrote a scene set at the Goldstone radio telescope in Barstow, California. In the scene, we learn that the Mayflower Project has been beaming the five tones out into space and receiving a puzzling set of numbers in return. Steven had been pleased with Bob Balaban's work in the rest of the movie and wanted to give the actor more to do, so Hal and Matthew changed his character's backstory. Instead of being a professional interpreter, David Laughlin would now be a Mayflower Project cartographer who happens to speak French and is drafted to serve as Lacombe's translator. Laughlin's map-reading skills allow him to recognize that the mysterious numbers are actually the latitude and longitude of Devils Tower (which the film erroneously identifies as 40°36'10"N, 104°44'30"W. The real coordinates are 44°35'25"N, 104°42'55"W). Finally, Barwood and Robbins wrote a scene that brought back Major Walsh and showed him brainstorming with a group of dirty tricksters to plot the nerve gas hoax, which Walsh hopes will clear the area around Devils Tower of "every living Christian soul."

Because Francois Truffaut wouldn't be available until late spring, the new scenes were scheduled to be shot in May 1977. By now it was obvious that *Close Encounters* was not going to be ready for release in June, so the decision was made to push the opening back to the end of the year. Steven wanted the film to premiere at Christmas, but Columbia wanted it to debut just before Thanksgiving. Spielberg didn't like this plan, because it meant that he would need to finish post-production by October. He wanted more time, but Columbia was adamant: the film would be released in November.

A new cinematographer was brought in to photograph the additions. Born in 1923, William A. Fraker was a third-generation cameraman—his grandmother, father, and uncle were still photographers (his father at Columbia Pictures in the 1930s). After serving in World War II, Fraker enrolled in USC's film school, where he became interested in cinematography. After spending several years on the fringes of the industry, he worked on a few early television shows (*The Lone Ranger, The Adventures of Ozzie and Harriet*) and eventually became a camera operator. Fraker started working as a cinematographer on television commercials in 1965 and earned his first feature credit on 1967's *Games*. He went on to photograph films such as *Rosemary's Baby* (1968), *Bullitt* (1968), and *Looking for Mr. Goodbar* (1977), and to direct *Monte Walsh* (1970) and *A Reflection of Fear* (1973). Fraker was recommended to Spielberg by set decorator Phil Abramson, who had worked with him on *Bullitt, Monte Walsh*, and *A Reflection of Fear*.

There was a new producer for the scenes as well—or rather an old producer who had now returned. Julia's drug problem had worsened throughout the post-production period and was taking a toll on her job performance. She came late to meetings or missed them altogether and was becoming increasingly disorganized and inattentive, which made it hard for her to fulfill her many duties and responsibilities. By the beginning of May, Steven—whose patience for such antics was wearing thin—asked Michael Phillips to step back in and supervise the production of the additional scenes. Michael agreed, which was good news for the production but created a great deal of tension between him and his ex-wife.

With veteran Jerry Ziesmer (*Black Sunday, Apocalypse Now*) serving as first assistant director, cameras rolled on the Flight 19 scene on May 17, 1977 (exactly one year to the day after filming began in Wyoming), in the El Mirage Dry Lake, which was located in the Mojave Desert approximately sixty miles outside Los Angeles. A small junkyard set had been constructed and dressed with five vintage Navy Avenger Torpedo Bombers that had been rented from collectors and flown in the night before. François Truffaut (who had just finished work on *L'Homme qui aimait les femmes*, the film that he wrote during his time in Mobile), Bob Balaban, and J. Patrick McNamara were on hand to reprise their roles. McNamara's Project Leader was not originally supposed to appear in the scene—the script had a character called The Tall Man accompany Lacombe to the Mexican desert. By May 1977, however, Pat had moved from New Orleans to Los Angles to try his luck in Hollywood and had become a member of Steven's regular Thursday night skeet shooting party at the Oak Tree Gun Club in Newhall, California (a group that also included John Milius, Robert Zemeckis, Bob Gale, and actor Robert Stack). One evening just prior to the start of shooting, Steven was talking to McNamara about the scene and realized that it would be more logical to have the Project Leader, who was by now a major character in the film, accompany Lacombe instead. Thus, McNamara, who had started out with little more than a bit part, ended up with a major role and the film's opening line ("Are we the first?").

The morning was spent filming Lacombe and Laughlin's arrival at the junkyard. The sandstorm was created by using a half dozen or so large wind machines (giant fans fitted with airplane propellers) to blow bags of Fuller's earth—a fine, powdery clay—across the set (cast and crew all wore goggles and gas masks to keep from breathing the noxious stuff, which ended up getting into every nook and cranny of every piece of equipment and every human body on the set). The scene took a long time to shoot, because the actors and the cameramen couldn't see their marks through all of the dust, and the noise from the propellers made it hard to hear dialogue and directions. The afternoon was spent shooting the discovery of the Navy ATBs. The company stayed overnight in a local motel and then on May 18 shot the scene in which Lacombe interviews a sunburned old man who saw the UFOs return the planes. The old man was played by Eumenio Blanco, who had once been an opera singer and had a long career as a character actor in both Mexican and American movies. On May 19, the production relocated to the Burbank Studios Ranch, a small satellite lot just down the street from the main facility, where the radio telescope scene was shot on an unadorned soundstage using one of the trailers that had been sent back from the Big Set in Mobile. On May 20, the Kodály hand sign exchange was reshot on the same stage. Truffaut and Balaban were both present, but the star of the scene turned out to be Carlo Rambaldi's ET puppet, a beguiling creation that Steven nicknamed Puck.

Rambaldi had created Puck by sculpting a full-size model of the creature in clay—basing the face in part on pictures of Cary Guffey. Carlo then built a skeleton out of aluminum and steel and installed mechanical devices at various points on the frame to facilitate arm and hand movements. Next Rambaldi fashioned a skull for the extraterrestrial out of fiberglass and fitted it with mechanisms that would move the creature's eyes and allow it to make facial expressions. The torso and skull mechanisms were operated by fifteen thin, flexible cables that ran down through Puck's body, out its feet, and over to a control panel where they were attached to a series of levers. When the levers were moved, the mechanisms would be activated and the alien would come to life. Esophagus and chest movements were created by pumping air through tubes into cylinders built into the creature's chest. Rambaldi then generated a positive and negative mold from the initial clay sculpture and (with the help of American makeup artist Dick Cobos) used it to create a quarter-inch-thick polyurethane skin that was fitted over Puck's skull and skeleton. The polyurethane was extremely delicate and decomposed rapidly, so it was only manufactured and applied just before filming. Rambaldi constructed Puck in his workshop in Rome and brought it to the United States in March 1977, when he came to receive his Academy Award for *King Kong*. Spielberg was thrilled with Carlo's work (and by the fact that he was one of the few vendors on the film who delivered on time and on budget). Puck was placed on a small set that was filled with smoke and lit to replicate the backlit intensity of the Big Set in Mobile. It took a crew of seven operators to work the extraterrestrial's controls. Steven himself operated the levers that made Puck smile during the filming of the alien's close-up.

On May 21, the scene in which Major Walsh plots the poison gas hoax was filmed in the woodworking mill at The Burbank Studios, which was dressed to portray the Mayflower Project's secret warehouse. Shots were also filmed of Walsh's men loading equipment bound for Devils Tower into a convoy of tractor trailers disguised as chain store delivery trucks. With that, filming on *Close Encounters* had come to an end—again. As Michael Phillips recalls, "We had, if I remember correctly, half a dozen wrap parties. Each got smaller, but champagne was popped. Each time it looked like that was it. Each time, it wasn't." (It wouldn't be this time, either—a few weeks later, Steven returned to the mill to film another scene showing the team of pilgrims—the red jumpsuited astronauts who were supposed to go aboard the Mothership—arriving at the Mayflower warehouse and boarding a chartered bus headed for Wyoming. John Alonzo returned to photograph this scene.)

After filming on the additional scenes wrapped, Spielberg took a few days off and went to Hawaii with his friend George Lucas, who wanted to get away from all the hoopla surrounding the release of *Star Wars*, which opened on May 25, 1977. Steven had mixed feelings about Lucas's film. On the one hand, he loved the movie itself and thought that it would be a big hit (he was right—the movie would gross $165 million in its initial run and overtake *Jaws* as the highest-grossing picture of all time in November 1977). On the other hand, he was not thrilled that it was coming out before *Close Encounters* (which would not have happened if *CE3K* had made its original Easter release date). Although the two were very different movies, they were both science fiction, and Steven was worried that if audiences got their fill of the genre with *Star Wars*, they might not want to come and see his film. However, whatever misgivings he might have had took a back seat to friendship, and he and Lucas had a terrific time (it was during this vacation that they cooked up the idea for *Raiders of the Lost Ark*).

After the additional scenes had been cut into the film, John Williams began composing his score. Williams was eager to work on *Close Encounters* because he loved the idea of doing a film about contact with extraterrestrial life. Initially, however, some of the executives at Columbia felt that, because John had just done the music for *Star Wars*, he shouldn't do the score for *Close Encounters*. They were worried that the music would end up sounding the same. Spielberg, of course, insisted on Williams, who had no intention of repeating what he had done on *Star Wars*. Whereas the score for that film was "very classical...almost operatic," Williams felt that the music for *Close Encounters* needed to be "abstract and impressionistic and otherworldly." Williams ultimately composed a score that consisted of two types of music: romantic—"where the notes are recognizable as notes and have tonal harmonies"—and non-tonal—"where there's no tonal relationship from phrase to phrase, note to note...a kind of a chaos." John felt that "the film demanded both of these approaches one on top of the other"—the romantic music for action sequences and emotional scenes (such as The Experience) and the non-tonal sounds for scenes of fear and confusion (such as Barry's kidnapping). The romantic portions of the score were based on three elements: the five tones, a four-note motif that Williams composed for Neary, and a musical theme for the Mayflower Project. The non-tonal sections were created by combining a variety of discordant musical phrases, with the occasional sound effect mixed in. After Herbert Spencer prepared the orchestrations, Williams recorded the score at Twentieth Century-Fox, conducting a 110-piece orchestra composed of professional studio musicians. Steven Spielberg called the result "airborne and awe-inspiring...a great symphony...and one of my favorite scores that John has ever written."

Once the music was finished, all of the film's audio elements—the score, effects, and dialogue—were mixed together reel by reel over a twelve-week period at the state-of-the-art Todd-AO sound facility in Hollywood. Re-recording mixers Robert "Buzz" Knudson, Don MacDougall, and Robert Glass mixed the tracks under the supervision of Spielberg, Williams, and Frank Warner. Although it is customary for a picture to be "locked" (i.e., finished with no further changes) at this stage, Steven was still making alterations—trimming shots and scenes, shooting more inserts, etc.—as the mix progressed. Warner kept a synthesizer on the dubbing stage to generate new sounds if required, and John Williams's longtime music editor Kenneth Wannberg was on hand to lengthen or shorten the score to accommodate Spielberg's changes.

The *Close Encounters* mix was recorded in stereo. Since the beginning of talkies, most movie sound had been monaural. It was generated by an optical track—a visual representation of the film's sound waves that was printed alongside the picture on a strip of film. A device on the projector translated the visual sound waves into audio that emerged from a single speaker located behind the screen in front of the theater. Over the years, a number of different systems were developed that used a number of tracks to create multi-channel sound, but most of those were extremely complicated and/or expensive and were therefore never deployed on a wide basis. In 1976, however, the San Francisco-based Dolby Laboratories introduced a new technology that encoded four different channels of sound—left, right, center, and surround (which was used for ambient sound and special effects and played over speakers located on the sides and in the rear of the theater)—on a single optical track. The Dolby system had two great advantages over previous cinematic stereo formats. The first was that the cost of manufacturing a Dolby soundtrack was approximately the same as that of a regular optical track, which made the cost-conscious studios more receptive to using it. In addition, a 35mm Dolby Stereo print could be played in a theater equipped with Dolby cinema decoders and a four-channel playback system, but it could also be run in a conventional mono auditorium. This meant that only one type of print needed to be made (as opposed to multiple formats, as had previously been required), which also saved a lot of money. *A Star Is Born* (1976) was the first film to use the new system, with *Star Wars* following soon afterward. At this same time, Dolby also introduced a system for 70mm prints called Dolby Stereo 70 mm Six

Track, which used six channels of sound recorded on magnetic strips that were attached to either side of the print. Since *Close Encounters* was going to be released in 35mm and 70mm, it would employ both systems.

Preparing a four-channel soundtrack was a more complicated task than preparing a mono mix, because the engineers had to decide which channel each effect would go on. They would sometimes have to move the sounds from one channel to another in order to track certain on-screen moves (for example, in shots in which helicopters flew into frame from over the camera, the sound would begin in the rear speakers, move to the middle speakers, and finish in the front to give the impression that the chopper was actually zooming over the heads of the audience). The mix was done using Dolby's A-Type noise reduction process, which reduced background hiss and made the track and all the sounds on it clearer and sharper.

As the movie neared completion, the production had to weather a number of crises and controversies. The first concerned the film's writing credit. The screenplay credits on all Hollywood feature films are determined by the Writers Guild of America, the union that represents screenwriters. When a movie has finished shooting, the production company is required to notify the Guild and all of the writers who worked on the screenplay and list the names of the people it intends to credit on the final film. If any of the writers disagree with the company's proposal, or if a director or a production executive associated with the project claims a writing credit, then the matter goes to arbitration. (The director/production executive rule was established to prevent directors, producers, and studio executives from using their power positions to put their names on movies they hadn't written, something that happened frequently during the heyday of the studio system). When it does, a select WGA committee reads all drafts of the script, along with any supporting materials, to determine who wrote what. Credit is almost always awarded to the first writer on a project, on the assumption that his or her work was the basis of all that followed. Any subsequent scribe must be deemed to have written fifty percent or more of the final story in order to receive on-screen recognition. A writer is free to withdraw from the arbitration process and forgo credit if he or she so chooses.

After *Close Encounters* wrapped, Columbia sent out a notice giving Steven sole screenplay credit. The rationale for this was that Spielberg had authored the primary drafts of the screenplay that had been filmed (an assertion that a comparison of the various scripts confirms—although many changes and additions were made along the way, Spielberg's first few drafts lay out the plot of the final film almost exactly). Paul Schrader and John Hill were not credited, because they had written a story that wasn't used. Jerry Belson was omitted because, while he had certainly done good work on the characters and dialogue, he had not contributed substantially to the overall story. Finally, Hal Barwood and Matthew Robbins were left off the list, because they had never been officially hired to work on the script and their names did not appear on any of the drafts (all of the versions that the duo worked on with Steven were credited solely to Spielberg). Both Barwood and Robbins were fine with this—in their view, they had simply been helping out a pal. This was something that all of the Movie Brats did regularly for one another without credit or compensation—unless their contribution was unusually significant, in which case they were sometimes given a small piece of the project's profits. In accordance with this tradition, Steven gave Hal and Matthew points to thank them for their help (Hal Barwood comments: "We each had a small net percentage. I put my kids through college on it, so I'm happy").

Because Spielberg was claiming a credit, the WGA insisted that the script go to arbitration. However, Schrader, Hill, and Belson all withdrew from the process before it got started. Years later, Julia Phillips wrote that they had done so because Steven, wanting to take full credit for the screenplay, "made me pressure every writer who made a contribution to the script...to back off their right to credits." Paul Schrader appeared to confirm this when he told author Peter Biskind that he withdrew from the arbitration process because Julia pressured him into doing so, so that Steven could get sole credit. In other interviews, however, Schrader has said that he withdrew voluntarily because there was nothing of his left in the final script except the idea that Roy's encounter with the UFO should be a spiritual one.

In "My Close Encounter with *Close Encounters,*" John Hill reports that his withdrawal was completely voluntary: "When the time came for the obligatory Whiners Guild writing credits to be determined, I got a chance to read the shooting script of CLOSE ENCOUNTERS, and compare it to my own. Yeah, I wrote some similar scenes to what was in the film—but they were told to me by Steven. They were not my ideas. The tone was different, the main character, the point of it all, etc., so I didn't even try for a credit arbitration. I'm not sure the final film has a *the* or an *and* in it that I wrote or contributed." In an interview with the author, Jerry Belson said that he had never expected to receive a credit because the story was all Steven's (although he was disappointed that a promised "thank you" never appeared in the end credits).

As for Spielberg himself, in several interviews given at the time of the film's release, he made it very clear that he considered himself the principal author of the *Close Encounters* script, but he was also quite up-front about the early participation of Schrader and Hill and freely acknowledged the contributions of Barwood, Robbins, and Belson. Ultimately, the Writers Guild awarded Steven sole credit for the script, which Michael Phillips feels was warranted. As he told Spielberg biographer Joseph McBride: "*Close Encounters* is really Steven's script. He got help from his friends and colleagues here and there, but 99.9 percent is Steven Spielberg."

In September 1977, *Close Encounters* lost two of its prime movers. The first was Julia Phillips, whose behavior had become increasingly problematic as the summer progressed. Her drug use was more flagrant (on one occasion, she brought cocaine to a meeting at Columbia and shocked all of the executives by casually tossing it out onto the table in front of them), her tardiness and absences increased, and she got into a number of heated confrontations with her colleagues (including Steven) and with a few studio executives. She tried to take control of the studio's advertising and marketing campaigns for the film—areas in which producers usually just consult—and her interference kept many people in those departments from being able to do their jobs. She had also begun demanding that the studio renegotiate her contract and give her a significant portion of the film's merchandising revenue. Things became so chaotic that David Begelman finally decided he had to take action. On September 13, 1977, Begelman fired Julia and banned her from the Burbank Studios lot. Michael Phillips supervised the rest of the post-production process and Julia went to Hawaii, where she slipped deeper and deeper into drug use. "It's too bad," Joe Alves says today, echoing the opinion of many of his *CE3K* colleagues. "Julia was a terrific producer when she was on her game. I think she could have been first female president of a studio. She was so sharp...[but] she just couldn't control her life."

The second loss was David Begelman. Back in February 1977, actor

Cliff Robertson (*PT 109* [1963], *Charley* [1967], *Three Days of the Condor* [1975]) had received an IRS Form 1099 (Statement of Miscellaneous Income) from Columbia Pictures indicating that he had been paid $10,000 for work he did for the studio in 1976. Knowing that he hadn't worked for Columbia that year, Robertson and his accountant began an investigation that lasted for several months and ultimately led to the startling discovery that Begelman (who had once been Robertson's agent) had ordered the studio's accounting department to issue Robertson a check. Begelman then forged Robertson's signature, cashed the check, and kept the money for himself. In August 1977, Robertson reported the matter to the Beverly Hills and Burbank police and to the FBI. The Beverly Hills police contacted Alan Hirschfield, who launched an internal investigation that revealed that Begelman had embezzled from the studio on at least two other occasions, bringing the total of the stolen funds to $60,000. The investigation turned up a number of expense account irregularities and conflict-of-interest business deals on Begelman's part as well. Hirschfield reported his findings to the CPI board, and in late September Begelman was given a leave of absence. Daniel Melnick was named acting production president while Hirschfield and the board tried to figure out what to do about their larcenous studio chief. The board quickly split into two factions. The first, led by Hirschfield, wanted to fire Begelman and turn the matter over to the authorities. The other, led by Herbert Allen—at the urging of his close friend and confidant, producer Ray Stark, who was also a close friend of Begelman's—wanted to give Begelman a second chance. The split sparked a boardroom battle that would rage for months.

By the beginning of October, most of the visual effects had been finished and inserted into the movie, and on Wednesday, October 5, 1977, Steven screened it for Alan Hirschfield, Daniel Melnick, and other top Columbia executives. This was the first time that any of them had seen the picture in its entirety. Because they had no idea whether it was any good or not, they were understandably nervous. The final cost of the film had turned out to be $19,400,870, making it the most expensive film in Columbia Pictures' history (and one of the most expensive in Hollywood history). Although the studio was in much better financial shape than it had been when the project first started (thanks to hits like *Shampoo*, *The Wind and the Lion*, *Taxi Driver*, and *The Deep*), it still wasn't out of the woods. If *Close Encounters* was a hit, then the studio's financial troubles would be a thing of the past, but if it flopped, the studio would be crippled and might even go under. As soon as the executives saw the film, their anxiety dissipated. They all thought that the movie was wonderful and had the potential to be a huge blockbuster. A nervous Steven wasn't so sure. Hollywood rule of thumb was that a film needed to gross three times its cost to break even, which meant that *CE3K* would need to make $60 million and become one of the highest-grossing films of all time just to break even. To be considered a hit, it was going to have to earn even more, something Steven wasn't as certain would happen as the studio brass seemed to be. Knowing that the odds of him having two *Jaws*-like blockbusters in a row were slim, the most he dared to hope was that the film would make its money back and not sink the studio.

Test screenings were scheduled for Wednesday, October 19 and Thursday, October 20 at the Medallion Theatre in Dallas, Texas (Steven had had a successful preview of *Jaws* at the Medallion and considered it his lucky theater, so he wanted to test *Close Encounters* there as well). A week or so before the screenings, Spielberg became concerned that the initial appearance of the aliens wasn't dramatic enough, so he decided to include the Bob Baker marionette after all, beginning the final part of The Experience with the lanky, transparent alien emerging from the Mothership and spreading its arms in a benevolent greeting. Steven wanted the five-foot-tall puppet to appear to be at least twice that height, so Greg Jein supervised the construction of a half-scale version of the hatch. Busy with all of his other postproduction chores, Steven didn't have time to direct the scene himself, so he asked Doug Trumbull to do it instead. With Richard Yuricich photographing and Baker's team manipulating the marionette, Trumbull filmed the scene on a stage at The Burbank Studios in a single day, after which it was turned over to Michael Kahn to cut into the movie.

At the first Dallas screening, the audience response was tremendous. Michael Phillips recalls: "They were with the picture from the opening second, when we had the crescendo...just those strings over...and opening to that blast of white and the music. The audience applauded—that! I never saw an audience applaud an opening. So we thought we did pretty well." The second screening went even better, and the Columbia executives were thrilled.

Following the Dallas showings, Steven made a few more changes. He cut seven and a half minutes out of the film to improve the pacing and inserted a few more bits to better emphasize certain points. One of those points was Roy's obsession with the mountain. Feeling that it needed to be underscored further, Spielberg asked Barwood and Robbins to write a new speech for Neary that could be cut into a previously filmed scene in which Roy and Jillian help Barry build a miniature mountain out of mud on Crescendo Summit. In the original version of the scene, Roy and Jillian talk about the effect that their close encounters have had on their lives. In the new speech, Neary tells Jillian that he has been seeing the shape of the mountain everywhere and (using a line that both he and Lacombe will repeat later in the film) insists that "This means something. This is important." Richard Dreyfuss was recalled to film the new speech. In the year since principal photography had ended, Dreyfuss had lost a considerable amount of weight. So that Richard would match the way he looked in the rest of the scene, Steven's instruction to new cinematographer Frank Stanley was to "make him look fatter."

The major change that Steven made following the Dallas screenings was to cut the song "When You Wish Upon a Star" out of the movie. From the very conception of the project, he had intended to play the song over the final moments of The Experience—he had written it into every draft of the script, obtained all the permissions required to use it, and inserted a number of *Pinocchio* references into the film to pave the way. However, the preview audiences hadn't responded well to the tune—they took its inclusion to mean that the film was a fantasy, and they wanted to believe in its reality. Since this is what Steven wanted as well, he made the difficult decision to remove the song and replace it with original music composed by John Williams (although Williams did interpolate two brief quotes from the song into his score).

After these changes were made, a final sound mix was done, and by the end of October 1977, *Close Encounters* was finished. For the time being, anyway.

| *Close Encounters,*
Scene by Scene

Sonora Desert, Mexico—Present Day: The thunderous music cue that opens the film is called "Let There Be Light." • Lacombe and Laughlin's first meeting originally took place in the Air East 31 scene, but when that was cut, it was necessary to have them meet again in this added scene. • The wind blows constantly throughout this seven-minute sequence. Rather than run the same sound effect for the entire scene, Frank Warner used a different one for each shot in order to give the storm more character and each cut more force.

Air Traffic Control, Indianapolis Center: The light level was so low in the Air Route Traffic Control Center that Vilmos Zsigmond had to shoot with a wide-open camera lens. This greatly reduced the depth of field and made it impossible to keep more than a sliver of each shot in focus at one time. As the ATCs monitor the near-collision between Air East 31 and a UFO, camera operator Nick McLean had to subtly shift focus from one character to another depending on who was talking, a technique that added a great deal of tension to an already tense scene.

Barry Meets the Extraterrestrials: The establishing shot of the Guiler farmhouse was created by putting a 65mm image of the house together with a matte painting of the surrounding countryside and horizon and then burning the stars into the sky above. • Steven Poster photographed the individual shots of Barry's toys coming to life. • Frank Warner created the sounds for the ETs' culinary investigations by recording himself as he rifled through a real kitchen opening drawers, playing with silverware, popping the tops on soda cans, etc. • To get the proper reactions from Cary Guffey when he first encounters the (offscreen) aliens, Steven Spielberg put makeup man Bob Westmoreland (who was friendly with Cary) in a gorilla suit, dressed another crew member up as a clown, and then put them both behind cardboard blinds. When Guffey entered the kitchen, Steven dropped the first blind and revealed the clown, which caused Cary to startle. Spielberg then revealed the gorilla and Guffey got scared. At this point, Westmoreland removed his mask. When Cary recognized his friend, he smiled and then laughed. • Jillian is supposed to be suffering from the flu, which is why she looks so miserable and has fallen asleep with her clothes on. • Jillian's backstory is never explained. Melinda Dillon said she was under the impression that Jillian was supposed to be some sort of artist, but she never knew any more than that. Guiler is a single mother, but although Columbia's press notes describe Jillian as "young widow," neither the script nor the film ever clarifies her marital status. There's a Bekins Moving box in her bedroom, but we don't know if she and Barry have just moved into the house or are getting ready to move out (in an interview in *American Cinematographer*, Joe Alves says that the house belongs to Jillian's mother and that Jillian is staying there temporarily, while her mother is staying at Jillian's place in town). As Jillian leans out her bedroom window to call Barry, a single tiny light can be seen moving in the star-filled sky above her. Created by the animation department, this light was called a "missile" and was to subtly tip the audience that a UFO was coming.

Meet the Nearys: To prepare 1613 Carlisle Drive East for filming, Joe Alves and his team put in a lawn and installed a number of yellow and avocado-colored appliances. Steven encouraged Teri Garr to buy things for the house so that she would feel more at home there, so she picked out a lot of the furniture (mostly cheap French provincial), bought a bunch of knick-knacks, and even put up her own chore charts • Filled with gadgets and hobby accessories, the Neary's family room was extremely cramped. To place the camera far enough back to position it properly for certain shots, some of the walls had to be removed. Ultimately, Alves felt that they probably should have built the room as a set on a soundstage.

The Blackout: To create the initial shot of the blackout, the team at Future General photographed a suburban neighborhood from the top of a bank building in Culver City, California. A night sky and distant horizon were painted in. During filming, the lighted windows and the streetlights were painted black block by block (by Rocco Gioffre). • The lights that go dark in the long shot that ends the sequence were pieces of artwork photographed on the Oxberry and composited with a shot of a miniature landscape.

Roy Reports to Work: This scene was filmed in a real power station in Mobile. • It was originally followed by another scene in which Neary drives out to the site where the blackout began and discovers that the power lines have been stolen right off the poles (presumably by the ETs). Hearing reports that lights (UFOs) have been spotted in an area that the DWP's monitors indicate is dark, Roy worries that the linemen working there will be hurt if they touch a live wire. Roy wants to drive out to the area and warn them, but his supervisor order him to stay put. Roy decides to go anyway and deserts his post. In the script, it is this action that gets him fired. In the final cut of the film, this scene is dropped and Roy gets fired for not having made it out to his post in the first place.

Jillian Searches for Barry: This scene was filmed in some woods adjacent to the Guiler farmhouse. The isolated house and grounds were so eerie that they prompted Julia Phillips to proclaim that "Ghosts live here."

Roy's First Encounter: All of the long shots of Roy driving along the lonely back road were filmed in 65mm by Steve Poster. Because the camera was so far away, the truck's headlights couldn't be seen, so Poster wired a piece of white wood to one of the lights. The lamp illuminated the board, which from a distance looked like a beam of light shooting forward from the front of the truck. • In the long shot that follows the "jackass/turkey" scene, another missile can be seen in the sky behind Roy's truck. • The over-the-shoulder shot of Neary looking at the pull-down map in the cab of his truck after he arrives at the railroad crossing was filmed during post-production at Future General, with a miniature landscape placed positioned in front of the truck to create the horizon. Animation cameraman Alan Harding doubled Dreyfuss. • The UFO that appears behind Neary's truck and then rises up into the sky was created by mounting a bank of lights on a camera crane that was driven up behind the truck and elevated while the camera rolled. • The mailboxes and railroad signal were vibrated with electronically controlled pneumatic devices. • The blinding ray of light that blasts down onto Roy's truck from above was created using a collection of powerful HMI spotlights suspended above the truck by a crane. • The multicolored UFO underbelly that burns Roy when he looks up at it was a full-scale mock-up filmed in Hangar 2 at Brookley Field. • The sound of the vibrating railroad signal was a slowed-down recording of the squeak of Frank Warner's editing room chair. • The shot in which all of the items in Roy's truck cab fly up toward the ceiling was created by mounting the cab on a gimbal and turning it upside down, causing all of the junk in the cab to fall down to the ceiling. The camera was mounted to the side of the cab and so moved along with it, making it appear as if the truck had remained upright throughout the shot. The turnover was filmed four times. By the time they were done, Dreyfuss and camera operator Nick McLean were both extremely nauseated. Crew members later took turns riding on the rig for fun. • The four-way intersection that Saucer H explores as it moves down the road was another tabletop miniature built by Greg Jein and his team.

Roy Speeds Along the Highway: These shots were filmed in Alabama. The tunnel that Roy drives through is the Bankhead tunnel in downtown Mobile, which had a sign for the Harper Valley (Indiana) exit affixed to it.

Crescendo Summit # 1: The backgrounds of all the shots in this sequence were the front-projected eight-by-ten plates of Greg Jein's miniature Indiana landscape, with stars burned in during post-production. • The front-projection screen was portable and could be positioned at various points around the set to accommodate any camera angle that Steven chose to use. • A stunt double replaced Cary Guffey for the shot in which Roy's truck almost hits Barry. The double is noticeably taller than Guffey. • Originally, full-size saucers were going to be used to film the UFOs' initial appearance. The saucers were created by attaching lights to a metal frame. The plan was to use cables to attach the saucers to the arm of a crane that would then swing them through the set. However, because the crane was positioned behind the set (so that it wouldn't appear on camera), the operator couldn't see what he was doing, which is not a good thing when one is whipping a heavy piece of metal around fragile human actors. The danger inherent in this approach became apparent five minutes into the initial test, and it was immediately agreed to scrap the full-size UFO and use models instead. Interactive lighting for the models was created by running lights through the set while the shots were being filmed. • For the shot of the UFOs tumbling down the road and disappearing around a bend, a miniature (five feet by five feet) portion of the highway was created, with the original Indiana landscape miniature positioned behind it to provide an extended background. Because the highway model contained a McDonald's billboard, this scene was dubbed "The Quarter Pounder Shot."

The Tollbooth: In the shooting script, this scene begins with the sleepy toll taker being awakened by alarms that have been (presumably) triggered by the UFOs. While the scene was being shot, however, Spielberg decided that he actually wanted to see the UFOs fly through the toll plaza. Since this was literally a last-minute decision, there was no time to prepare the necessary interactive lighting effects that would marry the UFO models to the live-action footage, so Richard Yuricich decided to create the lighting effects in post-production instead. To avoid at least seven weeks of tedious rotoscoping and matte work, Yuricich had Greg Jein build a miniature four-foot-by-four-foot toll plaza in forced perspective so that it would look exactly like the real toll plaza as it appeared in the production footage (Jein even adjusted the lines of the model to reflect the visual distortion created by the lens used to shoot the production footage). The model was painted gray and dressed with Plexiglas windows. Jein also built a quartet of forced-perspective saucers that were outfitted with internal and external lights. When the time came to film the shot, the stage was filled with smoke. The saucers were attached to an I-beam and driven through the miniature on a motorized track. As the glowing UFOs traveled up to and through the plaza, they created reflections in the Plexiglas windows and light patterns on the gray tollbooths. The resulting footage was made into an interpositive and double-exposed with the live-action shot, thus adding the reflections and lighting effects to the real-life toll plaza without a matte. The whole thing took a week to do, and Richard Yuricich identifies the final shot as his favorite in the film.

The Chase: When the police car drives off the cliff, the cruiser and the section of the guardrail that it smashes through are real. The rest of the shot is a matte painting, except for the UFOs, which were matted in. • The shot in which the camera rises into the air as Roy and the two remaining policemen get out of their vehicles and move to the edge of the cliff in order to watch the saucers fly off into the distance was filmed on the Crescendo Summit set. As with all of the other Summit shots, the background was projected onto the large front-projection screen. Beyond some minimal panning and tilting, the camera usually wasn't moved during a front-projection shot, because the camera and the projector had to maintain a constant ninety-degree relationship or else the camera/reflection alignment would have been off and it wouldn't have been possible to photograph the projected image. However, Doug Trumbull realized that, since their camera and front projector were locked together on a camera crane, they could be moved together at the same time and still maintain the proper relationship. This allowed the *Close Encounters* team to do what no one had ever done before: make a crane shot with front projection. The cloud effects and the UFOs were matted in later. The lights coming on in the distance as the power is restored were pieces of artwork photographed on the animation stand and composited with the Indiana countryside miniature. • A scene was cut that followed this one in which Roy and the cops go to a local police station to fill out incident reports. When the precinct captain chews the officers out for writing about flying saucers, they decide not to report the UFOs after all, which makes Roy realize that there's no point in him doing so either.

Crescendo Summit #2: The close shot of Ronnie's clogs as she pesters Roy with questions is devastatingly funny. When Teri Garr saw the finished film, she was surprised to find that so many of her scenes were so amusing, since she had approached the role in a very serious manner. • This scene was originally supposed to end with Ronnie jokingly asking Roy if he would climb aboard a UFO if one came by. Caught up in the excitement of the moment, Roy's reply is an emphatic "Jesus Christ, yes!!!" This upsets Ronnie, who stomps back to the car. Richard Dreyfuss regretted that this bit was dropped, because he felt it said a lot about Neary's character and showed how desperate he was for an escape from his dreary suburban existence.

"This Isn't a Moonburn..." : This scene shows the first crack in Roy and Ronnie's relationship, which Spielberg conceived as a very tenuous one. In his mind, the who had been together since high school and there wasn't much holding them together anymore besides their routine. When Roy disrupts that, things begin to crumble. • In the rough cut, this scene was followed by one that showed Ronnie and Roy attending a neighborhood block party (this is why the image-conscious Ronnie is so anxious to come up with a plausible-sounding explanation for Roy's burn that they can give to their future friends). As Ronnie keeps an eye on him to make sure he won't say anything that will embarrass her, Roy engages in small talk with the local menfolk, but quickly becomes bored and shifts his gaze to the sky. This prompts everyone else to look up as well, although none of them can figure out what it is they're supposed to be looking at. The sequence ends with Roy becoming intrigued with a Jello mold that reminds him of the mountain.

Crescendo Summit #3: Several bits that showed Roy interacting with the UFO true believers were cut. In one, he gets involved in a discussion with the eccentric farmer, who tells him about the three kinds of close encounters—the only time the phrase "close encounters of the third kind" was uttered. In the final cut of the movie, there is no mention or explanation of the film's title. In another bit, Roy talks to an elderly lady named Gracey, who shows him some blurry photos that she claims are of UFOs (Gracey and her husband reappear later in the film as two of the "gatecrashers" who are put aboard the evac helicopter with Roy in the Devils Tower base camp sequence). • A mysterious man (who later turns out to be a member of the Mayflower Project) seen taking pictures of the true believers was also cut from the sequence. His only remaining bit is when Jillian admonishes him for photographing Barry by saying "He's a little young for a record, don't you think?". • The lights seen in the first three shots of the helicopter approach are animation effects produced by Robert Swarthe and his team. In the fourth shot, they are actual lights—produced by mounting post scanners on the motion-control rig and aiming them into the camera to create lens flares—matted over the Indiana landscape model. In the fifth and final shot of the approach, the lens flares were matted over the front-projected background plate. Once the lights are revealed to be helicopters, the rest of the scene intercuts shots of a real chopper filmed outdoors at Brookley Field with special effects created by spotlights and wind machines on the Crescendo Summit set. • Like the mailboxes and railroad signal, the shaking road sign Roy sees at the end of the scene was vibrated with pneumatic devices.

India: In the script, Lacombe and his team are introduced watching the crowd chant the five tones. The scene ends with their leader telling Lacombe (in Hindi) that "The sky sings to us," and Lacombe replying, "It sings to us, too, my friend." During filming, the action was revised to show Lacombe arriving in the village and rushing through the crowd to ask the leader where the sounds came from. The ending was changed to have the crowd answer Lacombe's question visually by pointing to sky in unison.

The Auditorium: This scene was filmed in the Mobile Civic Center the day after Elvis Presley had performed there. It was Truffaut's longest scene in English. Nervous, he asked Steven if he could do it in French instead, but Steven said no.

Goldstone Radio Telescope, Station 14: The establishing shots of the telescope dish are images of the real thing, photographed by writer/director/cinematographer Richard E. Cunha (*Frankenstein's Daughter* [1958]) and then enhanced with matte paintings, lighting effects, and stars. • For the first shot of the scene in which the technicians steal a globe from the county supervisor's darkened office, Steven asked William Fraker to set the lamps in a way that would make the light pouring into the room from the hallway look like the sun illuminating the earth.

Barry Is Kidnapped: The images of the roiling clouds were created in the cloud tank and composited with a matte painting of the field and the horizon. The clouds were illuminated with colored light bulbs mounted on sticks that were plunged into the cloud tank. • To create the look of anticipation on Barry's face as he waits to see what will come out of the clouds, Steven climbed up on a ladder and began unwrapping a colorful gift box in front of Cary Guffey. Once Cary saw what was inside the box, he exploded with delight, which is why he shouts the word "toys" so enthusiastically in the scene. • In the production footage, the sky in the long shot of Jillian crossing back to the house was too light, so it was replaced with a matte painting of a darker sky. The clouds and saucer models were matted in. • Frank Warner added a low-end rumble behind all of the scene's other noises in order to create the sense of a great presence surrounding the house. • The sounds the aliens make as they move across the roof were created by vibrating a wooden board on the seat of a wooden chair, and the sounds the creatures make as they fuss around in the chimney were created by scratching a pane of glass with pieces of dry ice. • The screws in the floor grate were turned by a crew member positioned under the grate. • The close-up of Barry's feet as he jumps up and down during the grate scene was shot using Cary Guffey's double. • A few shots were filmed of the ETs running around inside the house, but Steven cut them because he didn't think they looked good. • For the kitchen scene, Roy Arbogast and his team rigged the appliances with pneumatics that would shake them furiously. • Steven didn't rehearse the scene with Melinda, so she didn't know what was going to happen. When Steven called "action" and the kitchen erupted, Dillon was terrified and began screaming. Meanwhile, Steven had told Cary what was going to happen, so the little boy wasn't scared at all. • Guffey's mother pulled him through the doggie door for the shot in which the aliens take Barry.

The Air Force Base Debunking: Early drafts of this scene had Roy meeting with Major Benchley alone and showed Benchley aggressively debunking Roy's story using the Project Blue Book techniques described in Hynek's book. The scene was later reconceived as a group meeting and the confrontational quality was softened considerably. • The scene originally ended with Roy, frustrated at being blown off by Benchley, going down into the basement of the building and flipping circuit breakers to turn off some of the lights in the building. As Roy and Ronnie drive away from the base, we see that the lights he left on cause the building's windows to glow in a pattern that forms the letters U-F-O.

The Warehouse: The scene of the trucks rolling out of the warehouse was filmed at Brookley Field. One of the *Close Encounters* hangars can be seen in the background of the last shot in the sequence.

The Mashed Potato Scene: This scene originally began with Roy being called down to dinner from a stargazing platform he had erected on the roof of 1613 Carlisle Drive East. • Although set at night, this scene was shot during the day, so the windows were covered with heavy black tarps in order to keep out the sunlight. As a result, the interior of the house became incredibly hot. There was no air conditioning, so Clark Paylow set up some fans in front of buckets of dry ice to cool the place off. • Steven shot a lot of takes of Roy obsessively sculpting his mashed potatoes—so many that the scene took almost fourteen hours to film. • Justin Dreyfuss ruined a few takes by laughing when he saw his uncle playing with his food. • To make himself cry, Shawn Bishop thought about his dog, which had recently died. • Adrienne Campbell saw a dead fly in the mashed potatoes on her plate and announced it repeatedly during filming. Steven thought this was funny and left it in the movie. • This scene was a hard one for Richard Dreyfuss because "I personally have an enormous desire to articulate an experience...[but] during the mashed potato scene, it was critical that Roy not be able to successfully articulate, and that was very difficult for me."

Roy Cracks Up: The mashed potato scene was originally followed by one in which a distraught Roy locks himself in the bathroom and turns on the shower so that his family can't hear him sob. Frightened, Ronnie forces her way in and the two get into a massive fight that upsets the household and traumatizes the kids. In the shooting script, the scene ended with a bizarre moment in which Ronnie's nightgown gets torn and the shape of her exposed breasts inspires Roy to begin building his massive replica of Devils Tower. This bit was dropped during filming and replaced by one in which Roy goes into the family room after the fight and falls asleep in front of a small clay model of a mountain that he has been sculpting but can't seem to get right. The next morning, Roy awakens to discover his daughter watching the Warner Bros. cartoon *Duck Dodgers in the 24th½ Century* (1953) on TV. The absurdity of Daffy Duck confronting Marvin Martian wakes Roy up to the absurdity of his own recent behavior. Neary begins to gather up all of his UFO-related material with the intention of throwing it out. In doing so, he accidentally pulls the peak off of his clay mountain, giving it a flat top. The sight of this moves him to begin building his giant model of Devils Tower. (Steven's use of the *Duck Dodgers* soundtrack to underscore Roy's final break is similar to a scene in *The Sugarland Express* in which the explosive finale of a Road Runner cartoon foreshadows the tragic fate of the fugitive couple.) • Spielberg eventually cut the shower scene out of the film, feeling that it was much too dark, intense, and "so powerful, it was almost another movie."

Roy Tears Up the Yard and Ronnie Leaves: A second unit directed by Matthew Robbins and photographed by Steven Poster filmed insert shots of dirt, bricks, and plants being tossed into the Nearys' kitchen window. Robbins and Poster also did some additional mashed potato shots. • Roy's rooftop stargazing platform is visible in the shot in which the station wagon backs out of the driveway and sends the Big Wheel bike flying.

Roy Builds Devils Tower: The large Devils Tower model was carved out of Styrofoam and covered in plaster. • Joe Alves and his team built the model at Brookley Field and brought it to 1613 Carlisle Drive East, but when they got there they found that it was too big to fit through the front door. They cut it in half to get it inside and then reassembled it. • A brief line in the ABC News report mentions that Devils Tower has been closed for three weeks for renovations. This line was inserted to explain how the Mayflower Project was able to construct the Box Canyon landing zone undetected, although Joe Alves concedes that "it must have been an awfully efficient three weeks." • The on-location portion of the news report was filmed during the Wyoming shoot (a smoke cloud was generated in a ditch several miles away from Devils Tower to simulate the nerve gas leak) before it was known that Walter Cronkite would not appear in the picture, which is why the report ends with the correspondent saying, "This means order your steak well done, Walter."

The Southwestern Motel: Joe Alves was a great admirer of François Truffaut and had hoped that the legendary French director would be impressed with the awesome Box Canyon set, but, much to his disappointment, Truffaut never said a word about it. However, when François saw the motel room that Alves assembled for the scene in which Jillian sees the Devils Tower report on TV, he was thrilled. "Now this is a set!" Truffaut exclaimed. At first Alves couldn't understand how Truffaut could be more impressed with this simple room that had been thrown together in a few days than by the biggest indoor set in motion picture history, but he ultimately reasoned that Box Canyon was simply beyond Truffaut's comprehension—the French don't make movies on the scale of *Close Encounters*, and François had no idea how to relate to it.

Wyoming: Scenes showing Roy flying to Wyoming and renting a car were cut. • The evacuation scene took two days to film. Because Vilmos Zsigmond was busy pre-lighting the Box Canyon set, he and Steven Poster split the shoot between them: Zsigmond photographed one day's work and Poster the other. • During filming of the scene in which Roy crashes his car through a barbed wire fence as he and Jillian make their way toward Devils Tower, a long strand of the barbed wire snaked out and snagged one of the crew members. As the wire was being dragged by the car, the crew member was, too. He was pulled along for several yards until the stunt driver behind the wheel stopped the vehicle. Luckily, the man was wearing a heavy leather jacket and so wasn't hurt. • As scripted, Roy and Jillian were supposed to catch their first sight of Devils Tower through the window of their car as they drove along the highway, but when the company arrived on location, Spielberg came up with a better idea—he would have them stop the car, get out, and climb a small hill. The camera would crane up with them, revealing the Tower in the distance. The only problem was that they didn't have a crane, so Clark Paylow had to rent one—not an easy task way out in the middle of nowhere. • A scene was shot to follow this one that showed Roy and Jillian stopping for gas at an abandoned service station. Several Army helicopters fly overhead and spot them, prompting Roy to put some money on top of the gas pump to show that he is not looting. The scene was eventually cut. • The "dead" animals that Roy and Jillian see lying on the side of the road were local livestock tranquilized by a local veterinarian.

The Interrogation: The interrogation was filmed in an abandoned office at Brookley Field. Like the news report, it was shot before it was known that Walter Cronkite wasn't going to be in the film—hence Roy's line: "Do you think I investigate every Walter Cronkite story there is?" • This is the only scene in the finished film in which the words "close encounter" are spoken.

The Base Camp: During the early part of pre-production, when the drive was on to keep costs down, Joe Alves was told that he could only spend $5,000 on the Base Camp set. Alves went to Clark Paylow and said he couldn't do it. "I knew if I only spent $5,000, Steven would get up there and say 'What's this? I can't shoot this.'" Paylow asked Alves how much he needed. When Joe replied that he would need at least $50,000, Paylow told him to go ahead. Alves was tremendously impressed with Paylow, for whom the good of the film always came first. "He [Clark] was such a cool guy...a fun guy and a knowledgeable guy," Alves says today. "And a wonderful man." • While they were preparing to film the scene in which Roy is taken out of the interrogation room and put on board the evacuation helicopter, Steven came up a novel idea for a shot: he wanted to begin the scene with the camera outside the chopper, focused on Neary as he is led over to the aircraft, and then, as Roy climbs inside, pull the camera back through the body of the helicopter and out the other side. It sounded simple enough, but it was incredibly difficult to execute because there was no way to move the camera smoothly through the helicopter—dollies and cranes couldn't fit inside the cabin, and hand-holding the camera would make the image look too shaky. The crew was stumped until key grip Bobby Moore suggested that they mount the camera on the end of a ten-foot-long wooden plank. The plank was narrow enough to fit inside the helicopter and long enough to be able to move the camera from one side of the aircraft to the other. The other end of the plank was attached to a dolly that was placed on rails set up outside the chopper to facilitate smooth movement. Moore called his invention the "Ubangi." Vilmos Zsigmond called this shot the most difficult of his entire career. • The scene in which Roy, Jillian, and Larry escape from the helicopter was Melinda Dillon's first on the picture. Dillon had sprained her ankle prior to the start of filming and injured it again when she jumped out of the helicopter. As a result, she limped through most of the Wyoming shoot.

Climbing Devils Tower: When the first unit left Wyoming on May 28, 1976, certain key shots in the sequence in which the army choppers fly over and spray Roy, Jillian, and Larry with EZ-4 had not been completed. Steven asked Doug Trumbull and Richard Yuricich if they would stay behind and make them. The assignment was complicated ; Trumbull and Yuricich had to make five shots (including several of the chopper approaching from behind Devils Tower, several of it departing, an aerial close-up of it dispensing the gas, and a shot of a stunt man—filling in for actor Josef Sommer—sitting on the mountain watching as the chopper flies overhead), all at magic hour and all with a helicopter that was only available for a single day. Doug and Richard decided that the only way to get the job done was to film all of the shots at the same time. Five cameras were set up (including one attached to the outside of the helicopter in order to shoot the close-up of the gas canister) to cover all of the angles. They spent a day rehearsing and then, when dusk came, all of the cameras rolled simultaneously as the helicopter flew by and dusted the hillside. The plan worked, and they got all of the shots but one in a single take. The shot they missed—a tilt-down showing birds dropping from the trees after they had been anesthetized—was redone in post-production by cinematographer Jim Dickson. • The shot of Devils Tower at dusk with spotlights appearing on either side of it is a 65mm image of the real mountain composited with a matte painting of the cloudy sky and beams of light produced in the smoke room. • Wide shots of Roy and Jillian climbing up a slope in the back of the Notch set were augmented with matte paintings of the sky and the surrounding countryside. • As the army helicopter comes around for a second pass to gas Roy and Jillian, shots of a real helicopter filmed in Wyoming are intercut with a shot of a miniature chopper—a Monogram model kit of a Phantom Huey that was tricked out with a small motor to run the rotors. The helicopter was the first model shot on the motion-control rig, before any of the saucers. The model footage was then composited with images of Dreyfuss and Dillon filmed on the slope and a matte painting of the countryside and the horizon.

The Notch: The wide shots showing Roy and Jillian looking down at the base of operations consist of footage shot in the Notch set composited with reduction shots of the base of operations. All of the surrounding imagery—the sky, the boulder field, the mountains in the distance, and the top of the stadium lights—are matte paintings. An extended portion of the runway lights are also painted. • The closer shots that do not feature Roy and Jillian are reduction shots of the base composited with matte paintings.

The Big Dipper: The points of light that arrange themselves to form the Big Dipper are animated. Each light was a piece of artwork that was placed on the bed of the Oxberry and illuminated from below. Using a series of cranks, the bed could be moved incrementally up and down, right and left, or even rotated a full 360 degrees. The animators used the cranks to move each point frame by frame along a predetermined path. (The missiles were produced using this same technique.) Each of the seven lights was photographed separately on the same negative. An interpositive was made of the effect and optically combined with a retouched still photograph of the real Devils Tower onto a dupe negative. After that was done, the rest of the stars were burned into the dupe. The Big Dipper was the first effects shot Future General finished for the film. When it was screened for Steven at the Annex, he said, "I've been waiting to see that shot all my life."

The Three Scout Saucers Arrive: The shooting star that flies over Devils Tower and splits into four separate lights was created in the same manner as the Big Dipper and the missiles. The Devils Tower featured in that shot was a model built by Greg Jein. The real Devils Tower is taller than it is wide. To better accommodate the widescreen movie frame, which is wider than it is tall, Jein adjusted the proportions of the model, which ended up being more squat than its real-life counterpart. A miniature landscape of the surrounding countryside was placed in front of the Devils Tower model, and both were augmented by matte paintings. A base-of-operations reduction was matted in at the foot of the Tower and the stars were burned into the sky above. • The shot of Lacombe, Laughlin, and Robert coming out of the cubicle and walking out onto the tarmac as the scout saucers float down into the frame is the first shot in the film that utilized the motion-control system to incorporate model effects into a moving live-action shot. The very next shot showing Jean-Claude walking over to the ARP 2500 and tripping as he watches the saucers is the second. The shot in which an impatient Lacombe walks out to the saucers and insists that they respond to the five tones is the third. • In the isolated shots that show the three scout saucers hovering over the tarmac, the runway is a Rocco Gioffre matte painting.

The Barnstorming Scene: The long shot of the clouds forming shows them billowing around Greg Jein's model. The medium shots show them billowing around the slope of the real mountain, with some trees painted in for effect. • The shot of Truffaut moving to the front of the crowd and looking up at the clouds as the scout saucers signal in the background is another motion-control shot. • For the shot in which the UFOs burst out of the clouds, five technicians stood behind the cloud tank holding fiber-optic probes. As the camera rolled, each technician pushed a probe through the paint to the edge of the cloud. Footage of the UFOs was then lined up to match the probes so that the saucers would appear to emerge from the light. • The scene required a wide variety of UFOs. The saucer kit was used to build a number of them. Others were created by attaching lights to everyday objects, including a Tonka truck, a rubber oxygen mask, and a toilet seat lid. Saucers seen far in the distance are animated. • Fiber optics were used to throw searchlight patterns onto Devils Tower and the surrounding landscape miniature to create interactive lighting for the UFOs. • John Williams scored some parts of this scene with to include recordings of car horns, played both forward and backward. • A number of shots of technicians reacting to the saucers were originally intended to be part of the cuboid sequence (they can be identified by their incredibly bright, overexposed white lighting). • The shot of Saucer H hovering above a group of technicians who attempt to monitor it with various pieces of equipment is a motion-control shot, as is a subsequent bit in which Lacombe reaches up and tries to touch its hull. • J. Allen Hynek did not like the tumbling motions of some of the saucers in this sequence, since no such motions had ever been reported by UFO witnesses.

The Arrival of the Mothership: The miniature R2-D2 can be seen as the Mothership rises up behind Jillian in the Notch. • To evoke a proper reaction for the moment when Jillian first sees the Mothership, Steven held up a piece of paper and told Melinda Dillon to look at it and imagine the biggest, most wondrous thing she had ever seen. Conjuring up a vision of her late grandmother at age thirty, hovering over Melinda as a little girl, Melinda gasped and said, "Oh, my God," which was just what Steven wanted. • The original concept for the Mothership's arrival was to have the giant craft come gliding across the sky from the horizon, but when the sequence was being storyboarded Steven came up with the idea to have it rise up from behind Devils Tower instead. While this idea is completely illogical (in order for the Mothership to be able to do this it would had have to risen undetected from a massive crater dug deep into the earth on the other side of the Tower), it is such an incredibly striking and powerful image that it really doesn't matter. • To film the shot in which the Mothership turns over, the model was rigged on a pipe that allowed it to pivot toward the camera. • A miniature hatch was used to film the shot in which the hatch descends from the underbelly as the Mothership touches down. The miniature hatch did not have the same row of rectangular yellow windows running across the top of it that the full-scale version did, so the animation department created some using slot gags and then burned them into the footage of the miniature hatch.

The Jam Session: Many of the rocks above or on either side of the colorboard are matte paintings. • Richard Yuricich superimposed a row of flares over the shot of Jean-Claude walking toward the Mothership as the ARP is moved forward in order to create the impression that the brilliantly illuminated Mothership is hovering overhead. • Columbia refused to pay the $10,000 it would cost to realize the gag in which the Mothership's ear-splitting response to the five tones blows the glass window out of one of the landing zone cubicles, so Steven paid for it himself. The window was made from Polystyrene #2, a plastic with a low-impact breaking point. Mike Wood, a member of Roy Arbogast's special effects team, used an air mortar to fire tiny pieces of glass at the window in order to shatter it. It required three takes and three panes of windows to get the shot.

The Returnees: Although never identified on screen, the group of return-ees included some famous "disappeared" people, including Amelia Earhart and Judge Crater. • The list of returnee names being read over the public address system include one David A. Erickson, the brother of production assistant Glenn Erickson • When filming Barry's reaction to the aliens' departure, Steven told Cary that he wanted him to be sad because his friends were going away. Cary thought Spielberg was referring to his real-life friends and started to cry. This in turn prompted Melinda—and quite a few members of the crew—to cry as well.

The ETs Emerge: The crew nicknamed Bob Baker's marionette the "Je-sus Alien" because of the messianic pose it strikes when it emerges from the hatch. During filming, Greg Jein had to hold the puppet's feet down because its lightweight legs kept blowing around. The marionette didn't look particularly realistic, so Robert Swarthe superimposed an animated lens flare over it in order to obscure its artificial appearance. • To explain why there are so many different kinds of aliens in the movie, Steven has said that he wanted to show that there are many different races of extrater-restrials just as there are many different races of humans. • The scientist with the pipe and the gray Van Dyke beard who pushes forward to see the

ETs is Dr. J. Allen Hynek. • The music for the last thirty or so minutes of the movie is the part of the score that John Williams himself likes best: "There's a sense of deliverance in it. An absence of tension. [That] everything is really going to be all right. Our world and their world are going to come together. There's nothing to fear. That's the part of the music that I find most successful, even today."

Roy Goes Aboard the Mothership: Originally, Roy was supposed to take a few steps up the ramp of the Mothership, enter the ship's anti-gravity zone, and then fly the rest of the way up. Dreyfuss was rigged with a harness and pulled up into the hatch for several takes, but the effect was never convincing, so Steven opted to have him walk up instead. • Spielberg on Roy's decision to go aboard the Mothership: "Neary got in touch with himself...he goes into that ship knowing what he's doing.... He makes the most important decision in the history of the world."

"Goodbye!": In the shot of the lead alien walking up to Lacombe just prior to the farewell exchange of Kodály signs, the creature is played by one of the Mobile ballet students. The exchange itself and the smile that follows are performed by Carlo Rambaldi's Puck—but it is the little girl we see again afterward, walking back to the Mothership. The appearance of the puppet and the child do not match at all, but the scene is so effective that it doesn't matter in the least.

ABOVE: The Future General team a
work filming the "Quarter Pounde
shot. *From left*: special visual
effects coordinator Larry Robinson
unknown, Gregory Jein, Douglas
Trumbull, Robert Swarthe, directo
of photography–photographic
effects Richard Yuricich (partially
hidden by the camera), camera
technician and assistant Robert
Hollister, special consultant Peter
Anderson, model maker Michael
McMillen. *Photograph by Glenn Erickson.*

LEFT: Future General's jack-of-all-
trades, project assistant Glenn
Erickson *Photograph courtesy of Glenn Erickson*

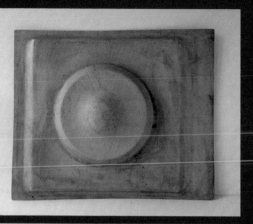

ABOVE: An unused vacuform plastic shroud of the sort used to create *Close Encounters*'s flying saucers. The excess plastic was trimmed away so that only the saucer shape remained. Different shapes were mixed and matched to create the various saucers.

LEFT: The hollow underside of the shroud.

BELOW: A side view showing the shroud's contour.

LEFT: The motion-control camera ready to film one of the UFO models. *Photograph by Glenn Erickson.*

BELOW: Dave Stewart preparing to film one of the saucers. *Photograph by Glenn Erickson.*

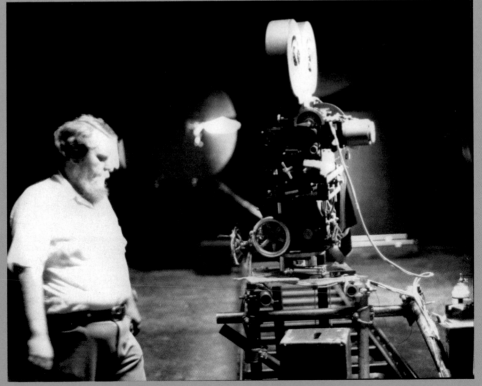

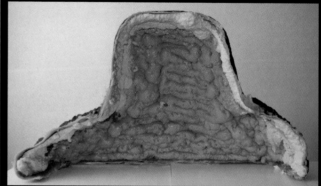

ABOVE: A duplicate model of the 3' x 2' Devils Tower miniature created by Gregory Jein for the movie's final sequence.

BELOW, LEFT: A side view of the Devils Tower miniature. The proportions of the actual tower were adjusted to accommodate the widescreen motion picture frame. As a result, the model mountain is more squat than its real-life counterpart.

BELOW, RIGHT: A rear view showing the miniature mountain's fiberglass and foam innards.

LEFT: A mock-up of the Mothership constructed by Gregory Jein based on Ralph McQuarrie's painting of the ship. Jein used this mock-up as a guide when constructing the full-size model.

BELOW: A side view of the Mothership mock-up.

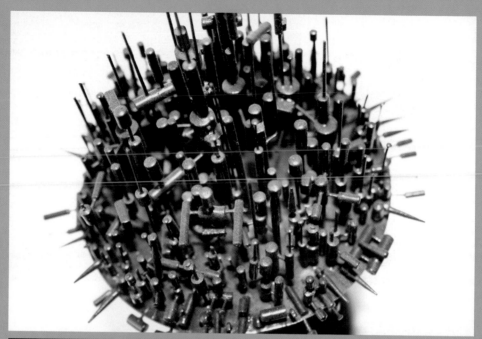

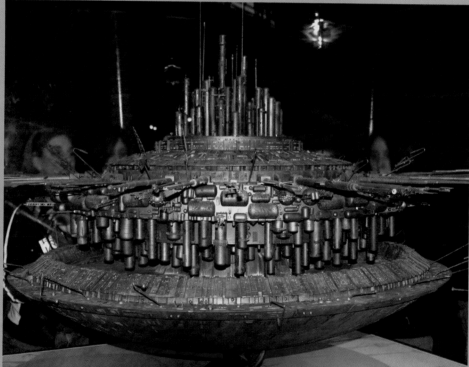

ABOVE: A close shot of the Mothership mock-up's intricate detail.

BELOW: The full-size Mothership model, currently on display at the Steven F. Udvar-Hazy Center of the National Air and Space Museum of the Smithsonian Institution in Virginia. *Photograph by Christine Van Bloem.*

ABOVE: A close-up of the towers (made from aluminum tubes) atop the Mothership. *Photograph by Paul Van Bloem.*

BELOW: The miniature R2-D2 model perched on the edge of one of the Mothership's lower levels. *Photograph by Paul Van Bloem.*

ABOVE: A miniature fighter plane—one piece of the Mothership's intricate surface detail. *Photograph by Paul Van Bloem.*

BELOW: A close shot of a detailed section of one of the Mothership's many tiers.

ABOVE: The miniature hatch used to film the Mothership's landing. A row of yellow rectangular lights were superimposed over this model in the final film so that it would match the full-size hatch that was built on the Box Canyon set in Mobile, Alabama.

BELOW: One of the diplomas given to the Future General visual effects staff to thank them for their hard work on *Close Encounters*. *Photograph courtesy of Robert Swarthe.*

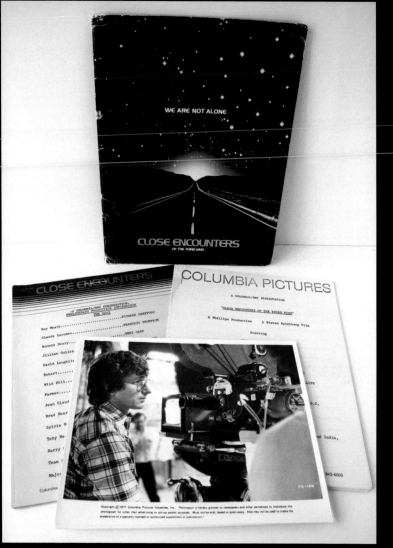

ABOVE: One of the press kits prepared by Columbia Pictures and distributed to newspapers and magazines in the run-up to the film's release. The kit contained a cast and crew list, detailed information about the production, and stills from the movie.

BELOW: The Ziegfeld Theatre in New York City, where *Close Encounters* premiered on November 15, 1977, and ran in an exclusive East Coast engagement from November 18, 1977, until December 13, 1977. *Photograph by Andrew Morton.*

ABOVE: The Cinerama Dome on Sunset Boulevard in Los Angeles, where *Close Encounters* ran during its exclusive West Coast engagement.

BELOW: A printed list of credits given out at the film's premiere.

ABOVE: The *CE3K* soundtrack album was issued on LP and eight-track tape.

BELOW: *Close Encounters*–related paperbacks.

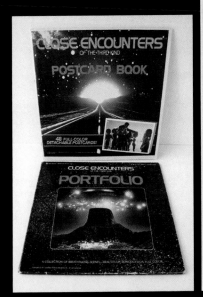

ABOVE, LEFT: The postcard book and portfolio, each featuring stills and artwork from the movie.

ABOVE, RIGHT: A *CE3K* Frisbee. *Photograph courtesy of Robert Swarthe.*

BELOW: A board game from Parker Brothers.

ABOVE: *Close Encounters* puzzles.

RIGHT: The bendable Puck doll.

BELOW: *CE3K* trading cards and 3D Viewmaster reels by GAF.

MAYFLOWER PROJECT

NAME: BOB SWARTHE
I.D.NO.:
PROJECT AREA: DIR
SECURITY RATING: A

AUTHORIZATION

MAYFLOWER PROJECT

NAME: KATHY CAMPBELL
I.D.NO.:
PROJECT AREA: SFX ED
SECURITY RATING: A

AUTHORIZATION

ABOVE, LEFT: ID badge worn by visual effects supervisor Robert Swarthe during the making of *The Special Edition*. *Photograph courtesy of Robert Swarthe.*

ABOVE, RIGHT: ID badge worn by *The Special Edition* visual effects editor Kathryn Campbell. *Photograph courtesy of Kathryn Campbell.*

MIDDLE: One of the thousands of miniature aliens featured in the "Alien Wall" shot that appears during the "Ballroom" sequence at the end of *The Special Edition*.

BELOW: *Close Encounters* on VHS and DVD.

"Goodbye!"

CHAPTER 25 | **Release**

By the time *Close Encounters* was finished, Steven Spielberg was exhausted (he was quoted as saying that the only UFO he wanted to see at that point was one that would take him to the Virgin Islands). But his labors were well worth it, for, with the help of his incredibly talented team, he had created a wonderful film.

Spielberg had taken his modest idea for a cynical thriller about a government cover-up and turned it into a terrifically entertaining adventure—full of action, suspense, fright, and humor—about the agony and ecstasy of pursuing a vision and the terror and excitement of confronting the unknown. The movie is extremely well made—the cinematography, production design, editing, sound, and music are all top notch, and the special photographic effects are brilliantly designed and executed, completely convincing, and often breathtakingly beautiful—the product of a team of abundantly talented artists and craftspeople working at the absolute top of their game. The acting is equally good: Dreyfuss is great as a man caught in the grip of a compulsion he can't understand and looking desperately for a way to make sense of it all; Truffaut is a wonderfully warm and human presence, full of infectious enthusiasm and unexpected humor; Melinda Dillon infuses Jillian with an affecting combination of pained fragility and resilient strength; Teri Garr takes a character who, as written, is rather harsh and unsympathetic, and, by emphasizing Ronnie's confusion and fear at the strange events that have overtaken her family, makes her very sympathetic indeed; Cary Guffey is enchanting and, along with the rest of the children—Shawn Bishop, Justin Dreyfuss, and Adrienne

Campbell—extremely believable and real; Bob Balaban brings an appealing sincerity to the stalwart David Laughlin; and J. Patrick McNamara, Warren Kemmerling, and Merrill Connally all make vivid impressions in their small but pivotal roles.

Ultimately, however, this is the director's show. Steven Spielberg is arguably the most gifted visual storyteller to ever work in movies, and his considerable talent for creating complex compositions, compelling camera movement, and dynamic pacing and editing are on full display here. He does an excellent job of rooting the film's fantastic events in an extremely believable reality—in this case, an incredibly honest and accurate depiction of suburban American life, free of the condescension or idealization that marks most portrayals of this misunderstood milieu. He then infuses this reality with a very real and very genuine sense of wonder—Spielberg is alert to the awesome magic and mystery present in the everyday world around us (so much so that *New York Times* film critic Vincent Canby dubbed him "the poet of suburbia") and incorporates it into his film in a way that makes us believe that amazing things can happen to us right in our own backyards. As strong as all of these elements are, it is the film's sweet spirit that makes it special. In *Close Encounters*, Spielberg offers us a generous, optimistic vision—one in which belief and persistence are rewarded and the terrifying unknown that we fear so much turns out to be a peaceful, childlike presence that wants nothing more than to be our friend and make our dreams come true. All of these pieces come together in the film's last forty minutes, as Spielberg harnesses the incredible power of the cinema—combining light and sound in a beautiful and joyous display that moves the viewer in a very real and genuinely profound way.

The film certainly has its flaws—the plot has a number of holes, there is some inconsistency and confusion, and some of the scenes are staged and played a bit too broadly—but the assets outweigh the deficits by a wide margin. Everyone involved knew that they had made something quite special. Now all they needed to do was get people to come and see it.

The promotional campaign for *Close Encounters*—which was the biggest and (at a cost of approximately $7.5 million) the most expensive in Columbia Pictures' history—began well in advance of the film's release. Everyone involved—Steven, the Phillipses, and Columbia—knew that one of the biggest challenges they faced in selling the film to the public was explaining its unusual title. In December 1976, Columbia took the first step by running an advertisement in newspapers and magazines across the country. Created by the advertising firm of Smolen, Smith, and Connelly, a company that specialized in film promotion (cofounder Donald Smolen had supervised the marketing for many of the James Bond films, and the company had recently done work on *The Omen* [1976] and *Star Wars*), the ad featured simplified versions of Dr. J. Allen Hynek's definitions of the three kinds of close encounters:

> Close Encounter of the First Kind: Sighting of an unidentified flying object
>
> Close Encounter of the Second Kind: Physical evidence after a sighting
>
> Close Encounter of the Third Kind: Contact with alien beings

The terms were laid over an image of a deep space nebula and supplemented with additional copy about the film and its makers. Since this layout was designed when Columbia was still planning to release the movie at Easter, a line at the bottom indicated that *Close Encounters* would be coming to theaters in the spring of 1977. When the release was pushed back, the studio ran a new ad on Sunday, April 10, 1977 to announce that the movie would be coming at Christmas instead. This two-page spread used an even simpler version of Hynek's terms ("Sighting"/"Evidence"/"Contact") and was accompanied by text that explained the UFO phenomenon and ended as follows: "It will start in an Indiana town and lead to four words which are becoming more and more apparent to all of us every day: We are not alone." Steven loved the last four words, and "We Are Not Alone" became the film's official tagline. The nebula was ditched and replaced by an all-new graphic—one that would soon become known the world over.

From the inception of the project, Spielberg, the producers, and the studio were eager to develop a distinctive logo for the film—a unique, powerful image that would symbolize the movie and represent it on posters, in advertisements, and on merchandise. Steven had been intrigued with a photograph called "Infinity Road" that had appeared in an issue of *Esquire* magazine—a picture of a deserted, divided Nevada highway that ran from the foreground of the frame straight back to a mountain range in the far distance. The photographer, Pete Turner—known for using strong, graphic composition; vibrant color; and sophisticated visual effects to create bold, striking images—was hired to create a variation on "Infinity Road" that could serve as the key art for *Close Encounters*. Given unfettered access to all areas of the production, including the Mobile hangars and the smoke room and cloud tank at Future General, Turner produced a string of pictures that incorporated his lonesome road with elements from *CE3K*, including Devils Tower, the saucers, Richard Dreyfuss, and the landing zone. In the end, however, none of these images were used. Instead, Smolen, Smith, and Connelly decided to adapt Turner's original photo: the road, mountains, and sky were painted over in tones of deep blue and black, stars were put in the sky, and a glow was placed at the end of the highway. Married to a special typeface designed by artist Dan Perri for the film's titles, it was this image that became the official logo for *Close Encounters of the Third Kind*.

Once the movie's release date had been set, Columbia began making deals with theater owners who wanted to exhibit the movie. With expectations for the film running high, the studio was in the position to drive a hard bargain, and it did. Each theater was required to play the film for a minimum of twelve weeks and to guarantee the studio a specific financial return (the amount varied by the theater and market). This guarantee would be taken from the theater's box office gross, which (minus house expenses) would be split ninety-ten in Columbia's favor until the promised amount was paid off (the formula would be incrementally adjusted in the theater's favor after that). Each theater was required to spend $1,000 per week to advertise the film in its market for the first four weeks of the engagement, and two hundred theaters had to agree to install the Dolby Stereo Sound System at a cost of $4,000 per theater.

Throughout the summer and fall, the promotional campaign continued. A trailer was produced and sent to the theaters to play in front of their current attractions. This trailer featured a live-action version of the key art: a camera moving along a deserted highway toward a glowing horizon (the road used in the trailer was a tabletop model filmed in the smoke room at Future General by Dave Stewart). Press kits containing photos and information about the film were created and distributed to the media, and Steven and other key members of the production began doing interviews with newspaper and magazine reporters who were preparing stories about the movie that would be published to coincide with its release (many of these stories focused on Steven and his status as cinema's reigning wunderkind). As that date grew closer, Columbia began placing ads in magazines and newspapers and on radio and television announcing the film's imminent arrival. The promotional campaign was a tremendous success. By the beginning of November, awareness of the film among the members of the public was extremely high, as was its "want-to-see" factor.

This was good news for the filmmakers and for Columbia, because throughout the production and post-production periods, *Close Encounters* had received a great deal of negative publicity—much of it generated by the terrific budget and schedule overruns, the numerous delays in release, and the news of Julia's firing. Occurrences such as these are usually signs that a film is in trouble, and word began to spread in Hollywood that the movie was a potential disaster (Michael Phillips feels that some of these rumors were instigated by jealous competitors who were rooting for the film to fail). The general public picked up on a lot of this, so the movie had a lot to overcome. Things began to turn around after the Dallas test screenings, when word began to spread that the picture was actually good. This enthusiastic buzz and the anticipation generated by the promotional campaign had a positive effect on Columbia's stock, which on Friday, November 4, 1977, closed at $18 per share, up from $7 per share just a few short months before—an increase attributed to the excitement that was building around *Close Encounters*. However, excitement turned to panic the next Monday when the November 7 issue of *New York* magazine hit the newsstands.

Although journalists were prohibited, *New York* financial writer William Flanagan had managed to sneak into one of the Dallas test screenings by bribing someone he had met in the line outside the Medallion Theater to let him take his place. Flanagan didn't like the movie and wrote a review called "An Encounter with *Close Encounters*." Illustrated with a drawing of a UFO landing atop Devils Tower and laying a big egg, the article was not encouraging: "I can understand all the apprehension. In my humble opinion, the picture will be a colossal flop. It lacks the dazzle, charm, wit, imagination and broad audience appeal of *Star Wars*.... R2-D2, where are you when we need you?" Flanagan's pan had an immediate impact. Nervous investors began to sell their shares of Columbia Pictures Industries stock that very day. A positive review by *Time* magazine movie critic Frank Rich (who had also sneaked into one of the Dallas screenings—although he probably didn't have to go to the same lengths that Flanagan did, since Time, Inc. was an investor in the movie) published the same day and assuring readers that the film would "certainly be a big enough hit to keep Columbia's stockholders happy," did little to stop the slide. By the time trading ended on Monday evening, the price of CPI's stock had fallen to $17. On Tuesday morning, so many "sell" orders had come in for CPI stock that the New York Stock Exchange refused to permit trading to open until noon Tuesday, by which point the price had had fallen to $15.50 per share. Approximately 185,000 shares were traded that afternoon, and Columbia's future was once again looking bleak.

The company issued a press release that defended the film's (and by extension its own) prospects—"Based upon exhibitor reaction, plus the fact that the company will have over $20 million in guarantees (more than the film's negative cost) before the film opens, as well as the results of two previews held two weeks ago, the company continues to believe that *Close Encounters* will be financially successful, justifying the company's faith in backing Steven Spielberg and the rest of the creative team who are responsible for a most unique film experience." But, as confident as they tried to appear in public, behind the scenes everyone associated with the film and the studio was very anxious and hoped that the rest of the reviews would be positive enough to bind the wound that Flanagan had inflicted.

A special advance screening for critics and the media had originally been scheduled for October 24, 1977, but was postponed when Steven decided to make some changes to the film following the Dallas tests. A screening for East Coast critics was finally held on Sunday, November 6, 1977 at the 1,131 seat, state-of-the-art Ziegfeld Theater in midtown Manhattan. Many members of the cast and production team were present, although one key member of the team wasn't: Steven Spielberg. Anxious about how the film would be received in this, its first public showing, Spielberg stayed back in his hotel room. A press conference was held the next day at the Americana Hotel, which Steven did attend, along with Michael Phillips, Douglas Trumbull, Teri Garr, Melinda Dillon, Cary Guffey, J. Allen Hynek, and John Williams. Julia Phillips was there as well. By her own report, she arrived late and, under the influence, slurred her words

while answering questions. All of the reporters present received a tape
recorder and a *CE3K* paperweight as gifts. The ritual was repeated on the
West Coast with a screening at the Cinerama Dome in Hollywood on
Wednesday, November 8, and a press conference at the Burbank Studios
on Friday, November 10.

In the days and weeks that followed, the reviews began to appear. A
few of them were mixed: writing as "Murf," *Variety*'s Art Murphy praised
the film's last thirty-five minutes, but complained that its first hundred
were "somewhat redundant in exposition and irritating in tone;" Charles
Champlin of the *Los Angeles Times* characterized Steven as "a director...
of effects rather than characters or relationships;" and although the *New
York Daily News*'s Kathleen Carroll gave it three stars, she also called the
film "curiously uneven." There were also some outright pans: Judith Crist
of the *New York Post* complained that "[*Close Encounters*] has a simple-
minded approach to a subject worthy of serious and contemplative comment;" the *Village Voice*'s Andrew Sarris wrote that "[*CE3K*] is a gooey,
melted marshmallow of a movie with nothing at the core but more gooey-
ness masquerading as godliness;" and his wife, *New York*'s Molly Haskell,
titled her review "The Dumbest Story Ever Told." The majority of the reviews, however, were extremely enthusiastic:

> **Vincent Canby—*The New York Times*:** "Steven Spielberg's giant, spec-
> tacular *Close Encounters of the Third Kind*...is the best—the most elabo-
> rate —1950s science fiction movie ever made.... If, indeed, we are not
> alone, it would be fun to believe that the creatures who may one day
> visit us are of the order that Mr. Spielberg has conceived.... The final
> thirty to forty minutes of the film...are breathtaking.... this climax in-
> volves the imagination in surprising, moving ways."
>
> In a follow-up assessment written after the film's release, Canby
> went on to say: "*Close Encounters*...comes close to apotheosizing a
> movie genre of the second kind...[it] makes no attempt to be anything
> but the science fiction it is, and it succeeds in doing this better, more
> thoroughly, than anyone else has done to date."
>
> **Jack Kroll—*Newsweek*:** "*Close Encounters*...[is] a genuine work of the
> popular imagination.... Spielberg...starts with the classic genre of the
> 1950s "It Came From Outer Space" [science fiction] flick, but stretches

its scale and resonance with brilliant special effects until the film flares up into something approaching awe."

Frank Rich—*Time*: "[Spielberg's] new movie is far richer and more ambitious than *Jaws* and it reaches the viewer at a far more profound level than *Star Wars*...at the end of *Close Encounters*, the audience is sitting with [Spielberg] in the lap of the universe, ready and waiting for new magic to fall into their lives."

Richard Corliss—*New Times*: "Although the film's hardware...is spectacularly rendered...the special effects are only part of the film's very special effect. It's more important that we're left with the feeling of potential human value radiated by the movie.... This is a triumph of an extraordinary kind: a drama not of good and evil, but of good and the possibility for greater good...."

Arthur Knight—*The Hollywood Reporter*: "*Close Encounters* is...a film of incredible power and intensity. It is also, and ultimately, reassuring."

Steven had taken a considerable risk making a film that wore its hopefulness and optimism so blatantly on its sleeve, and the critics could easily have ridiculed him and dismissed the film for doing so. That they didn't shows how desperately the world—after decades of corruption, violence, fear, and disillusionment—needed and welcomed such a message.

While the critics were writing their reviews, the film lab at MGM was busy turning out prints of the film in 35mm (for regular theaters) and 70mm (for large-screen showcase houses). Originally the plan had been to take advantage of the incredible beauty of the 65mm special photographic effects by blowing up all of the scenes that had originally been filmed in 35mm to 65mm and marrying them with the full-size visual effects shots. Unfortunately, this approach proved to be too time-consuming and expensive, so in the end, a 35mm version of the entire film (including the reduced-to-35mm effects shots) was blown up to 70mm instead. For the Future General team, this was a disappointment, because they felt that the reduced effects never looked quite as good as the originals.

The film's official world premiere was held on Tuesday, November 15, 1977 at 7:30 P.M. at the Ziegfeld Theater. Following the screening, a dinner dance was held across the street in the New York Hilton's Trianon Ballroom. The event was a benefit for the Cancer Research Institute, of which Columbia Pictures Industries CEO Alan Hirschfield was a trustee. Although it was a wonderful evening, there was an undercurrent of tension among the Columbia brass. The CPI board was scheduled to meet the following morning to decide the fate of David Begelman. As CEO, it was ultimately Alan Hirschfield's decision, and at that meeting he announced that he was going to fire Begelman. The pro-Begelman faction of the board was extremely upset about this and began pressuring Hirschfield to change his mind by questioning his character, criticizing his job performance, and even accusing him of impropriety (because Columbia did business with a market research company for which Hirschfield's wife had once worked—an arrangement the board had approved). After several weeks of this, Hirschfield changed his mind and reinstated Begelman.

Hirschfield's decision to allow an admitted forger and embezzler back at the helm of Columbia Pictures set off a firestorm of controversy both within the company and without. Cliff Robertson expressed his outrage in an interview in the *Washington Post*, and articles exposing all of the sordid details of the case began appearing in the *New York Times* and the *Wall Street Journal*. The Burbank and Beverly Hills police launched new investigations into the matter, as did the Securities and Exchange Commission, and a number of lawsuits were filed against the company. Eventually, Begelman's position became untenable, and on Sunday, February 5, 1978, he resigned (Daniel Melnick took his place). In April 1978, Begelman was arrested and charged with one count of grand theft and three counts of forgery. He pleaded No Contest to the grand theft charge (the forgery charges were dropped) and was ultimately sentenced to three years of probation. In addition, he was required to pay a $5,000 fine, seek psychiatric care, and to do community service, which he eventually fulfilled by producing an anti-drug film about PCP (a.k.a. angel dust) called *Angel Death*. The rift that the Begelman affair had opened between Alan Hirschfield and the CPI board continued to widen until July 1978, when the board fired Hirschfield and replaced him with Fay Vincent, the associate director of the division of corporate finance of the Securities and Exchange Commission.

Close Encounters began exclusive 70mm East Coast and West Coast engagements on November 18, 1977 at the Ziegfeld and the Dome. Audiences were turned on by Spielberg's optimistic epic, and the film was an instant hit. At $4 per ticket, the film made approximately $21,000 on its first day at both theaters. These exclusive engagements ran until December 13, 1977, during which time the combined gross from both theaters was $1,076,927. The film went into general release on December 14, 1977 in 272 theaters in the United States and Canada, in a mixture of 35mm and 70mm engagements. By the end of the month, it had grossed $24,695,317; by the end of January 1978, it had grossed $62,033,815; and by the end of February, it had grossed $72 million and become the seventh-highest-grossing film of all time.

In the wake of the film's release, numerous pieces of *Close Encounters*–related merchandise appeared in stores: Arista Records released an album of John Williams' score for the film on LP and eight-track tape that included a disco single incorporating the five tones. Another disco single—this one of the score's main themes—was created by dance music producer Meco Monardo, who had released a similar version of the *Star Wars* theme that had reached number one on the pop music charts the previous summer. Dell Books published two *Close Encounters*–themed paperbacks: a novelization of the film's screenplay by thriller writer Leslie Waller, which was credited to Steven Spielberg (this sort of attribution was in vogue at the time—earlier in the year George Lucas had been credited as the author of Alan Dean Foster's novelization of *Star Wars*); and a Fotonovel version of the movie produced by Mandala Productions (Fotonovels were a late-1970s novelty that retold the stories of popular movies using frame enlargements from the films, accompanied by dialogue balloons and action captions). Marvel Comics put out a comic book adaptation of the story. Denied permission to use the likenesses of the actors, Marvel's version of *Close Encounters* starred a much older, beefier Roy Neary; a leaner, hawk-faced Lacombe; and a Jillian who was much more...um...buxom than her big-screen counterpart. The inability to use the actors' likenesses also affected the Topps Chewing Gum Company, which produced a fifty-five-card set of *CE3K* trading cards. While the company did have permission to use pictures of Teri Garr, Melinda Dillon, and Cary Guffey, both Richard Dreyfuss and François Truffaut had refused to let their images be used. As a result, Topps's retelling of *Close Encounters* omits both Roy Neary and Claude Lacombe.

Ariel Books published *Close Encounters of the Third Kind: A Document of the Film*—an elaborate appreciation of the film consisting of hundreds of behind-the-scenes pictures and quotes from the cast and crew—and the *Close Encounters of the Third Kind Portfolio*, a collection of large-format stills and production art (including some of the unused Pete Turner photos). Paradise Press put out the *Close Encounters of the Third Kind Diary*—Bob Balaban's account of his experiences working on the film—as well as a behind-the-scenes magazine and several monthly issues of a *CE3K* poster magazine. Warren Publications also issued a behind-the-scenes magazine, this one edited by *Famous Monsters of Filmland* creator Forrest J. Ackerman. George Fenmore Associates produced a souvenir program that was sold in theaters; Grosset & Dunlop put out a book of *CE3K* puzzles and brainteasers; and Prime Press published a collection of postcards made from the behind-the-scenes stills and more of the Turner photos. J. Allen Hynek's Center for UFO Studies sponsored (with Columbia) the *CE3K* Skywatchers Association, a club that allowed members to receive updates from the Center and provided a pre-printed form for them to use to report a UFO sighting. A lot of *Close Encounters* toys were manufactured as well, including a Parker Brothers board game, Milton Bradley jigsaw puzzles, 3D Viewmaster reels from GAF, a pinball game from D. Gottlieb & Company, and a vinyl Puck doll produced by the Imperial Toy Company. There were also *CE3K* T-shirts, posters, buttons, belt buckles, stickers, iron-on transfers, Halloween costumes, ET masks, Frisbees, sleeping bags, lunch boxes, drinking straws, and pajamas.

The film began its international release on February 25, 1978 in Tokyo and made its European debut in March 1978 at London's Odeon Leicester Square, with Queen Elizabeth II in the audience. The film did just as well in the foreign markets as it had done in the United States, and by April 1978, the film's total earnings had reached $100 million. The film finished its run in the summer of 1978, by which point it had earned a remarkable $116,395,460, making it the highest-grossing film in Columbia Pictures' history and one of the top five highest-grossing films of all time. As David Begelman had hoped when he first approved the project, *Close Encounters*' success solved Columbia's money woes. In the quarter ending in April 1978, the company's profits had risen 169 percent over the previous quarter—to $16.1 million, most of which had come from *Close Encounters*. By July 1978, the film had freed the company from debt and allowed it to pay cash dividends for the first time since 1970. Although by then Begelman was gone, Columbia Pictures was back and would remain on solid ground for some time to come, thanks to Steven Spielberg and his (in the words of François Truffaut) "film of flying saucers." Apparently, the only person who was (a little bit) disappointed in *Close Encounters'* performance was Spielberg himself. According to some of the people who worked on the production, Steven felt that *Star Wars* had stolen some of his movie's thunder and that *CE3K* would have done even better if it had, as originally scheduled, reached theaters first. (Many people who worked on the film share Spielberg's opinion, although Michael Phillips does not—he feels that *Star Wars* did not detract from *Close Encounters'* success at all, but may have actually helped it by priming the sci-fi pump.) Still, Steven had every reason to be happy when he received his first check from Columbia (which the company blew up to poster size) for his 13.5 percent share of the film's net profits. The amount: $4.5 million.

When the Academy Award nominations for 1977 were announced in February 1978, *Close Encounters* received nine nods: Best Director (Steven Spielberg), Best Actress in a Supporting Role (Melinda Dillon), Best Art Direction - Set Decoration (Joe Alves, Daniel A. Lomino, Phil Abramson), Best Film Editing (Michael Kahn), Best Music, Best Original Score (John Williams), Best Sound (Robert Knudson, Robert Glass, Don MacDougall, Gene S. Cantamessa), Best Visual Effects (Douglas Trumbull, Richard Yuricich, Matthew Yuricich, Gregory Jein, Roy Arbogast), and Best Cinematography (Vilmos Zsigmond). It was also announced that Frank Warner would receive a Special Achievement Award for Sound Effects Editing.

The nomination for Best Cinematography presented a dilemma for the board of the Academy of Motion Picture Arts and Sciences' Cinematography Branch, because—although their members had voted to place *CE3K* in contention—they didn't know whom to give the nomination to. Academy rules stipulated that anyone who received a Director of Photography credit on a film was eligible. Normally, though, only one cinematographer earns this designation on a given film. If other cameramen work on that same movie (shooting inserts, pickup scenes, etc.), they usually receive an "Additional Photography by" credit. However, on *Close Encounters*, five people were identified as a Director of Photography: Vilmos Zsigmond, William A. Fraker (who was credited as Director of Photography of Additional American Scenes), Douglas Slocombe (Director of Photography of India Sequence), John A. Alonzo (Additional Director of Photography), and László Kovács (ditto). Not relishing the prospect of having five people crowd up on stage should the film win, the board of the Cinematography Branch adopted a suggestion put forth by board member William A. Fraker, who suggested that they limit the nomination to the cinematographer with the principal credit, who in this case was Vilmos Zsigmond. In proposing this rule (which still stands today), Fraker was putting himself out of contention, but he felt it was the fair thing to do.

The fiftieth Academy Awards Ceremony was held at the Dorothy Chandler Pavilion in downtown Los Angeles on Monday, April 3, 1978. Going up against the likes of *Star Wars* and *Annie Hall*, *Close Encounters* unfortunately ended up only winning one of the awards—apart from Frank Warner's special achievement honor—that it was nominated for: Best Cinematography.

When Vilmos Zsigmond accepted his Oscar, he thanked the Academy, his film school teachers, and America for giving him a new start when he arrived from Hungary as a refugee, but, in a major breach of Hollywood etiquette, he did not thank his director or his producer. The reason was that, by the time the awards rolled around, Zsigmond was not feeling particularly generous when it came to *Close Encounters*. Still smarting from the difficult time he had had during production and from not being asked back to photograph the additional scenes, he had been further hurt by the prominent credits that had been given to Fraker, Slocombe, Alonzo, and Kovács on the movie. Vilmos felt that giving them all "Directors of Photography" credits (as opposed to just "Additional Photography by") was a deliberate attempt to diminish his contribution to the film. (As it turned out, he was correct. In her book, Julia Phillips wrote that she pushed to give the other cinematographers DP credits in order to "let the world know how he [Vilmos] sandbagged us.") Certain that *Close Encounters* was going to win most of the awards it had been nominated for, Vilmos imagined that Steven and Julia were going to be thanked and praised numerous times that evening, and he didn't feel like adding to the deluge. As Zsigmond explains, "With all of the pressure that I experienced, I didn't feel like I had to thank the producers or Spielberg.... Why should I give them extra when they weren't really that nice to me?" However, as the night wore on and *Close Encounters* did not win the expected number of statues, Zsigmond began to feel bad. "I really thought that *Close Encounters* was going to get five or six major awards...I [really] thought Steven was going to win. And if I would have known that [mine] was going to be the only award, then my speech would have been totally different. It was a very bad thing to have done...and I was sorry."

In addition to the Oscars, *Close Encounters* was nominated for four Golden Globes—Best Motion Picture (Drama), Director, Screenplay, and Original Score—and nine BAFTA (British Academy of Film and Television Arts) Awards—Best Film, Direction, Screenplay, Production Design, Cinematography, Film Editing, Sound, Supporting Actor (François Truffaut), and the Anthony Asquith Award for Film Music. Joe Alves actually won the BAFTA for his production design, but, since no one had ever informed him that he had been nominated, he wasn't there to collect it. Steven was nominated for a Directors Guild of America Award for his direction and a Writers Guild of America Award for his script. Michael Kahn was nominated for a Best Edited Feature Award from the American Cinema Editors Association. John Williams won a Grammy for Best Album of Original Score Written for a Motion Picture or Television Special for his soundtrack album, Frank Warner won a Golden Reel Award for Best Sound Effects Editing from the Motion Picture Sound Editors Association, and the film itself received a citation from the National Board of Review for the special effects and Italy's David Di Donatello Award for Best Foreign Film.

Close Encounters was not just an artistic and financial success—it made a big impact on pop culture as well. As J. Allen Hynek had hoped, the movie created a greater awareness of and respect for the entire UFO phenomenon. In the years immediately following the film's release, the number of sighting reports increased significantly. Hynek didn't think that more people were necessarily seeing Unidentified Flying Objects, but he did feel that those who did were—thanks to *CE3K*—more willing to come forward and talk about it. Also during this time, a number of serious books and articles were written by reputable scientists that gave serious consideration to the possibilities of contact with extraterrestrial life. Inevitably, of course, the movie also egged on the fringe element—several UFO cults spread the rumor that Steven had been hired by a shadow organization within the U.S. government to make *Close Encounters* as a way of preparing the public at large for a soon-to-occur arrival of extraterrestrial life.

The film itself was referenced in opinion columns, editorial cartoons, Johnny Carson monologues, and James Bond movies (when Agent 007 taps a security keypad in 1979's *Moonraker*, the buttons on the pad sound out the five tones. Steven Spielberg, a huge Bond fan, gave 007 producer

Albert R. Broccoli permission to use the tones in the gag). It was spoofed in the July 1978 issue of *Mad* magazine, the cover of which featured caricatures of all of the film's main characters, with Puck's face replaced by that of Alfred E. Neuman. It was also spoofed on television: when Richard Dreyfuss guest-hosted *Saturday Night Live* in May 1978, he appeared in a sketch called "Cone Encounters of the Third Kind," in which Roy Neary becomes obsessed with the shape of the Conehead family's unusually shaped pates. Later in the same episode, Bill Murray's Nick the Lounge Singer entertains an audience by singing the *Close Encounters* theme (which he does by actually singing the words "close," "encounters," and "theme" to the tune of the five tones). In an episode of *Happy Days* called "My Favorite Orkan," Richie Cunningham has a close encounter of the first kind, but no one believes him until an extraterrestrial named Mork shows up to do battle with The Fonz. Mork was played by a newcomer named Robin Williams, and it was this episode that led directly to the creation of his breakthrough series *Mork and Mindy*. A number of other movies ripped off the film's title, including a Jerry Lewis movie about aliens (based on a novel by Kurt Vonnegut) called *Slapstick of Another Kind* (1982); *Cheech & Chong's Next Movie* (1980), which was released in the U.K. as *High Encounters of the Ultimate Kind* (1980); a made-in-Hong Kong movie about vampire-battling martial artists, called *Close Encounters of the Spooky Kind* (1980), the success of which led to the inevitable *Close Encounters of the Spooky Kind 2* (1990); and several soft-core porno films, including *Erotic Encounters of the Fourth Kind* (a 1975 film originally titled *Wham Bam, Thank You Spaceman*) and *Very Close Encounters of the Fourth Kind* (1978).

The tremendous success of both *Star Wars* and *Close Encounters* sparked a cycle of big-budget science fiction and fantasy films filled with high-tech special effects, including *Superman: The Movie* (1978), *Alien* (1979), *Star Trek: The Motion Picture* (1979), and *Blade Runner* (1982), which, along with their many sequels, spin-offs, and imitators, transformed genres that were once dismissed as low-budget, grade-B schlock into mainstream Hollywood staples worthy of big budgets and the attention of significant A-list talent.

In light of all of *Close Encounters'* tremendous commercial, artistic, and cultural success, Michael Phillips is able to look back on William Flanagan's dire predictions for the film's fate with a chuckle, saying, "I think we had the last laugh."

| **The Special Editions**

The Special Edition

As *Close Encounters'* theatrical run came to an end in the summer of 1978, Columbia Pictures began to make tentative plans for a re-release. In those pre–home video days, a studio would release a film to theaters, send it out again a year or two later (often as part of a double bill), and then sell it to television. When a title was re-released, new prints were struck and a new ad campaign mounted, but no changes were made to the actual movie. When it came to *Close Encounters*, however, Steven had other ideas.

As generally pleased as he had been with *CE3K*'s critical and commercial success, Spielberg was dissatisfied with the film itself. In his opinion, the movie had a number of problems that he felt he could have solved if he had been given a few more weeks to work on them—a chance he was denied by Columbia's insistence on a November 1977 premiere. To begin with, Steven wasn't happy with the juxtaposition between Roy Neary's story and that of the Mayflower Project. In addition, there were some things that he had put into the movie but now wished he had left out, as well as some things that he left out but now wished he had included. Spielberg was also still unhappy that he had not been able to shoot the scene in which the *S.S. Marine Sulphur Queen* is discovered in the middle of the Gobi Desert. The sequence had been cut for budgetary reasons, but now that the film had done so well, he wondered if the studio might now be willing to fund it. Finally, Spielberg wanted to give "When You Wish Upon a Star" another try to see if he could get it to work.

In August 1978, Steven approached Columbia (which was now being run by Dan Melnick and new head of production Frank Price) and asked to rework the film—to reedit it and add the Gobi Desert sequence. The executives were amenable as long as the cost of the revamp remained reasonable. As they began to discuss the particulars, the trio decided to add another new scene—one that would take the audience inside the Mothership. In a number of interviews, Steven has said that this idea came about when the Columbia executives asked him to give them something special that they could use to advertise the reissue (although some people associated with the production think that Spielberg may have actually come up with the concept sometime earlier). They knew this would be a good enticement because many viewers and critics had expressed a desire to see what happened to Roy Neary after he went aboard the giant starship.

A budget of $2 million was set for the project. Steven would produce the revision (neither Julia nor Michael Phillips was involved) and John Veitch would supervise the project for the studio. At this point, Steven was hard at work preparing his next film—the World War II comedy spectacular *1941*, a coproduction between Columbia and Universal Pictures on which he was joined by a number of his *CE3K* compatriots, including Michael Kahn, John Williams, William Fraker, J. Patrick McNamara, Sally Dennison, Chuck Meyers, Bob Westmoreland, George Jensen, Gene Cantamessa, Greg Jein, and Matthew Yuricich. With shooting on that picture scheduled to begin in October 1978, Steven didn't have time to tackle the *Close Encounters* revision right then, so it was agreed that he would do the bulk of the work after *1941* was finished. There was one exception: to take advantage of an opening in Richard Dreyfuss's schedule, it was agreed that the live-action portions of Roy's trip inside the Mothership would be filmed early in 1979. A set representing the interior of the Mothership's hatch was constructed on a soundstage at The Burbank Studios, and on Saturday, February 10, 1979, Steven spent the day filming Richard Dreyfuss (wearing the same red jumpsuit he had worn eighteen months earlier on the Big Set in Mobile) walking up the ramp and entering the hatch, where he was greeted by a welcoming committee made up of a number of extraterrestrials (a whole new group of young girls had been recruited to don the ET leotards and masks). Working with Director of Photography Michael Butler (*The Missouri Breaks*, *Jaws 2*)—the son of *CE3K* special effects adviser Larry Butler—Steven next filmed a few shots of Dreyfuss looking around, followed by then one of him looking straight up at a black ceiling, which some months later would be replaced with a visual effect showing the vast interior of the Mothership.

That brief weekend aside, Steven spent the period from October 1978 until May 1979 filming *1941*—a gigantic, chaotic production that, like *Close Encounters*, went far over schedule and far over budget. After shooting had wrapped and the movie entered post-production, Steven turned his attention back to *Close Encounters*. To design the interior of the Mothership, he hired noted cartoonist/conceptual artist/production designer Ron Cobb (*Dark Star, Star Wars,* and *Alien*). Cobb came up with the concept for a huge interior space that would eventually be nicknamed "the Ballroom." The Mothership's curved underbelly served as the floor of the Ballroom, and hundreds of brilliantly illuminated cylinders (presumably the lower portions of the towers seen jutting from the top of the ship in the exterior shots) would serve as the ceiling. Hanging down from that ceiling in the middle of the vast chamber was a massive cylindrical dock to which the scout saucers would attach themselves as the ship prepared to lift off. Once the Ballroom had been conceived, Spielberg and Cobb began developing storyboards to show what would actually happen there. The scene they came up with went as follows: Entering the hatch, Neary would find himself in large circular room—nicknamed "the Roundhouse"—that contained a number of high-intensity spotlights. As Roy watched, the ceiling of the Roundhouse would begin to rise and the spotlights would angle upward to reveal that the circular chamber was located at the very bottom of the giant, majestic Ballroom. The three primary scout saucers and the little red whoosh would converge on the dock and attach themselves as a series of claw-like doors closed down to cover them. At that point, thousands of tiny points of light reminiscent of the micro-cuboids that had originally been intended to appear in The Experience would burst from the dock and rain down upon Roy like a shower of fairy dust.

To bring these storyboards to life, Steven once again approached Douglas Trumbull, who at that point (the summer of 1979) was busy supervising the creation of the visual effects for Paramount Pictures' gargantuan production of *Star Trek: The Motion Picture*. Following his work on *Close Encounters* (which Trumbull considered a "detour" from his directing and technological development pursuits) Doug had attempted to persuade Paramount to let him direct a feature film utilizing the Showscan process, but the studio—feeling that the process was too expensive and too impractical—had refused. Frustrated with Paramount's lack of support for his revolutionary process and for his directorial ambitions, Trumbull agreed to supervise the effects for *Star Trek* (an assignment he had originally turned down) in exchange for Paramount agreeing to release him from his exclusive employment contract and turn Showscan over to him. Most of the *Close Encounters* team had joined Trumbull to work on *Trek*, including Richard Yuricich, Matthew Yuricich, Robert Swarthe, Dave Stewart, Scott Squires, and Rocco Gioffre.

Trumbull agreed to supervise the creation of the new effects shots for *Close Encounters*, but when he attempted to work out a deal for his services with Columbia, he was surprised to find that the studio expected him to work on the project for free. As part of his compensation for *Close Encounters*, Trumbull had received a participation in the film's profits. Since the re-release would presumably generate additional profits in which Trumbull would share, the studio felt that this should be compensation enough, but Trumbull didn't see it that way. His profit participation was in addition to his fee, not in lieu of it. Everyone else working on the revision was being paid and Trumbull wanted to be paid, too. Columbia refused, so, while Future General would still produce the effects, Trumbull himself declined to work on the project. Exhausted after working on *Star Trek* (which had been a notoriously grueling project), Richard Yuricich agreed to get the *CE3K* revamp up and running, but then departed for a well-deserved vacation. With Trumbull and Yuricich not participating, the project found itself in need of a new effects supervisor. After consulting with Spielberg, Trumbull and Yuricich offered the job to Robert Swarthe, with Dave Stewart being asked to supervise the photography. Swarthe and Stewart talked it over and decided that they had no choice but to accept— they didn't want someone else to come in and tamper with the stellar work that they had labored so intently to create.

Future General's portion of *Close Encounters* Mach II got under way in the summer of 1979, as Greg Jein and his team began putting together the Ballroom, which actually consisted of three separate models: a miniature of the Roundhouse, eight feet in diameter, that came complete with motorized searchlights and a six-inch-tall Roy Neary doll (wearing a Richard Dreyfuss mask that took Greg Jein many hours to sculpt) that was motorized to create just enough movement so that it would look alive; a separate Roundhouse ceiling, three feet in diameter; and the fifteen-foot-by-twelve-foot Ballroom itself, which consisted of a variety of fiberglass shapes that were attached to an elaborate wooden frame, painted, detailed with bits and pieces of plastic, and then wired with thousands of strands of fiber optics (Rocco Gioffre later added some matte-painted lighting effects as well). The illuminated cylinders that hung from the ceiling were created by wrapping sheets of acrylic around fluorescent tubes (the acrylic sheets had holes punched in them to let the light shine through). The full Ballroom model had a tiny Roundhouse at the bottom that was only a few inches in diameter and in which stood a half-inch-tall Roy Neary. The flying saucers that would be seen soaring through the giant chamber were the same models that had been created for the original shoot three years before. After the original production wrapped, Steven Spielberg took the models home and stored them in his garage. As the new shoot was gearing up, Future General retrieved the models and refurbished them. The burst of micro-cuboids that descend upon Roy consisted of six separate pieces of artwork, created by animator Leslie Ekker, that were designed to be photographed in combination with one another to create elaborate moiré patterns.

Work on the new effects shots got under way in January 1980 and continued until April. Dave Stewart photographed the Roundhouse models and the saucers, while cinematographer Don Baker photographed the Ballroom miniature and animation cameraman Mike Peed shot the cuboid effects. As each element was completed, it would be turned over to visual effects editor M. Kathryn Campbell, who had joined Future General during the production of *Star Trek*. Campbell assembled all of the elements required for each shot and then gave them to the optical department for line-up and compositing.

As the model and animation elements were being created, Robert Swarthe was busy reworking the shots of Richard Dreyfuss entering the Mothership hatch that had been photographed in 1979. This footage had been filmed before the details of the Ballroom sequence had been nailed down, and some adjustments needed to be made so that it would fit in smoothly with the new concept. To begin with, the alien welcoming committee had to be removed because Steven had decided that it looked too comedic. A light bar that ran across the bottom of the entryway on the hatch set needed to be removed as well, because there was no such bar in the Roundhouse model. To eliminate both of these elements, Swarthe optically enlarged all of the shots in which the bar and/or the aliens appeared, moving in closer on Dreyfuss so that he would fill the frame and they would be pushed out. Light flares needed to be added to some of the shots to tie them in with the spotlights. There was also a big continuity problem that needed to be addressed. When Roy enters the Mothership in the footage that was filmed on the Big Set in 1976, he is seen walking into a blazing inferno of light, but in the 1979 footage, he is shown walking into a very dark room. To fit the two shots together, Swarthe overexposed the portion of the 1979 shot that showed Dreyfuss walking up the ramp. As he enters the Roundhouse, Swarthe gradually brought the exposure back down to normal to make it look as if Neary had walked past a brilliant light source and entered a darkened space on the other side. The storyboards called for a shot of Neary from behind, looking up as the Roundhouse ceiling starts to rise. Since Dreyfuss was not available, a double was hired and photographed on the blue screen stage at Apogee Productions, Inc.—the visual effects company that John Dykstra started after he left Industrial Light & Magic. A plate of the ceiling was inserted later (this was the only blue screen shot in the movie). Finally, after the micro-cuboid burst, Swarthe had wanted the camera to tilt down onto Roy Neary. Unfortunately, no such shot had been filmed, so Swarthe took the tilt-up that had been photographed and reverse-printed it so that, instead of moving up off of Dreyfuss, the camera now moved down onto him. Lens flares also had to be added to some shots to tie Dreyfuss in with the searchlights.

As work on the Ballroom sequence was winding down, Steven decided that they had better show some ETs after all (he figured that audiences would want to know where they were), so a shot was designed in which the camera would move up one of the walls of the Ballroom. The wall would have many openings in it, through which would be seen thousands upon thousands of extraterrestrials. Greg Jein had moved on to his next project by that point, so modelmaker Mitch Suskin was given the task of creating what came to be known as the "Alien Wall." The fifteen-foot-tall model was assembled from pieces of the Ballroom miniature. The ETs that appeared in the openings were half-inch-tall alien plastic models, attached to little rods that were used to move them back and forth so that they would look alive. Over ten thousand of the little creatures were manufactured in three distinct styles (to match the three different alien races seen outside the ship in the original footage). When the time came to photograph the wall, it was placed on its side to make it easier to shoot (the camera was mounted sideways and run along a track that had been set up parallel to the model). Dave Stewart filmed the model in smoke and used a lot of backlight so that the aliens would appear in silhouette. The entire shot was done in-camera, and no optical effects were used to enhance it. Since the Alien Wall hadn't been included in the original plan or budget, Steven paid for it himself.

In addition to the Ballroom sequence, Swarthe and his team had several other shots to complete. Steven wanted to show the shadow of Saucer H flying over Neary's truck as Roy drives away from the railroad crossing after his first encounter, so Greg Jein and his team built a miniature landscape that came complete with a road and a miniature truck. A light was rigged above the set and the saucer was flown past the light on wires to create the shadow. The entire shot was done in-camera—no optical effects at all were used. Steven also wanted to add an insert of one of the three scout saucers shining its headlights on the McDonald's sign during the Quarter Pounder shot. The sign in the original bend-of-the-road miniature was approximately three inches high, but the model used for the insert was one foot by two feet.

Steven began work on the new live-action scenes in January 1980. By then, *1941* had opened (in December 1979—to bad reviews and less-than-expected box office) and Spielberg was in the early stages of pre-production on his next film, *Raiders of the Lost Ark* (1981), which was scheduled to begin filming in June 1980. First up was the Gobi Desert sequence. Steven had worked out a new version of the scene—the original version had featured Claude Lacombe, but since François Truffaut was unavailable (in January 1980 he had just begun directing his latest film, *Le Dernier Métro* [*The Last Metro*]), Spielberg refocused the action around David Laughlin and the Project Leader. He also decided to drop the *S.S. Marine Sulphur Queen* and replace it with the *S.S. Cotopaxi*—a tramp steamer that disappeared in December 1925 while en route from Charleston, South Carolina to Havana and soon afterward became part of Bermuda Triangle lore.

Rather than employ a lot of complex (and expensive) photographic effects, Steven and the Future General team opted to take a much simpler, more low-tech approach to the scene and do a forced-perspective shot by placing a miniature *Cotopaxi* close to the camera, positioning the actors a considerable distance away, and then employing a judicious camera angle to make it look as if there were a lot of little people standing next to a very big ship. It was Greg Jein's job to build the *Cotopaxi*. He began by purchasing a very old miniature ship from Twentieth Century-Fox. The model was in such dilapidated condition that only the hull was usable, so Greg tore off the superstructure and began rebuilding it using plywood and plastic. To guide him in his efforts, Jein looked for a picture of the *Cotopaxi* but couldn't find one, so he had to use his imagination. When the model was almost finished, a picture of the *Cotopaxi*'s sister ship was finally located. As it turned out, Greg's model didn't look anything like the real *Cotopaxi*, but Jein didn't mind, because he thought his version actually looked much better.

The Gobi Desert sequence was filmed on January 29 and 30, 1980, in the Dumont Dunes near Death Valley. Ronald L. Schwary (*The Electric Horseman* [1979], *Ordinary People* [1980]) was the production manager, and Allen Daviau, who had shot *Amblin'* for Steven back in 1968, was the Director of Photography. Jein and his team spent the first day moving the *Cotopaxi* model into position. In the meantime, the rest of the unit filmed shots of three UN jeeps and two helicopters carrying Mayflower Project personnel as they race across the desert toward the derelict ship. Unfortunately, the day got off to a rough start. In the introductory shot of the jeeps, the three vehicles were supposed to come bounding over the top of a dune, one after another. The first jeep made it over and continued down the dune's sandy slope as intended. However, when the second jeep came over the hill, it got stuck in the sand at the top of the crest, and when the third jeep came zooming over a few seconds later, it crashed into the back of the second jeep. A few of the people riding in the jeeps were injured and were flown by helicopter to a nearby hospital. Later on, a team of camels appearing in the scene got loose, and it took almost half a day for the crew to round up the escaped dromedaries. Things went much better the second day—the *Cotopaxi* model looked great and had been positioned perfectly, so the forced-perspective shots went off without a hitch. Bob Balaban reprised his role of David Laughlin in the sequence. At the time, Balaban had been appearing in a production of Wallace Shawn's play *Marie and Bruce* at the Public Theater in New York City, so Columbia bought out a number of the performances so that Balaban would have the time to fly to California and join J. Patrick McNamara, who had just finished appearing in *1941*, in the scene. Both men wore the same costumes they had worn when the filmed the Flight 19 sequence almost three years earlier.

After the company returned to The Burbank Studios, work began on another new scene that Steven had dreamed up—one in which Roy stops at a gas station during the blackout that occurs at the beginning of the movie. While he is there, shafts of light from the UFOs (which are hovering behind some trees) come streaming in through the station's windows, at which point all of the electrical equipment in the place goes haywire and Roy gets pelted with cans fired out of a Coke machine. Second unit director Matthew Robbins directed the scene, which was ultimately cut after Steven saw a similar scene in John Carpenter's movie *The Fog* (which was released at the beginning of February 1980) and decided to abandon the sequence.

Once all of the new footage had been completed, Steven and Michael Kahn started to reedit the movie. The first thing they did was restructure the middle portion of the film in order to effect a better balance between Roy's story and the Mayflower tale. Beginning with the second Crescendo Summit scene (the one in which Roy takes his family out in the middle of the night to look for UFOs), the scene progression in the original 1977 version of the film was as follows: Roy gets fired; Roy goes out to Crescendo Summit for a third time and sees the mysterious lights that turn out to be helicopters; the India sequence; the auditorium scene (in which Lacombe introduces the five tones and the Kodály hand signals), the radio telescope scene (in which the Devils Tower coordinates are discovered); and Barry's kidnapping. In the restructured 1980 version, the second Crescendo Summit scene is followed by the new Gobi Desert sequence, and then: Roy gets fired; India; the auditorium scene; Crescendo Summit 3; the radio telescope scene; and Barry's kidnapping. In addition to this restructuring, Steven cut out sixteen minutes of footage that had appeared in the first version of the movie and added seven minutes of fresh material (including the new sequences and several bits that had been filmed in 1976 but never used).

The first addition and deletion were made to the scene in which Roy Neary is first introduced. In the 1977 version, this scene begins with close shots of Roy's model train running through a miniature landscape, an insert of a Pinocchio music box, and a close-up of Roy's face as he watches the train crash. These close shots are followed by a wide shot of the family room as Ronnie answers the phone and Roy is called in to work. In the 1980 re-vamp, the model railroad and Pinocchio shots are dropped. The scene now begins with an aerial view of the Nearys' suburban Indiana neighborhood (a recycling of the blackout shot), and Roy is introduced as he unsuccess-fully tries to help Brad with his math homework. This is followed by an argument over whether the family should go out to play miniature golf or to see a re-release of *Pinocchio*. From there, the scene plays as it did in 1977. • The entire scene in which Roy reports to work at the power station was cut. • The new effects shot of Saucer H flying over Neary's truck was inserted after Roy's first encounter. • The close-up of the McDonald's sign was added to the Quarter Pounder shot. • The eccentric farmer's line "They can fly rings around the moon, but we're years ahead of 'em on the highway" was removed. • The tail end of the scene in which Roy loses his job was also removed. In the 1977 version, Roy lies down on the bed after Ronnie tells him he got fired and begins studying one of the pillows. After looking at it intently for a few minutes, he mutters, "That's not right."

Footage of the Mayflower Project members giving Lacombe a standing ovation were added to the end of the auditorium scene. • The entire Air Force Base debunking scene was cut. • A few shots showing Roy entering the dining room and sitting down as the family begins to pass the dinner dishes were removed from the beginning of the mashed potato scene. • The sequence that had been filmed in 1976 but never used (in which Roy locks himself in the bathroom and Ronnie breaks in to find him crying in the shower) was inserted into the film right after the scene in which a frus-trated Roy looks up at the heavens and cries, "What is it?" Apparently this was done to balance out the removal of the scene in which Roy tears up the yard to collect the material with which to make his large model of Devils Tower (when the film was first released, many critics objected to this scene, complaining that it was much too broad and farcical and should never had been included). In the 1980 version of the movie, Roy's Looneytoon-scored moment of inspiration is followed by Ronnie and the kids leaving him, now presumably in response to the shower scene. Ronnie's departure plays as it does in the original version, although it now ends with her driving away. The scene's original tag, in which Roy enters the house by climbing though the kitchen window, was cut. A brief bit in which Roy watches some of his neighbors playing baseball was cut from the scene in which Neary's Devils Tower model is revealed. • A shot of the gas mask salesman giving his spiel at the start of the evacuation scene was replaced by an alternate take in which he makes his pitch while using his dog as a model. The scene in which Roy is questioned by a suspicious soldier as he tries to figure out how to get past the roadblock was dropped, as was one in which Neary carries a newly purchased gas mask and cage of canaries to his car. • In the base camp scene, a brief bit in which Roy, Jillian, and Larry shove aside a guard and jump out of the evacuation helicopter was cut. The revamp doesn't show how the trio escapes from the helicopter, but simply joins them already on the run. • The Ballroom sequence was added to the film directly after Roy ascends the ramp into the Mothership. • The heavy influence that Disney movies had on the picture, which was only suggested in the 1977 version, was made explicit when John Williams added a *Snow White*-like chorus to the Roundhouse scene and then played "When You Wish Upon a Star" directly over the shot of the Alien Wall. • After the micro-cuboids burst out of the bottom of the dock and shower down upon Roy, the revamped version of the film goes directly to the scene in which Puck approaches Lacombe for the farewell exchange of Kodály signs, a cut that gave many viewers the mistaken impression that the micro-cuboid "fairy dust" had somehow transformed Roy into Puck. • The final change came during the end credits, when the original music was replaced by a gentle, instrumental version of "When You Wish Upon a Star." As a result of all of the alterations, the 1980 version of the film had a running time of two hours and twelve minutes (the 1977 version was two hours and fifteen minutes long).

Steven delivered the negative of what was now called *The Special Edition of Close Encounters of the Third Kind* (although only in the promotional materials. The title on the film itself didn't change) to Columbia in April 1980 and then went off to London to make *Raiders*. The reissue had originally been scheduled for Easter 1980, but was pushed back until summer. Columbia prepared for the re-release by mounting a new advertising campaign. The "Infinity Road" key art was replaced by a still of Roy being led into the Mothership by the ETs. The copy in all of the promotional materials announced that "Now, for the first time, filmgoers will be able to share the ultimate experience of being *inside!*" *The Special Edition* was screened for the press in the Samuel Goldwyn Theater at the Academy of Motion Picture Arts and Sciences headquarters in Beverly Hills on July 31, 1980. The reviews were mixed:

David Ansen—*Newsweek*: "The tinkering was worth it: a terrific film has been fine-tuned into a great one.... The new *Close Encounters* is not just sleeker now, it has an emotional charge and coherence that were missing before."

Charles Champlin—*The Los Angeles Times*: "The new version of *Close Encounters of the Third Kind*...is better, surer, swifter and clearer than the original film."

Arthur Knight—*The Hollywood Reporter*: "Director Steven Spielberg has taken his 1977 flawed masterpiece and, by judicious editing and the addition of several scenes...has turned his work into an authentic masterpiece."

Stanley Kauffmann—*The New Republic*: "It's a mistake. The second encounter isn't as good as the first.... Nothing that Spielberg could show match what he made us imagine. Seeing is believing less."

Pauline Kael—*The New Yorker*: "I wish Steven Spielberg had trusted his first instincts and left *Close Encounters of the Third Kind* alone.... When you remember something with pleasure and it's gone, you feel as if your memories have been mugged."

The Special Edition opened on August 1, 1980 in 750 theaters in the United States and Canada and on later dates around the world. Audience reaction was mixed. Although some fans liked the changes, many didn't like the fact that one of their favorite films had been tampered with, no matter how flawed it was or was perceived to be. The reaction to the Ballroom scene was especially lukewarm. Even those people who liked it conceded that it didn't add much of substance to the movie, and those who didn't felt that it ruined much of the ending's magic and mystery by making explicit what should have been left to the imagination. Steven himself later said that the Ballroom scene was a mistake. As Michael Phillips comments, "People thought they wanted to see the inside of the Mothership. As it turns out, they didn't." By the end of its run, *The Special Edition* had grossed approximately $16 million, which was decent money for a reissue, although perhaps not as much as Columbia had hoped it would make.

Super-8mm

As was the custom in those pre-video days, highlight reels of scenes from *Close Encounters* were released on Super-8MM film in various versions (black-and-white and color; sound and silent) for the home market at the end of 1978.

The Television Edition

Close Encounters made its U.S. television debut on the ABC television network on November 15, 1981. The version shown that night was basically *The Special Edition*, but in order to pad the film out so that it could run in a three-hour time slot, a number of cut scenes were restored, including the Air Force debunking and the scene in which Roy tears up his backyard. Steven later told Hal Barwood that this was his favorite version of the movie because it included everything.

Videotape

The Special Edition was released in a pan-and-scan version on VHS and Betamax in 1982 and then again on VHS in 1988.

Laserdisc

The Criterion Collection issued the film on Laserdisc in 1990. Although this edition was advertised as being the original 1977 version of the film, it wasn't. The shot in which the shadow of Saucer H passes over Neary's truck produced for *The Special Edition* was included, and the bits in which Roy watches his neighbors play baseball as he is building the Devils Tower replica, and in which Roy, Jillian, and Larry escape from the helicopter in the base camp scene (which were cut for *The Special Edition*), were not restored. As a bonus, the Criterion disc included a documentary about the making of the movie that featured interviews with many members of the creative team, including Steven Spielberg and Doug Trumbull.

The Definitive Director's Version

In 1998, Steven put together yet another iteration of the film. Essentially a polished version of the television cut, *The Definitive Director's Version* was *The Special Edition* with a few significant changes: the close-up of the McDonald's sign that had been added to the Quarter Pounder shot for *The Special Edition* was removed, as was the standing ovation at the end of the auditorium scene. • Both the Air Force debunking and the scene in which Roy tears up his backyard were restored (the removal of both scenes for *The Special Edition* had been applauded by critics but decried by many fans). • The Ballroom scene was cut. • Finally, "When You Wish Upon a Star" was removed and the original end title music restored. • The running time of this new edition is two hours and seventeen minutes.

The Definitive Director's Version premiered at a special screening held at the Academy of Motion Picture Arts and Sciences on January 12, 1999. The screening was followed by a reunion of many members of the cast and crew (including Julia Phillips, who had by then recovered considerably from many of her problems) and a panel discussion about the making of the movie. Following this event, *The Definitive Director's Version* was given a limited theatrical release in a few major cities. Retitled *The Collector's Edition*, it was released on VHS and Laserdisc in 1999 (the Laserdisc version was accompanied by a new account of the making of the film produced by documentarian Laurent Bouzereau) and on DVD in 2001 (in a package that included the Bouzereau documentary, along with a number of deleted scenes, trailers, and promotional materials). A CD release of John Williams' complete score for the film (due to technical limitations, the original LP release contained only forty-five minutes of music) was released at the same time as the DVD. Called *Close Encounters of the Third Kind: The Collector's Edition Soundtrack*, the CD contained a lengthy interview with John Williams and the "When You Wish Upon a Star" version of the end title music.

The Thirtieth Anniversary Ultimate Edition

In November 2007, Sony Pictures Home Entertainment rereleased *CE3K* in a special Thirtieth Anniversary DVD and Blu-ray Disc that contained all three editions of the film on a single disc. This marks the first time that the original 1977 release version of *Close Encounters of the Third Kind* has been available on any home video format.

Aftermath

The Special Edition of Close Encounters of the Third Kind was the first time that a major motion picture had been reworked so extensively after it had been successfully released. Its relative critical and commercial success, as well as the success of the subsequent versions of the film, led to a string

of theatrical "special editions" and "director's cuts" that have included revisions of *A Star Is Born* (1954), *The Exorcist* (1973), *New York, New York*
(1977), *Star Wars* (1977), and *Blade Runner* (1982). With the advent of
home video and especially DVD, the practice of issuing multiple editions
of the same movie has now become commonplace (and, in the opinion of
some, epidemic).

| Close Encounters
of the Fourth Kind

IN A NUMBER OF INTERVIEWS given just prior to the original release of *Close Encounters* in November 1977, Steven Spielberg announced that he was already at work on a sequel. In some of those interviews, he said he was writing a screenplay; in others he said that the script was already finished. He told one reporter that he would direct the new movie and many others that he would probably only produce it. One one occasion he said he intended to start production on the follow-up by the summer of 1978 and have it in theaters by the summer of 1980. As it turns out, Steven's enthusiasm for continuing the *Close Encounters* experience may have caused him to get a little bit carried away, because, while Spielberg and Michael Phillips had talked about the possibility of doing a sequel, no story had been conceived, no script had been written, and no production was imminent.

After the film opened, Steven and Michael spent some time brainstorming to see if they could come up with an idea for a second film, but, as Phillips reports, "Nothing revealed itself as an obvious way to go. We talked about going to the ETs' home world, but we couldn't figure out what would happen once we got there. After a while, we just let it go." Eventually, Spielberg decided that the story of *Close Encounters* was not one that should be continued. In a July 1982 interview in *American Premiere* magazine, he told writer Susan Royal that a *CE3K II* would be "...forced...the movie essentially ended in the best way it could possibly end, with Richard going away, never to return. If I made a sequel and Richard returned, it would be undermining the uniqueness of the first story." It is likely that Columbia Pictures wanted a sequel to their high-est-grossing film ever and may have even pressed Steven on the point (it has been suggested that one of the reasons Spielberg did *The Special Edition* was to give Columbia more *Close Encounters* without actually having to make another movie), but by the end of 1978, the notion that there were going to be further adventures of Roy Neary and his extraterrestrial friends was pretty much dead. This did not mean, however, that Spielberg was finished making movies about aliens.

During the production of *Close Encounters*, J. Allen Hynek told Steven the tale of a Kentucky family that in 1955 claimed to have been terror-ized by a group of malevolent extraterrestrials who had come to earth and invaded their farm. It was an intriguing story, and Steven immediately recognized that it had the potential to make an exciting movie, albeit a very different one from *Close Encounters*—quite a bit darker and certainly much more horrific. Although it was not necessarily something that Steven wanted to direct himself, it was something that he was interested in producing (after years of working solely as a director, Spielberg had recently made his producing debut with a Robert Zemeckis film about Beatlemania, called *I Wanna Hold Your Hand* [1978]). He discussed the idea with an enthusiastic Ron Cobb while they were preparing *The Special Edition*, and the two eventually worked up a rough treatment with a very familiar title: *Watch the Skies*. Steven pitched the project to Columbia, and the studio—more than happy to be in business with Steven Spielberg on another movie about visitors from outer space—agreed to make it.

To write the script, Spielberg hired John Sayles, a novelist (*Pride of the Bimbos* [1975], *Union Dues* [1977]) and future independent film pioneer (*Return of the Secaucus Seven* [1980], *Matwan* [1987]), who had also writ-ten a number of very entertaining horror and science fiction scripts for exploitation movie king Roger Corman, including a takeoff on *Jaws* that Spielberg had really enjoyed called *Piranha* (1978). Basing his screenplay on the classic John Ford western *Drums Along the Mohawk* (1939)—a film about a group of frontier settlers menaced by a group of marauding Indi-ans—Sayles came up with the story of a group of eleven insectoid extra-terrestrials that land on an isolated backwoods farm. The members of the frightened family that owns the farm barricade themselves inside their house as as the aliens proceed to turn the farm upside down—playing with the equipment, trying to communicate with the livestock, etc. As it turns out, some of the ETs are curious, some are mischievous, and a few, led by a villain nicknamed "Scar" (after the main bad guy in another Ford classic, *The Searchers*) are downright hostile. After killing a number of farm animals, Scar and his minions focus their attention on the house and its occupants. With the help of an amiable alien nicknamed "Buddy," who has befriended the family's autistic son, the family pulls together and fights back against the alien attack. While Sayles was writing, Spielberg began to assemble the rest of his creative team. Ron Cobb was hired to direct, and special makeup effects wizard Rick Baker (who was currently at work on director John Landis's horror/comedy *An American Werewolf in London* [1981]) was given the daunting task of creating eleven lifelike extraterrestrials (although as soon as the expense and complexity of this task became apparent, the number was reduced to five).

John Sayles finished *Night Skies* (the title was changed when it was discovered that someone else owned the rights to *Watch the Skies*) in the summer of 1980 and sent it to Spielberg, who was then in Tunisia filming the desert portions of *Raiders of the Lost Ark*. Although Steven thought that Sayles had written a very good script, he began to have second thoughts about making such a dark and gruesome film (at one point in the story, the aliens dissect a cow and then later attempt to do the same thing to a human). He was, however, quite taken with the subplot involving Buddy and the little boy, and began thinking about turning it into a movie of its own—something more in tune with his own sensibilities and more reflective of his personal beliefs about the peaceful nature of extraterrestrial life.

Steven worked on the idea with screenwriter Melissa Mathison, who had coauthored the script for the classic children's film *The Black Stallion* (1979) and was currently in Tunisia visiting her boyfriend, Harrison Ford. Using the last scene of *Night Skies*—in which Buddy is left behind on Earth—as a jumping-off point, Spielberg and Mathison developed a new story about a gentle, sweet-natured extraterrestrial named (naturally) ET, who comes to Earth to collect plants, but gets stranded in the American suburbs when his shipmates are forced to leave in a hurry in order to avoid being captured by a group of UFO investigators that bear more than a passing resemblence to Claude Lacombe and and his Mayflower team. ET is befriended by a lonely young boy named Elliot Taylor (note the similarity in initials) who is struggling to cope with the breakup of his parents' marriage, and the two eventually develop a very close, symbiotic releationship. As *ET & Me* took shape, Steven fell in love with the project and eventually decided that he wanted to direct it himself.

Upon returning to the United States in the fall of 1980, Steven shelved *Night Skies* (although many of its elements would turn up in other Spielberg productions: the family menaced by evil forces was featured in *Poltergeist* [1982], and a band of marauding creatures [in this case led by a creature named Stripe] creating havoc was the focus of *Gremlins* [1984]). Sayles and Cobb, after having been compensated for their contributions to the project, moved on to other assignments, Mathison got to work on the *ET & Me* screenplay, and Steven pitched the new concept to Columbia. The change of direction presented the studio with a dilemma. Columbia was already developing a script about a friendly alien who comes to Earth and becomes involved in a relationship with a human being, called *Starman*. Since it made neither creative nor economic sense for the studio to make two movies with essentially the same story, the executives had to choose one over the other. As they evaluated both projects, they reasoned that *Starman* would appeal to a wider audience because it was about adults and contained a love story, whereas *ET & Me* was, in their opinion, nothing more than a kiddie movie that would play only to a very narrow family audience and generate returns that were modest at best. Based on this logic, Columbia decided to go ahead with *Starman* and, in February 1981, put *ET & Me* into turnaround.

Steven took the project to Universal, which picked it up immediately. Spielberg prepared the film throughout the spring and summer while promoting *Raiders*, which became a smash hit when it opened on June 12, 1981. *ET & Me* began filming in September 1981 under the code name *A Boy's Life* (this was another one of Steven's security precautions—as with *Close Encounters*, he didn't want any details about the film to leak out before it was released). The film's production team included a number of *Close Encounters* veterans, such as Allen Daviau, Gene Cantamessa, and John Williams. Matthew Robbins did an uncredited rewrite on the script, Ralph McQuarrie designed ET's spaceship, and the film's visual effects were supervised by former Mothership cinematographer Dennis Muren. After Spielberg and Rick Baker had a falling-out over concepts and costs, Steven called on yet another *CE3K* alumnus—Puck's creator, Carlo Rambaldi—to bring ET to life. Other holdovers included a few ideas that Spielberg had developed for *Close Encounters* but hadn't been able to use, such as giving the alien a long, telescoping neck, transparent skin through which its internal organs could be seen, and a whimsical-looking spaceship to fly around in that could have been designed by Dr. Seuss. Both films also featured wonderfully naturalistic performances from a group of child actors. But the primary connection between the two films was the gentle, optimistic spirit and powerful sense of wonder that Steven brought to both of them.

The retitled *ET: The Extra-Terrestrial* debuted at the Cannes Film Festival in May 1982 and was released to theaters in the U.S. and Canada on June 11, 1982. It quickly became both a smash hit (earning $352 million in the domestic marketplace alone, making it the highest-grossing film ever until that time) and a cultural phenomenon. While *ET* did not continue the story of *Close Encounters*, the new film did carry forward its warm, reassuring vision, and the incredibly positive response that the movie generated was proof that this was something that audiences not only responded to, but actually craved on a very deep level, just as they had in 1977.

Although no official sequel to *Close Encounters* has ever been made, many of its themes and concepts, and much of its imagery, have been reprised. Following the film's successful first release, the NBC television network began airing a series called *Project UFO* (1978–1979). Produced by Jack Webb of *Dragnet* fame, the show was about a team of dedicated Air Force officers who investigate UFO reports (J. Allen Hynek was no doubt amused by their extreme diligence and lack of agenda). In the 1990s, the Fox Network took the concept a quantum leap further with *The X-Files*, an incredibly popular series about two FBI agents who investigate paranormal activity, much of it centering around a plot by villainous extraterrestrials to take over the earth. Abduction by aliens was the subject of 1993's *Fire in the Sky*, a film based on a true story about a logger who claims to have been kidnapped by the occupants of a flying saucer. When the film first opened, it was promoted as being a realistic version of *CE3K*.

Benign, spiritual encounters with friendly extraterrestrials were at the core of a number of popular films and television shows that appeared in *CE3K*'s wake, including the original 1979 *Battlestar Galactica* television series (in one episode, glowing beings in a massive luminescent starship set the lost travelers of ABC's *Star Wars* rip-off on the right path to Earth). A 1979 Italian film called *Uno Sceriffo extraterrestre—poco extra e molto terrestre* (*The Sheriff and the Satellite Kid*) and its 1980 sequel,

Chissa perche...capitano tutte a me (*Everything Happens to Me*) chronicle the adventures of a Smalltown, U.S.A. sheriff—played by Bud Spencer, the English screen name of popular spaghetti western star Carlo Pedersoli—who comes in contact with an alien being who looks just like an eight-year-old boy. The *Close Encounters* connection was bolstered by the fact that the boy was played by Cary Guffey. The title character in the 1981 series *The Greatest American Hero* is given a magical superhero costume by aliens who travel about in UFOs that cause car engines to conk out). There were also the previously mentioned *Starman* (1984), which, although popular, never earned anything near what *ET* did, much to Columbia's chagrin and embarrassment; 1985's geriatrics-meet-the spacemen fantasy *Cocoon* and its 1988 sequel, *Cocoon: The Return*, both of which were brought to the screen by *Jaws* producers Richard D. Zanuck and David Brown; **batteries not included*, a 1987 film produced by Steven Spielberg and directed by Matthew Robbins, about living machines from outer space that come to the aid of a group of inner-city New Yorkers; and *The Abyss* (1989), James Cameron's epic about a group of underwater oil rig workers who discover an extraterrestrial ship buried deep beneath the sea.

Less friendly meetings with aliens of a more sinister nature were the subject of *Independence Day* (1996), a movie about an alien takeover of Earth that has more in common with the "invaders from Mars" flicks of the 1950s than it does with Steven's film, but that is nevertheless filled with a number of *Close Encounters* references; *The X Files* (1998), a big-screen adaptation of the television series that ends with a hostile encounter between alien and man in the frozen north; and M. Night Shyamalan's *Signs* (2002), an awkward attempt to combine the *Night Skies* concept of a family whose isolated farm is besieged by aliens with *Close Encounters'* transcendent spirituality. Almost all of these movies and shows feature some variation on *CE3K*'s Mothership, often with a very similar design.

The production of *Close Encounters'* brilliant visual effects are a major element of writer/director Patrick Read Johnson's film *5/25/77*. Based on Johnson's real-life experiences, this 2007 movie chronicles the adventures of a movie-obsessed teenager who gets the opportunity to visit Industrial Light & Magic during the making of *Star Wars* and Future General during the making of *Close Encounters*. Actor Kevin J. Stephens portrays Steven Spielberg in the movie, Michael Pawluck appears as Doug Trumbull, and

Dave Shin plays Greg Jein. Richard Yuricich served as a special effects adviser on the film.

Twenty-eight years after *Close Encounters* and twenty-three years after *ET: The Extra-Terrestrial*, Steven Spielberg made another film about aliens coming to Earth: *War of the Worlds*, his 2005 adaptation of H.G. Wells's novel about a hostile invasion from outer space. To the surprise of many, Spielberg's third extraterrestrial film was as dark, threatening, and bleak as his first two were light, benign, and hopeful. In recent years, Spielberg has distanced himself a bit from the positive vision of *Close Encounters of the Third Kind* and *ET: The Extra-Terrestrial*, identifying that vision as stemming from a youthful optimism that he doesn't necessarily feel any more.

If indeed Spielberg has lost some of that wonderful spirit, then we can certainly mourn the loss of any new work that it might have produced. At the same time, however, we can be cheered by the fact that, thanks to the miracle of cinema, we will always be able to turn to that joyful light that was first committed to film over thirty years ago and continues to shine today.

CHAPTER 28 | After the Glow

STEVEN SPIELBERG'S post–*Close Encounters* career has been nothing short of phenomenal. Following the back-to-back successes of *Raiders of the Lost Ark* and *ET: The Extra-Terrestrial*, Steven directed the "Kick the Can" segment of *Twilight Zone: The Movie* (1983), *Indiana Jones and the Temple of Doom* (1984), *The Color Purple* (1985), *Empire of the Sun* (1987), *Indiana Jones and the Last Crusade* (1989), *Always* (1989), *Hook* (1991), *Jurassic Park* (1993), *Schindler's List* (1993), *The Lost World: Jurassic Park* (1997), *Amistad* (1997), *Saving Private Ryan* (1998), *The Unfinished Journey* (1999), *AI: Artificial Intelligence* (2001—for which he also wrote the screenplay), *Minority Report* (2002), *Catch Me If You Can* (2002), *The Terminal* (2004), *War of the Worlds* (2005), and *Munich* (2005). In addition to many of his own films, Spielberg has produced dozens of successful movies, including *Poltergeist* (1982), *Gremlins* (1984), *The Goonies* (1985), *Back to the Future* (1985) and its two sequels, *Who Framed Roger Rabbit* (1988), *Men in Black* (1997), *Flags of Our Fathers* (2006), and *Letters from Iwo Jima* (2006), as well as the television series *Amazing Stories* (1995), *SeaQuest DSV* (1993), *ER* (1994), *Band of Brothers* (2001), and *Taken* (2002)—a show about UFO abductees.

Spielberg was nominated for an Academy Award as Best Director for *Close Encounters, Raiders of the Lost Ark, ET: The Extra-Terrestrial, The Color Purple,* and *Munich* and won for directing *Schindler's List* and *Saving Private Ryan.* In 1987, the Academy of Motion Pictures Arts and Sciences honored Steven for his work as a producer by giving him the prestigious Irving G. Thalberg Award. In 1994 Spielberg joined with David Geffen and Jeffrey Katzenberg to found Dreamworks SKG—a movie studio that produced three consecutive Best Picture winners (*American Beauty* [1999], *Gladiator* [2000], and *A Beautiful Mind* [2001]), as well as the very successful *Shrek* series. In that same year, Steven used the profits from *Schindler's List* to start the Survivors of the Shoah Visual History Foundation, an organization that records the testimonies of Holocaust survivors. In 1995 Spielberg received the American Film Institute's Life Achievement Award, and in 2001 he was named a Knight Commander of the British Empire by Queen Elizabeth II. In 2002 he returned to college and finally graduated from the California State University at Long Beach with a degree in film. As of this writing, he is currently directing a fourth Indiana Jones adventure, which is scheduled for release in 2008. According to his public statements on the matter, he has yet to see a UFO.

The Producers

Julia Phillips spent the decade following her departure from *Close Encounters* struggling with her various substance abuse problems. She finally returned to producing in 1988 with two low-budget films—*The Beat* and *The Boost*. After earning her final screen credit as an executive producer (with Michael Phillips) on 1991's *Don't Tell Mom the Babysitter's Dead*, Phillips wrote *You'll Never Eat Lunch in This Town Again*, a memoir of her life in Hollywood in which she bad-mouthed just about everyone she had ever known or worked with, including many people involved with *Close Encounters*. The scandal surrounding the book brought Julia an enormous amount of publicity but put a permanent end to her career. She died of cancer on January 1, 2002. Several members of the *Close Encounters* company report that Julia reached out to them before her death in an attempt to mend some of the many fences she had broken.

    Michael Phillips made his debut as a solo producer in 1981 with *Heartbeeps*, a science fiction comedy written by John Hill about two robots that fall in love. Since then, Phillips has produced or executive produced *Cannery Row* (1982), *The Flamingo Kid* (1984), *Eyes of an Angel* (1991), *Mom and Dad Save the World* (1992), *Mimic* (1997), *Imposter* (2002), and *The Last Mimzy* (2007). He currently runs Lighthouse Productions with his wife, Julia Maio.

    Clark Paylow served as the production manager for the Jack Nicholson–directed *Goin' South* in 1978 and then executive produced Oliver Stone's directorial debut, *The Hand*, in 1981. He produced two more films—*Savannah Smiles* (1982) and *Bog* (1983)—before his death on September 25, 1985.

The Writers

Paul Schrader wrote many more screenplays, including *Raging Bull* (1980) and *The Last Temptation of Christ* (1988). He also directed a number of movies, including *Blue Collar* (1978), *American Gigolo* (1980), *Cat People* (1982), *Mishima: A Life in Four Chapters* (1985), *Affliction* (1997) and *The Walker* (2007), many of which he also wrote or cowrote. His brother, Leonard, who earned an Academy Award nomination for his script for *Kiss of the Spider Woman* (1985), died on November 2, 2006.

John Hill wrote the television movie *Griffin and Phoenix: A Love Story* in 1976 and spent the next twenty-five years as a full-time screen and television writer. In addition to *Heartbeeps*, he wrote or cowrote the scripts for *Little Nikita* (1989), *Quigley Down Under* (1990), *Steel Justice* (1992), and a remake of *Griffin and Phoenix* (2006). He sold a number of spec scripts, was a supervising producer on the television series *Quantum Leap*, and won an Emmy as a producer of *L.A. Law*. He currently lives in Nevada, where he writes novels and teaches writing at the University of Nevada in Las Vegas. He says that *Close Encounters* is still one of his favorite movies.

Jerry Belson used the education in screenwriting that he received working on *Close Encounters* to good effect—in the years that followed, he wrote or cowrote the screenplays for *Fun with Dick and Jane* (1977), *The End* (1978), and *Smokey and the Bandit II* (1980) before turning to directing with *Jekyll and Hyde...Together Again* (1982) and *Surrender* (1987), both of which he also authored. Belson worked with Steven Spielberg again when he wrote the screenplay for *Always*. Jerry also remained active in television, writing and producing for a number of series including *The Tracy Ullman Show*, *The Norm Show*, and *The Drew Carey Show*. He died on October 10, 2006.

Hal Barwood and Matthew Robbins followed *Stingray* (which was released in 1978 as *Corvette Summer*) with the scripts for *Dragonslayer* (1981), which Robbins directed, and *Warning Sign* (1985), which Barwood directed. Combining a lifelong interest in games with a burgeoning interest in computers, Hal Barwood left the film industry in the late 1980s and became a very successful video game designer. Matthew Robbins remained in the movies, cowriting and directing *The Legend of Billy Jean* (1985) and **batteries not included* (1987). He also directed the 1991 family film *Bingo*, many television commercials, and a music video for Paul McCartney. In 1997 Robbins cowrote the screenplay for *Mimic* with director Guillermo del Toro and in 2007 cowrote *The Rangoon Express* with director Vishal Bhardwaj.

The Art Department

Joe Alves followed up his extraordinary work on *Close Encounters* by serving as the production designer, associate producer, and second unit director on *Jaws 2* (1978). After designing John Carpenter's *Escape from New York* (1981), he directed the third installment in the *Jaws* series, *Jaws 3-D* (1983). He directed the second unit on Carpenter's *Starman* and then returned to production design for *Everybody's All-American* (1988), *Freejack* (1992), *Geronimo* (1993), *Drop Zone* (1994), *Shadow Conspiracy* (1997), *Fire Down Below* (1997), and *Sinbad: Beyond the Veil of Mists* (2000). Alves, now semi-retired, lives in Southern California.

   George Jensen was the production illustrator on a number of high-profile films in the 1980s and 1990s, including *Romancing the Stone* (1984), *Dune* (1984), and *Terminator 2: Judgment Day* (1991). He also served as the visual effects art director for *2010* (1984), *Big Trouble in Little China* (1986) and *The Boy Who Could Fly* (1986) before retiring from the film industry in the 1990s. **Dan Lomino** has been both an art director and production designer on a long string of films and television programs, including *Fast Times at Ridgemont High* (1982), *Christine* (1983), *Starman*, *They Live* (1988), *Child's Play* (1988), *Buddy* (1997), *Baywatch,* and *Joan of Arcadia*, and is still active in the film industry. **Phil Abramson** did the set decoration for (among many others) *Jaws 2, Raging Bull* (1980), *Legend of the Lone Ranger* (1981), *Howard the Duck* (1986), and *Tin Men* (1987). He passed away several years ago.

The Cinematographers

Vilmos Zsigmond has photographed almost forty feature films since winning his Oscar for *Close Encounters*, including *The Rose* (1979), *Heaven's Gate* (1980), *Blow Out* (1981), *The Witches of Eastwick* (1987), *The Ghost and the Darkness* (1996), and *Melinda and Melinda* (2004). He received

Academy Award nominations for his work on *The Deer Hunter* (1978), *The River* (1984), and *The Black Dahlia* (2006), and in 1999 the American Society of Cinematographers honored him with its Lifetime Achievement Award. **Nick McLean** earned his first credit as a Director of Photography on *Cheech & Chong's Next Movie* and has since shot numerous features, including *Staying Alive* (1983), *The Goonies*, and *Spaceballs* (1987), as well as the television series *Cybill*, *Veronica's Closet*, and *Friends*. **Earl Gilbert** set the lights on many more films including *Norma Rae* (1979), *The Jerk* (1979), *Mr. Mom* (1983), *Fletch Lives* (1989), and *The Butcher's Wife* (1991) before retiring in the early 1990s. **Steven Poster** earned his first feature film DP credit on 1983's *Spring Break* and has since photographed *Strange Brew* (1983), *The Boy Who Could Fly* (1986), *Rocky V* (1990), and *Donnie Darko* (2001). He headed the American Society of Cinematographers from 2002–2003, and was elected president of the International Cinematographers Guild in 2007.

William A. Fraker received Academy Award nominations for his work on *Looking for Mr. Goodbar* (1977), *Heaven Can Wait* (1978), *1941* (for which he was also nominated, along with A.D. Flowers and Greg Jein, for Best Visual Effects), *War Games* (1983), and *Murphy's Romance* (1985). He directed *The Legend of the Lone Ranger* (1981), was President of the American Society of Cinematographers from 1979–1980, from 1984–1985, and from 1991–1992, and received the ASC Lifetime Achievement Award in 2000. **Douglas Slocombe** photographed the three Indiana Jones films for Steven Spielberg, as well as a number of other films—including *Nijinsky* (1980), *The Pirates of Penzance* (1983), *Never Say Never Again* (1983), and *Lady Jane* (1986)—and commercials before retiring in 1994. **John A. Alonzo**'s further credits included *Blue Thunder* (1983), *Steel Magnolias* (1989), and *Star Trek: Generations* (1994). He passed away in 2001. **Laszló Kovács** shot (among many others) *New York, New York* (1977), *The Legend of the Lone Ranger*, *Ghostbusters* (1984), *Say Anything* (1989), *Multiplicity* (1996), and *Two Weeks' Notice* (2002), and received the ASC Lifetime Achievement Award in 2002. He passed away on July 21, 2007. **Frank Stanley** photographed *The Big Fix* (1978), *"10"* (1978), and *Grease 2* (1982) before retiring in the mid-1980s. He died in December 1999. **Michael Butler** filmed *Small Circle of Friends* (1980), *Smokey and the Bandit II*, and *Megaforce* (1982). **Allen Daviau** was nominated for an Academy Award for *ET: The Extra-Terrestrial*, *The Color Purple*, and *Empire of the Sun*, as well as for *Avalon* (1990) and *Bugsy* (1991), and received the ASC Lifetime Achievement Award in 2007.

Editing, Sound, and Music

Michael Kahn has edited every Steven Spielberg film since *Close Encounters* with the exception of *ET: The Extra-Terrestrial* (which was edited by Carol Littleton while Kahn was busy working on *Poltergeist*). He also edited a number of non-Spielberg films, including *Falling in Love* (1984), *Alive* (1993), and *Laura Croft Tomb Raider: The Cradle of Life* (2003). He was nominated for an Academy Award for his work on *Empire of the Sun*, *Fatal Attraction* (1997), and *Munich*, and won for *Raiders of the Lost Ark*, *Schindler's List*, and *Saving Private Ryan*.

Gene Cantamessa received Oscar nominations for *1941*, *2010*, *Star Trek IV: The Voyage Home*, and won for *ET*. After working on 1999's *End of Days*, he retired ("*End of Days* was the end of my working days," he quips) and now spends his time enjoying his family and traveling the world with his wife. **Frank Warner** continued to create compelling soundtracks for films such as *Coming Home* (1978), *Rocky II* and *III*, *Being There*, *Raging Bull*, and *The King of Comedy*. He retired after working on *Everybody's All-American* (1988).

John Williams has composed the score for every Steven Spielberg film since *Close Encounters* except for *The Color Purple* (the music for which was written by Quincy Jones), as well as for over thirty other films, including the five *Star Wars* sequels, two *Harry Potter* films, *Jaws 2*, *Superman* (1978), *Dracula* (1979), *The River* (1984), *The Witches of Eastwick* (1987), *The Accidental Tourist* (1988), *Home Alone* (1990), *JFK* (1991), *Far and Away* (1992), *Angela's Ashes* (1999), and *Memoirs of a Geisha* (2005). He has also written a number of concert pieces and themes for the 1984, 1988, 1996, and 2002 Olympic games. From 1980 to 1993, Williams was the principal conductor of the Boston Pops Orchestra and is now its laureate conductor. In the years following his nomination for *Close Encounters*, Williams has received twenty-one additional Academy Award nominations (for a lifetime total of forty-five—more than any other person except for Walt Disney) and has won Oscars for *Star Wars*, *ET: The Extra-Terrestrial*, and *Schindler's List*.

The Production Team

Charles Meyers continued to work as a first assistant director on films such as *Coming Home* (1978), *The Right Stuff* (1984), *Young Guns* (1988),

The Fabulous Baker Boys (1989), *Wild at Heart* (1990), and *Bram Stoker's Dracula* (1992) until he passed away on February 12, 1995. **Jim Bloom** served as the second assistant director on *Coming Home* and as the First AD on *Corvette Summer* and *Invasion of the Body Snatchers* (1978). He was the associate producer of *The Empire Strikes Back* (1980) and *Return of the Jedi* (1983), produced *Warning Signs*, and was the executive producer of *Fires Within* (1991). He is currently an independent producer living and working in San Francisco. **Charlsie Bryant** died in 1979. *Close Encounters* was her last feature, and *1941* is dedicated to her memory.

Juliette Taylor and **Shari Rhodes** both continue to cast actors in film and television productions. Taylor works frequently for directors Woody Allen and Mike Nichols, while Rhodes has done the location casting for *Urban Cowboy* (1980), *Terms of Endearment* (1983), and *Mississippi Burning* (1988) and the primary casting for *Raggedy Man* (1981), *Passenger 57* (1992), *The Patriot* (2000), and *Have Dreams Will Travel* (2007). After spending the summer of 1976 wrangling extraterrestrial ballerinas, **Sally Dennison** became a full-fledged casting director, working on *1941, Endless Love* (1981), *Robocop* (1987), *The Accused* (1988), *Heathers* (1989), and *Love Field* (1992).

Bob Westmoreland worked as both a makeup artist in features (*Straight Time* [1978], *Invasion of the Body Snatchers* [1978], *The Island* [1980]) and in television (*Hill Street Blues*), and as an actor (*The Island, Inside Moves* [1980]) until he retired in the late 1980s. **James Linn** worked on a number of other science fiction films, including *The Last Starfighter* (1984), *Star Trek II: The Wrath of Khan*, and *Star Trek III: The Search for Spock*, and earned his final feature film credit on 1986's *Star Trek IV: The Voyage Home*. **Edie Panda** went on to do hair for *Goin' South* (1978), *Invasion of the Body Snatchers* (1978), *Being There* (1979), *Thief* (1981), and *Real Genius* (1985). **Frank Griffin** continued to work as a makeup artist and collaborated with Steve Martin on almost all of the actor's films from *The Three Amigos* (1985) through *Cheaper by the Dozen* (2003).

Roy Arbogast joined Joe Alves on *Jaws 2*, which he followed with *Dracula* (1979), *The Incredible Shrinking Woman* (1979), *Escape from New York, The Thing* (1982), *Return of the Jedi* (1983), *Starman, Silverado* (1985), *Midnight Run* (1988), *The Fugitive* (1993), *The River Wild* (1994), *Village of the Damned* (1995), and *Master of Disguise* (2001).

Carlo Rambaldi won an Academy Award for his creature effects on

Alien (1979) and *ET: The Extra-Terrestrial*. He worked on several more films for producer Dino De Laurentiis, including *Dune, Conan the Destroyer* (1984), and *King Kong Lives* (1986) and then retired. He lives in Italy. **Tom Burman** has created makeup effects for *Invasion of the Body Snatchers*, *Heaven's Gate, Cat People, The Goonies, Howard the Duck, Last Action Hero* (1993), *The X-Files*, and *Nip/Tuck* and was nominated for an Academy Award for his work on *Scrooged* (1988). **Ellis Burman** has worked on numerous iterations of *Star Trek*, including *Star Trek V: The Final Frontier* (1989), *Star Trek: First Contact* (1996), *Star Trek: Insurrection* (1998), *Star Trek: Nemesis* (2002), *Star Trek: Deep Space Nine*, and *Enterprise*

Buddy Joe Hooker has arranged and performed stunts on over 130 movies since *Close Encounters*, the latest of which was 2007's *Death Proof*. After recovering from his accident, **Craig R. Baxley** became a stunt arranger, a second unit director, and then a first unit director on films (*Action Jackson* [1988]) and television shows (*Storm of the Century* [1999]).

In November 1978, **Dr. J. Allen Hynek**—*Close Encounters'* Technical Adviser—presented a statement written by himself, Dr. Jacques Vallée, and Dr. Claude Poher to the United Nations General Assembly, proposing the establishment of a United Nations UFO authority—a proposal upon which the UN failed to act. In his later years, Hynek began to have doubts about the notion that UFOs were spacecraft visiting earth from other worlds. Feeling that it didn't make much sense for super-intelligent beings to travel millions of miles just to stop cars, collect soil samples, and frighten people, he began considering other explanations for the phenomenon, including the idea that the manifestations witnessed by those who encounter UFOs might actually be psychic projections of some sort—perhaps from another dimension, perhaps from another world. Hyenk died of a brain tumor in 1986. Interest and belief in UFOs, while no longer at the peaks reached in the 1950s and 1970s, continues.

Special Photographic Effects

Star Trek: The Motion Picture earned **Douglas Trumbull**, **Richard Yuricich**, **Robert Swarthe**, and **Dave Stewart** (along with John Dykstra and Grant McCune) an Academy Award nomination for Best Visual Effects. Liberated from Paramount following that film's completion, Trumbull and Yuricich established the Entertainment Effects Group (EEG) in 1980. The company's first project was Ridley Scott's *Blade Runner* (1982), which brought Doug and Richard (along with effects co-supervisor David Dryer) yet another Oscar nomination.

In 1981, Trumbull returned to directing with a film for MGM about virtual reality, called *Brainstorm*, with Yuricich serving as the director of photography. Tragically, the movie's costar Natalie Wood died during shooting, throwing the production into chaos. Doug wanted to finish the film by employing a body double and cutting some of Wood's scenes, but MGM preferred to cancel the project altogether so that it could claim the insurance money. Trumbull opposed this decision, but it was only after a two-year battle with the studio that he was able to finish his movie—which the studio then released with little promotion or support, thus ensuring its failure at the box office. Looking to take a break from Hollywood, Doug and Richard brought former ILM effects supervisor Richard Edlund in as a partner in EEG and turned the operation over to him. Edlund ran the company under the name Boss Film, and Trumbull and Yuricich both left California and moved to Massachusetts—Doug to the Berkshires and Richard to Cape Cod.

In 1983, Trumbull cofounded the Showscan Film Corporation, through which he produced and directed a number of large-format shorts that were exhibited in specially designed theaters. Trumbull left Showscan in 1989 and started a company that created simulator rides for theme parks, through which he produced, cowrote, and directed the innovative *Back to the Future...The Ride* (1991) for Universal Studios Hollywood and Florida. In 1993, Doug—along with Geoffrey Williamson, Robert Auguste, and Edmund DiGiulio—was awarded a technical achievement Oscar for the development of the Showscan process. Trumbull's firm was acquired by IMAX in 1994, and he became co-chairman of that company. In 1996, Doug created, produced, and directed an elaborate three-part show that incorporated live onstage action with filmed IMAX elements for the Luxor Hotel and Casino in Las Vegas. As of this writing, Trumbull is currently at work on new feature film projects and continues to pioneer new entertainment formats.

After leaving EEG, Richard Yuricich was partnered for a time with Doug Trumbull in Showscan and later became a freelance visual effects supervisor on films such as *Field of Dreams* (1989), *Ghost Dad* (1990), *Mission Impossible* (1996), *Event Horizon* (1997), *Mission Impossible 2* (2000), *Resident Evil* (2002), and *The Reaping* (2007). Following the completion of

The Special Edition, **Robert Swarthe** supervised the visual effects for *One from the Heart* (1982) and *The Outsiders* (1983) for director Francis Ford Coppola. He continues to direct television commercials and short films and in recent years has moved from Los Angeles to New York, where he lives with his wife, *The Special Edition*'s visual effects editor (and now film editor) M. Kathryn Campbell. **Dave Stewart** worked with Bob Swarthe on *One from the Heart* and *The Outsiders* and on various EEG and Boss Films projects (*Blade Runner, Brainstorm, 2010, Alien 3*) as well as other projects for Douglas Trumbull (*Back to the Future...The Ride*) and Richard Yuricich (*Event Horizon*) until he passed away in 1997. All of the people interviewed for this book who knew him emphasized repeatedly their liking and respect for Stewart and made it clear that they miss him terribly.

Greg Jein remains one of the film industry's most respected and sought-after effects artists. Following *The Special Edition*, he has continued to construct miniatures, models, and special props for films such as *One from the Heart, *batteries not included, The Hunt for Red October* (1990), and *Fantastic Four* (2005), as well as for a large number of *Star Trek* projects, including *Star Trek V: The Final Frontier* (1989), *Star Trek VI: The Undiscovered Country; Star Trek: Insurrection, Star Trek: The Next Generation, Star Trek: Deep Space Nine,* and *Star Trek: Voyager*. He also builds concept models for set designers and for the Walt Disney Company's Imagineering division. Jein was nominated for an Academy Award for the spectacular miniature Los Angeles that he conjured up for *1941* and is currently working on the new Indiana Jones film.

Matthew Yuricich followed *1941* with *Blade Runner, My Favorite Year* (1982), *Brainstorm, Ghostbusters, 2010, Die Hard, Field of Dreams,* and *Dances with Wolves* (1990). He is currently retired and living in Washington State.

Dennis Muren relocated to northern California when George Lucas moved Industrial Light & Magic to Marin Country in 1979. In the ensuing twenty-seven years, Muren has worked on dozens of films, including many directed by Steven Spielberg, and has become one of the leading pioneers in the digital effects revolution. He has received Academy Award nominations for his innovative work on *Young Sherlock Holmes* (1985), *Willow* (1987), *The Lost World: Jurassic Park* (1997), *Star Wars Episode I: The Phantom Menace* (1999), *AI: Artificial Intelligence,* and *War of the Worlds*, and won for *ET: The Extra-Terrestrial, Indiana Jones and the Temple* *of Doom, The Abyss, Jurassic Park*, and *Terminator 2: Judgment Day*. He also received a Special Achievement Award for *The Empire Strikes Back* and a Technical Achievement Award for *Dragonslayer*.

Following *Star Trek: The Motion Picture*, **Rocco Gioffre**, **Scott Squires**, and **Hoyt Yeatman** teamed up to start their own visual effects company, called Dream Quest Images, through which each contributed his talents to films such as *Caddyshack* (1980), *Caveman* (1981), *Once from the Heart* (1982), *Blue Thunder* (1983), *Vacation* (1983), *The Adventures of Buckaroo Banzai Across the 8th Dimenson* (1984), and *The Fly* (1986). Gioffre left the company in the mid-1980s and went on to create matte paintings for *RoboCop 2* (1990), *City Slickers* (1991), *Cliffhanger* (1993), *What Dreams May Come* (1998), *The Scorpion King* (2002), *Terminator 3: Rise of the Machines* (2003), and many other movies. In 2003 he founded Svengali Visual Effects, which has done matte painting and effects work for *Garden State* (2004), *Van Helsing* (2004), *The Chronicles of Narnia: The Lion, the Witch, and the Wardrobe* (2005), and *Apocalypto* (2006). As of this writing he has still not paid Future General back for his plane ticket. Scott Squires also left Dream Quest in the mid-1980s and joined Industrial Light & Magic, where he has helped to create effects for films such as *The Witches of Eastwick* (1987), *Willow* (1988), *The Hunt for Red October* (1990), *The Mask* (1994), *Dragonheart* (1996), *Van Helsing* (2004), and *Fantastic Four: The Rise of the Silver Surfer* (2007). Squires is now one of ILM's senior effects supervisors and was nominated for an Academy Award for his work on *Star Wars Episode I: The Phantom Menace* (1999). When Dream Quest was acquired by the Walt Disney Company in the 1990s, Hoyt Yeatman remained with the company (which Disney renamed The Secret Lab) working on films such as *The Rock* (1996), *Armageddon* (1998), *Mighty Joe Young* (1998), and *Mission to Mars* (2000) until it closed in 2002. Yeatman won an Oscar for his work on *The Abyss* (1989) and is currently supervising the effects for *Underdog* (2007).

Robert Shepherd was a member of John Dykstra's Apogee Productions until the company closed in the early 1990s. He continues to work as a visual effects producer (*Ghosts of Mars* [2001]). **Robert Hall** worked on *Blade Runner, Brainstorm, Short Circuit, The Fly*, and *Predator*. Both he and **Don Jarel** are now retired. **Ralph McQuarrie** followed his work on *ET* by continuing to do concept designs for films such as *Return of the Jedi, Star Trek IV: The Voyage Home, *batteries not included*, and *Back to the

Future...The Ride. He won an Oscar for his work on *Cocoon* and is now retired. **Glenn Erickson** was a member of Greg Jein's miniature unit on *1941* and co-wrote a book on the making of that movie. He is now an Emmy-nominated film editor, the author of the DVD Savant web column, and a film reviewer for Turner Classic Movies Online. **Don Trumbull** worked at Apogee for many years on projects such as *Firefox* (1982), *Lifeforce*, and *Spaceballs* (1987). He passed away in 2004.

Most of the rest of the Future General team—the modelmakers (**J. Richard Dow, Michael McMillen, Kenneth Swenson, Jor Van Kline**, and **Robert Worthington**), the animation staff (**Harry Moreau, Cy DidJurgis, Alan Harding, Max Morgan, Carol Boardman, Connie Morgan, Eleanor Dahlen, Tom Koester**, and **Bill Millar**), the camera assistants, grips, and electricians—went on to have long careers in effects work and animation. Some are retired and some are no longer with us, but those who remain recall the time they spent working on *Close Encounters* as one of the most exciting times of their lives. Sadly, the photochemical approach to creating visual effects that Future General perfected is no more, rendered obsolete by the digital revolution. Elements for effects shots are now created and composited primarily in a computer. The ability to conjure up entire worlds on a hard drive has made visual effects easier and cheaper to produce and, as a result, much more plentiful. It has also, in the opinion of some, robbed the process and the final product of much of its magic. As Richard Yuricich observes: "The business has moved past the technology. You can do anything now with CGI. But anything's not much anymore..."

The Cast

Richard Dreyfuss followed *Close Encounters* by playing the energetic male lead in Neil Simon's romantic comedy *The Goodbye Girl* (1977), for which the thirty-year-old won an Academy Award as Best Actor (making him the youngest actor ever to do so, a distinction he kept until twenty-nine-year-old Adrien Brody won for *The Pianist* in 2003). After his win, Dreyfuss starred in *The Big Fix* (1978), *The Competition* (1980), *Whose Life Is It Anyway?* (1981), *Down and Out in Beverly Hills* (1986), *Stand By Me* (1986), *Tin Men* (1987), and *Stakeout* (1987), and in 1989 reunited with Steven Spielberg when he played the lead in *Always*. Since then, Dreyfuss has appeared in *Once Around* (1991), *What About Bob?* (1991), *The American*

President (1994), *Mr. Holland's Opus* (1995), *The Day Reagan Was Shot* (2001), and *Poseidon* (2006). He starred in the 2001–2002 television series *The Education of Max Bickford* and in a 2004 Broadway revival of Larry Gelbart's *Sly Fox*. He is also a Senior Associate Member of St. Antony's College, University of Oxford.

François Truffaut directed five more films following the completion of his stint on *Close Encounters*: 1978's *La Chambre verte* (*The Green Room*—in which he also played the lead), 1979's *L' Amour en fruite* (*Love on the Run*—the final Antoine Doinel film), 1980's *Le Derner métro* (*The Last Metro*), 1981's *La Femme d'à côté* (*The Woman Next Door*) (1980) and 1983's *Vivement Dimanche!* (*Confidentially Yours!*). Although Truffaut had enjoyed working with Steven Spielberg, the long periods of inactivity he experienced on the *Close Encounters* set made him vow to never act for another director again—a vow he kept. The vast complexity and politics of American filmmaking also convinced him never to make a movie for a major Hollywood studio, and he didn't (shortly after the completion of *Close Encounters*, Stanley Jaffe asked Truffaut to direct *Kramer vs. Kramer*. He declined). François Truffaut died of a brain tumor in 1984.

Melinda Dillon appeared in *F.I.S.T.* (1978), *Absence of Malice* (1981—for which she received another Academy Award nomination as Best Supporting Actress), *A Christmas Story* (1983), *Harry and the Hendersons* (1987), *The Prince of Tides* (1991), *How to Make an American Quilt* (1995). *Magnolia* (1999), *Reign Over Me* (2007), and many, many episodes of network television.

Teri Garr starred in *The Black Stallion* (1979), *One from the Heart*, *Tootsie* (1982—for which she also received a Best Supporting Actress nomination), *Mr. Mom* (1983), *Firstborn* (1984), and *After Hours* (1985). Throughout the 1990s, she had regular and recurring roles on the television series *Good and Evil*, *Good Advice*, *Women of the House*, and *Friends*. In October 2002, Garr announced that she has multiple sclerosis and has spent much of her time since then working to raise awareness about the illness and its treatment. In December 2006 she suffered a brain aneurysm from which, at the time of this writing, she is reported to be making a strong recovery.

Cary Guffey followed his Italian adventure with roles in *Cross Creek* (1983), *Stroker Ace* (1983), *The Bear* (1984), *Chiefs* (1983), *Poison Ivy* (1985), and *North and South* (1985), after which he retired from acting. Guffey graduated from University of Florida with a degree in marketing and from Jackson State University in Alabama with an MBA and became a financial planner for Merrill Lynch. **Shawn Bishop** continued to act into the 1990s and is currently a sound effects editor. *Close Encounters* marked the only film appearances for both **Justin Dreyfuss** and **Adrienne Campbell**.

Bob Balaban has given memorable performances on screen in *Altered States* (1980), *Prince of the City* (1981), *Absence of Malice* (1981), *Whose Life Is It, Anyway* (1981), *2010* (1985), *Waiting for Guffman* (1996), *Best in Show* (2000), *A Mighty Wind* (2003), *Ghost World* (2001), and *Capote* (2005), and on television in episodes of *Miami Vice, Seinfeld,* and *The West Wing.* As a director, Balaban has helmed episodes of *Tales from the Darkside, Amazing Stories, Oz, Deadline,* and *Strangers with Candy,* the television movie *The Brass Ring,* and the feature films *Parents* (1985), *My Boyfriend's Back* (1993), *The Last Good Time* (1994—which he also wrote), and *Bernard and Doris* (2007). With director Robert Altman, Balaban conceived the idea for and produced *Gosford Park* (2001), which was nominated for an Academy Award as Best Picture. He is the author of a series of children's books featuring a bionic dog named McGrowl and in 2003 reissued his account of his experiences during the making of *Close Encounters* under the title *Spielberg, Truffaut & Me: An Actor's Diary.*

J. Patrick McNamara appeared in many movies (*Blow Out* [1981], *Warning Sign* [1985], *Some Kind of Wonderful* [1987], *Bill & Ted's Excellent Adventure* [1989], *Bill & Ted's Bogus Journey* [1991]) and television shows (*Dallas, The A-Team, Hill Street Blues, Knot's Landing, Star Trek: The Next Generation*). In 1995, he moved back to New Orleans, where he acts in local theater and teaches at New Orleans Center for Creative Arts. **Josef Sommer** became a highly in-demand character actor and has appeared in dozens of films and television shows, including *Hide in Plain Sight* (1980), *Absence of Malice* (1981), *Sophie's Choice* (1982), *Silkwood* (1983), *Witness* (1985), *Shadows and Fog* (1992), *The Mighty Ducks* (1992), *Nobody's Fool* (1994), *Patch Adams* (1998), *X-Men: The Last Stand* (2006), *The Equalizer, Law & Order,* and *The West Wing.* **Lance Henriksen** followed *CE3K* with strong supporting parts in *Damien: Omen II* (1978), *Prince of the City* (1981), *The Right Stuff* (1984), *The Terminator* (1984), *Aliens* (1986), *Near Dark* (1987), *Pumpkinhead* (1989), *Alien 3* (1992), *Jennifer Eight* (1992), *The Quick and the Dead* (1995), and *Alien vs. Predator* (2004). He also starred in the 1996–1999 television series *Millennium.* **Warren Kemmerling** continued to appear on television in programs such as *How the West Was Won, King, The A-Team, Murder, She Wrote,* and *L.A. Law,* and in the feature films *The Dark* (1979) and *Godzilla 1985* (1984). He died on January 3, 2005. **Roberts Blossom** worked with Steven Spielberg again in an episode of *Amazing Stories* and in *Always.* He also appeared in *Escape from Alcatraz* (1979), *Christine* (1983), *Reuben, Reuben* (1983), *The Last Temptation of Christ* (1988), *Home Alone* (1990), *Doc Hollywood* (1991), and *The Quick and the Dead* (1995). Now retired, he lives in Berkeley, California. **Merrill Connally** played Davy Crockett in 1988's *Alamo: The Price of Freedom* and also appeared in *Rush* (1991) and *Heaven & Hell: North & South, Book III* (1994). He died on September 4, 2001.

The Studio

David Begelman bounced back from disgrace in 1980 when studio owner Kirk Kerkorian hired him to be the CEO and President of MGM, where he greenlit films such as *Clash of the Titans* (1981), *Pennies from Heaven* (1981), *Poltergeist,* and *My Favorite Year* (1982). After leaving MGM, Begelman ran a number of smaller companies and produced films such as *Mr. Mom* (1983) and *The Adventures of Buckaroo Banzai Across the 8th Dimension, Mannequin* (1987), *Weekend at Bernie's,* and *The Fabulous Baker Boys* (1989). After suffering a number of business reversals and declaring bankruptcy, David Begelman committed suicide in 1995. He once said that he considered *Close Encounters* to be his crowning achievement. **John Veitch** remained with Columbia Pictures until the mid-1980s, when he left to become a producer on films such as *Fast Forward* (1985), *Suspect* (1987), *Bram Stoker's Dracula* (1992), *Mary Shelley's Frankenstein* (1994) and *Fly Away Home* (1996). He died on December 8, 1998. **Alan Hirschfield** went to work at Warner Brothers, where shortly thereafter he was hired to serve as the movie division president. Eventually he became chairman and CEO of Twentieth Century-Fox, a position he retained until Rupert Murdoch bought the company in 1984. Since leaving Fox, Hirschfield has held a number of executive and board positions at media-related companies and is now a private investor. **Stanley Jaffe** produced *Kramer vs. Kramer,* which won the Academy Award as the Best Picture of 1979. Since then he has produced *Taps* (1981), *Without a Trace* (1983—which he also directed), *Firstborn* (1984), *Fatal Attraction* (1987), *The Accused* (1988), *Black Rain* (1989), *School Ties* (1992), *Madeline* (1998), *I Dreamed of Africa* (2000), and *The Four Feathers* (2002). **Daniel Melnick** produced or executive produced (among others) *All That Jazz* (1979), *Altered States*, *Footloose* (1984), *Roxanne* (1987), *Punchline* (1988), *Air America* (1990), and *L.A. Story* (1991).

In 1982, Allen & Company sold the (thanks to *CE3K*) newly vibrant Columbia Pictures Industries to the Coca-Cola Company for approximately $800 million. The studio initially flourished with hits such as *Tootsie* (1982) and *Ghostbusters* (1984), but after a few rough years in the late 1980s (which included the notoriously expensive flops *Leonard, Part VI* [1987] and *Ishtar* [1987]), Coke decided to get out of the entertainment business and sold the company (now know as Columbia Pictures Entertainment) to Japan's Sony Corporation (which eventually renamed it Sony Pictures Entertainment). To run the studio, Sony hired former producer **Peter Guber**—who had been Columbia's production chief when *Close Encounters* went into production—and Jon Peters, who had just scored a tremendous box office success of *Batman* (1989), as co-heads of production. At the time, the two were under exclusive contract to Warner Brothers. To release them, Warner insisted that Sony buy the former MGM Studio facility in Culver City, which Warner had inherited when it purchased the lots previous owner, Lorimar-Telepictures, a few years before.

Sony agreed and moved Columbia to Culver City. Warner bought out Columbia's interest in The Burbank Studios, which once again became known as the Warner Brothers Studios. The Guber/Peters years were rocky ones with few hits and some major flops (the biggest one being 1993's notorious Arnold Swarzenegger bomb *Last Action Hero*). Eventually, Guber and Peters were ousted and the studio, with new management teams led by John Calley and then Amy Pascal, rebounded with a number of major hits, including the *Spider-Man* series.

Most of the people who worked on *Close Encounters* consider it to be one of the highlights of their careers in motion pictures.

The Film

Thirty years after its release, *Close Encounters of the Third Kind* continues to endure. Since the movie didn't generate numerous sequels and a perpetual merchandising campaign, it never achieved the cult status of *Star Wars*, but it remains highly regarded by cinema buffs (in 1997 it was ranked number sixty-four in the American Film Institute's *100 Years...100 Movies* list of the greatest American films of all time), Steven Spielberg fans (who consider it one the director's best and most personal works), and special effects aficionados (many of whom feel that the work Future General did for the movie has never been surpassed, even in this modern digital era). The film plays frequently on television, sells well on home video, and has become such a piece of Americana that the Mothership model is now on permanent display at the Smithsonian Institution (when it was damaged several years ago in a fire, Greg Jein was called in to repair it). Best of all, the film retains its remarkable power to enthrall (at a recent screening in Los Angeles, several audience members were in tears by the end of the movie and one young man leaped to his feet and quite sincerely implored the Mothership to "Take me with you"). Steven Spielberg's goal in making *Close Encounters* was to produce a remarkable movie. He succeeded, and the results are ours to enjoy forever. And in that, we are not alone.

Credits: Cast and Crew

**A Columbia Presentation
In Association with EMI**
Close Encounters of the Third Kind
**A Phillips Production
A Steven Spielberg Film**

Credits

Produced by	Julia Phillips, Michael Phillips
Written & Directed by	Steven Spielberg
Director of Photography	Vilmos Zsigmond, ASC
Special Photographic Effects by	Douglas Trumbull
Music by	John Williams
Director of Photography of Additional American Scenes	William A. Fraker, ASC
Director of Photography India Sequence	Douglas Slocombe, BSC
Production Designer	Joe Alves
Edited by	Michael Kahn, ACE
Associate Producer	Clark Paylow
Visual Effects Concepts by	Steven Spielberg
Unit Production Manager	Clark Paylow
Additional Directors of Photography	John Alonzo, ASC Laszló Kovács, ASC
Technical Advisor	Dr. J. Allen Hynek
Set Decoration	Phil Abramson

Realization of "Extraterrestrial" by	Carlo Rambaldi
Art Director	Dan Lomino
Assistant Director	Chuck Meyers
2nd Assistant Director	Jim Bloom
Assistant Film Editors	Geoffrey Rowland, Charles Bornstein
Music Editor	Kenneth Wannberg
Supervising Sound Effects Editor	Frank Warner
Sound Effects Editorial Staff	Richard Oswald, David Horten, Sam Gemette, Gary S. Gerlich, Chet Slomka, Neil Burrow
Production Illustrator	George Jensen
Dolby Sound Supervisor	Steve Katz
Supervising Dialogue Editor	Jack Schrader
Dialogue Editorial Staff	Dick Friedman
Assistant Dialogue Staff	Robert A. Reich, Bill Jackson
Technical Dialogue	Colin Cantwell
Production Sound Mixer	Gene Cantamessa
Music Scoring Mixer	John Neal
Mothership Tuba Solo	Tommy Johnson
Light Board Oboe Solo	John Ellis
Video Technician	"Fast" Eddie Mahler
Camera Operator	Nick McLean
Construction Manager	Bill Parks
Special Mechanical Effects	Roy Arbogast
Re-recording Mixers	Buzz Knudson, Don MacDougall, Robert Glass
Assistant to the Producers	Kendall Cooper
2nd Assistant to the Producers	Judy Bornstein
Assistant to Mr. Spielberg	Rick Fields
Assistant to François Truffaut	Françoise Forget
Production Secretary	Gail Siemers
Production Staff	Janet Healey, Pat Burns
Makeup Supervisor	Bob Westmoreland
Hairdresser	Edie Panda
Property Master	Sam Gordon
Wardrobe Supervisor	Jim Linn
AFI Intern	Seth Winston

Casting	Shari Rhodes, Juliette Taylor
Additional Casting	Sally Dennison
Stunt Coordinator	Buddy Joe Hooker
Script Supervision	Charlsie Bryant
Publicity	Al Ebner, Murray Weissman, Pickwick Public Relations
Still Photographers	Pete Sorel, Jim Coe, Pete Turner
Title Design	Dan Perri
2nd Unit Director of Photography	Steve Poster
Location Auditor	Steve Warner
Location Manager	Joe O'Har
Gaffer	Earl Gilbert
Special Photographic Effects Supervised by	Douglas Trumbull
Director of Photography/ Photographic Effects	Richard Yuricich
Matte Artist	Matthew Yuricich
Effects Unit Production Manager	Robert Shepherd
Special Visual Effects Coordinator	Larry Robinson
UFO Photography	Dave Stewart
Chief Model Maker	Gregory Jein
Animation Supervisor	Robert Swarthe
Optical Photography	Robert Hall
Matte Photography	Don Jarel
Mothership Photography	Dennis Muren
Project Coordinator	Mona Thal Benefiel
Camera Operators	Dave Berry, Eugene Eyerly, Maxwell Morgan, Ron Peterson, Eldon Rickman
Technician	Robert Hollister
Assistant Cameramen	David Hardberger, Alan Harding, Bruce Nicholson, Richard Rippel, Scott Squires
Still Photography	Marcia Reid
Model Shop Coordinator	J. Richard Dow
Model Makers	Jor Van Kline, Michael McMillen, Kenneth Swenson, Robert Worthington
Camera and Mechanical Design	Don Trumbull (B.G. Engineering), John Russell, Fries Engineering

Mechanical Special Effects	George Polkinghorne
Electronics Design	Jerry L. Jeffress, Alvah J. Miller, Peter Regla, Dan Slater
Assistant Matte Artist	Rocco Gioffre
Effects Electrician	David Gold
Key Grip	Ray Rich
Laboratory Expeditor	Charles Hinkle
Animator	Harry Moreau
Animation Staff	Carol Boardman, Eleanor Dahlen, Cy DidJurgis, Tom Koester, Bill Millar, Connie Morgan
Production Secretary	Joyce Goldberg
Production Accountant	Peggy Rosson
Project Assistants	Glenn Erickson, Hoyt Yeatman
Editorial Assistant	Joseph Ippolito
Transportation	Bill Bethea
Laboratory Technicians	Don Dow, Tom Hollister
Effects Negative Cutter	Barbara Morrison
Special Consultants	Peter Anderson, Larry Albright, Richard Bennett, Ken Ebert, Paul Huston, David M. Jones, Kevin Kelly, Jim Lutes, George Randle, Jeff Shapiro, Rourke Engineering

Filmed in Panavision
Metrocolor
Color Consultant: Robert M. McMillian
Dolby System
Special Thanks to Johnny Mathis

Cast

Roy Neary	Richard Dreyfuss
Claude Lacombe	François Truffaut
Ronnie Neary	Teri Garr
David Laughlin	Bob Balaban
Project Leader	J. Patrick McNamara
Wild Bill	Warren Kemmerling
Farmer	Roberts Blossom

Jean Claude	Philip Dodds
Barry Guiler	Cary Guffey
Brad Neary	Shawn Bishop
Sylvia Neary	Adrienne Campbell
Toby Neary	Justin Dreyfuss
Robert	Lance Henriksen
Team Leader	Merrill Connally
Major Benchley	George DiCenzo
Implantee	Amy Douglass
Implantee	Alexander Lockwood
Mrs. Harris	Mary Gafrey
Ohio Tolls	Norman Bartold
Larry Butler	Josef Sommer
Self	Rev. Michael J. Dyer
Highway Patrolman	Roger Ernest
Military Police	Carl Weathers
ARP Project Member	F.J. O'Neil
ARP Musician	Phil Dodds
Returnee #1 Flt. 19	Randy Herman
Returnee #2 Flt. 19	Hal Barwood
Returnee #3 Flt. 19	Matthew Robbins
Air Traffic Controller	David Anderson
Air Traffic Controller	Richard L. Hawkins
Air Traffic	Craig Shreeve
Air Traffic Controller	Bill Thurman
Air East Pilot	Roy E. Richards
Hawker	Gene Rader
Old Man	Eumenio Blanco
Federale	Daniel Nunez
Federale	Chuy Franco
Federale	Luis Contreras
Radio Telescope Team	James Keane
Radio Telescope Team	Dennis McMullen
Radio Telescope Team	Cy Young
Radio Telescope Team	Tom Howard
Truck Dispatcher	Richard Stuart
Load Dispatcher	Bob Westmoreland

Support Leader	Matt Emery
Special Forces	Galen Thompson
Special Forces	John Dennis Johnston
Dirty Tricks #1	John Ewing
Dirty Tricks #2	Keith Atkinson
Dirty Tricks #3	Robert Broyles
Dirty Tricks #4	Kirk Raymond

Additional Credits

The following worked on *Close Encounters* but did not receive screen credit:

Additional Director of Photography	Frank Stanley, ASC
Additional Photography	Richard E. Cunha
Additional Photography	James Dickson
Additional Photography	Joseph Westheimer
Additional Photography	Rexford L. Metz
Assistant Director for Additional Scenes	Jerry Zeismer
"Extraterrestrial" Mask Design	Frank Griffin
"Extraterrestrial" Mask Fabrication	The Burman Studio
Alien Marionette	Bob Baker Marionettes
Mothership Concept Painting	Ralph McQuarrie
Orchestrator	Herbert Spencer
Boom Operator	Raul A. Bruce
Production Manager (India)	Baba Shaik
Focus Puller (India)	Robin Vidgeon
Camera Operator (India)	Chic Waterston
Production Counsel	Norman Brokaw
Production Counsel	Norman Garey

Additional Cast

Officer Longley	Basil Hoffman
Self	J. Allen Hynek
Self	Howard K. Smith
Stunt Driver	Craig R. Baxley
Stunt Driver	Jerry Brutsche
Stunts	Bobby Bass

Stunts	Steven Burnett
Stunts	Jeannie Epper
Stunts	Monty Jordan
Stunts	Stephen Powers

Additional Credits for *The Special Edition*

Unit Production Manager	Ronald L. Schwary
Director of Photography for Additional Material (*The Special Edition*)	Allen Daviau
Additional Photography	Michael C. Butler
Second Unit Director	Matthew Robbins
Supervisor of Visual Effects for *The Special Edition*	Robert Swarthe
Director of Photography/ Photographic Effects	Dave Stewart
Animator	Leslie Ekker
Additional Matte Painting	Rocco Gioffre
Model Maker	Mitch Suskin
Additional Effects	Robert Shourt
Additional Effects Photography	Don Baker
Animation Photography	Mike Peed
Visual Effects Editor	M. Kathryn Campbell

Notes

Chapter 1

Page 1: "I looked, and I saw a windstorm coming out of the north..." Ezekiel 1:4–5. *The Holy Bible, New International Version.*

Page 3: "like the tail of a Chinese kite." Bequette, Bill. "Boise Flyer Maintains He Saw 'Em." *East Oregonian,* 26 June 1947.

Page 5: "being a natural-born American..." "The *Case for Flying Saucers.*" CBS Radio. 7 April 1950.

Chapter 2

Page 15: "I wait for them to walk out of the room" Hirschberg, Lynn. "Will Hollywood's Mr. Perfect Ever Grow Up?" *Rolling Stone,* 19 July/2 August 1984.

Page 20: "My first introduction to the world beyond the earth..." Bouzerau, Laurent (director). "The Making of *Close Encounters of the Third Kind.*" *Close Encounters of the Third Kind: The Collector's Edition* DVD. Columbia/Tri Star Home Video, Inc., 2001.

Page 23: "I love to grip an audience and watch them lean forward in their seats..." Bobrow, Andrew C. "Filming *The Sugarland Express*: An Interview with Steven Spielberg." *Filmmakers Newsletter,* Summer 1974.

Page 23: "I knew after my third or fourth little 8mm epic that this was going to be a career, not just a hobby..." McBride, Joseph. *Steven Spielberg: A Biography.* New York: Simon & Schuster, 1997

Chapter 3

Page 28: "We're not interested in making small, critical successes nobody goes to see..." Lindsey, Robert. "The New Wave of Filmmakers." *New York Times Magazine,* 28 May 1978.

Page 31: "I think you should be a director," Hirschberg, Lynn. "Will Hollywood's Mr. Perfect Ever Grow Up?" *Rolling Stone,* 19 July/2 August 1984.

Page 31: "I think so too," *Ibid.*

Page 32: "Do you wanna graduate college or do you wanna be a film director?" *Ibid.*

Page 39: "an innate sense of the visual mechanics..." McBride, Joseph. *Steven Spielberg: A Biography.* New York: Simon & Schuster, 1997.

Page 39: "The way he directs a film makes you think he must have..." Lightman, Herb A. "The New Panaflex Camera Makes Its Production Debut." *American Cinematographer*, May 1973.

Page 41: "UFOs and Watergate." Interview with Michael Phillips by the author.

Chapter 4

Page 41: "I was just as interested in...why people looked to the skies..." Combs, Richard. "Primal Scream: An Interview with Steven Spielberg." *Sight and Sound*, Spring 1977.

Page 41: "cultural phenomenon" Maslin, Janet. "Spielberg's Journey from Sharks to the Stars." *New York Times*, 13 November 1977.

Page 41: "Whether they're real or not real, they have certainly affected everybody's life." *Ibid.*

Page 41: "I'm convinced something's going on..." Crawley, Tony. *The Steven Spielberg Story.* London: Zomba Books, 1983.

Page 41: "the jury's still out." Sanello, Frank: *Spielberg: The Man, the Movies, The Mythology.* Dallas: Taylor Publishing Company, 1996.

Page 47: "No direct evidence whatever of a convincing nature now exists..." University of Colorado, under Contract No. 44620-67-C-0035 from the United States Air Force (Dr. Edward U. Condon—Scientific Director). *Scientific Study of Unidentified Flying Objects.* 1968.

Page 50: "Who wants to be a shark and truck director?" Gottlieb, Carl. *The Jaws Log: 25th Anniversary Edition.* New York: Newmarket Press, 2001.

Page 52: "a political thriller." Helpern, David. "At Sea with Steven Spielberg." *Take One*, March/April 1974.

Chapter 5

Page 57: "gave us [the three producers]—against editors guild rules..." Interview with Michael Phillips by the author.

Page 59: "Everything was carefully prepared..." Ford, Luke. "Producer Michael Phillips Still Eats Lunch in This Town." *Luke Ford.Net.* http://www.lukeford.net/profiles/profiles/michael_phillips.htm.

Page 60: "ride on our coattails" Interview with Michael Phillips by the author.

Page 60: "knew [he] was something special." *Ibid.*

Page 61: "*The Road Warrior* with trains." Interview with Hal Barwood by the author.

Page 63: "they felt that my sensibility, being extremely Germanic and moralistic,..." Jackson, Kevin (ed). *Schrader on Schrader and Other Writings.* London: Faber and Faber, 1990.

Page 63: "It was an incredibly pure and true piece of work." Ford, Luke. "Producer Michael Phillips Still Eats Lunch in This Town." *Luke Ford.Net.* http://www.lukeford.net/profiles/profiles/michael_phillips.htm.

Chapter 7

Page 74: "solved a big story issue." Interview with Michael Phillips by the author.

Page 75: "It was a bad script..." Shay, Don. "Steven Spielberg on *Close Encounters*." *Cinefantastique*, Volume 7, Number 3/4, 1978, 20–29.

Page 76: "...wasn't joyful...[and] we weren't getting the excitement." Interview with Michael Phillips by the author.

Page 76: "the arrival of an extraordinary young filmmaker." Zimmerman, Paul D. "Hard Riders." *Newsweek*, 18 April 1974.

Page 76: "...one of the most phenomenal debuts in the history of movies." Kael, Pauline. "Sugarlands and Badlands." *The New Yorker*, 18 March 1974.

Page 78: "the correct day of the year to try to become a screenwriter." Hill, John. My Close Encounter with *Close Encounters*." Unpublished. 2006.

Page 78: "I was informed by my agent that I got the job to write *Close Encounters*..." Hill, John. "My Close Encounter with *Close Encounters*." Unpublished. 2006.

Page 85: "I mean, why would they? It always struck me as ridiculous..." Interview with Michael Phillips by the author.

Page 85: "So I finished my first draft..." Hill, John. "My Close Encounter with *Close Encounters*." Unpublished. 2006.

Chapter 8

Page 88: "...fish movie..." Petrou, David Michael. *The Making of* Superman: The Movie. New York: Warner Books, 1978.

Page 90: "I said, 'Boy, that sounds a lot more interesting than this baseball thing..." Interview with Joe Alves by the author.

Page 93: "There was a moment when he (Steven) said, 'I have to write this..." Interview with Michael Phillips by the author.

Chapter 9

Page 95: "The first step was writing a series of encounter sequences..." Tracy, Dick. "Alien Visions." *New Musical Express*, 20 May 1978.

Page 95: "I'm not a writer and I don't enjoy..." Combs, Richard. "Primal Scream: An Interview with Steven Spielberg." *Sight and Sound*, Spring 1977.

Page 95: "I find it much more difficult than directing..." Lightman, Herb A. "Spielberg Speaks About *Close Encounters*." *American Cinematographer*, January 1978.

Page 99: "I think he was a little bit unsure..." Interview with Michael Phillips by the author.

Page 99: "believer in benevolent aliens," *Ibid.*

Page 99: "I was always a strong advocate of that if they..." *Ibid.*

Page 99: "Steven was always asking the question: 'Do you think it's enough..." *Ibid.*

Page 100: "...a cornucopia. It just kind of washes over you..." *Ibid.*

Page 101: "Being enthusiastic about flying saucers..." Interview with Hal Barwood by the author.

Page 101: "It's...[the ideal ending]...and it's really hard to resist." *Ibid.*

Page 101: "...Glad that [Steven's movie] got made and that these ideas got expressed as well as they did"). *Ibid.*

Page 104: "It was a very strange...very impressive...piece of topography..." Interview with Joe Alves by the author.

Page 104: When Steven saw the pictures, Alves reports that he "...immediately chose Devils Tower..." *Ibid.*

Page 105: "When I heard...'When You Wish Upon a Star'..." Tracy, Dick. "Alien Visions." *New Musical Express*, 20 May 1978.

Page 105: "I pretty much hung my story on the mood that song created..." "Dialogue on Film: Steven Spielberg." *American Film*, September 1978.

Page 105: "It became what we now recognize as a Steven Spielberg film..." Interview with Michael Phillips by the author.

Page 113: "a science fiction thriller based on an original story by Steven Spielberg..." "Columbia Announces *Encounters*." *Hollywood Reporter*, 12 August 1975.

Chapter 10

Page 118: "I try to work from my imagination day-to-day..." Poster, Steve. "The Mind Behind *Close Encounters of the Third Kind*." *American Cinematographer*, February 1978.

Page 118: "When I was first planning the movie..." Hodenfield, Chris. "The Sky Is Full of Questions: Science Fiction in Steven Spielberg's Suburbia." *Rolling Stone*, 26 January 1978.

Page 124: "It was a fantastic score...a very American score..." Crawley, Tony. *The Steven Spielberg Story*. London: Zomba Books, 1983.

Chapter 11

Page 133: "The sheer luminescence of his [Jensen's] style..." Spielberg, Steven. "The Unsung Heroes or Credit Where Credit Is Due." *American Cinematographer*, January 1978.

Page 133: "I needed [a space] 300 feet by 450 feet..." Interview with Joe Alves by the author.

Page 137: I figured...that I might as well take advantage of that success..." Shay, Don. "Steven Spielberg on *Close Encounters*." *Cinefantastique*, Volume 7, Number 3/4, 1978.

Chapter 12

Page 142: "I'm not a special effects person..." Shay, Don. "A Close Encounter with Steven Spielberg." *Cinefex* # 53, February 1993.

Page 142: "We didn't know what the hell we were doing." Interview with Joe Alves by the author.

Page 148: "You can't live on development deals..." Interview with Douglas Trumbull by the author.

Page 150: "The surface of the screen disappears..."Axmaker, Sean. "From the Drawing Board to Immersive Media with Douglas Trumbull." *Green Cine.* http://www.greencine.com/article?action=view&articleID=267.

Page 150: "I was just sitting around, twiddling my thumbs..." Interview with Douglas Trumbull by the author.

Page 151: "terrific. I liked what the movie had to say..." Shay, Don. "Close Encounters at Future General: Interviews with Doug Trumbull and His Future General Effects Staff." *Cinefantastique*, Volume 7, Number 3/4, 1978.

Chapter 13

Page 158: "I felt...that this particular project had a noble agenda..." Bouzerau, Laurent (director). "The Making of *Close Encounters of the Third Kind*." *Close Encounters of the Third Kind: The Collector's Edition* DVD. Columbia/Tri Star Home Video, Inc., 2001.

Page 159: "a child...a child and yet a man" *Ibid.*

Page 160: "I worked very hard in developing this character..." Interview with Teri Garr by the author.

Page 163: "learn to write movies." Interview with Jerry Belson by the author.

Page 165: "...a lot of fun. We'd get together in the morning and pitch..." *Ibid.*

Page 166: "Il y a avait longtemps depuis que j'aie parlé français..." Balaban, Bob. Close Encounters of the Third Kind *Diary*. Los Angeles: Paradise Press, 1978.

Page 174: "I felt that he was a tremendous human presence in that film..." Bouzerau, Laurent (director). "The Making of *Close Encounters of the Third Kind*." *Close Encounters of the Third Kind: The Collector's Edition* DVD. Columbia/Tri Star Home Video, Inc., 2001.

Page 174: "I needed a man who would have the soul of a child..." de Baecque, Antoine, and Serge Toubiana. *Truffaut: A Biography.* New York: Alfred A. Knopf, Inc., 1999.

Page 174: "I like the script and I like Lacombe," *Ibid.*

Page 175: "Mostly, I stood around smiling stupidly..." Spielberg, Steven. "He Was the Movies." *Film Comment*, February 1985.

Page 176: "I was absolutely certain that he was the Lacombe I had envisioned..." *Ibid.*

Chapter 14

Page 183: "a doorbell." Bouzereau, Laurent. "An Interview with John Williams." *Close Encounters of the Third Kind: The Collector's Edition Soundtrack.* Arista Records, 1998.

Page 184: "a CIA spook movie..." Interview with Hal Barwood by the author.

Page 185: "We wrote all day and all night..." *Ibid.*

Page 185: "mechanics..." *Ibid.*

Page 188: "I'd much rather collaborate..." Combs, Richard. "Primal Scream: An Interview with Steven Spielberg." *Sight and Sound*, Spring 1977.

Page 190: "I went in and he said, 'Are you a good editor?...'" Bernard, Tommy.

"Cutting with Feeling: An Interview with Michael Kahn." *Spielberg Films. Com.* 5 March, 2006. http://www.spielbergfilms.com/munich/19

Chapter 15

Page 192: "Every time I make a movie, it's like starting over again..." Dialogue on Film: Steven Spielberg." *American Film*, September 1978, 44–53.

Page 192: "The conception of the story is the most exciting part of making a picture for me..." Helpern, David. "At Sea with Steven Spielberg." *Take One*, March/April 1974.

Page 195: "film of flying saucers" Jacob, Gilles, and Claude de Givray (eds). *François Truffaut: Correspondence*. Lanham: Cooper Square Press, 2000.

Page 195: "He was very curious about the way I set up shots..." Spielberg, Steven. "He Was the Movies." *Film Comment*, February 1985.

Page 195: "superb." de Baecque, Antoine, and Serge Toubiana. *Truffaut: A Biography*. New York: Alfred A. Knopf, Inc., 1999.

Page 199: "What the hell is this?..." Interview with Matthew Robbins by the author.

Chapter 16

Page 206: "I didn't clamp the lid down because of egocentric reasons..." Cook, Bruce. "Close Encounters with Steven Spielberg." *American Film*, November 1977.

Page 207: "like a movie—a *movie* movie." Interview with Vilmos Zsigmond by the author.

Page 207: "More light," *Ibid.*

Page 211: "Look at Light number one..." Interview with Jim Bloom by the author.

Page 213: "...a crack in the tarp. It got bigger and bigger..." Interview with Joe Alves by the author.

Page 215: "They blamed Vilmos because he had never lit a set like this before..." Interview with a *Close Encounters* crew member by the author.

Chapter 17

Page 218: "Much has been written about his boyish grin and childlike delight..." Lightman, Herb A. "My Close Encounter with *CE3K*." *American Cinematographer*, January 1978.

Page 218: "He [Steven] shoots scenes again and again..." Janos, Leo. "Steven Spielberg: L'Enfant Directeur." *Cosmopolitan*, June 1980.

Page 218: "He has unlimited patience..." *Ibid.*

Page 218: "I don't have the best sense of humor when I'm making a film," Swires, Steve. "A Conversation with Steven Spielberg." *Future*, October 1978.

Page 218: "I'm usually the first person who loses his temper..." Royal, Susan. "Steven Spielberg in His Adventure on Earth." *American Premiere*, July 1982.

Page 219: "I'm not the most fun to work with unless the people I hire can sit on their egos..." Cook, Bruce. "Close Encounters with Steven Spielberg." *American Film*, November 1977.

Page 219: "...I'm a real stickler for having things my way." Tuchman, Mitch. "Close Encounter with Steven Spielberg." *Film Comment*, January/February 1978.

Page 219: "He didn't need my help anymore." Interview with Vilmos Zsigmond by the author.

Page 220: "Steve is not what you would call an actor's director in the classical sense..." Durwood, Thomas (ed). *Close Encounters of the Third Kind: A Document of the Film.* Kansas City: Ariel Books / New York: Ballantine Books, 1978.

Page 221: "I would rather let the actors inspire me..." Poster, Steve. "The Mind Behind *Close Encounters of the Third Kind.*" *American Cinematographer*, February 1978.

Page 221: "Steven did force me to act..." Thomas, Kevin. "Catching Up with Truffaut's Latest Wave." *Los Angeles Times*, 24 January 1977.

Page 221: "Several times during the shooting..." McBride, Joseph. *Steven Spielberg: A Biography.* New York: Simon & Schuster, 1997.

Page 222: "...always worried that what I planned isn't working..." Poster, Steve. "The Mind Behind *Close Encounters of the Third Kind.*" *American Cinematographer*, February 1978.

Page 222: "this film's shark..." Lightman, Herb A. "Spielberg Speaks About Close Encounters." *American Cinematographer*, January 1978.

Page 223: "He [Steven was] pretty improvisational..."Cook, Bruce. "Close Encounters with Steven Spielberg." *American Film*, November 1977.

Page 223: "You'd see him [Spielberg] just kind of walking back and forth..." Shay, Don. "*Close Encounters* Extraterrestrials." *Cinefantastique*, Volume 7, Number 3/4, 1978.

Page 223: "I'm almost at my most improvisatory..." Tuchman, Mitch. "Close Encounter with Steven Spielberg." *Film Comment*, January/February 1978.

Page 223: "If you would stop watching those..." Interview with Vilmos Zsigmond by the author.

Page 227: "He really goes for the home run, the amazing thing..." Cook, Bruce. "Close Encounters with Steven Spielberg." *American Film*, November 1977.

Page 227: "Spielberg gives you all you can imagine..." *Ibid.*

Chapter 18

Page 228: "this wondrous, quiet, soft, attentive, *listening* child." Bouzerau, Laurent (director). "The Making of *Close Encounters of the Third Kind.*" *Close Encounters of the Third Kind: The Collector's Edition* DVD. Columbia/Tri Star Home Video, Inc., 2001.

Page 230: "I was working nights, drinking a little scotch..." Interview with Joe Alves by the author.

Page 233: "We were working on the script..." Interview with Hal Barwood by the author.

Page 237: "You have forty-nine. You don't need fifty." Spielberg, Steven. "He Was the Movies." *Film Comment*, February 1985.

Page 238: "I told them it was going to cost $250,000..." Interview with Joe Alves by the author.

Page 239: "im-Mobile-ized" Jacob, Gilles, and Claude de Givray (eds). *François Truffaut: Correspondence*. Lanham: Cooper Square Press, 2000.

Page 245: "We were just happy to get the hell out of there." Phillips, Julia. *You'll Never Eat Lunch in This Town Again*. New York: Random House, Inc., 1991.

Chapter 19

Page 249: "satanic." Biskind, Peter. *Easy Riders, Raging Bulls: How the Sex-Drugs-and-Rock 'n' Roll Generation Saved Hollywood*. New York: Simon & Schuster, 1998.

Page 250: "She is incompetent. Unprofessional..." Clarity, James F. "François Truffaut—A Man for All Festivals." *New York Times*, 26 September 1976.

Page 251: "rather unkind..." Spielberg, Steven. "Letter to the Editor." *New York Times*, 24 October, 1976.

Page 260: "I found it extremely easy to get on with [Steven]..." Interview with Douglas Slocombe, BSC by Tim Partridge.

Chapter 20

Page 262: "the most gifted photographer working today," Trumbull, Douglas. "Creating the Photographic Special Effects for *Close Encounters of the Third Kind*." *American Cinematographer*, January 1978.

Page 262: "*Close Encounters* would have been impossible." *Ibid*.

Page 268: "The bottom layer was salt water and the top layer was fresh water..." Interview with Scott Squires by the author.

Page 269: "We'd fill the tank half full of salt water..." *Ibid*.

Page 270: "Where are they?" Interview with Douglas Trumbull by the author.

Page 270: "That was one of the most fun moments for me." *Ibid*.

Page 273: "best buddy." Interview with Richard Yuricich by the author.

Page 274: "When you do it well enough..." Shay, Don. "Close Encounters at Future General: Interviews with Doug Trumbull and His Future General Effects Staff." *Cinefantastique*, Volume 7, Number 3/4, 1978.

Chapter 21

Page 275: "terrible." Interview with Douglas Trumbull by the author.

Page 275: "The technology just wasn't ready," *Ibid*.

Page 282: "We wanted to project a feeling of involvement with some being..." Shay, Don. "Close Encounters at Future General: Interviews with Doug Trumbull and His Future General Effects Staff." *Cinefantastique*, Volume 7, Number 3/4, 1978

Page 287: "An oddball type of machine that..." Irvin, Sam. *Close Encounters of the Third Kind*. Second Draft screenplay, 2 September 1975.

Page 293: "babysitter" Interview with Dennis Muren by the author.
Page 293: "city of lights." Interview with Joe Alves by the author.

Chapter 22

Page 312: "The Stars in *Close Encounters*, with very rare exceptions..." Swarthe, Robert. "Animation Effects for *Close Encounters of the Third Kind*." Unpublished, 1977 (Revised 2007).

Page 314: "the next Walt Disney..." *Close Encounters of the Third Kind* Press Kit (1977).

Page 314: "a turn-on...I would give Doug an idea, and then he would give me an idea..." Shay, Don. "Steven Spielberg on *Close Encounters*." *Cinefantastique*, Volume 7, Number 3/4, 1978.

Page 314: "a creative collaborator..." Spielberg, Steven. "The Unsung Heroes or Credit Where Credit Is Due." *American Cinematographer*, January 1978.

Page 315: "...thought we were out of control. We looked it, but we weren't. We were always under control." Interview with Richard Yuricich by the author.

Page 316: "a very positive presence" *Ibid.*

Page 316: "John had a room somewhere where he could go and scream." Interview with Rocco Gioffre by the author.

Page 317: "very rewarding" Interview with Douglas Trumbull by the author.

Page 317: "How did you do that?" "Creating the Photographic Special Effects for *Close Encounters of the Third Kind*." *American Cinematographer*, January 1978.

Page 317: "The Class of *2001*." Interview with Richard Yuricich by the author.

Page 318: "successfully completed creative activities and requirements for graduation" *Close Encounters of the Third Kind* special effects staff diplomas awarded to Rocco Gioffre and Robert Swarthe.

Page 318: "The Class of *CE3K*." Interview with Richard Yuricich by the author.

Page 318: "the most believable and sophisticated visual effects ever put on film." Trumbull, Douglas. "Creating the Photographic Special Effects for *Close Encounters of the Third Kind*." *American Cinematographer*, January 1978.

Chapter 23

Page 320: "the images came fast and furious." Durwood, Thomas (ed). *Close Encounters of the Third Kind: A Document of the Film*. Kansas City: Ariel Books / New York: Ballantine Books, 1978.

Page 320: "irrepressible.... His enthusiasm for this project bordered on the ridiculous..." "The Unsung Heroes or Credit Where Credit Is Due." *American Cinematographer*, January 1978.

Page 321: "We got so paranoid after a while..." Bouzerau, Laurent (director). "The Making of *Close Encounters of the Third Kind*." *Close Encounters of the Third Kind: The Collector's Edition* DVD. Columbia/Tri Star Home Video, Inc., 2001.

Page 330: "We had, if I remember correctly, half a dozen wrap parties..." Interview with Michael Phillips by the author.

Page 332: "very classical...almost operatic..." Bouzereau, Laurent. "An Interview with John Williams." *Close Encounters of the Third Kind: The Collectors Edition Soundtrack.* Arista Records, 1998.

Page 332: "airborne and awe-inspiring..." Bouzerau, Laurent (director). "The Making of *Close Encounters of the Third Kind.*" *Close Encounters of the Third Kind: The Collector's Edition* DVD. Columbia/Tri Star Home Video, Inc., 2001.

Page 336: "made me pressure every writer who made a contribution to the script..." Phillips, Julia. *You'll Never Eat Lunch in This Town Again.* New York: Random House, Inc., 1991.

Page 336: "When the time came for the obligatory Whiners Guild..." Hill, John. "My Close Encounter with *Close Encounters.*" Unpublished. 2006.

Page 337: "*Close Encounters* is really Steven's script..." McBride, Joseph. *Steven Spielberg: A Biography.* New York: Simon & Schuster, 1997.

Page 338: "It's too bad.... Julia was a terrific producer..." Interview with Joe Alves by the author.

Page 341: "They were with the picture from the opening second, when we had the crescendo..." Interview with Michael Phillips by the author.

Page 342: "make him look fatter." "The Unsung Heroes or Credit Where Credit Is Due." *American Cinematographer,* January 1978.

Chapter 24

Page 346: "Ghosts live here." Phillips, Julia. *You'll Never Eat Lunch in This Town Again.* New York: Random House, Inc., 1991.

Page 355: "I personally have an enormous desire to articulate an experience..." Durwood, Thomas (ed). *Close Encounters of the Third Kind: A Document of the Film.* Kansas City: Ariel Books / New York: Ballantine Books, 1978.

Page 356: "it was so powerful, it was almost another movie." Shay, Don. "Steven Spielberg on *Close Encounters.*" *Cinefantastique,* Volume 7, Number 3/4, 1978.

Page 357: "it must have been an awfully efficient three weeks." Interview with Joe Alves by the author.

Page 357: "Now this is a set!" *Ibid.*

Page 359: "I knew if I only spent $5,000, Steven would get up there and say..." *Ibid.*

Page 359: "He [Clark] was such a cool guy..." *Ibid.*

Page 362: "I've been waiting to see that shot all my life." Phillips, Julia. *You'll Never Eat Lunch in This Town Again.* New York: Random House, Inc., 1991.

Page 364: "Oh, my God..." Balaban, Bob. *Close Encounters of the Third Kind Diary.* Los Angeles: Paradise Press, 1978.

Page 366: "There's a sense of deliverance in it..." Bouzerau, Laurent (director). "The Making of *Close Encounters of the Third Kind.*" *Close Encounters of the Third Kind: The Collector's Edition* DVD. Columbia/Tri Star Home Video, Inc., 2001.

Page 366: "Neary got in touch with himself..." Durwood, Thomas (ed). *Close Encounters of the Third Kind: A Document of the Film.* Kansas City: Ariel Books / New York: Ballantine Books, 1978.

Chapter 25

Page 368: "the poet of suburbia" Siskel, Gene, and Roger Ebert. *The Future of the Movies*. Riverside (NJ): Andrews McMeel Publishing, 1991.

Page 373: "I can understand all the apprehension..." Flanagan, William. "An Encounter With *Close Encounters*." *New York*, 7 November 1977.

Page 373: "certainly be a big enough hit to keep Columbia's stockholders happy" Rich, Frank. "The Aliens Are Coming!" *Time*, 7 November 1977.

Page 374: "Based upon exhibitor reaction..." McClintick, David. *Indecent Exposure: A True Story of Hollywood and Wall Street*. New York: William Morrow and Company, 1982.

Page 375: "somewhat redundant in exposition and irritating in tone;" Murf. "*Close Encounters of the Third Kind*." *Variety*, 4 November 1977.

Page 375: "a director...of effects rather than characters or relationships;" Champlin, Charles. "Saucer Sorcery." *Los Angeles Times*, 18 November 1977.

Page 375: "curiously uneven." Carroll, Kathleen. "*Close Encounters of the Third Kind* Review." *New York News*, 17 November 1977.

Page 375: "(*Close Encounters*) has a simple-minded approach..." Crist, Judith. "*Close Encounters of the Third Kind* Review." *New York Post*, 17 November 1977.

Page 375: "[CE3K] is a gooey, melted marshmallow of a movie..." Sarris, Andrew. "Hyped Hopes." *Village Voice*, 28 November 1977.

Page 375: "The Dumbest Story Ever Told." Haskell, Molly. "The Dumbest Story Ever Told." *New York*, 5 December 1977.

Page 376: "Steven Spielberg's giant, spectacular *Close Encounters of the Third Kind*"...is the best..." Canby, Vincent. "An Encounter That's Out of This World." *New York Times*, 17 November 1977, C:19.

Page 376: "*Close Encounters*...comes close to apotheosizing a movie genre..." Canby, Vincent. "Rediscovering the Secrets That Made Hollywood Corn Grow." *New York Times*, 20 November 1977.

Page 376: "*Close Encounters*...[is] a genuine work of the popular imagination..." Kroll, Jack. "The UFOs Are Coming!" *Newsweek*, 21 November 1977.

Page 376: "[Spielberg's] new movie is far richer..." Rich, Frank. "The Aliens Are Coming!" *Time*, 7 November 1977.

Page 377: "...Although the film's hardware...is spectacularly rendered..." Corliss, Richard. "An Encounter of the Best Kind." *New Times*, 12 December 1977.

Page 377: "*Close Encounters* is...a film of incredible power and intensity..." Knight, Arthur. "*Close Encounters of the Third Kind*." *The Hollywood Reporter*, 4 November 1977.

Page 382: "film of flying saucers" Jacob, Gilles, and Claude de Givray (eds). *François Truffaut: Correspondence*. Lanham: Cooper Square Press, 2000.

Page 385: "let the world know how he [Vilmos] sandbagged us." Phillips, Julia. *You'll Never Eat Lunch in This Town Again*. New York: Random House, Inc., 1991.

Page 385: "With all of the pressure that I experienced..." Interview with Vilmos Zsigmond by the author.

Page 385: "I really thought that *Close Encounters* was going to get five or six major awards..." *Ibid*.

Page 388: "I think we had the last laugh." Interview with Michael Phillips by the author.

Chapter 26

Page 403: "The tinkering was worth it..."Ansen, David. "An Even Better 'Encounter'." *Newsweek*, 18 August 1980.

Page 403: "The new version of *Close Encounters of the Third Kind*...is better, surer..."

Champlin, Charles. "*Encounters* Even Closer in Revision." *Los Angeles Times*, 3 August 1980.

Page 403: "Director Steven Spielberg has taken his 1977 flawed masterpiece..." Knight, Arthur. "*Special Edition of Close Encounters of the Third Kind.*" *The Hollywood Reporter*, 1 August 1980.

Page 403: "It's a mistake..." Kauffmann, Stanley. "Late Summer Round-up." *The New Republic*, August 1980.

Page 403: "I wish Steven Spielberg had trusted his first instincts..." Kael, Pauline. "Who and Who." *The New Yorker*, 1 September, 1980, 80–81.

Page 404: "People thought they wanted to see the inside of the mothership..." Interview with Michael Phillips by the author.

Chapter 27

Page 408: "Nothing revealed itself as an obvious way to go..." Interview with Michael Phillips by the author.

Page 408: "...forced...the movie essentially ended in the best way..." Royal, Susan. "Steven Spielberg in His Adventure on Earth." *American Premiere*, July 1982.

Chapter 28

Page 424: "*End of Days* was the end of my working days," Interview with Gene Cantamessa by the author.

Page 434: "The business has moved past the technology..." Interview with Richard Yuricich by the author.

Bibliography/ Source List

Books

Agel, Jerome (ed). *The Making of Kubrick's 2001*. New York: Signet, 1970.

Balaban, Bob. *Close Encounters of the Third Kind Diary*. Los Angeles: Paradise Press, 1978.

Bizony, Piers. *2001: Filming the Future*. London: Aurum Press, 1994.

Biskind, Peter. *Easy Riders, Raging Bulls: How the Sex-Drugs-and-Rock 'n' Roll Generation Saved Hollywood*. New York: Simon & Schuster, 1998.

Brode, Douglas. *The Films of Steven Spielberg*. New York: Citadel Press, 1995.

Crawley, Tony. *The Steven Spielberg Story*. London: Zomba Books, 1983.

de Baecque, Antoine, and Serge Toubiana. *Truffaut: A Biography*. New York: Alfred A. Knopf, Inc., 1999.

Durwood, Thomas (ed). *Close Encounters of the Third Kind: A Document of the Film*. Kansas City: Ariel Books / New York: Ballantine Books, 1978.

Friedman, Lester D., and Brent Notbohm (eds). *Steven Spielberg Interviews*. Jackson: University Press of Mississippi, 2000.

Garr, Teri, with Henriette Mantel. *Speedbumps: Flooring It Through Hollywood*. New York: Hudson Street Press, 2005.

Griffin, Nancy, and Kim Masters. *Hit and Run: How Jon Peters and Peter Guber Took Sony for a Ride in Hollywood*. New York: Simon & Schuster, 1996.

Gottlieb, Carl. *The Jaws Log: 25th Anniversary Edition*. New York: Newmarket Press, 2001.

Hynek, J. Allen. *The UFO Experience: A Scientific Inquiry*. Chicago: Henry Regnery Company, 1972.

Jackson, Kevin (ed). *Schrader on Schrader and Other Writings*. London: Faber and Faber, 1990.

Jacob, Gilles, and Claude de Givray (eds). *François Truffaut: Correspondence*. Lanham: Cooper Square Press, 2000.

Kelly, Mary Pat. *Martin Scorsese: A Journey*. New York: Thunder's Mouth Press, 1991.

McBride, Joseph. *Steven Spielberg: A Biography*. New York: Simon & Schuster, 1997.

McAllister, Michael J. *The Language of Visual Effects*. Los Angeles: Lone Eagle Publishing, 1993.

McClintick, David. *Indecent Exposure: A True Story of Hollywood and Wall Street* New York: William Morrow and Company, 1982.

Medavoy, Mike, with Josh Young. *You're Only As Good As Your Next One: 100 Great Films, 100 Good Films and 100 for Which I Should Be Shot*. New York: Atria Books, 2002.

Petrou, David Michael. *The Making of* Superman: The Movie. New York: Warner Books, 1978.

Phillips, Julia. *You'll Never Eat Lunch in This Town Again*. New York: Random House, Inc., 1991.

Pye, Michael, and Linda Myles. *The Movie Brats: How the Film Generation Took Over Hollywood*. New York: Holt, Rinehart and Winston, 1979.

Sanello, Frank: *Spielberg: The Man, the Movies, The Mythology*. Dallas: Taylor Publishing Company, 1996.

Siskel, Gene, and Roger Ebert. *The Future of the Movies*. Riverside (NJ): Andrews McMeel Publishing, 1991.

Sunshine, Linda (ed). *ET: The Extra-Terrestrial: From Concept to Classic: The Illustrated Story of the Film and the Filmmakers*. New York: Newmarket Press, 2002.

Yule, Andrew. *Fast Fade: David Puttnam, Columbia Pictures and the Battle for Hollywood*. New York: Delacorte Press, 1989.

Zierold, Norman. *The Moguls: Hollywood's Merchants of Myth*. Los Angeles: Silman-James Press, 1991.

Periodicals

Alves, Joe. "Designing a World for UFOs, Extraterrestrials and Mere Mortals." *American Cinematographer*, January 1978, 34–35, 60–62, 84–85.

Ansen, David. "An Even Better 'Encounter'." *Newsweek*, 18 August 1980, 87.

Becker, Scott. "Dr. J. Allen Hynek: An Interview." *Science Fantasy Film Classics*, Spring 1978, 22–23; 62.

"Behind the Scenes of *Close Encounters of the Third Kind*." *American Cinematographer*, January 1978, 26; 52–53; 86–87.

Bequette, Bill. "Boise Flyer Maintains He Saw 'Em." *East Oregonian*, 26 June 1947.

Bobrow, Andrew C. "Filming *The Sugarland Express*: An Interview with Steven Spielberg." *Filmmakers Newsletter*, Summer 1974.

Canby, Vincent. "An Encounter That's Out of This World." *New York Times*, 17 November 1977, C:19.

Canby, Vincent. "Rediscovering the Secrets That Made Hollywood Corn Grow." *New York Times*, 20 November 1977, Arts & Leisure: 15; 30.

Carroll, Kathleen. "*Close Encounters of the Third Kind* Review." *New York News*, 17 November 1977.

Champlin, Charles. "A Close Encounter with the Energetic Truffaut." *Los Angeles Times*, 1 January 1978, Calendar: 24.

Champlin, Charles. "*Encounters* Even Closer in Revision." *Los Angeles Times*, 3 August 1980, Calendar: 1; 36.

Champlin, Charles. "Saucer Sorcery." *Los Angeles Times*, 18 November 1977, IV: 1; 22.

Clarity, James F. "Francois Truffaut—A Man for All Festivals." *New York Times*, 26 September 1976, 15; 35.

"Columbia Announces *Encounters*." *Hollywood Reporter*, 12 August 1975.

Combs, Richard. "Primal Scream: An Interview with Steven Spielberg." *Sight and Sound*, Spring 1977.

Cook, Bruce. "Close Encounters with Steven Spielberg." *American Film*, November 1977, 24–29.

Corliss, Richard. "An Encounter of the Best Kind." *New Times*, 12 December 1977, 76.

Crist, Judith. "*Close Encounters of the Third Kind* Review." *New York Post*, 17 November 1977.

"Dialogue on Film: Steven Spielberg." *American Film*, September 1978, 44–53.

Flanagan, William. "An Encounter With *Close Encounters*." *New York*, 7 November 1977, 48–49.

Fox, Jordan. "Roy Arbogast." *Cinefex* #5, July 1981, 42–53.

Gelmis, Joseph. "If at First You Don't Succeed." *Newsday*, 10 August 1980.

Gwynne, Peter, with Katrine Ames. "The Galileo of UFOlogy." *Newsweek*, 21 November 1977, 97.

Haskell, Molly. "The Dumbest Story Ever Told." *New York*, 5 December 1977, 143–144.

Helpern, David. "At Sea with Steven Spielberg." *Take One*, March/April 1974.

Hill, John. "My Close Encounter with *Close Encounters*." Unpublished. 2006.

Hirschberg, Lynn. "Will Hollywood's Mr. Perfect Ever Grow Up?" *Rolling Stone*, 19 July/2 August 1984, 32–38.

Hodenfield, Chris. "*1941*: Bombs Away." *Rolling Stone*, 24 January, 1980.

Hodenfield, Chris. "The Sky Is Full of Questions: Science Fiction in Steven Spielberg's Suburbia." *Rolling Stone*, 26 January, 1978, 33.

Jameson, Richard T. "Wild Child, Movie Master." *Film Comment*, February 1985, 34–39.

Janos, Leo. "Steven Spielberg: L'Enfant Directeur." *Cosmopolitan*, June 1980, 236–239; 345.

"Junket to Spielberg." *Variety*, 31 August 1977.

Kael, Pauline. "Sugarlands and Badlands." *The New Yorker*, 18 March 1974, 130.

Kael, Pauline. "The Greening of the Solar System." *The New Yorker*, 28 November 1977, 174-176.

Kael, Pauline. "Who and Who." *The New Yorker*, 1 September 1980, 80–81.

Kauffmann, Stanley. "Late Summer Round-up." *The New Republic*, August 1980, 24.

Kilday, Gregg. " 'Close Encounters' Third Degree." *Los Angeles Times*, 11 November 1977, II:7

Klemesrud, Judy. "Can He Make the *Jaws* of Science Fiction?" *New York Times*, 15 May 1977, Arts & Leisure: 13; 25.

Knight, Arthur. "*Close Encounters of the Third Kind*." *The Hollywood Reporter*, 4 November 1977.

Knight, Arthur. "*Special Edition of Close Encounters of the Third Kind.*" *The Hollywood Reporter*, 1 August 1980, 3.

Kroll, Jack. "Close Encounter with Spielberg." *Newsweek*, 21 November 1977, 98-99.

Kroll, Jack. "The UFOs Are Coming!" *Newsweek*, 21 November 1977, 88–92; 97.

Kroll, Jack, with Martin Kasindorf. "Wizard of Special Effects." *Newsweek*, 21 November 1977, 99.

Lewis, Fiona. "A Close Encounter with Steven Spielberg." *Los Angeles Times*, 13 November 1977, Calendar: 41.

Lindsey, Robert. "The New Wave of Filmmakers." *New York Times Magazine*, 28 May 1978, 6:11–15, 33–36.

Lightman, Herb A. "My Close Encounter with *CE3K.*" *American Cinematographer*, January 1978, 28; 56–57; 88–91.

Lightman, Herb A. "Spielberg Speaks About *Close Encounters.*" *American Cinematographer*, January 1978, 39–42; 58–59; 95.

Lightman, Herb A. "The New Panaflex Camera Makes Its Production Debut." *American Cinematographer*, May 1973, 567; 61.

Maslin, Janet. "Spielberg's Journey from Sharks to the Stars." *New York Times*, 13 November 1977, Arts & Leisure: 15; 29.

McCarthy, Todd. "*Close Encounters* Revision." *Variety*, 6 August 1980, 22; 33.

McCarthy, Todd. "The Man Who Loved." *Film Comment*, February 1985, 44–47.

McGilligan, Patrick. "Stars Behind the Lens." *Take One*, January 1979, 23–28; 41.

McLellan, Dennis. "Jerry Belson, 68; Comedy Writer Set the Standard for TV Shows of '60s, '70s." *Los Angeles Times*, 13 October 2006, B10.

Mitchell, Steve. "Douglas Trumbull." *Science Fantasy Film Classics*, Spring 1978, 45–48; 52

Munson, Brad. "Greg Jein: Miniature Giant." *Cinefex* #2, August 1980, 1–49.

Murf. "*Close Encounters of the Third Kind.*" *Variety*, 4 November 1977.

Palmer, Randy. "Trumbull's Showscan Is a Hit—Sort Of." *Cinefantastique*, Volume 14, Number 4/5, 1984, 108.

Phillips, Julia, and Michael Phillips. "From the Producers' Point of View." *American Cinematographer*, January 1978, 48–49, 106.

Poster, Steve. "The Mind Behind *Close Encounters of the Third Kind.*" *American Cinematographer*, February 1978.

Reed, Rex. "Columbia's *Close Encounters* Sets World Press Preview." *Entertainment Today*, 9 September 1977, 8.

Rich, Frank. "The Aliens Are Coming!" *Time*, 7 November 1977, 102–105.

Royal, Susan. "Steven Spielberg in His Adventure on Earth." *American Premiere*, July 1982.

Sammon, Paul. "*Brainstorm*: Douglas Trumbull's Fight for Survival Against the MGM Lion." *Cinefantastique*, Volume 12, Number 5/6, 1982, 14.

Sammon, Paul. "Greetings from Ridleyville." *Cinefantastique*, Volume 12, Number 5/6, 1982, 20-46.

Sammon, Paul M. "Turn On Your Heartlight: Inside *E.T.*" *Cinefex* #11, January 1983, 4–49.

Sarris, Andrew. "Hyped Hopes." *Village Voice*, 28 November 1977, 47–48.

Schickel, Richard. "No, But I Saw the Rough Cut." *Time*, 18 August 1980, 58–59.

Segers, Frank. "Columbia Asking Pretty Stiff N.Y. 'Encounters' Guarantees." *Variety*, 24 August 1977, 4.

Sragow, Michael. "A Conversation with Steven Spielberg." *Rolling Stone*, 22 July, 1982, 25–28.

Shay, Don. "A Close Encounter with Steven Spielberg." *Cinefex* #53, February 1993, 54–69.

Shay, Don. "Close Encounters at Future General: Interviews with Doug Trumbull and His Future General Effects Staff." *Cinefantastique*, Volume 7, Number 3/4, 1978, 30–57; 80–95.

Shay, Don. "*Close Encounters* Extraterrestrials." *Cinefantastique*, Volume 7, Number 3/4, 1978, 4–19.

Shay, Don. "Dennis Muren: Playing It Unsafe." *Cinefex* #65, March 1996, 98–111.

Shay, Don. "Into the V'Ger Maw with Douglas Trumbull." *Cinefex* #1, March 1980, 5–33.

Shay, Don. "Robert Swarthe." *Cinefex* #11, January 1983, 50–71.

Shay, Don. "Steven Spielberg on *Close Encounters*." *Cinefantastique*, Volume 7, Number 3/4, 1978, 20–29.

Silberg, Jon. "Master of Light: Vilmos Zsigmond, ASC Shares Some Thoughts About the Art and Craft of Motion-Picture Lighting." *American Cinematographer*, October 2004.

Spielberg, Steven. "He Was the Movies." *Film Comment*, February 1985, 40–41.

Spielberg, Steven. "To the Editor." *New York Times*, 24 October, 1976, 15.

Spielberg, Steven. "The Unsung Heroes or Credit Where Credit Is Due." *American Cinematographer*, January 1978, 68–70, 88.

Swarthe, Robert. "Animation Effects for *Close Encounters of the Third Kind*." Unpublished, 1977 (Revised 2007), 1–6.

Swires, Steve. "A Conversation with Steven Spielberg." *Future*, October 1978, 55–57; 62.

Swires, Steve. "Filming the Fantastic: Steven Spielberg." *Starlog*, October 1978, 22–26.

Thomas, Kevin. "Catching Up with Truffaut's Latest Wave." *Los Angeles Times*, 24 January 1977, IV: 1; 8.

Tracy, Dick. "Alien Visions." *New Musical Express*, 20 May 1978.

Trumbull, Douglas. "Creating the Photographic Special Effects for *Close Encounters of the Third Kind*." *American Cinematographer*, January 1978, 72–83; 96–97.

Tuchman, Mitch. "Close Encounter with Steven Spielberg." *Film Comment*, January/February 1978, 49–55.

Warner, Frank. "The Sounds of Silence and Things That Go 'Flash' in the Night." *American Cinematographer*, January 1978, 44–45; 92–94.

Yakir, Dan. "Looking Back." *Film Comment*, February 1985, 48–53.

Zimmerman, Paul D. "Hard Riders." *Newsweek*, 18 April 1974, 82.

Zsigmond, Vilmos. "Lights! Camera! Action! For *CE3K*." *American Cinematographer*, January 1978, 30–33; 64–65; 98–104.

Internet

Axmaker, Sean. "From the Drawing Board to Immersive Media with Douglas Trumbull." *Green Cine.* http://www.greencine.com/article?action=view&arti cleID=267.

Bernard, Tommy. "Cutting with Feeling: An Interview with Michael Kahn." *Spielberg Films.Com.* 5 March, 2006. http://www.spielbergfilms.com/munich/19

Coate, Michael, and William Kallay (compilers). "70mm in New York." *From Script to Screen.* http://www.fromscripttodvd.com/70mm_in_new_york_main_page.htm

Coate, Michael, and William Kallay (compilers). "70mm in Los Angeles." *From Script to Screen.* http://www.fromscripttodvd.com/70mm_in_los_angeles_main_page.htm

Dove, Linda. "Rhythm and Attitude: Michael Kahn Speaks at ASC Seminar." *Editors Guild Newsletter.* May–June 1998. http://www.editorsguild.com/v2/magazine/Newsletter/kahn.html

Erickson, Glenn. "Review of *Close Encounters of the Third Kind.*" *DVD Savant.* http://www.dvdtalk.com/dvdsavant/s26oce3k.html.

Ford, Luke. "Producer Michael Phillips Still Eats Lunch in This Town." *Luke Ford.Net.* http://www.lukeford.net/profiles/profiles/michael_phillips.htm.

"Live Chat with Vilmos Zsigmond Transcript." *International Cinematographers Guild.* http://www.cameraguild.com/index.html?interviews/chat_zsigmond/index.htm~top.main_hp.

McDonald, Liza. "Zen Mind/Experienced Mind: Fireside Chatting with Michael Kahn." *Editors Guild Newsletter.* May–June 1998. http://www.editorsguild.com/v2/magazine/Newsletter/MayJun98/kahn.html

Regös, István, "A Close Encounter with Vilmos Zsigmond." *Spielberg Films. Com.* http://www.spielbergfilms.com/ce3k/900

Reports

University of Colorado, under Contract No. 44620-67-C-0035 from the United States Air Force (Dr. Edward U. Condon—Scientific Director). *Scientific Study of Unidentified Flying Objects.* 1968.

Documentaries

Bouzerau, Laurent (director). "The Making of *The Andromeda Strain.*" *The Andromeda Strain* DVD. Universal Studios Home Entertainment, 2003.

Bouzerau, Laurent (director). "Douglas Trumbull: Then and Now." *Silent Running* DVD. Universal Home Entertainment, 2001.

Bouzerau, Laurent (director). "The Making of *Close Encounters of the Third Kind.*" *Close Encounters of the Third Kind: The Collector's Edition* DVD. Columbia/Tri Star Home Video, Inc., 2001.

"The Case for Flying Saucers." CBS Radio. 7 April 1950.

Screenplays

Irvin, Sam. Close Encounters of the Third Kind. Second Draft, 2 September 1975.

Spielberg, Steven. *Close Encounters of the Third Kind*. Revised (SS changes included)—contains all revisions up to 4/22/76.

Spielberg, Steven. *Close Encounters of the Third Kind*. Revised (SS changes included)—contains all revisions up to 5/14/76.

Additional Materials

Bouzereau, Laurent. "An Interview with John Williams." *Close Encounters of the Third Kind: The Collector's Edition Soundtrack*. Arista Records, 1998.

Bouzereau, Laurent. "When You Wish Upon a Note." *Close Encounters of the Third Kind: The Collector's Edition Soundtrack*. Arista Records, 1998.

Close Encounters of the Third Kind Shooting Schedule (May 6, 1976).

Close Encounters of the Third Kind Storyboards (1976/1977).

Close Encounters of the Third Kind Press Kit (1977).

Close Encounters of the Third Kind Merchandising and Advertising Manual (1977).

Close Encounters of the Third Kind special effects staff diplomas awarded to Rocco Gioffre and Robert Swarthe.

Index